Dreaming

All the Time

The Recapitulation Diaries

Volume 5

January - July 2004

J. E. Ketchel

Riverwalker Press

Copyright ©2021 by J. E. Ketchel.

All rights reserved.

No part of this book may be used or reproduced in any manner whatsoever without the written permission of the publisher except in the case of brief quotations embodied within a review.

Cover design by J. E. Ketchel

Cover photo by Chuck Ketchel

Riverwalker Press: www.riverwalkerpress.com

ISBN: 978-0-9800506-8-4

MEDICAL DISCLAIMER: The information in this book is intended for educational and informational purposes only. It is not meant to diagnose or treat any mental health disorder whatsoever, nor is it intended to replace treatment with a competent mental healthcare provider. Please seek appropriate support and put the book aside if it proves to be too disruptive. Any application of the material presented in this book is the reader's responsibility. The author and publisher are in no way responsible or liable for misuse of this information.

INTRODUCTION
  By Chuck Ketchel, LCSW I
PROLOGUE
  This Beautiful Thing Called Love VII
CHAPTER 1
  Old Ghosts 1
CHAPTER 2
  I Tell Chuck About Jeanne 65
CHAPTER 3
  Apprenticeship 139
CHAPTER 4
  Stalking a New Self 203
CHAPTER 5
  War 279
CHAPTER 6
  Redeployment of Energy 333
CHAPTER 7
  Completion 401
EPILOGUE 489
ACKNOWLEDGMENTS 497

Introduction

By Chuck Ketchel, LCSW

Jan Ketchel's five volume series, *The Recapitulation Diaries*, provides an unprecedented documentation of the daily experiences of a three-year-long healing journey that eventuated in a complete healing from Complex PTSD (Post-traumatic Stress Disorder). What distinguishes Complex PTSD from PTSD is the frequency of traumatic experiences encountered. Jan was sexually abused hundreds of times over a sixteen-year period, from ages two through eighteen. Though she had one primary abuser, he exposed her many times to organized group rapes from which he collected fees from participants.

Jan initiated her healing journey in earnest at the age of forty-nine, triggered by her shock at her complete non-feeling reaction to the traumatic attack upon the United States on September 11, 2001. For her entire life, up to that date, the events of her traumatic past, including the cognitive, physical and emotional dimensions, had remained frozen and inaccessible to her memory. This type of amnesia is common in Complex PTSD, as some agency within the psyche protects the developing ego by employing the psychological defense of dissociation, which immediately removes from consciousness the occurrence and details of a traumatic experience just encountered. A story is immediately unconsciously conjured to rationally and non-threateningly account for the appearance of body pains, torn clothing and other effects actually resulting from the traumatic episode.

These split-off traumatic events are then stored in the depths of the unconscious, as well as in various parts of the physical body, until they are triggered into consciousness, generally in piecemeal parcels eventuating in flashbacks and full body re-experiences at a later time in life. In my experience, as a clinician, it seems as if some higher agency in the psyche determines the time and triggering event to prompt consciousness to initiate the reclaiming of its lost wholeness. I have come to trust the judgment of this higher agency, which determines that the ego is now sufficiently matured to undertake its journey to recover its traumatic history. For Jan, this meant the breaking out of the robotic mold that had contained her trauma and held her together for her entire life. My own simultaneous emergence from a seven-year saturation in the shamanic world of Carlos Castaneda intersected with Jan's need to undertake a soul retrieval. Thus, I was well primed to be her guide through her awesome recapitulation journey of discovery and transformation.

Breaking with the shamanic tradition of secrecy, Carlos Castaneda, in the 1990's, openly taught the basic practices of his ancient shamanic line in his launching of Tensegrity. Central to his teaching is the Magical Pass of Recapitulation, a practice in which modern practitioners relive the core interactions of their lives. The Magical Pass of Recapitulation is accompanied by a bilateral sweeping breath in which lost energy is retrieved, inhaled, and the energy of others is released, exhaled. This practice also enables practitioners to explore infinity while in human life, with sobriety, unencumbered by the weight of unresolved human entanglements.

My first wife, Jeanne, and I were lifelong Castaneda followers, eagerly awaiting each new book. When Carlos and his fellow cohorts went public with Tensegrity, we dove into every training opportunity we could, participating in countless seminars throughout the world over a seven-year period. When we first encountered the practice of Recapitulation, we synchronistically encountered advertisements for training in EMDR (Eye Movement Desensitization and Reprocessing), a clinical mind body technique to resolve trauma. At first, EMDR struck me as just another clinical fad, which I automatically dismissed. However, I soon discovered that it used a bilateral mechanism, similar to the Magical Pass of Recapitulation, to enable healing. On the strength of this bilateral similarity, Jeanne and I, both psychotherapists, quickly became trained and certified in EMDR. The efficacy of EMDR in the treatment of PTSD is well documented and clinically accepted as the best treatment method available to date.

Carlos himself was emphatic that Recapitulation was an energetic process, not to be confused with psychotherapy. Nonetheless, as I deepened my practice with EMDR, I incorporated the intent of Recapitulation and the Recapitulation breath into my practice, with startling results. Jeanne had similar

Introduction

success in her practice; however, her life in this world ended in 2001 after a long journey with breast cancer.

I first met Jan in 2001, shortly before Jeanne's death. At first glance I knew she had been sexually abused. Clients who had dealt with sexual abuse had dominated my practice since I began my professional career in 1984. This was hardly my intention, at least not consciously; they just appeared. I believe we attract the clients with issues we are destined to tackle.

For many years, I had relied upon the use of indigenous conscious dreaming practices gleaned from Patricia Garfield's classic work, *Creative Dreaming*, to help clients master the traumas they were recovering. The soul retrieval opportunity offered by the Recapitulation process was the natural evolution of this early work.

The most unique quality of Recapitulation that I have encountered many times, is that once the intent to recapitulate has been established the flow of memory retrieval takes on a life of its own. Jan's documentation of this process is representative of many people I have worked with. The healing sequence of memory retrieval is directed by a higher center in the personality, well beyond the conscious ego. Jan could have a memory from very early life followed by a teenage memory, followed next by another from early childhood. We learned to trust the forces that decided the order as the necessary building blocks for the retrieved self. I am convinced that anyone who invokes the intent to heal through the practice of Recapitulation will be supported and guided by the higher Self within the personality, as well as the living energy of the intent of the shamans of Ancient Mexico.

Jan's soul retrieval journey of Recapitulation resulted in the complete experiential retrieval of hundreds of abusive encounters from her childhood. Utilizing the bilateral breathing technique of the Magical Pass of Recapitulation, she restored her innocent energy that had been lost in those abusive encounters, released long-repressed emotions, and gained complete cognitive clarity of the truth of every encounter. Today, she can recall any memory with full clarity and complete emotional neutrality; there are no triggers to be avoided. Jan offers her deeply personal story, to all who suffer, to demonstrate the possibility of complete healing from Complex PTSD.

Equally important for Jan, in the telling of her story, was the need to document explicit details of the types of sexual molestation perpetrated upon very young children, which, for most people, are both unbelievable and unfathomable. In order to address the reality of sexual abuse, especially to children, the full truth of it must be known. Jan is no longer triggered by these memories, as her recapitulation completely depotentiated their power over her. However, most people recoil in terror and denial at the mention of such possibilities. Freud himself was overwhelmed with reports of countless episodes of childhood sexual abuse revealed to him by patients in his consulting room. Unfortunately, he ultimately relegated this material to fantasy, setting the field back a century. *The Recapitulation Diaries* are a major contribution to documenting the full truth of the sexual abuse of very young children.

Jan's books represent one person's experience as a sexually abused person. From the vantage point of my own clinical practice, I can contribute a much broader truth: Jan's experience of sexual abuse, in its entirety, is not uncommon. The truth is that in a very large sample of cases I have worked with, over the past thirty-six years, individuals have recovered memories of networks of sexually abusing predators who live and operate in the shadows of their communities. I would add that these include communities of all races and socioeconomic status, in widely diverse locations, around the country and the world.

In many cases, family members who sexually abuse their child relatives introduce them to these wider networks, often in exchange for money or access to other children. Frequently, however, there is no direct family linkage, as children's innocence makes them vulnerable to exploitation by almost anyone. The fact that children, generally, become instantly amnesic to their traumatic abuse sets the stage for repeated abuse with ease by the predator.

Though I believe that the truth of these individual predators and these networks of predators must be outed, and criminals prosecuted, the underlying issue of sexual abuse itself is a collective human problem that won't be solved with jail sentences. Sexual abuse has its roots in the dissociation of the

Introduction

sexual instinct from the human being. The human sexual instinct has not been squared with. Centuries of repression have elevated the spiritual side of humanity but left the dissociated and repressed instinct to fend for itself in the life of the human shadow. The innocence of children has become the target of the cravings of this disenfranchised sexual instinct. Although people are having sex, it doesn't mean they are truly satisfying the instinct. The fullness of sexual desire must be known and honestly accepted in the light of day to avoid its predatory activity in the shadows.

At a shamanic level, Jan's recapitulation process well attests to the fullness of human potential. Trauma, in some form, is often used to initiate shamans on shamanic journeys of heightened awareness, into out-of-body experiences beyond the solid world of everyday reality, from which they often return with a greater understanding of life, as well as enhanced healing and psychic abilities. As with all soul retrieval journeys, the key is in the full remembering of one's experiences, as in recapitulation. Jan's books are replete with such out-of-body experiences and their full recapitulation, as she explored beyond the physical and connected with a higher state of awareness. Sexually abused individuals are frequently afforded such out-of-body and psychic experiences. Some people are terrified by such experiences, others are enthralled and seek to enhance them. I issue the following warning: to pursue psychic abilities without a thorough recapitulation risks psychosis, as the ego may be overtaken by its unknown dissociated self. Anyone seeking to pursue psychic abilities should put themselves under the guidance of those truly versed in the art they seek to pursue.

In summary, *The Recapitulation Diaries* indeed validate the truth of full healing from Complex PTSD, report the truth of sexual abuse of very young children, document the existence of networks of sexual predators, and demonstrate how healing from trauma can lead to human transformation at a very high level of wisdom and ability.

Thank you, Jan, for gifting the world with your most private experiences, demonstrating the freedom and lightness of being that is fully available through total transparency.

Prologue

This Beautiful Thing Called Love

"I have turned you into this beautiful thing called love."

I hear these words one morning while washing the breakfast dishes, looking out into the dense woods on our property in the Blue Ridge Mountains of Virginia.

"Who are you?" I ask, but I already know. It's a part of me, my Spirit, letting me know that I'm doing well on this journey through Earth School.

This is the final book in *The Recapitulation Diaries*; five books that document my struggle to know myself on the deepest of levels, to find and integrate the lost parts of myself, and the healing journey I embarked upon beginning in 2001 as a novice of the inner world, and from which I emerged three years later, a greatly changed person. At the time I began my recapitulation journey, I did not really know what love was, not in the sense I know it now, but it marked the beginning of a new path. In the end, I discovered that love is what this whole journey through life is about. It's about finding love, but it's also about discovering the true meaning of love, by learning about, experiencing, and practicing loving compassion. First, however, my journey took me to the dark side of myself where I learned to confront what I feared the most, where I learned to passionately hate, to be angry with a vengeance, to be a fully emotional human being. For I had to become fully, expressively human before I could go anywhere near understanding and fully being love.

Much has changed in the few years since the publication of my last book, *Place of No Pity*, in 2017. Another phase of the magical journey I call life has catapulted me to another place on the map, to new experiences, and to new possibilities. Spirit came knocking. Choices were made, one thing led to another, a leap was taken. And so, I write these words from a place I never knew of, a place I never expected to land in, but here I am, in a new dream. It all began when my husband, Chuck, and I attended a Gateway Program at the Monroe Institute, in Virginia, in April of 2018, the premier educational setting for explorations of consciousness, and home of the great out-of-body explorer Robert Monroe. Actually, it began a lot earlier than that, but this was where things really cranked up. We had some profound experiences during our week there, at a time when we were both ready for new adventures.

"Everything will be different after Monroe," I kept saying, for weeks before we attended the workshop. "Everything will be different." I don't know how I knew this, but, as with all things *knowing*, it proved to be quite true.

Now, I often stop and wonder what I'm doing here in the Blue Ridge Mountains, and at the same time I have never felt more at home in my life. The life I have always envisioned for myself is realized here, all the tiny aspects of wishes, dreams, and imaginings from many different phases of my life are fulfilled here, both physical and spiritual. I could not have landed in a better place. I feel more deeply grounded every day in the stillness of the mountains, where the profound silence of winter is contrasted by the busy sounds of summer, the incessant calling, cackling, chattering, pecking, buzzing, chirping of cicadas, crickets, birds, the honking of geese on the nearby lake, the shriek of the barn owl, the gentle whinnying of the tiny screech owl and the hoot of the great horned.

Why am I here? I belong here. As much as the deer that wander the land, as much as the bear that scramble past my window in the middle of the night, I am home. That I am sure of. And so, I feel great privilege in being able to complete my final book of *The Recapitulation Diaries* here, in the Blue Ridge Mountains, surrounded by the great groundedness of nature and in the spiritual energy of this special place on Earth where Robert Monroe also lived and wrote his last book.

As I finish the writing of this book the Covid-19 pandemic is raging. I'm feeling deeply the pain of loss and devastation happening to so many people around the world, to our collective civilization, to our planet, and to our greater wholeness. Even so, I remain in a state of awe, filled with gratitude and love for all who share this planet, for this is a time of great change, and I am sure that we are all here together, at this time in history, for a reason.

This Beautiful Thing Called Love

We are all part of the whole, the good and the bad of it, just as I was once part of a sexual predator's world; my journey through childhood sexual abuse was part of the wholeness of life itself. We are all that, part of the wholeness.

Indeed, our individual journeys on Earth are meaningful in that we are all charged with learning the true meaning of love, and being that love.

J. E. Ketchel

February 2021

Chapter 1

Old Ghosts

January 1, 2004

Memories of being violently raped course through me as I awaken, every fiber in my body burning with pain. Clenched against the pain, I hang by a thread to this healing practice as my saving grace, to this shamanic art of recapitulation that has taken me on so many journeys over the last few years. My days and nights have been steeped in it, my body and soul wrung dry by it. And yet, though in pain, I awaken to a new day, feeling alive and grateful, hopeful, so ready and willing to see where this healing journey takes me next. What a way to start the New Year!

Last night was another busy night of dreaming, as I took care of things that needed attention. I dreamed of simplifying, sorting, deciding what should go, wheedling down an enormous box of stuff to one small envelope that easily fit into the palm of my hand, no bigger than a matchbox. Then I realized I didn't even need that, and so I moved on empty-handed to a new house where nothing from my past existed. There were only beds for the many children I'd rescued and took care of, my exhausted inner children, whom I made sure were safe and well. The truth is, they still need me. And me? I constantly seek a good balance between taking care of them, as well as myself, as I take this journey to its natural and peaceful end.

I dreamed also of being followed along a deserted road at night by a car driving at a slow and determined pace, clearly tracking me. I knew there was evil inside, men who wanted to get me. I was tense with fear, but at the same time I felt strong, and so I turned and confronted them, shouting: "What do you want?" There was no answer. Only dark silence. All my instincts went on heightened alert then, telling me to escape before it was too late, telling me I could get away now because I knew the way.

"Yes," I thought, "I do know the way," and so I sprinted away into the safety of the nearby woods, running as fast as I could, quick as lightning, until I was back at the new house from which I had started. Once there, I put an exhausted child to bed while others called out to me. I calmed them down and then I too went to bed, rolling into the depths of the fetal pose, feeling how thin and fragile, how utterly breakable I still am. I was aware of being in the old pose but knew I had to be there, that wrapped in that fetal pose lay the final remnants of my recapitulation and the sadness I've been avoiding too. I can't go on without releasing the sadness, I told myself.

"Tears but also laughter helps heal," a voice told me, as the dream ended.

I've been on break from meetings with Chuck over the holidays, on my own with the recapitulation, finding ways, in dreams and in daily practices, to continue the process as best I can. It's been a bit of a rollercoaster ride, the ups and downs of dealing with shattering memories and almost constant pain, while struggling to stay grounded and sane. I think I've been doing pretty well, but I long for our work to begin again soon.

I meditate. I'm down inside myself, sitting before my alchemical cauldron, my inner place of recapitulation, burning off the things that hurt. My inner children are here with me, all sixteen of them. We're hiding, but at the same time yearning to be found. We hide because we have to. If someone came along and said, "you don't have to hide anymore," would we believe them? When here, I'm not really an adult who can take care of anyone else, I'm just another frightened child, afraid to trust. I want to trust Chuck, but even with him I've been wary, cautious, and afraid. Why?

Old scenarios play out before me, dancing in the flames of the cauldron fire, and the old voices come too, warning me to beware, that no one *really* cares. Maybe I don't even care, but I sit by the cauldron with the children and wait with a certain eagerness for what will happen next, for surely something will.

Part of me never really made it into life. As the flames dance, I see the false, stoic me who did go out into the world, but the real me is still hiding out, frightened of life and yet always waiting for it to begin. The false me, the guardian self, is very good at deflecting anything that tries to get in. She's having a hard time giving up her position. She knows how dangerous life can be and how painful it has been to let others get close. She doesn't want me to suffer anymore. I know that's all she really cares about, but she's tired now, she's weakening, and even though she's a false persona, she has been my savior. She's the reason I've survived. As I look at her serious demeanor, flickering in the flames of the fire in the cauldron, I realize just how strong a protector she has been.

"You don't have to fight for me anymore. You've been fighting my whole life, but you can stop now," I tell her, but I'm certain that the only way she'll stop, and the only thing that's going to allow this process to move forward, is to patiently wait for her to succumb to pure and utter exhaustion.

I'm living a strange and wild life now, going where I'm led, following my spirit, and although I'm afraid, I also know that fear is my guide too, showing me where I need to go next. And so, I sit beside my frightened little inner children and peer into the alchemical cauldron and face what I see flickering in the flames.

What do I fear the most? That those men in the car of my dream are still after me? I have to take the dream seriously; it's showing me where I'm still caught. I confronted the men, but what I really need to do is get rid of them, once and for all. I can't just burn them in the fire of the alchemical cauldron; I have to eliminate them from my psyche in a real way, otherwise they'll still have power. I have to stop running away from them as I did in the dream. The new me wants to confront them and the old me wants to keep protecting myself from them and what they represent. Those two parts of myself are facing each other now; the old has to relax her grip and the new has to really step up and take charge now.

"Believe, that's the key to everything," Chuck once said to me, and he's right. I have to believe that I can take care of this, within myself.

"Tonight, go after them," I tell myself. "Go after the men. You're light and fast and that's your advantage. They are big and bulky, wearing heavy suits, but you are like a dragonfly buzzing about their heads, distracting and teasing. Go in for the sting. Kill them."

"Be strong. Dream strong dreams," I tell myself. "Trust yourself. Believe!"

January 2, 2004

I dream that I'm standing in a house, looking out a large picture window at cloud formations, x and y letter formations, like chromosomes floating in the sky. I'm the only one who can see them. I'm building a house. Sometimes I work outside on top of the roof and sometimes I'm working inside. I'm strong and powerful. Then I see another cloud formation floating by, a vampire woman. When I point her out to a little boy, she turns immediately into a cow and runs into a pasture, then suddenly transforms back into a vampire woman again. I sense evil oozing from her. I tell the boy not to respond to her, that she's a trickster, but that we must bear the tension of her presence.

"Don't run from her, but stand your ground and face her," I say. I take the little boy's hand and lead him away without turning my back on the vampire woman.

Noon. It's raining. I was hoping to take a walk. Instead, I'm in bed, reading, thinking, a little unhappy, but hopeful. That old stalwart protector in me is exhausted! She's still down by the cauldron, hiding out. It's irresponsible to hide, not fair to those who depend on me, and not fair to myself, but it still feels like the safest place in the world, warm and comfortable too. I'm safely isolated and that feels good. I feel safest when I'm alone.

I've been thinking about training myself to handle the onslaught from the unconscious in a better and more healing way. I don't want to keep getting exhausted by it or keep running and hiding from it. I want to be prepared to meet it head on with a new kind of strength and determination, like I did in my dream. I felt strong as I worked on my house in the dream and as I faced the evil vampire woman. I actually do feel that same strength inside me and I know I can access it sometimes, but not all the time. Yet.

I'm considering implementing a more conscious physical healing and training program. It would involve resting more, eating better, and doing some kind of physical strengthening practice, maybe *tai chi*. I'd take up running again, but that's an old method that proved far better at keeping things at bay, as rather than confront things I literally ran from them. This time I intend healing as the ultimate goal, a restorative practice rather than an exhaustive one. My real goal overall is to take better care of myself.

    I notice the progress one of our cats has made. When we first rescued her, many years ago, she hid under the television stand for four days, in a three-inch high space, before coming out to snoop around. I knew she was getting used to us, our sounds, our habits, our smells, testing our goodness and getting used to our voices. She was skittish, nervous, and terribly afraid for many months after that too. Now she knows we care about her and she trusts us enough to slowly crawl into our laps when she wants a cuddle, knowing that we accept her neediness. I feel bad if I have to push her away, like I'm being cruel, because I know what it means to have come that far, to be able to trust that much. It's what I'm hoping for, to be able to open my heart and become so trusting.

    I want to trust Chuck, and yet I still hold back. Where is the difficulty? He guides without harming me in any way, doesn't push unnecessarily, and I only move forward because I'm ready. As I advance, I really am learning what it means to trust another human being, without fear of being violated. I also know that in order to go further, to fully heal, I will have to one day allow myself to intimately and fully trust another human being with my body and my soul. First, I must be able to trust myself to not fall back into an old complacency, thinking that just ANY relationship is better than being alone. I must protect myself from making THAT mistake. I must not move into a relationship until I'm really ready, and until the right person shows up. And how will I know it's the right person? I'll *know*.

    I go to the video store and bump into a guy who likes me. Suddenly he's standing next to me, appearing as silently as an apparition. We had coffee and took walks together a few times last summer and fall, and then I broke off contact with him. I found him too needy, too sad, though he made it pretty clear that he was interested in a relationship. He's been in the area again for about a week, he says. I'm relieved he didn't call, though he suggests he might stop in for a visit at the studio. I don't say anything to that. I'm just so glad I didn't start anything with him because as soon as he starts talking, I'm bored. No interest there. My intention to be in a good place within myself before venturing forth into the world of relationship remains good advice. And I just proved to myself that indeed, I *will* know when I meet the right person!

In my dream last night, the sun shone brightly on those x and y chromosomes, clearly highlighting them. What did they represent, a male/female connection? Giving birth to some new form? They morphed into the evil vampire woman, who tried to trick me, before morphing into a docile cow, and then back into a vampire again, perhaps showing me her two sides, the spirit and the shadow, the calm and the angry, the giver and the taker, life and death. I confronted her. I didn't run but stood my ground, aware of her trickery, warning the child too. But who was she?

My dream seems to be showing me what's happening in my life right now, as I experience the highs and lows of my night sea journey, one moment as happy as a cow and in the next raging like a vampire queen. It's showing me what I do to myself, or what this stage of my recapitulation is teaching me about myself, as I seek to reconcile my many moods and emotions, all the feelings I've never dealt with, and especially as I seek to untangle and make sense of the anger that lies deep within me. I too have more than one side.

The vampire woman is a figment of my dreaming imagination so she represents what comes from within, from the unconscious, and all that is yet to be resolved. At the same time, she may also represent a fear I haven't yet faced, like those men in the car. I have a feeling I'll be seeing more of her, in one form or another!

I must constantly confront myself as I take this unfolding journey, just as I confronted her in the dream. I must not allow my emotions or feelings to overwhelm me. Exhausted or not, I have to be my own healer now, for the only true possibility of rescue lies within myself. I have to be my own savior.

Perhaps I'll dream myself out of the depression I've been in all day. The darkness within pulls so strongly, and yet I know full well that it's only old energy that pulls me down, the vampire woman within, as last night's dream points out. I get angry at myself for sitting all day by the cauldron, dark thoughts firing away. I should fight it by feeding myself good nourishing thoughts, but I'm exhausted, and that has led to no appetite for new foods of any kind now, no appetite for change, though that's exactly the main course I must indulge in. The only way I can go forward is by changing.

In my dreams I intend to be strong and, if need be, I will call for help, but I won't run. *I won't run.*

January 3, 2004

I fight a long battle against the vampire woman and her army from the sky. All night long I fight ferociously and bravely, expertly wielding a long sword, but I am no match for her and her powerful army. Eventually, I am taken prisoner. As the dream ends, my legs are clamped into a wooden torture machine and, unable to move, I am left to die.

I really did sleep like a prisoner, my legs clamped tightly together, in great pain. But the reality is that I'm keeping *myself* a prisoner, staying sequestered and alone. I hide away from the world unless I have to actually be somewhere or do something. I can't stand to be around people for very long so I hide out, avoiding interactions as much as possible, even if I say I'm not. What the fuck is wrong with me!

It's nothing new, this agoraphobia, nothing I haven't already experienced, in fact it's the way I've always preferred to be. I go out into the world for a little while but can't wait to get home again. I'm not quite ready to be a part of the world yet. As much as I've been changing, and as much as the world beckons me to new life, I don't know if I can fully embrace it yet. But the truth is, I'm no longer as comfortable in the old world as I once was either. I'm trapped between a desire to retreat and a desire to forge ahead, and even though I fought valiantly against the vampire woman and her army, I failed to advance or save myself.

As soon as I got captured, my physical body accepted the sentence of torture, falling right back into an old pattern. But for the rest of the night, though my body stayed a prisoner in the torture rack, I was aware of nonstop dream action and interaction. In spite of being clamped into a torture machine, another part of me moved about freely and easily, without pain. It's the truth of the place I'm in now; part of me is still a prisoner of the old world while another part of me has already gone on into new life. I'm living a wild, uncertain life now, as two people entangled in two different worlds, the x and y of my own self.

It's a fragile state and I fear I'm going to break, that there won't be anything left of me, that the me I know now won't exist anymore. But, wait! Maybe I've already shattered. Maybe I've just been misinterpreting this stage, thinking that I'm about to disintegrate when actually I'm really on the mend! The truth is, I know I'm still holding onto something, though it's not clear what it is. But why do I still need to go back to the cauldron? What does it still hold for me? What have I missed? For I am still held captive by *something*, something as of yet unrecapitulated.

The only thing I find back there in an old-world comfort; it's the only place I know that still provides a deeply known sense of comfort and belonging. Even though it's a numbing and disturbing place, in its own way it's also a most warm and inviting place. It's probably not unusual that there's comfort in the same place where there's excruciating pain, and that there's pain in the tension of this time of change and transition too. As Chuck is fond of saying, something has to be sacrificed for there to be new life, something must give for something to grow; you can't have new life without first suffering the pain of birth.

It's three-thirty in the afternoon and I've been out in the world all day, managing okay. I walk and talk and act like a normal person. When in the darkness and alone I find nothing to hang onto, nothing that makes me feel real, yet I long for that dark loneliness the way an addict longs for a fix. I really am in between worlds, and I find that both worlds fill needs, yet I also notice that I don't feel quite safe in this new one yet, and I find nothing really meaningful in the old one either—only old fears greet me back there. But after being so present in the world, negotiating commissions today, I admit that I now long for the comforts of the past. I crave the safety of the old known fears, faraway from everything new that scares me in a different way. I'm not sure what it is about the new that scares me, nothing when I think about it, perhaps just the thought of not knowing what to expect.

This is what I most desire: to be able to paint quietly in my studio, to do what I do best and get paid for it, and to not feel like I have to apologize for wanting to work and earn an income that I can live comfortably on. Is that too much to ask? Why do I always think I don't deserve these basic things? This issue has plagued me forever, a leftover from my days of low self-esteem, and yet it plagues me still, that I am not worthy of such things. Is it still true, or is it just an old idea from the old world that was never true to begin with?

It's Saturday night. The kids are away with their dad for the weekend and I've been trying to deflect the pull to the comforts of the gloomy old world by watching movies and reading. Depression, like a desperate lover, comes calling in the night, its draw intense. I know how dangerous it is, and that every time I go back there, I lose some of the ground I've gained. So, I seek to stay present by focusing on sound and word and image, instead of the old known comfort of my own darkness.

I kept busy at the studio today too so I could forget for a while, forget the way the depression sneaks up on me and tells me I need it, that I'm happier with it, that I'm a failure and that only *it* matters. I'll be happy to be back to our family routine again on Monday, the kids back to school after the holidays, everything predictable, for the most part, the structure of each day mundanely known.

January 4, 2004

I dream that I move into a new house. I wander around looking into closets, deciding where to put things. It's a large fortress-like house on a mountain, built of stone, with flowering fruit trees outside; pawpaw, mulberry, and cherry. The house is protected at night by armed guards. It's my turn to stand guard, so

I dutifully pick up my sword and prepare myself. I'll fight if I have to, even though I don't really want to fight; I'm too tired. Chuck, standing quietly in the corner, tells me, very kindly, that it's okay, that I don't have to fight. As soon as he says this, I put my sword down, knowing that it's better to be prepared for new life by getting some rest. I then clearly see that the house is already a strong fortress and doesn't need additional protection. Besides, it's daytime, not nighttime. The fruit trees are in bloom and the sun is shining brightly. There's nothing to worry about. It's suddenly clear to me that nothing threatens my new sanctuary on the mountain. As the dream ends, I realize, very clearly, that there's nothing to fight.

    I must remember what it's like on the days when I feel good, when I'm relaxed and my thoughts don't weigh me down. There's a lightness in my brain and my body then, and I even feel hopeful. Maybe the depressed emptiness that I feel now is only the habitual nothingness that I've been fighting, the ghosts of fears and memories that don't really exist anymore. My dream tells me that it's time to shift my perspective, to notice what's real and what's illusory, only in my mind. The old fear is unnecessary now, the memories simply memories, nothing that I need. The truth is, I've been fighting ghosts, my own ghosts, ghosts of myself, ghosts of pain and fear and sadness, ghosts overloading me with their old energies, continuing to haunt me because I have not told them to stop. Perhaps they're just waiting for me to acknowledge and release them.

    In last night's dream, by putting down my sword, there suddenly was *nothing* to fight. Whatever I thought I needed to fight no longer existed; as soon as I took my energy and attention off it, it ceased to exist. In an instant the enemy was gone! I must merge this dream reality with this waking life. I must remember to put down my weapons when the urge to fight comes upon me. Otherwise, I'm just creating my own enemies.

    I take a walk in the mud and rain. It gives me time to think, and to feel myself in my body. I'm pretty relaxed, the fight gone out of me. During that dream I was sleeping on my right side and then, in my dream and in reality, I turned my body over to the left and said to myself: *right fight; left no fight*. That phrase, *right fight; left no fight*, goes through me as I walk, repeating itself like a mantra, taking over where the ghosts of fear and memory have been living.

 I've been sleeping on my right side lately, after I'd noticed I could fight better from that position when dreaming. If I lay on my left side while sleeping, I failed to fight back in dreams, I was more complacent. So, if I wanted to fight back in my dreams I instinctively went to sleep on my right side; I thought it was necessary. But maybe it isn't really necessary, maybe it incites fighting, keeps me bound in a fighting stance, which expends a lot of energy, both in dreaming and in real life. Maybe it's time to shift to the other side, especially if I intend to uphold the decision I've made to not fight anymore. The dream gave me such a brilliantly simple message: *if you don't want to fight, put down your weapon.* In so doing, I discovered there was indeed nothing to fight. Have I been the instigator all along, creating the enemy I have so feared and despised?

 The right side is masculine, aggressive, while the left side is feminine, gentler. The right is physical, the left is spiritual. I've noticed that if I sleep on my right side, I have more aggressive dreams and I tend to fight back. If I sleep on my left side I fail to fight; I just don't have any fight in me. And when I sleep in the middle, on my back, I am stuck between the two sides, my legs clenched, trapped in pain, unable to act in either direction, and my dreams reflect this. My sleeping positions are intricately tied in with what transpires in my dreams. How interesting!

 I am no longer breakable. I'm still fragile, but light and airy fragile, not brittle fragile. I'm tired too, exhausted by this inner work. In my dream, once I realized there wasn't anything to fight, I also realized that exhaustion had offered a key to shifting, that exhaustion offered an opportunity to change. It's what I've already deduced might be the ticket to unseating the old protectorate self, but I'm going to have to find a better method than exhaustion if I'm going to move forward. If I'm simply exhausted, I'll have no energy for anything. And I must remain strong because I know there's still more to come. The journey is far from over.

I'm grateful for the daily revelations I receive. They guide me and keep me focused on the path, looking forward, toward the new life that is waiting for me. I sometimes wonder what I'll do with what I've been learning, the lessons from all the worlds I've intersected with as I've taken this incredible journey, not just the guidance that I've discovered is available for the asking, but the true journey of accessing and bringing forth the spiritual Self. For the truth is, I've discovered that what I truly am is a little soul taking its journey through life, discovering what it's truly capable of. This, I truly believe, is the same journey we are all on. I feel that I must somehow use the knowledge I'm learning in a way that will reach as many people as possible, but also in a way that's comfortable and natural for me. Writing may be the way for me to teach what I've learned.

At other times, I wonder if I'm really learning anything new. It feels like ancient knowledge that everyone has access to. I'm not special, but for some reason I've found myself here, in this moment, having these extraordinary experiences.

Bad thoughts creep in every now and then as the day progresses, old ghosts trying to reassert themselves no doubt. I do my best to dispel them, focusing on getting back to work tomorrow and planning what I'll do in the future. I know now that I must write, in my own quiet way, for it has become a clear imperative. I also know that once I sit quietly and listen to the voices inside myself, I'll know how to begin and I'll know what to say. Those voices have been with me through this whole process, and they will remain in the future, allowing me to speak and write the right words. I sense that I will become a conduit of some sort for the silent voices that yearn to be heard, for the painful stories that must to be told, for the truths that must be spoken. I'm tired of the cruelty of silence.

January 5, 2004

I dreamed all night, aware of my position, sleeping mostly on my back, but it was far from a restful night. Jesus came in a dream and tried to convince me to stop being so stubborn. I had a long conversation with him. He kept urging me to give up, to stop holding in. I said something about it being my strength.

"Our strengths are also our weaknesses, but even I gave up after a while," he said.

"I give up on you!" he finally said, in exasperation, when I refused to give up holding in stuff that wasn't good for me.

"Well, at least I'm not fighting anymore," I said.

"Yes, you are," he said. *"You are fighting yourself and your destiny."*

"Give it up, Jan!" he said, repeatedly. *"Just give it up!"*

"I wash my hands of you," he said, as the dream ended, and he walked away in disgust, saying he was giving up the fight to save me. If I wouldn't help myself then neither would he.

Freezing rain in the night has left the world coated in ice, so there's a two-hour school delay for the kids, nice for the first day back after the holiday break. I accept the gift of the extra time to sit here in bed and write for a little while before I have to get the kids up.

I envision a proactive day today, as my intention is to do some positive things to kick off this New Year of new beginnings on the right foot. I ask my spiritual advisors to guide and help me, to keep me focused on my intentions so that my path may unfold naturally, unencumbered by financial worry, unplagued by old thoughts of self-defeat. I pray for confidence to keep going into the future unafraid, to never give up on myself as I seek to become all that I can be.

The kids are off to school by 9, and though I still feel somewhat depressed, with the old need to withdraw still present, I also know I have to really push myself through those old ghosts of feelings if I am to survive this time of transition, for I do know that during times of transition old fears within myself are apt to reappear, presenting their old challenges. Do I retreat into their comforts, or do I ignore them and push on? If I am to survive this crucial time, I must push through with all the fierceness I can muster. In that sense, I *am* still fighting; Jesus got it right.

Tomorrow I see Chuck for the first time in weeks, but I'm almost afraid to see him, afraid to start talking again, to get back into the routine of it, even though I know I need to keep moving forward with this recapitulation. I must go where it takes me, and so this is not the time to refuse to talk, or to quit. This recapitulation, which includes the process of speaking to another human being, is too necessary. And it's much bigger than I am, with a mind and a heart of its own.

January 6, 2004

The pain and discomfort in my legs was excruciating last night and I tossed and turned most of the night, not knowing which position to take, fight or no fight. I was able to get some sleep when on my left side and had dreams of apathy, not caring anymore, of giving up. I remember turning over to my right side to try and bring some fight back in. Then I fell into a vivid dream where my struggle coalesced and I was able to finally make a decision. I was in a beautiful cathedral filled with sunlight, too exhausted to care about anything. People followed me around, begging me to keep fighting, handing me weapons.

"No! I'm not fighting anymore," I said, lying down on the floor, exhausted. "I don't care. I just don't care. I'll just lie here and let it happen. It's going to happen anyway. I give up. Leave me alone. I'm not fighting anymore. I give up."

Obviously, the dream confronted my ambivalence over which stance to take, and the exhausted part of myself resolved the issue by lying down, similar to putting down my sword in that previous dream. I seemed to be all those people in my dream urging me to get back into the fight too. There's a part of me that always fights, no matter what, but in the dream another part of me spoke the bitter truth.

"What does my child self need?" I ask. "What does she want? What is she asking of me?"

"Love," Chuck says, and I know he's right, that the little girl inside me is looking for the love she's never had.

"Oh, I get it! I couldn't figure out what the great longing I've been feeling so strongly was for! A longing for *something* elusive, but now I get it. You're right, it's the need for love, to be loved. I thought I *had* experienced love in my life, but now I realize it wasn't REAL love. So, there isn't really anything to be afraid of. Love can't hurt me, at least not if it's REAL."

"Yes, but you can't be rescued, swept out of misery, you have to reach out for it," he says. "You have to meet it."

"How?"

"You have to let go of everything that's holding you back and accept the ride," says Chuck, "but you have to do it on your own. The truth is you're being rescued left and right. Even Jesus Christ himself came to rescue you, and you turned him down!"

"I realize I have to let go of all the old notions of love, be open to love in a different way, redefine it, or let it redefine itself as I experience it. I have no idea what real love means, but I have to stop looking for it in an old way, in the way my child self hoped for love from neglectful parents, or in the way I've projected it onto partners. I have to be open to it for my little girl self, as well as my adult self, in a totally new way."

"Yes, that's one of those metaphorical bridges you have to cross," Chuck says. "Whether you've had no love at all or were totally, unconditionally loved in childhood, it doesn't matter, because you are in the same dilemma. You have to allow yourself access to love by going out on your own, finding love and experiencing it in your own way. Once you walk across that bridge, you will find everything there waiting for you."

We schedule a Friday appointment but as soon as we do, I realize I'm afraid to meet with Chuck again, and I'm afraid not to as well. I've been so apprehensive about getting back into the intensity of the recapitulation, knowing that once I did, I would be thrown into it head over heels again. And true to form, here I am, challenged immediately to face the unknown, to let go of what has held me together and cross a new bridge, and be OPEN to what comes. Yikes! Just the thought and I'm shaking. But maybe I'm not being fair to myself and the journey I've already taken. I've accomplished a lot and learned to be really open over the past few years, and I've weathered through incredible trials. It's not like I haven't been here before.

I took control of the recapitulation over the holidays, and now I'm being challenged to let the process take control again, letting it take things to a new level. That's my dilemma with Chuck too, because meeting with him again means having to shift away from what kept me safe over the holidays, and there's both fear and excitement in that. But I face the real truth: I've had too much control over the holiday break. It truly is time to give that up and get back into the flow of things!

My dreams have been telling me to lay down my arms and let go of everything that I've held onto, even my fierceness, which has been my saving grace, and my worst enemy at times too. It seems almost anathema to this whole shamanic process, though. A warrior never gives in or gives up, which seems par for the course, but in a sense that's the type of warrior I've been my whole life. Now I think I'm being presented with a different kind of warriorhood, a gentle and loving kind. I have a feeling that if I slow everything down and pay attention to how I *feel*, and really listen to the voices and what they're saying, I'll get where I'm going faster and in a more compassionate way. I think I'm being taught to be a gentle warrior of loving kindness. That's the next bridge to cross and the next shift taking place.

There's an older, retired man who has appeared in my life. I had a premonition of meeting him in a dream I had on October 26, 2003, where he brought me food and coffee and told me he wanted to help me. Something about him felt familiar then and here I have met him in real life. He's a cancer survivor and his goal in life now is to help others, to do good where it's needed. He's chosen me to be the recipient of his goodness, he says. He wants to be my benefactor. He's very earnest about his reasons for having chosen me, through a mutual friend, to be the object of his giving. He's been offering to help me for weeks now, and this has freaked me out. I have been automatically saying, "no, but thank you," every time he says he wants to help me. He offers money, groceries, rides. He's happily married, he tells me, so there's no cause for alarm, but it's his goal to be good to me. He says he's totally available, unconditionally, without wanting anything in return. He's just happy to be alive.

I begin to see his offer in a different light now, especially after my conversation with Chuck today. I have, in fact, been asking my guides and helpers to send me someone, a mentor or benefactor, and here they've sent me this man! But I haven't realized it because he came so eagerly and in a manner that triggered some old fears in me, sending me into a negative place when, truthfully, I could use his offers of help. I've been refusing him the same way I refused Jesus in my dream. Just because something isn't coming as I imagine it should come, doesn't mean I'm not being offered something meaningful. He popped in to see me again today at the studio.

"Okay, let's talk," I said. "What I really need is more work. Can you help with that?"

"My offer of help is so easy, and it's free!" he said, and yes, he has a lot of connections and he'll be happy to hook me up with some work.

When I told Chuck about my leg pain today, he called it *memory pain*. It's not the posture that brings it on, he said, but habit. I admit that I'm still drawn to attaching to the familiar habits, simply because they are familiar, but I also know that they're no longer acceptable. Only the unfamiliar is acceptable now. I have to get used to the idea that when something new makes me uncomfortable, that's a GOOD sign. I'll try to remember that!

"You've instinctively discovered the right/aggressive, left/passive personality sides," he said. "Continue to balance them, as you did in dreaming, by turning to the right side during passive dreams to pump up the energy a little."

I hope to remember that as I dream.

January 7, 2004

I had asked my guides for help before sleep last night and then I dreamed about them. They urged me to seek the *unfamiliar*. They told me it was the next step. My legs won't hurt, they said, if I step in the right direction. They hurt now because I'm stuck, they said, and they, my legs, are yearning for me to turn in a new direction, while all I continue to do is hold them stiffly in an old stance, thus, the pain. If I turn in a new direction and accept the unfamiliar, the pain will ease. It's really that easy, they said.

If I turn to my Benefactor, whom I instinctively shy away from and become uncomfortable around, I am aware that he clearly lays his cards on the table, no hidden agenda. When he says he only wants to help, I believe that to be the truth. His offers are genuine and visible, not hidden or veiled. Perhaps it really is time to take a leap of faith and go for the unfamiliar, as my guides are telling me, as even Jesus told me, rather than engaging the same old stuff, which is so predictable. Which direction is really scarier?

The guidance is that all I have to do is turn; as simple as pivoting in a new direction and I'll be in the next phase of my life. I am assured that things *will* happen, but I can make them so much easier if I don't fight them. In fact, the other day my Benefactor encouraged me, quite abruptly, to "loosen up!" My studio partner was quite taken aback by this outburst, but I knew exactly what he meant. The challenge is that he's a stranger whom I am being encouraged to trust. The other person who continues to show up is the guy who likes me and whom I met in the video store a few days ago. He's been stopping at the studio to visit, though I remain uninterested and unencouraging.

I call Chuck and tell him I won't be coming on Friday, that I feel a need to take it slower, and that I think coming on Friday might be pushing too much, putting too much pressure on myself. I think he understands. I tell him about the dilemma with my Benefactor and the other guy who continues to pursue me. My Benefactor said, "I know I seem to be overly affectionate, but I mean to be!" The other guy looks at me with his hangdog, begging eyes and I realize the danger of falling into a relationship simply because something about it feels familiar, a certain neediness that I automatically fall into the habit of taking care of. The familiar is dangerous and the unknown, the unfamiliar, is the new direction to take, the only path now. I get it.

It's perfectly okay to say no, to keep people away, to detach, to retreat from what doesn't feel right. The one guy is a familiar self-centered, childish chump, a sad sack, while my Benefactor is a strong John Wayne type, big and tall, totally up front, with all his cards laid on the table in a straightforward, no bullshit manner. It's a type and approach I am definitely not used to!

I realize that what I took for granted as normal as a child, such as my parent's lack of emotional and physical expressions of love, was not normal at all. So now, when someone comes and very earnestly and truthfully asks what they can do for me, I immediately shy away and say, "nothing, I don't need anything," because that has been my attitude my entire life, that I don't need other people. I'm fine on my own; I can take care of myself. But underneath, the little girl in me has always remained hopeful that someone would come along and help her, but I have kept that little girl at a distance from the adult me, who proceeded through life as unattached and emotionless as my parents. Now I'm reconnecting with the needs of my little girl self, finding out that her needs are real and legitimate, that she's right to want to be loved and appreciated, protected and cared for. I'm meeting her now on a new level, from a place that neither of us has been able to achieve until now, and I'm trying to learn how to say yes, for both of us.

I expect I'll get tested and challenged by my old demons a while longer before I'm completely free of them, but I'll do what it takes to move things along, for the scent of new life is certainly in the air.

I do believe that someone in the universe is trying to tell me something. Last week, I swear I had four dollars in my wallet one day, but when I next looked, I had five singles. I spent three of them and when I looked next, I had four again. Today I had two single dollars, which I took out to buy a bagel and now when I just looked inside my wallet, I have two dollars again! What the heck is going on? Is this a sign, telling me to not worry about money? That I will have it when I need it? I hope so! I like the message. It seems to be saying, "calm down about money issues, it's not worth wasting energy on, the worry eats away at you. Just look, you have money!" It's not exactly a lot of money, and I don't spend much either, but it's teaching me to just relax and enjoy the playfulness of the universe. Rather than wrack my brain over whether or not I just didn't see those extra dollars each time I looked in my wallet, I'm just going to trust the message I most need right now, which is: don't worry, you'll be fine!

Trust, believe, and accept the help that comes.

January 8, 2004

"*Believe. Let yourself believe.*"

"*Slow down. Take it slow.*"

"*Let go, Jan. Just be a part of it,*" Jeanne says, "*be a part of the miracle that is unfolding in your life.*"

These words, spoken very clearly, hang in the air above my head as I awaken.

It *is* a miracle; my whole life is a miracle. That I survived is a miracle. That I forgot, blocked out the abuse, is a miracle. That I began to recall is a miracle. That I discovered I could trust Chuck is a miracle, and that I'm beginning to come alive is a miracle. For the first time in my life, I'm beginning to feel the essence of myself, an awareness of myself as real. I *am* real. I *do* exist. I'm a miracle too.

There really is nothing to be afraid of. The people I meet, the things that happen to me now have a different meaning because I'm different. I'm getting out of my head, out of the darkness in my own mind. I'm getting out of the prison of myself that I've upheld for so long. I'm doing what Jesus asked me to do in my dream last week: *letting go*. And in so doing, I discover that I'm a free being, free to have and enjoy the experiences that come to me in this miraculous life I'm in!

I feel loved. I guess I'm feeling *God*, there is no better name for it. God as Love. It's not so much something outside of me, but an awareness growing inside me. As I write those words, I feel my body puffing up. Suddenly I'm floating, and before I know what's happening, a conversation begins.

"Hello, Jan, this is God."

"Hi, God."

"*I'm here.*"

"That's really you? How did you find me?"

"*Through Chuck, I'm Chuck too.*"

"Chuck is God?"

"*Yes, and a lot of other people are too.*"

"My Benefactor?"

"Yes. That's how I find you, through other people; that's how I do my work."

"Thank you."

"You don't have to thank me. I have to go now. I have to help some others."

"Okay. I love you."

"*I love you, Jan.*"

Wow, so he works through other people. God works through all those good people. I've seen him in Chuck. I've seen light and truth shining through Chuck, God's goodness and love. And those dollar bills showing up in my wallet are just another sign that I'm going to be okay, that I'm on the right path, that I'm getting out of the darkness and experiencing new, fresh light. I'm learning to not question my experiences or wonder where I'm going, no longer judging but trusting.

Somewhere, a long time ago, as a small child I was happy. I remember laughing and delighting in life, completely innocent and unafraid, with a child's complete trust in her life and the people in her world. And then the darkness came like a heavy, dank curtain. My innocence was smothered and that happy memory was extinguished, until now, for I remember that I did once experience a baby's innocence and trust, that at one time I knew nothing but that. Maybe it didn't last very long, but the memory still exists. It makes me realize all that I can and will feel again, that one day I will reside in complete trust and love. I'm already granted the feel of it in the memory of my innocent child self, and I know it to be love, as God says.

We all have innocence in us at birth, but then we lose it. It's taken from us in so many different ways, but then some of us are lucky enough to find it again. In finding it we understand how fragile and important it is, how fragile and important we were as children, how fragile and important all children are, but also how essential innocence is. We just have to find our way back to it. It's innocence that we seek, and with innocence fully restored we can experience REAL love. That's the bridge to cross that I spoke of with Chuck at our last meeting. I need to be near him tomorrow; I need to meet with him after all.

I call him. We'll meet as usual.

I was emotional today, but quietly so, innerly feeling a lot of things. I'm feeling much more peaceful inside and the peace comes with the realization that I'm not alone. Even as I continue searching for connection, for my place in this world and the meaning of my life, I know I'm not alone. Plenty of messages are being dropped along the way to prove this to me.

I'm aware, through my meditation practice and my quiet, deep listening practice, that spiritual advisors have always been present. I understand that God uses whatever is available to communicate with us and aid us. I'm not afraid of mystical things. In fact, I expect them and I look forward to experiencing them. They're important to me, part of life, similar to what happens to me when I go into my creative bubble. Experiences in creative states are open communications with God, with the universe, with spirit, whatever you want to call it. They are all the same thing really, experiences of the mystical; loving energy seeking outlet in time and space.

I need to find a way to talk about this with Chuck tomorrow without feeling embarrassed or self-conscious. I know he'll understand. He never makes me feel absurd. God speaks through all kinds of beings, conduits, people, animals, wind, voices, and signs. He, God, told me this today, but I realize we only hear or see what we are ready for.

It's happening, *something* is happening. I'm not sure what it is, but I'm beginning to feel it.

January 9, 2004

Sleeping was a tiresome and difficult chore last night. I lay awake in a semi-conscious state, aware that I still struggle with the darkness. It tugged at me all night, attempting to pull me back when all I wanted to do was stay in the light, in the beauty of finally knowing God. I tossed and turned trying to get comfortable and ended up finally sleeping on my right side, giving in to the pull of the fight, just to get some sleep. I slept knowing that I had fallen back into an old place and I grew disappointed when I found myself back there fighting again.

Having only just discovered God, I'm disappointed that I already have to fight for my new thoughts and feelings. I know they don't quite belong to me yet. They're just beginning to coalesce and yet I feel such a strong coming together, a clash of truths and synchronicities that I couldn't have accepted before, shut down and shut off as I was. But the darkness is lifting now and I'm beginning to see the light. I'm discovering God.

Is this what a spiritual journey is all about, discovering the God in me? And here I thought I was all alone! Even as I write this, I feel a cry of forlornness welling up inside me, telling me that I AM alone, lonely and lonesome. But I have to trust and believe in my experiences, let them guide and lead me now, and they're telling me something else completely. I really understand what Chuck means when he says to believe! Believe in your own experiences, he's really telling me; they are all you have to go on. There's nothing else to believe in, only that which you personally experience and know in your own heart is real and meaningful.

I know this will all sound rather simple when I speak to Chuck, but there was so much more that was unspoken swirling through my conversation with God yesterday. There was so much more meaning than just a few little words can express, steeped as they were with unspoken visions that I intuited as we spoke. But I also know that Chuck will understand. He has to. God is, after all, working through him, as I was told!

I'm afraid to feel anything except wonder, afraid that it can all be taken away, this fragile touch of Oneness with the God image. It's as if I've touched the hand of God and yet can't believe that hand will remain in touch. I can't own any of this, nor fully take it in yet either, though I feel a dawning about to take place, a deep sense that something is finally about to come together, a new understanding, a revelation of some sort, but all I can abide at the moment is the wonder of it all. I'm trying hard to believe, to just be part of this miracle of my life as it unfolds.

There's constant struggle present in the mind. Whether one is in pain or bliss there's conflict. I see that in Chuck as he struggles to do the right thing, to listen and hear what I say, as he struggles to make sure he hears exactly what he's supposed to hear, to really get what I'm saying. And then I see him struggling to say the right words back to me in just the right way, to find the proper words of guidance, to let it come through him without judgment, without telling me what I must do but giving me the guidance that I can best use to help myself. I see how careful and thoughtful he is to never take ownership of my journey nor tell me what to do—it's my job to live my own life. And I'm thankful and grateful for his approach, because I see how important it has been for me to find my own way through the dark morass of my past into my own bright present.

"Yes, life is a constant struggle," Chuck says when we meet, "and the challenge is to not get caught in the struggle, but to continuously let it go."

He deals with it daily, he tells me, learning to trust the universe and that he too is in good hands, in God's hands. He says that for him, as with me, the struggle comes up around work, being self-employed. It's not about advertising and pushing an agenda in any way, he says, but trusting that he fills a need and that people will come; that those who are seeking will find him, just as I found him.

I ask him if he's aware that he's being used by God. He says he's aware of being a vessel for people who need something, and if they need it, he gives what comes through him. He says he always knew he was a seeker and it was either to do this, psychotherapy, or become a priest, but the priesthood wasn't right for him. And now he has elected to go outside the system in order to do what he feels needs to be done, into the shamanic world. It supports what he does and how he does it.

"Keep listening to those voices in your head," he says, laughing, knowing it's not what you'd expect a therapist to say!

He brings up the dream I had a long time ago, about his wife Jeanne, telling me I could trust him.

"Wow!" he says.

"Yes, that was really the beginning of all this," I say, but I don't tell him it wasn't a dream, that it was a vision, although as I sit with him, I hear Jeanne saying, "You should tell him!" But stubborn me, I don't. Instead, we continue talking about the magic that I've been experiencing, about just believing in it. Then it's my turn to laugh, because there's so much real magic I haven't had the nerve to tell him about yet!

"This is the big payoff now, for everything you've gone through," Chuck says. "This is when everything is in alignment and it all comes together."

I'm glad I came to see Chuck today. No matter what I say, he validates it in some unique way. He never makes me feel ridiculous or absurd, but always listens with kindness and compassion. Even so, I still feel the need to take it slow, to slow everything down, to let myself experience this new side of myself slowly, the side I always knew was there, but just couldn't reach.

"I feel like a prisoner suddenly let out of prison!" I say.

"You were a prisoner given a life sentence and then, once out in the real world, you wondered if it wasn't better back there in prison."

"Yes, that's exactly how I feel."

"Just let yourself experience it," he says. "Take it slow."

I'm not surprised that he uses the exact phrase that has been going through my own head. It's all the validation I need. Indeed, I will *take it slow*.

January 10, 2004

I dream that brown, muddy floodwaters swirl through a house. I watch as everything is carried rushing downstream. I have the feeling that it doesn't matter, that none of it matters, just let it go. Start over. You don't need any of it. And I have such a deeply visceral feeling of letting go as I watch things wash away and disappear. Afterwards, I see people walking around, naked, looking for things they lost in the flood and I know that none of it matters. Here we all are, stripped to nothing and with nothing, and why are we searching for things we can't get back?

"There's nothing here for us, nothing," I say, at dream's end. "Time to look in a new direction now."

Trust. I'm learning to trust. This is what comes to me as I wake up, sore from clenching, stiff and achy as usual. It feels like my body isn't quite with me on this trust issue yet. Though my spirit is making headway, my body is reluctant. The pain is as severe as ever.

The pain never released today, as if the cold icy chill in the air has settled into me like an old friend, reluctant to leave. I take a long hot bath at the end of the day, adding hot water several times, urging my tight muscles to let go. Even the heat of the bath does little to budge the pain. I get out of the tub and wrap myself in clothes and blankets. I think I'll talk to my yoga teacher about doing some healing yoga therapy with him. When I'm ready, of course!

I've been thinking again about writing my story, of publishing what I've been writing in my journals. I continue to feel how important it is that it be known, that sexual abuse of children happens and is happening now, right under our noses, horrible things, in idyllic settings as well as in the depths of poverty, inside families who are pillars of their communities and inside the institutions that we so depend on, dark, bitter tasting, secretive business. On a personal note, my own memories still reside in me. Writing them down, giving them form and shape with my own hands, may be the way to finally release them. Ultimately, to put them to rest between the pages of a book, organized, catalogued, stored away outside of my body, neatly packaged, nothing left undone, may be the way to finish with them once and for all.

I've also been pondering how inner voices can be totally misconstrued, how God/Spirit speaks to us in many ways, and how innocently sensitive and unafraid we must be to hear anything at all. Most of the time I feel I miss half of what I'm being guided to. I see my own spiritual advisors looking down on me from the floor of a great tower in the sky. There's a trio on the right; a woman, a man, and a child—my grandparents and my brother—and off to the left, a lone female, Jeanne, dark-haired and young looking, around thirty years of age. If the clouds clear, if the fog clears, I can see hundreds, perhaps thousands of other figures behind them, a universe of spiritual support, individuals just waiting to be assigned a human being to protect and guide.

Should I tell Chuck that Jeanne doesn't come to me in dreams as I once told him, but that she has come in the form of an apparition, in visions, in her energy body, and that she communicates through channeled messages? Should I tell him that I could reach out and put my hand through her ethereal substance? She came to me once when I was crying in my bed, when a memory was gripping me, and she calmed me, telling me that everything would work out just fine, that I was going to be okay. I felt the weight of her body on top of me and I've felt her beside me on numerous other occasions as well. She steadied me once in a yoga class, her hand pressing lightly but firmly on my shoulder, bringing immediate deep calmness.

Do I tell him these things? That she has appeared to me in person? That she speaks to me regularly too? That I have long conversations with her?

"*Sleep now,*" Jeanne says. "*TRUST is still the issue.*"

January 11, 2004

I dream that I'm on the roof of a building, lying half hanging over the edge while a man points a gun at me. A second man, on the ground below, also has a gun trained on me. I'm caught between them. I quickly roll away from the edge of the building, and as I look back, I see that another woman has taken my place, but she's standing up, holding a gun, which she's pointing straight at the man on the roof. The man is inches away from her, his own gun pointed at her head in a tense standoff.

"Shoot! Why don't you shoot!" I silently scream to the woman, but she doesn't shoot. Then I realize that I am both myself lying on the roof and the other woman with the gun. I can't move, my legs hurt like heck, and as the woman with the gun I can't pull the trigger either. In both cases I'm paralyzed. When I see the man reach out and take the gun away from the other woman, I feel so disappointed. Why didn't she shoot? The tension between them remains high as he leads her away, his hostage.

I wake up from this dream, my legs hurting so badly that I want to scream. I realize that this dream underscores the hostage situation I've gotten myself into with my inability to let go, my own stubbornness to trust that I will be okay, and to, as Jesus told me, stop holding in that which causes so much harm. I am only doing this to myself.

I fall back asleep and dream again. This time I rescue an old rocking horse. I buy it and bring it home to my children, but they're really too big for it. I'm really buying it for myself. I carry it around with me, afraid that if I put it down, I'll lose sight of it or forget about it. I need it; I'm deeply attached to it. I walk beside an empty four-lane highway, clutching the rocking horse. The only vehicle I see is a small child on a tricycle riding down the middle of the road. I remember another dream I had where the same child got run over by a truck and my immediate reaction is to yell to the child to be careful, but then I realize it isn't necessary now. There's no danger out there anymore. The cars are all gone, the road is completely open.

"Have fun!" I say instead.

I wake with tears running down my cheeks because of the pain in my rigid legs, which lie stiffly clamped, burning like two logs on fire, stiff as the rocking horse in my dream. Do I still think I need to salvage something from childhood? I have to let everything go, even my ideas of innocence, because it's a new and different world out there now, no longer dangerous. I feel the pull to let a lot of things go and a desperate need to hold onto something, somewhere, anything familiar will do, even a thing as innocuous as an old rocking horse, but the truth is that childhood is over and yes, it's safe to be in the world now. At the same time, I know how ridiculous it is to hold onto old stuff, especially the old habits of clenching and hiding that only cause me such pain. Chuck once compared me to a heroin addict needing a fix, and here I am again, filled with the raw desire for something familiar, the craving so intense I feel I could explode.

I'm replaying the same feelings and problems repeatedly, having the same inner fights, the same dreams, the same curses, just in different settings. I have a strong desire today to not get out of bed, to just stay here and hide, to never move again, the heroin addict deciding to go for the fix. However, now that I've tasted some of what's out there for me in the future, I know I'll go back for more, that I'll begin to crave that instead, more and more of it and less of this. Someday, all of this will be far away and I won't be in such pain or so sad, that's how things work. But today I'm still sad.

It's Sunday and for most of the day I rest, read, and do laundry. My daughter spends the day at a friend's house and my son goes to a music rehearsal. I try to not make too much of being sad, focusing instead on just living and getting through this trying time, as I break with the old and seek to embrace the new.

January 12, 2004

I dream that I'm back in the neighborhood where I grew up, driving and walking around the familiar landscape near the house of the man who abused me. I stand at the entrance to his driveway and look down the long hill that I drove up to get here. I stand for a long time, looking down the long, empty slope of road. I feel nothing.

I wake up in a bad mood, feeling like I'm on an endless loop, searching for who-knows-what. I've experienced a touch of where I'm going, been gifted with small insights into the possibilities before me, but mostly I feel stuck! I get to a plateau where I see everything clearly, but then fall off, back into dark canyons again, then drag myself out and back up to the top of the plateau again, in an endless looping of highs and lows. I'm looking for some stability here, but it's been tough going.

It snowed during the night and there's a two-hour school delay, so I've had a little extra time to tend to my big baby self, but it's time to get the sleepy kids up now.

I know what my problem is. I'm still not able to trust. It's the one thing I've never allowed myself to do. *Never trust* has been my lifelong motto, and now I'm trying to teach myself how to do it. How do I learn to really trust? How do I learn to trust the magic, the possibilities? How do I learn to trust the voices, and that there's love and goodness in the world? How do I learn to trust that everything will be okay? How do I trust that I'm safe, that no one can hurt me now, that I'm strong and capable, that I'm good, that I'm beautiful, and that I'm loved? How?

January 13, 2004

I meet with Chuck and all I do is talk about being angry and depressed, frustrated and wanting to give up. He thinks I'm doing great. Shit! He then speaks of his wife, Jeanne, dealing with cancer, taking each conventional and unconventional step as it seemed right, until the end when she accepted that the next step was death.

"It wasn't her inclination to blame herself because she wasn't going to make it," he says. "It's just the way it was going, and we accepted it."

"I'm not blaming myself," I say. "I'm stubborn! I don't seem to know when it's time to accept or time to shift. How long do I wait before insisting on doing things differently? What am I waiting for? What do I really want? And how do I get there? Do I let the magic do its thing? Of course! So far, I've seen the magic, but what's next?"

"I'm fighting the old stuff again, aren't I," I finally say, feeling deflated and defeated.

"Well, you didn't think it would give up so easily, did you?" Chuck says.

It's eleven at night now. I allowed myself time to go inside and get some answers today, sat around the old cauldron, where I hadn't been for a few days because it just seemed better for me to feel the anger.

As I recall the hostage dream of the other night, I know that I must shift my *intent,* rather than make any actual physical shifts right now. When I physically shifted in the dream I was still caught in the tension of the situation, still in the grips of my own stubbornness. Shifting now must happen on an energetic level, by focusing my intent on what's right.

This hostage situation won't last long, if I can shift my focus and align my intent with the universe. It will disarm the perpetrators enough so I can overpower them and finally get to where I need to go, all parts of myself in alignment with what the universe has in mind. I must remove the interferences from my path, the old habits and ideas that just keep me looping through old dream scenarios. When I stood at the top of the hill in my dream the other night, and looked down the long road outside the property of the man who abused me, I wondered what I was doing there. It didn't seem like the right place to be anymore, and it really isn't. It's time for new dreams to take over.

I'm discovering that I have the ability to "see." Chuck mentioned something today and I realized that it felt like an instance of déjà vu, as it was something I had already seen happening, weeks before. I've noticed that I have this power of vision, of clairvoyance, but I haven't really paid much attention to it, or really given it any thought. Perhaps it has frightened me a bit, but I'm getting used to it now, and I intend on paying more attention to it.

January 14, 2004

I'm on my way to see the "Oracle," my legs hurting all the way down to my knees while I dream. I'm seeking relief, going to the Oracle to ask her what I should do. I'm taking Chuck with me, whom I refer to as the "soft tissue salesman," which appears to refer to both paper tissues and the tissues of the human body. I bring him along to explain things to me, because everything is coded and I have to break the codes before I can move on to the next thing.

I told Chuck yesterday that I won't see him on Friday, for the second time, but now feel a desperate need to be near him. What am I doing to myself? I can't do this without him. I turn to Jeanne for guidance.

"Please, help me."

"*Jan, I'm here,*" Jeanne says. "*All you have to do is ask. Just believe and I'll be right here.*"

"It's so hard. Why does it have to be so hard?"

"*Because you deserve it.*"

"I deserve it? The pain?"

"*The reward! When it comes it will show you how much you deserve it, and you will know that it belongs to you and no one can ever take it away again because you have worked so hard for it, your entire life in fact.*"

"How do I get to the reward?"

"*Believe. That's all. Just believe.*"

"*We're all here for you,*" she says. "*You are not alone. I'm always waiting for you. Whenever you are ready.*"

I know it's not the time to cut myself off from Chuck. In fact, I have to be near him. Without hesitation, I give him a call and ask to meet on Friday after all.

"I keep telling myself I'll be okay," I say, "but I can't stand this tension and fear."

"We're back in *The Matrix*!" says Chuck.

"I slept on the wrong side," I say.

"The right?" he asks.

"Yes."

"Bring the energy back to the left now. Slow down. Slow everything down."

"I'm trying not to push."

"That's good. Go slow. See you Friday."

There was an Oracle in *The Matrix* and when Neo went to see her, she wouldn't give him answers, but only replied in riddles. I know the answer is not with Jeanne but within myself. She can't give me answers really, only support. She really is there when I need her, but I have to do life on my own.

"What should I do?" I ask, speaking to Jeanne again.

"*Seek.*"

"What will I find?"

"*The next step.*"

"Where does it take me?"

"The next step. And so on..."

"Will I ever arrive?"

"Each step is an arrival of sorts, until it's time to move on," she says. *"Perhaps some steps are resting steps and others are hopping stones, but all of them lead on to the next one. You don't ever get to a final place; you just keep going. If you stop for too long you are stuck and then it's too hard to move again and that is the danger. The moving forward, as each step comes into view, is not the danger. The danger lies in not being able to move forward. Being stuck in The Matrix is the past, being stuck in the control of something other than your own destiny, and that is dangerous. The code is: Keep moving forward, take the next step; don't get stuck."*

In spite of the terrible night and the frustration of the morning, I see that a certain amount of giving into a situation is required, enough to propel me forward without crushing me. So, if I'm actively engaged, I'm doing great—I get it! It's when I get stuck that I'm in a bad spot. On the other hand, I'm in such a heightened and tense state; the manic side rescuing me from the depressive side, but if I'm to function at all reasonably I have to tone it down to a quieter pace. Slow down and go quiet inside. I'll go to work now and get into my quiet creativity—that should help. Hopefully there will be heat at the studio!

In the evening, at the dinner table, I suddenly feel that I'm going to collapse. Oh God! Right now, in front of my kids, I'm going to crash!

"Do it!" I tell myself, "CRASH! Fall apart. Just crumble, because this holding on is so false, a real farce."

But I can't let it happen, not here and not now. I think about excusing myself, but I can't even stand up, much less walk down the hallway to my room. It seems so far away, in the hazy distance, so far that it doesn't really exist. Nothing seems real. I reach out to the glass of water in front of me, see my hand grasping it and lifting it to my mouth. I take a sip, and then another and another, trying to focus on the conversation the kids are having.

"This is it. I'm not going to survive. I'm going to break down, crying, a total mess," I think, expecting a full physical and emotional collapse, a most frightening and sickening explosion, but the cold water going down my throat is like liquid resolve and I notice that firmness pours into me with each sip, that I'm slowly returning to my body.

"Get ahold of yourself!" I think, and then I do, as if I've just magically floated through a dark tunnel and come out the other side, still in one piece.

Excusing myself from the table, I go to my room to get this experience written down in my journal. As I write, I reenter my physical body more fully, each word grounding me deeper, pulling me back into this reality.

"I'm exhausted," I tell myself, and that's what the experience felt like, total exhaustion and imminent collapse, but here I sit now, all in one piece again, ready to keep going. Wherever this journey is leading, I am determined to keep going, even into total collapse if need be. Just not today!

It's snowing heavily now, with another delay anticipated for tomorrow, which will give us two extra hours in the morning. The kids will sleep late and I'll have time to journal. I'm going to try and sleep on my left side tonight, the no-fight side. Maybe my dreams will be better as a result.

Thank you, everyone, for getting me through another day. I know I'm supported. I know you're there, Jeanne. Should I tell Chuck about you? Is he ready? I think I know him enough now to trust him, even with that, even with my secret of you.

January 15, 2004

I fall asleep on my left side and dream that I'm painting the same chair over and over again. While I paint, I talk about a rescue plan, repeatedly going over the plan until I have it memorized. I turn over to get out of that dream and end up lying on my right side. While dreaming on my right side, I find myself traveling with Chuck, still in the role of the soft tissue salesman. We're on our way to see the Oracle again. When we arrive, the Oracle instructs Chuck to take away my weapon, a large machete, which I have apparently been carrying around for a long time. This makes me angry. I protest vigorously because the idea seems like the most absurd thing I've ever heard. The Oracle says I don't really need it. Without the weapon, I am told, I won't be able to defend myself as I usually do. Instead, I'll just have to stand there and accept what comes at me, that I need to learn humility instead. I insist that I'm the humblest person in the world, that humility is the one thing I have in overabundance, that it's the one thing I don't need to learn.

"Oh, really!" Chuck and the Oracle shout in unison, and then begin taunting me, teasing and shouting insults at me until I get so angry that I'm fuming. I don't understand what they're doing to me. I know they want me to get something, but I'm just not getting it. I think maybe they want me to feel bad about myself. As the verbal abuse goes on it finally dawns on me that they're trying to break me down, to get me to lose all self-importance, that they really just want me to understand that I can do whatever I need to do without a weapon, *without an ego.*

And then it suddenly dawns on me that I don't need to fight anymore! I just need to soften myself and acquiesce to the process, to let all tension out of my body by doing deep-tissue work, by releasing my old demons, and by letting my strong true self emerge and take over.

"You must stop fighting," they tell me. "It's time to let the old stuff seep out of your body and your mind. You must become empty of everything you have previously upheld as important."

The ego is a weapon, and losing it is part of the cleansing process, they tell me, part of the releasing and healing process of this recapitulation. I must achieve total humility, which they explain as a *total lack of attachment* to needs, feelings, and emotions, a total absence of self-importance. Only when I am totally humble and empty will I fully heal, I am told. By the end of the dream my ego is totally shattered. I am utterly broken, as humble as can be!

We're snowed in, no school and no work, and so I have plenty of time to ponder the meaning of last night's dreams. My first thought is that I must now pick up the pieces, rebuild myself, create a new ego, and start over on a different track, but that doesn't seem right. I'm supposed to be egoless. That's the new plan, to proceed now without self-importance, stripped bare of any old ego permutations.

I also understand that I have to learn to pay attention to my body, especially when it screams at me that it's ready to give out like it did last night. I have to pay attention and really learn to listen to what it's trying to tell me, for its messages come in quite different forms from what comes through the mental plane. I must learn how to listen to my body over my mind now.

I learned, in my dream, that to be humble means to be an empty vessel, without impressions, a blank slate, empty of all preconceived notions, without judgments. To be egoless means lacking in self-importance, totally without attachments. I don't need to build myself up with thoughts of who I am anymore, or boost my ego, but must instead totally empty myself of all thoughts of the self, both my lowly self-doubts and my high self-aggrandizements, and instead experience the emptiness of true humility. In this manner, I'm forced to put down my old weapon, my ego, and all that it has done for me up until now. Humility is my new weapon now.

Humility is lack of ego, and I understand the necessity of it, for how can I begin anew if I'm carrying an old weapon? How can I heal if I'm constantly angry at myself? How can I transform if I'm full of preconceived ideas, whether true or not?

I'm gaining a broader understanding of the concept of *letting go* and it's becoming more important than ever. It's as if I'm just an inanimate object, a piece of clothing that needs laundering, a sack that has been filled with all sorts of things that are no longer important. I am put into the washing machine and thoroughly washed, inside and out. Not an inch of me is left untouched nor allowed to retain any trace of the old. All shadows and stains of who and what I once was are being washed away, every shade of previous existence washed clean in this letting go process, resulting in a total detachment from everything once believed, adhered to, and idealized. Letting go is freedom from the known. I will emerge from the wash a newly scrubbed being, with not the faintest stain of my previous self, nor any of the old ideas that once rattled around in my head, or the old pains that once wracked my body.

It's kind of like a baptism of the soul and the body, in which I am both the priestess and the saved.

At the same time that I'm being baptized into new life, I must also confront that I'm facing a kind of death, for this means death to the old self. In being reborn as an egoless being, the old ego self dies. This process of letting go must be similar to what happens at real death, as the body and the soul separate, and that which once lived is washed away in the dying process. Truths may at one time have been my strengths, false ideas may at one time have been my weaknesses, but in the end, everything is washing away during this time of transition so that a new beginning may take place. Humility is gained as everything that once defined and upheld life, and was declared important, is let go of. I'm in the final stages of detaching from what the shamans call the *foreign installation*, the known social order, all the ideas and agreements that have upheld my life up until now.

The earlier dream I had, while sleeping on my left side, painting the chair repeatedly, indicates the old process, the old life of PTSD, but it's an old idea of myself in an old world. I see that now. To complete this recapitulation, I must learn what total detachment is if I am to truly transform and move on into new life. I understand this in a monastic sense, as in leaving the known world to enter a monastery, entering an unknown world where the ego and the known self have no value. It's a process of letting go, as one takes vows to adhere to a new set of rules and walk a new path, shedding the past, totally detaching from an old self and an old life. It's the only way to get to the next step.

This is big! This is just what I needed to know. This is the light in the darkness I've been waiting for! This is what Chuck and the Oracle were teaching me in my dream; I have to break down so far that there's nothing left of me. Only then can I truly move on and discover the real reason for being here, and achieve some sense of purpose and meaning. This is true for everyone on a similar journey.

The dream of painting the chair was just a boring reiteration of the known truths about myself. My strengths, abilities, and knowledge are all there, why bother going over them again? Why bother hearing the same rhetoric again? Yes, I know that I'm strong, I'm capable, I'm talented, I'm good. I don't need to hear those things anymore. I know them already. Now I need to assimilate them, fully accept them, and let them go, just as I've been doing with all the memories! And likewise, I don't need to hear about my falsehoods anymore, the things I thought were true about myself but obviously are not.

This is also about living out and working through old karmic issues that I've carried from one life to another. It's time to be done with them, once and for all! My soul has been waiting for this moment for a long time. This is enlightenment unfolding, one step at a time, just as Jeanne insinuated!

True humility is realizing that I am nothing, that I neither need nor lack, that I am not special, that I am just a being who is going to die.

January 16, 2004

I dream all night of having heavy, stiff legs and feet, so heavy that I am unable to lift them. I struggle to walk up steps, and everywhere I go everything is covered in riddles and codes, the same secret codes of other dreams. I try to read the messages I see everywhere, while at the same time my feet and legs refuse to respond to my commands. I try to remember to not let this cumbersome body control me, even though I'm in its grip. I try to remember that fear prefers that I don't let go of the old stuff, prefers that I don't evolve. I try to remember that it wants me to stay its captive forever, so it can continue to feed off my energy.

"Getting rid of the ego self is exactly right," Chuck says when we meet.

"The ego self doesn't really matter," I say. "I get that now, though the physical self continues to be a challenge."

"The shamans say that all memory is stored in the legs," he says.

"The yogis say the same," I say, "and I have instinctively known it for a long time, in the soft tissue of the body, and you, Chuck, as the 'soft tissue salesman' in my dreams, have been alerting me to this fact."

"It's perfectly understandable that there's no stopping this recapitulation process, that it took on a life of its own," I tell him, "probably from the very moment I decided to embark on this journey. I'm not in control of how it's unfolding or where it's leading, and that's both the terror and the thrill of it."

"I'm determined to complete this recapitulation and fully allow myself to launch into a new future, undertaking this final leg of the journey with equal parts wonder and delight, and with a good dose of caution and respect too. Because even though I'm willing to let the universe guide me, I also know that I must make decisions and choices for myself, though based now on a new set of parameters and the knowledge I've gained over the past few years."

"I must stay fully present and aware, and yet also fully open and ready for what the universe presents me with, for in the long run it's all about changing and growing. I know that the only way my body will achieve release, that my mind will achieve calmness, and that my soul will achieve all that it longs for is in my continued attention to this healing process."

"An experience I had at the dinner table the other night was another of those shamanic moments, another shift of the assemblage point, where the universe showed me its vastness, as I experienced a collapse of the self and felt the real and frightening possibility of falling into its vast nothingness. It was similar to the experience I had driving into the fog on the bridge or feeling the undercurrent of energy at my mother's birthday party, both of which occurred last year. This time, however, I was not readily cognizant of it as magical or pleasant, or even appropriate, but found it instead to be a most disturbing incident. It had quite a different tone to it than those other experiences."

"It's another example to show you that you are not in control," Chuck says. "And this time it was focused on your body, which is where the work still needs to be done. The challenge now is to first empty the mind, then to empty the body."

I leave Chuck's office and spend a few hours at the studio. My studio partner stops in to work for a while and my Benefactor drops in too, looking pale, losing his hair to chemotherapy treatments. He brings a bottle of wine. The three of us sit in a circle, making awkward conversation, sipping out of tiny paper cups he's brought with him. I suspect it's his way of cementing our agreement, sealing the deal.

"Whatever I can do, let me know," he says, emphatically and with real vigor, in spite of his obviously poor health.

"I think something's wrong," I say to my studio partner after he leaves. "He came with a bottle of wine to celebrate, but it felt more like a funeral. I think he needs me more than I need him. I wonder what's really going on there?"

I meet the kids back home after school and take them over to their dad's house for the weekend. I notice how tightly clenched my body is on the short drive to his house. It's been so cold for the past few days, going below zero every night, though it warms up slightly during the day. It's been very windy too. Back home, the winds howl, buffeting against my little house, and my old physical response immediately kicks in. I hunch, a normal reaction perhaps, but I'm attempting to change how I react to things now. So, I leave the usual scramble of thoughts in my head alone while I concentrate on relaxing my body.

I do the recapitulation sweeping breath too, which Chuck had reminded me to use to expel negative emotions and physical tensions, as well as any residual memories or pain still lurking in my body. I feel lonely, sad, and scared as I breathe, sweeping my head from side to side, inhaling good energy, exhaling bad. I know I have to empty myself of all the old feelings, not cover them or hide from them anymore but empty myself of them once and for all, taking back my own power. I sense that if I can release the physical holdings then everything else will release as well. I can attest that my body does indeed hold everything, the stiff, heavy legs and feet of my dream pointing that out very clearly. I set my intention to seek humility, and an absence of self-importance and ego.

"What do I do now?" I ask, tired, almost to the point of tears, not self-indulgent tears but tired-body, releasing tears.

"*Trust me*," comes the answer from Jeanne.

"That's very hard."

"*I know it is, but you can do it, just trust me.*"

"Okay."

I empty my mind. I relax my body. I pray for guidance. I breathe. I inhale. I exhale. I leave myself open to accept whatever is coming my way. I will accept it because, as Chuck says, it's coming anyway; just let it happen.

"*Trust me,*" Jeanne says again, "*just trust me.*"

January 17, 2004

I dream that I'm with a group of children, swimming inside a moat that surrounds a lighthouse, playing a game. As part of the game, we have to create a hole in the moat, allowing access to the ocean that lies off to the left. It's clear that having a gap in the moat wall is the only way to access the great wide ocean. Then I see the opening, that it's been made, and although I'm frightened, aware of the dangers of the ocean deep, I dive right in and swim through the opening. As soon as I hit the cold ocean waters I wake up in the dream and clearly understand that I need not be afraid, that it's time to leave the confines of the moat and let the wide ocean take me where it will. I intuit that everything will be all right now, that everything in my life will unfold in a positive manner, that my money issues will resolve, that my life will be fulfilling and that there are many individuals ready and willing to help me; I just have to ask.

"Ride the current," I dream, "go with the flow."

All through the night I dreamed of emptying, allowing things to happen as they will, in the natural flow of life, trusting the journey as it unfolds. How did we, a few kids and myself, reconfigure that moat wall? We did it with *intent*. We intended that it be open, and it opened. I was afraid to enter the ocean, but I dove in anyway, and after waking up in the dream and gaining insight, I closed my eyes and let the ocean take me. I felt empty and filled at the same time, free and whole, at one with the ocean, totally unafraid and totally at peace in the great oneness of it all.

The episode at the dinner table the other night was yet another shamanic experience, where in the midst of inner turmoil I was shown the path to which I am naturally drawn, that of the spirit and experiences of the world as energy. It was an ushering into a new phase of awareness, just as last night's dream was. I'm being taught that there's nothing to be afraid of in that world of energetic oneness. A life that's all-inclusive and all-encompassing is my personal intent now, for I do in fact seek to have my inner and outer worlds in balance, both the spiritual and the physical world, for my life to be productive and fulfilling in whatever world I enter. Learning to go with the flow is part of that intent.

In my dream I learned that going with the flow means detaching from worry and fear, accepting and trusting my journey, believing in my process, and emptying the mind so the body can follow suit. And if I can empty the body, the heart will follow, and if I follow the heart, wherever it leads, I will naturally arrive at a place of inner peace, happiness, and fulfillment. It's the heart that matters.

All day, whenever anything started to enter my mind regarding the past, whenever fear intruded, I shifted away, recalling the sensation of diving into the ocean and going with the flow.

"Empty! Empty!" I'd say. "Like the moat flowing into the ocean, empty! Empty the mind and the body will follow. Empty the body and the heart will follow. Follow the heart wherever it leads. Just follow the heart."

These are the things I tell myself.

January 18, 2004

I slept on my right side again and dreamed of being a spiritual seeker. I then received awareness that my body needed release, so I turned onto my back to ease the pain. However, I wake up this morning in full body pain, my legs brittle and stiff, as if encased in cement casts. My arm hurts too, for months now a place of pain and tension, the residual memory of a rape not fully explored or recapitulated yet, but still in my body causing pain. It's taken me a long time to understand why I have the pain, and I understand that it will continue to manifest, staying with me, for as long as needed. That is, until I recapitulate it more fully, until I remember, relive, and release the ENTIRE memory. Unfortunately, I don't have the whole thing yet.

I've stopped going to yoga classes. I've even stopped doing yoga on my own, as I felt I couldn't and shouldn't do it while I'm recapitulating so deeply. It's not helping anymore. Last night I read in a book that yoga can, in extreme cases, cause further blockages while one is under great mental distress. And although yoga is a releasing therapy it also has a tendency to strengthen holdings. I feel much better about working on the reasons for the holdings with Chuck, and on my own too, employing the recapitulation breath and other gentle breathing passes in order to initiate release. This decision supports my instincts, my inner guides, and what my body tells me. I'll return to yoga when it feels right, but for now it isn't what I need.

I have other well-established means of caring for myself; walking, breathing, writing in my journals, taking relaxing baths, meditating, all of which are supportive without building further blockages. My dream work is the other most important aspect of this work. The same things that inform my mental and physical self when awake are also informing my dreams, stalking me night and day, in a good way, trying to wake me up and shift me, to alert me to what I must learn about myself so I can enter into the fullness of life.

I spend the day at the studio. Some visitors come in and wander around, fascinated by the mass of objects and art in different stages of production. They ask a lot of questions and a lively conversation ensues. A woman buys one of my painted footstools. Cash for my next session with Chuck! Thank you, universe!

January 19, 2004

I remember a dream. I remember French words on signs and the feeling that my legs will always be strong. I remember doing a backbend, completely folding over backwards, as if I were hinged at the waist, and the feeling that I had achieved something great. I remember the feeling that everything is going to be okay, that life is full of possibilities. I remember knowing my own strengths and being able to stick with my convictions, no matter what. A great sense of calmness came over me as I dreamed these things.

It's Monday morning, no school, Martin Luther King Day, and the kids are still asleep. I feel optimistic and successful, things I haven't felt in a long time. This contrasts greatly with how I felt last night. Something got into me after a fairly good day, and I cried last night, felt defeated and sad. I tried to empty my mind and relax my body so I could sleep, visualizing the dream of swimming in the moat, repeatedly diving into the water and then turning onto my back and letting the water take me out into the ocean blue, where I felt safe and supported while also open to all that the unconscious offers.

I finally slept on my right side, intentionally gathering strength, then turned onto my back where I had that backbend dream. I was happy then, but an old wariness entered the dream and told me not to be too happy. And I do have to admit that I'm still a little afraid of happiness, generally cautious about feeling too good. If I begin to relax and enjoy myself, I might become inattentive, I might miss something coming at me. If I begin to trust, my relaxed awareness might not catch the next trickery and I might end up hurt again. At least, that's what the old me expects, but I have to change the expectation that I could still be abused. It's an old fallacy, deeply embedded, but until I can unseat it nothing will change.

First, I must learn to trust myself, allow trust into my heart, engage it as a possibility to begin with, and as a potential asset in the long run, as a core virtue I'd like to possess. The challenge is to find a positive, safe and secure place within myself that I can tap into when needed. I must start within.

"What should I do and how should I proceed?"

"*Let it all go, all the old stuff,*" Jeanne says.

"And then what?"

"*Nothing, you don't have to do a thing, just let go and let yourself be carried into that ocean deep.*"

"Is it safe?"

"*Of course, it's safe. It's your destiny; it's where you belong. Just go there; you'll see.*"

"How do I deal with all the demands of this world, the business, the bills to pay, the kids to raise?"

"*It will all happen on its own, you just have to allow it. Let go. Go with the flow. Let yourself be taken on your journey. You're going there anyway. Make it easy on yourself by not fighting. You are going there anyway.*"

"But what about making decisions?"

"*The end result will be the same.*"

"And what's that?"

"*Your destiny. You just have to go there. You have to trust and allow yourself to go.*"

"Okay, I'm going to trust, and I'm going to allow myself to let go, to go with the flow of things. I'm going to join you, not fight you. I'm ready."

Thank you, Jeanne. I'm grateful for your guidance.

The kids have friends over for dinner. I feed them homemade soup, grilled cheese sandwiches and potato chips. Afterwards, I give them a big plate of chocolate chip cookies and they take over the living room, a lively bunch of kids playing video games.

Meanwhile, I prepare for my meeting with Chuck, and when the evening is over and the kids are in bed, I go to bed wishing to dream about prosperity, about good things to come, about flowing in the great wide ocean, emptying and releasing into the vast blueness of it all.

January 20, 2004

I meet with Chuck. He thinks I'm doing fine. I tell him that I need to feel stronger, that I'm trying to sleep on my back as much as possible, especially just before I wake up, so I can get myself into a strong position for the day. I tell him that I try to wake myself up at night, especially if I'm having bad dreams, so I can turn over and dream something better. It's been interesting watching the succession of dreams as I undergo this process. As I talk, something shifts and a certain apprehension or anxiety I'd awoken with wears off.

The shift holds through the session, and for the rest of the day I'm in a brighter, more positive mood too. I actually feel my inner confidence gaining strength, my intention to stay strong, both in waking and sleeping life, more firmly planting as the day goes on, and as I anchor more deeply in the new me.

My Benefactor stops in at the studio again and tells me he wants to be my surrogate husband because I don't have a husband. I tell him I don't need a husband. He insists that I should let him at least be my friend.

"I'm not much of a talker," he says, "but I talk to you because I like you. Friends are good to have."

It all sounds a little weird to me, almost creepy, but I also know that he's a sincere guy. In the end, I agree we can be friends and not just business associates.

January 21, 2004

I slept mostly on my right side and then turned onto my back and dreamed that I was splitting apart. All the pieces of what had once been me went tumbling into nothingness. When I jolted awake, my heart was beating so loudly I could hear it!

I don't want to die, which is what that dream felt like, the end of life as I know it in human form. I want to fully live, to feel joy and happiness, a deep sense of accomplishment, prosperity, and that certain kind of solidity that I've experienced in some of my recent dreams. If I can maintain a calm sense of happiness and equilibrium, I know I'll be happy. There will always be conflict, and challenges to tackle too, that's life, but I'm learning that I don't have to engage every one of them. I can pick my battles, decide which are most important and worth putting my energy into.

Every day I feel support from people around me. A friend told me he has no worries or doubts that I will continue to support myself with my talents. I felt such positive energy when he said this, a realization that I will be fine, that in fact I *am* fine. I'm clearer as a result of his declaration, determined to stay doing what I'm doing, with no big changes in my life now. I've had enough changes to last a long time. Chuck is helping me find the right direction in my inner world, allowing me access to his knowledge and insight while I figure out my outer world. So far, things are looking pretty good in both worlds!

Throughout my life I've heard and recognized the quiet voice inside myself, what I've always thought of as my ancient knowing self. Occasionally I would contact her, be able to reach her, as if on a transcontinental phone line with a bad connection, but every now and then it would be crystal clear. This recapitulation has been a bit like discovering how to get back to her intentionally, reconnecting to a long time ago when I was innocent and happy. I feel as if I've been looking for the way back there ever since earliest childhood. I intend to hold onto that ancient self now, for she belongs to me, the long-lost treasure I have been seeking all along—Myself!

I have so much energy right now, a kind of euphoria that I haven't felt in a long time and it's lasting for longer than a day. It's a good feeling. So good that I'd thought of cancelling my visit with Chuck on Friday, but then I thought, "What? Can't I see him if I'm in a good mood too?" I have so much to talk about, even when I'm happy. Wow, I'm actually letting myself feel happy!

It was a good day, my inner energy of a high frequency combined with an almost manic intensity, but by day's end I was in so much pain, every tiny movement agonizing. I guess it's the expected result of being so high. It doesn't mean I've failed, just that I don't quite have myself regulated yet.

January 22, 2004

Every day now I gain further insight into what it really means to be an energetically available being. I've observed that when I put energy into my intentions, when I do something that *feels* right, and when I listen to my guides, life is generally successful and I feel good about myself. There are always stumbling blocks, but I see those as tests, and as long as I keep mentally and energetically focused, and don't let outside things interfere, I'm fine. I know that in the long run I'll be fine too. As usual though, I still have to find better ways to physically attend to what my body is holding, to better aid it in letting go. It's a slow process, overall taking more time and more tests than expected, but I admit that I'm much more in tune with and aware of my body and how it speaks to me now. I'm careful to check in with it when pain arises, asking it to tell me what's happening, asking it for guidance on how best to address it in ways that are productive and healing.

The last of the painful memories will work through me over time. And so, I must be patient at the same time that I must also push ahead and complete this inner journey.

I'm so thankful for Jeanne, for her being in my life, for teaching me to trust Chuck, and for helping me get to where I am now. She has been a fantastic traveling partner!

January 23, 2004

I sleep steeped in bad thoughts, on my left side, but then I dream of letting them go, of volitionally changing my attitude about myself.

"I'm good," I tell myself, "not bad at all. I'm really good," and then I become aware that the physical tensions and pains that I suffer every night, even in my dreams, are connected to my increased desire to release. I become aware that my intentions have been clearing the way for a new me, that my attitude and my mental thoughts have all turned away from the old and are working toward the new, but my physical body, the great holder-on, doesn't want to let go. The old stubbornness, the refusal to change is still so dominant, kicking in as soon as I make up my mind that it's okay to let go.

"There's no need to be so strong that way anymore, strength is needed in other places now," I tell my sleeping body.

As I awaken, I know that if I keep holding everything in, I'm going to get sick. And I don't want to be sick. I need to release so I can get better. I have so much knowledge about myself at this point, a much clearer view of who I am and where I've been, and I see the path ahead of me so clearly now too. The final release must come from, and through, my poor body so that I can walk the new path without this debilitating old stuff dragging me down. I feel as if I've spent the entire week fighting off a pesky virus that I just want to be rid of.

"Away! Get out!" I shout, flicking it off, and then I do feel a little bit better.

My father's cancer is back, aggressively attacking and spreading. I notice that I don't even have room in myself for compassion. I am so filled with what I carry inside myself that I have no room for anything else. My focus remains this work on myself.

When I meet with Chuck he suggests breathing and walking to release the tension in my body, so after our session I head out to take a walk, but it's only nine degrees out, too bitterly cold for much of a walk. I run a short distance and then run back home again, just enough to loosen up and get the blood flowing.

I discover I have an extra hundred dollars in my bank account. I haven't made a deposit since Christmas Eve and my last bank statement and my checkbook matched on that day. I've only written three checks since then. I've checked the numbers over and over again and I still have an extra hundred. Nice! So, okay, I believe. I believe everything.

January, 24, 2004

It was a good day. We had a sale at the studio and I made five hundred dollars and cultivated some potential new clients. I have a new painting job lined up for next week, compliments of my Benefactor, and almost two thousand dollars in outstanding invoices to collect, so things are looking pretty good. I'm beginning to feel prosperous, and much more confident too. I'll be fine. My kids have been great too. As Jeanne has been telling me for so long: *everything will work out just fine!*

I haven't had wine to drink in quite a while, but tonight I celebrated and bought a bottle, and picked up food from the local Chinese restaurant too. The kids and I were sitting down to a nice meal together when the old stuff struck, sneaking in with the usual crotch pain, and I had to go to my room for a few minutes.

"Oh well, it's just a part of my life," I thought, as soon as I felt the attack beginning.

I took it in stride, sat on my bed, breathing into it, breathing it out, waiting for it to ease. No images or memories came, just the pain passing through me, my body letting it go, as I asked it to. I've noticed that as soon as I begin to feel a little positive, even just a little up, I get pulled back down. Just when I feel as if I'm finally getting somewhere, the recapitulation pops in and brings me right back to the real work at hand. Never a dull moment! I just have to accept it as it comes, not fight it, but move over and give it the room and the time it needs, until I'm done with it once and for all, which will be soon, I hope!

Exhaustion seeped into my body after the experience, my energy and enthusiasm done for the night. I do have to admit though, that overall, I continue to feel a bit stronger and healthier every day.

January 25, 2004

I dream that the doorbell rings. I answer the door and a strange man throws a blanket over my head.

"You don't want me! I'm not who you think I am!" I yell, insinuating that I'm not worth anything to anyone, but at the same time I feel incredibly strong, and positive feelings of value and self-worth course through me. The man pulls the blanket off my head and stands there staring at me, listening attentively, seemingly fascinated, as I explain the way things are now.

"You are no longer after me," I say. The dream shifts then and I'm throwing a giant net over a field of rabbits, entrapping them. They immediately freeze with fear, except one baby bunny that struggles to escape. While the baby bunny struggles, the rest of the rabbits lie under the net, unable to react, in frozen, scared-rabbit poses.

I dream this same dream three times, tossing out the net, seeing the scared rabbits under the net, with only one baby bunny trying to escape. My daughter and two other little girls are present throughout this rabbit dream. Each time I toss the net, I instruct one of the girls to collect the struggling baby bunny and take it to my daughter's bedroom, saying that we have to save it. I tell the girls that they must make a circular nest for the bunnies to feel safe, that they need protection. When I look in on them, I see that each girl has made a nest with blankets for their bunny. They are lying on the floor of my daughter's bedroom, three little girls curling their bodies around the nests, protecting the three baby bunnies.

My dreams reveal my evolved state. I am no longer like those frozen rabbits, unable to react, but strong and confident now. As I've worked my way through this recapitulation process, I've rescued myself time and time again, just as I guided the three little girls to rescue the baby bunnies in my dream. And my reaction to the man in the first dream reflects the strong and confident emotional state I've cultivated. I am no longer a numb, traumatized being but reactive and self-preserving. My tender and caring attention to myself over the past few years has finally paid off!

I feel lighter and happier after these dreams. And yesterday's successful studio sale leaves me feeling confident of plenty of business to come. Yesterday, when a client came to pick up a child's table and chair set that I'd painted for her, she said she could feel the flow of creative energy in it. To me it has felt like creative *healing* energy, and it's pouring out of me into everything I do. I really am making progress.

I make a furniture delivery in the morning and then head home to spend a quiet Sunday with the kids, attending to their needs. My daughter wants help rearranging her room and my son wants a haircut. As the day goes on the usual pain comes, but I don't let it take over. My arm hurts again too, related to that partially recapitulated memory of being held down so many years ago, a strong physical memory still hanging on. I just have to think of it and I feel the pain, as if my abuser is grabbing me once again, digging his fingers into my upper arm. When I push the memory away, the pain goes away too.

"Let it pass, it's only temporary," I tell myself each time the pain returns, but it's rough going. I know I have to be craftier than it is, carry myself through it without getting caught by it. I breathe and relax into it, but it exhausts me. A part of me just wants to be left alone to cry, to roll up in a ball and howl, but there is life to do. So, I push it away and help my daughter move her furniture around and give my son his haircut.

We're off to bed early tonight, all of us tired, my son suffering from a slight fever. I lie still in bed for a while, unable to move, unable to pull myself away from the bad feelings that have circled around all day looking for a way in. Like the rabbits in my dream, I lie frozen and stiff, caught in the glare of a memory I can't quite see. I also know that whatever this memory is, it was once a real event in my life, that this pain is guiding me to know and understand what has been repressed. Something still haunts me.

January 26, 2004

I sit in bed dealing with my usual morning pain, my daughter off to school, my son staying in bed, not feeling well, his fever higher today. Even this late into my recapitulation the pain arrives with its usual nagging and uncomfortable anxiety, wondering why I don't immediately understand it, why I don't get what it's trying to tell me. I can't believe I still have another memory to uncover, at this late stage! But I know the drill, know I should let it happen, assume the position and let it rip.

Whatever this memory is, it's been nagging at me for days now. It gives me the usual physical hints, the pains that normally precede a memory, but no visuals. All I can think to do is acquiesce, just allow it to come, as it will. It's like suddenly discovering that I'm pregnant, and no memory of intercourse ever having happened, a virgin birth of sorts. I only have the arm pain that has plagued me for weeks to go on, only the feeling of my abuser's hand clamped on my upper arm. Some last attempt to draw me back? Even if I do go back, it will be brief, long enough to learn what I need to know. I don't belong there anymore. I've moved on. I have things of more importance to attend to now.

If I relax my body, I feel the memory trying to take over. Rather than acquiesce, I find myself tensing up physically in an attempt to fight it off, to keep it out. I know it's the wrong tactic. I lie down, try to relax, hoping it will flow better, release, and be over with faster, but I can't stand the tension. I sit up, break away from the recapitulation and away from the hand on my arm, take a shower, try to pull myself together. It's frightening, but has it ever been different?

It's eleven at night and snowing lightly. I spent a weird day, depressed, fighting the memory's emergence while trying to hold onto the new, happier me. I was in a bad mood though, lost in a wasteland for much of the day, incapable of reacting to the pull to recapitulate. All I could do was feel sorry for myself. So pathetic!

I meet with Chuck tomorrow and a part of me wonders why I still bother going to see him. A part of me feels like just giving up. Maybe that's what I'll do, just stop now. I'm not getting anywhere; I'm just fighting the same old stuff. Why fucking bother!

January 27, 2004

"As soon as I was feeling good about myself and things in my life were progressing nicely, the recapitulation came back at me full force again," I tell Chuck when we meet.

"That seems to be the pattern," he says.

"I gave up fighting it last night and was finally able to release some of the pain," I say.

"But it also got you depressed," he says, which is true.

He suggests that my dreams are fully supporting the progress I've made, but that they also seem to be implying that my inner child still needs me, that I'm not done recapitulating yet. He's referring to the rabbit dream and the nagging, unrecapitulated arm pain, and I know he's right, of course.

"Are you coming on Friday?" he asks at the session's end.

"What, you're going to give up?" he says, when I don't immediately answer.

"Well, yes, actually, I was going to give up," I say, but I notice that I feel a lot lighter, especially in my head where the intensity of the depression is already lifting.

"I'll see you on Friday, as usual," I say.

I go to the studio and write up an estimate for a new job, staying positive by focusing on the tasks of the day. I deliver a completed furniture job and then head back home to care for my sick son. After a while I'm in a much better mood.

I have to admit that I feel a great change coming on, an excitement building, but also a feeling of dread too, and I wonder what it refers to. Is it the past pushing into the present? The memory that's looming? I'm not sure, but I have a sense of something unsettling on the horizon, aware that in the midst of this sense of foreboding I must remain calm and steady. I must look forward with a straight gaze, go about my business with unbending intent. On the other hand, maybe I'm just feeling the approaching snowstorm, predicted for tonight.

In order to stay firm and steady I do some Tensegrity movements that Chuck taught me today, for intent, even though I wanted to tell him to stop. "Please," I wanted to say, feeling saturated, "don't teach me anything more, no more karate moves, no more magical passes," but I didn't. And I'm glad I didn't because as I do the moves, I begin to feel more solid, more rooted, and more determined.

I've lost most of my old frameworks of denial, my old habits and behaviors, my old comforts, and I haven't found anything to replace them with. I've had hints of new structure perhaps, but no solid foundation on which to depend, to feel safe within. I float, uncertainly, seeking salvation, while carrying my two children and my inner child forward with me, all of whom trust and depend on me for everything. And yet, I sometimes think that the boat we think we're all sailing in doesn't even exist and at any minute we'll find ourselves sinking, plunging into dark waters. But then, I'll suddenly feel strong and determined again, totally dedicated to trusting the journey, fully aware that we won't sink, that in fact our little boat is quite solid, a sturdy craft capable of carrying us through any storm. And, yes, I'm certain there's another storm up ahead; there are always storms ahead, and yet we will weather through them just fine.

Pain coursing through my body brings me back to three years of age. Already I'm used to him, to the man who abused me. Already I can read his energy. Already I have a sense of his vileness and his evil intent. Already I know how to escape too, how to dissociate, to separate myself from my body. Already an old hand, at three years of age!

I come from a long line of women, on my mother's side, who have kept secrets for generations, things that are never to be spoken of. I see them all holding them in. Why have they been forced to keep these secrets, passing them from mother to daughter, a tight bundle of stoicism that has grown larger and larger until it landed in my lap? It's large enough to kill me, to smother and drown me in its suffocating memories and devastating pain. I can't keep the secrets any longer. I refuse to hide behind silence and intellectual pursuits, behind good works and mindless actions. I refuse. I won't pass this habitual stoicism onto my own daughter. I will free it from the bloodlines, breaking the chain, the silent pact of generations of women who never dare speak of the pain they carry.

My beautiful, lovely, lively daughter does not deserve this. None of us have deserved it. It's my duty and my desire to stop this habit that has been perpetrated upon us, to end it now. It's my duty to pass on only freedom to my daughter, the freedom I never had, the freedom to speak. And in doing this, I too will become free of the weight that has pushed me down, cheek to the ground, for decades. It's now a known weight, but at one time it was unknown, the brutal strength of a grown man, abusing and violating the innocence of a tiny girl, stealing her soul, robbing her life, leaving her mired in pain and self-hatred, hatred of her own body and her own thoughts. I'm not alone in such pain. Words, spoken and written, as well as this recapitulation, are my healing balm, as they could and should be for all women, for it's my belief that every woman has suffered.

It's imperative now that I replace the old habits with new healthy habits and allow myself to be open to life and all its gifts. The irony was, I thought I *was* living, I thought I *was* alive, but the truth is I had no idea what that really meant. Now I seek to know what that means; I seek to truly live. I have to replace what once gave me comfort with new comforts that bring joy and contentment, because if I don't, I'm left with a dangerous gaping hole inside me, a powerful vortex. That's where I am, still on the edge of that vortex, still on the verge of getting sucked down into its swirling darkness. And the truth is, I still find comfort there, comfort I can't find anywhere else, comfort that meets me when I'm at my darkest and most dissociated. I haven't replaced it with something more nurturing yet. There's a gaping dark hole inside me that must somehow be filled. But with what?

It's nighttime and snowing heavily now. I'm still in the grips of the memory, my arm still hurting. I can barely move without feeling pain, feeling like my arm is being wrenched, held by an unseen hand, constantly tugging at me to remember, remember. The ghost of the man who abused me haunts me still. As far as I know he's not dead, but it's the ghost of him in me, the ghost of who he was then, the ghost who knows what he did.

What do I have to do, so he'll let me go? Forgive him? Tell him it's okay? That I forgive him? I'm still trying to deal with the knowledge of these painful memories within myself. How do I forgive him when I have hardly had time to forgive myself, much less fathom it all? Is that all it takes to end this hell, forgiveness? I don't think so.

January 28, 2004

A foot of fluffy snow fell during the night and it's still coming down, so no school today. We'll be out there shoveling soon. The physical activity will do me good, and my mental state could use the perk-up too.

Old Ghosts

Please, please, please, stay with me, Jeanne. I know you are there even though I haven't been to visit you in a while. I've gotten dragged away from who I really am, a spiritual being, by the recent encounter with the past. But I know you are there for me and I still need you. Thank you to my other spiritual advisors for being there too. I plan on remaining open to all of you, for I'm aware of your presences, and always ready to listen to what you have to say. Your guidance is crucial to me.

As I write these words I begin to dissociate, my entire body puffing up into a huge bloated pillow, my tongue and teeth enormous, my lips incredibly large. Why is this happening? Am I still so haunted by what happened in my childhood that I need to escape? Because that's what this dissociative experience is, it's a means of escape, an old means. I take note that though my body turns into a large, soft pillow, nothing hurts. I can't feel a thing. I am nothing and I am nowhere, lost in some void.

Focusing on my breath, breathing slowly into my lungs, I am able to bring myself back into my body. I know that if I can stay focused on the present, stay in the moment, I'll be okay. It's when I lose touch with reality that I get dragged back into the past where that void is, right there, waiting.

When I'm depressed, I have a hard time remembering who I am, the spiritual being I really am. Only the sad and depressed me exists then and I so easily get lost in an old idea of my life as hard, as ugly, as unbearable and despicable. I become trapped once again with all my sixteen sad little girls, one of whom has memories of being happy and innocent once. It's hardest for her because she knows what was stolen, what was destroyed, what was lost. It's the cruel reality of life that she finds so hard, for she holds the truth of a happier time that the others don't have access to, that they never realized in their numbness.

As I go back and re-experience that first abrupt moment, the day my life changed forever, I now know that everything else, the rest of my life, was determined by it, that everything else unfolded out of that crucial moment. Life changed that day and nothing was ever the same again. My inability to trust, to ever be truly innocent and happy again, goes back to the very beginning when I was two and a man stuck his fingers into my vagina and told me I was a dirty little girl. To this day, I have to remind myself that what he said is not true. And I have to keep remembering that I survived because there was a part of me that always knew the truth and was not going to be destroyed by the cards life so cruelly dealt me.

This new memory, triggered by arm pain, going back to the earliest years of the abuse, is slowly beginning to emerge, the pains in my body signaling that the time to fully remember is getting close. I feel that the little child inside myself is still lost in a darkness that had no end, a tunnel full of terrible encounters with evil. There's no light at the end of that dark tunnel. For my life, as I once experienced and knew it, my child's happy innocent life, is over.

I realize that everything is magically being taken care of, one day at a time. The bills get paid and there is always an extra ten or twenty dollars in my wallet for other things we might need. God, the angels, my guides, and Jeanne—whomever they may be—are taking care of us. I'm counting on things beginning to flow even better now, as the daily worry is removed, as I continue to trust the universe, and as I complete this inner work.

I really am going to be okay. I need to keep relaxing into the life I'm being granted and keep trusting that everything will work out just fine, as Jeanne constantly counsels me.

January 29, 2004

In dreams, I walked down endless school corridors, kept moving because of pain in my legs. I felt the pain and said to myself, "relax, relax," while at the same time I knew it was necessary to keep moving, though the pain was excruciating, almost disabling. I slept mostly on my right/fight side, staying optimistic. Now I must do the same in my waking life, for as I awaken my legs are still burning with pain. My goal today is to encapsulate that pain and let it go, to replace the pain with my own energy and my own positive strengths.

In spite of the good intentions I started out with, I had a terrible day, full of self-doubt and self-hatred. I was tired when I left the house this morning, which probably didn't help. Perhaps I should have stayed home and rested. Instead, I got caught in a vortex of misery. Everything I've been trying to keep separate and compartmentalized caved in on me—work, home life, my children, the past—it all fell together into a huge, swirling mess. I finally realized how useless it was to struggle against it. Far better to use my energy to find a way back into my own calm center, to reconnect and anchor within myself. If I can relocate to my strong center, I know I'll be okay, but I somehow got thrown today and lost sight of my intentions.

Maybe a little chaos will do me good. Maybe I'm just being asked to acquiesce to the way this is unfolding, to go with the flow, as my dream of the ocean suggested was the way to proceed. Perhaps it's this memory that's slowly emerging, that I can't see or feel clearly yet, that's creating the disturbances. Maybe this is how I'm being asked to let go and let the universe determine the next step. Maybe this is my next lesson.

January 30, 2004

I meet with Chuck. He pulls out the *I Ching* and I ask for guidance on how to weather through this time of frustration and chaos, as I acquiesce to how this letting go process is unfolding. *What is the best way to proceed?* I write on the notepad that Chuck hands me. When I hand it back, I notice that he doesn't even glance at my question, as if he already knows it. I throw the coins and the answer I get is hexagram #32: Duration.

Persevere, the *I Ching* says; in the long run there will be success. Duration is a self-contained state of union within the self, a state of endurance with a calm center. My intention to get back to my calm self is supported by this image. As the *I Ching* says, there may be a thunderous storm outside, but what's happening on the inside is in accordance with what's right. There is meaningfulness at the calm center, which is guided by a knowingness of the true self and true meaning.

All is in accordance with the laws of nature, the *I Ching* says. All I have to do is breathe. Just breathing in and out will bring newness and change. Contraction and expansion are all very natural. I must stand firm, stay connected to my intent, and to the deeper meaning of this process, to this recapitulation as it flows along at its natural pace, taking me through its natural laws of change. When things change, it's good to change along with them, the *I Ching* suggests. Exactly what I'm attempting to do!

"You must look to yourself for what you need," Chuck says. "All is contained within."

The reading from the *I Ching* is right in alignment with what I've already decided; I must seek calmness within myself, maintain a strong, calm inner center. I do have the strength and endurance to persevere, though this process's unfolding may not be as expected. But it never really has been!

"I'll be fine. I can weather any storm," I tell Chuck, and I leave the session feeling much better.

I have a good day. I feel more open, as I allow myself to vent a lot more than usual, feeling like I'm getting a lot of stuff out. It's as if I'm a jug that I've uncorked, and throughout the day I pour out a little bit more of what's inside me, what's been blocking the flow. I'll keep pouring until I'm empty.

I feel like I'm starting to get in touch with myself again, to find my way back to the self I've felt distanced from lately. I must not give up on myself but forge ahead! It feels like I got my head flossed today!

This weekend my goal is to continue re-centering myself, to find that calm place within again, even as the storm rages on around me, even as chaos ensues. Let it rage. Let chaos come if it must. It will only go on for as long as it needs to, but I intend to find my calm place at the center of my being where the voices of my guides, and my own inner spirit, speak words of truth to me, the place where I know I'm truly safe, no matter what's going on around me.

January 31, 2004

I dream that I'm visiting a woman therapist. I'm stiff but trying to unwind and talk. She's kind. I'm scared. I want to let go, but letting go is so painful. She speaks soothingly, urging me to relax. I have a black shoulder bag across my body, the strap bulky and the bag in the way as I try to lie down.

"Take it off," the therapist says, but I don't want to because it's filled with personal stuff I don't want to part with. The therapist tells me I'll be more comfortable without it and I realize this is true. That realization alone feels like a small but significant step. But even so, I still cannot relax.

The dream shifts and I'm in a very comfortable house with a library filled with books. I walk along a hallway and come to a set of stairs. I try shimmying down them by putting my hands and feet on the railings and walls, straddling the steps, trying not to knock down pictures and sculptures attached to the walls. All of a sudden it dawns on me, I can WALK down the stairs, one step at a time! I never imagined it could really be that easy, to take the steps in a normal way! I am blind to what is right before my eyes. And when I walk down the stairs there is Chuck at the bottom, waiting for me, with a delightful expression on his face, that says, well, it's about time! And then I realize that there are indeed easier ways to do things, that life doesn't have to be so hard. I can take the easy, more practical way for a change, the way that's right in front of me rather than making everything so hard on myself. It's just not necessary. It's an old stubborn tactic that has outlived its time.

The dream shifts again and I'm standing in line, waiting for ice cream. I discover the comfort of this simple, normal act. I realize my fears are not gone, but I'm getting better.

Last night, as I attempted to sleep, early memories of my abuser kept rolling through my mind, like thunder rumbling on the horizon. I was stricken with panic and fear, and I kept hearing the screams of a tiny child, whom I knew was being brutally raped. There was no talk, no chance to say no or protest in this memory. There was just brutal, painful rape. This seems to be the memory that I must recapitulate.

That memory was contrasted by the dreams I had, their themes pretty obvious, showing me how far I've come and where I'm still stuck. The dream that strikes me the most is the house in the second dream, beautifully built with light streaming in the windows. Everything was finished, no more construction, each room exquisitely decorated and finished down to the last detail. There was artwork on the walls, a library filled with books, comfortable furniture, a wonderful house filled with everything I could wish for. I felt that I had at last found a place I could stay, a place I belonged in. The only problem was that I was still in my old body, still in the stiff-with-memory body that couldn't take in what was right before it, suspecting the stairs weren't done yet, that nothing was really finished, safe, or stable. That old body doesn't trust anything, but when I saw that the house was totally and completely done, right down to the pictures on the walls, the meaning became clear: I have achieved completion; it's time to wake up to the truth and trust that the work I have done on myself has produced a strong and sturdy, beautiful, safe structure—Me.

Maybe I'll learn to put that black bag down soon too. Maybe I won't have to keep carrying all that "important" stuff around, the burdens of a lifetime, self-imposed and otherwise!

It's been a very long day! This morning I went to the studio for about an hour and the check I was expecting was not in the mail. I ranted a little bit, called the client and left a message, then went to the kid's band and choral concerts. Afterwards they went home with their dad for the rest of the weekend and I went to visit my parents who live near the concert venue. On the way to their house, I saw the barn where I had been raped many times, now almost totally collapsed, but still a small section stood standing, tucked back into the woods. If you didn't know it was there you probably wouldn't see it at all, but I just happened to glance in that direction and saw it.

Then I drove straight past my parent's place, down the road to the property of the man who abused me, somehow knowing I was ready to face it. I saw again how it has changed, bulldozed into lots for sale, and then devastated further by a tornado that came through last fall. It's all gone now; everything I remember from a long time ago, the fields, the woods, the stream; everything totally removed, buried, by man and by nature. I took in the ugliness of it all.

"It was the ugly beginning and now it's the ugly end," I told myself.

Just as I did in a dream a few weeks ago, when I stood in the same spot and looked at the changed setting without attachment, I sat there in my car for a few minutes on the side of the road and realized that it doesn't affect me anymore in reality either. Although I still have this new memory pending, although I expect that more memories may still come, the place itself doesn't affect me. I have successfully disconnected my energy from it. Now my job is to disconnect the memories from my body so they no longer hold any power either.

Overall, when I think about the memories, about what happened to me in my childhood, I think and feel differently now. I don't suppress the memories or reject them. And there's something else happening too; I'm okay with the memories. I can let myself feel the brutality of them, but also the sadness of them, and not get triggered. The most important and striking new aspect, however, is that now when I reflect on the memories I react with *feeling*. I can actually feel things, even emotions that come to me, and be okay with them. That's progress!

I visited with my parents for a little while today. Their energy was low, and they felt as closed and uninterested in life as ever. My dad wanted to know if I had a man in my life. He thinks a man is the answer to everything. I finally gave up on them, drove home, and called two girlfriends, who don't have a man in their lives either, and invited them over. We sat around, conversing over wine and food until one this morning, talking about everything: men, kids, jobs, our place and our mission in the world. Now I'm tired, but wound up too. We all seemed to need the experience; we all seemed to need each other.

I do know that my father is partly right, that I need to love someone and be able to receive love in return, because the truth is that I do want a man in my life, but it won't be because I can't take care of myself or because I can't be alone, but because it's the right man and because I'm ready for him.

Chapter 2

I Tell Chuck About Jeanne

February 1, 2004

It was a difficult night. I woke several times in pain, paralyzed and unable to move. I breathe into my aching heart and hear Jeanne's voice.

"Everything will be fine," she says. *"Be honest with yourself and your situation and know that you are strong. You can do incredible things. You have already proved it. You proved it a hundred times, even as a tiny child you proved your strength, strength of endurance. You can hold on for the duration. You don't have to resort to out-of-body or dissociative techniques anymore. Just stay in the calm center of your being."*

"Empty the bowl of your mind and be calm, be calm, be calm. Everything will work out. Everything will be fine. You have strength of endurance. Be aware of the gifts that are being offered. Be aware of the friends who are knocking at your door. Be aware of who they are and be friends back. Those two women were lonely, sitting at home just like you last night. If you hadn't called them, they would have been alone."

So, I didn't get to have the alone time I so often crave, though perhaps the time with friends last night was more important. I opened myself during a very vulnerable stage when normally I would have shut the world out. My life is fuller because I did something I haven't done in a very long time.

On the drive to the old neighborhood yesterday I entered one of those strange time warps. I felt, as I have all weekend, that someone else was in control. It was as if someone else was driving my car yesterday. They took me to the property of the man who abused me, to the tornado destroyed woods where everything has changed, while I sat in a daze the whole time, unsure of what I was feeling, except an agreement that, yes, it *has* all changed. I took in the changes, noting that nothing exists as it once did, except in my memory. My memories are wholly intact, and yet I was given insight into the fact that they don't trigger me as they once did, and the sight of that property didn't trigger me either.

I had a similar experience with my parents. The past doesn't exist there either, not even between them anymore. They seem to be in a different place now, old and worried about each other in a new way. They are certainly living in the present, with no desire to go back into the past. So, after I left them, I felt that I had gained even more clarity. Then I felt that other "someone" directing me the rest of the night too, calling the women and inviting them over, totally out of character for me, for I haven't socialized in such a long time. I mostly just want to be alone and I did want to be alone last night too, but something made me abandon my habitual tendency for introversion.

Today, I had a similar experience when driving, that same feeling that I was not in control. So, I get it, I'm *not* in control. But what does that really mean? Does it mean that Jeanne and the fates will be taking over? Do I just let things happen because they will anyway? Is it safe to give over my autonomy to these unseen forces?

The truth is, I really am not in control, even if I think I am. I realize I did things this past weekend that were destined to be done. I had actually visualized the women sitting in my living room earlier in the day, long before I called them. I knew ahead of time what was going to unfold, before it happened, even though I'm not in control. I'm shown a picture of the future, and then it happens. I'm not surprised, but I am amazed! The magic keeps happening, even as I get pulled back into old depression.

Just as I write the word "depression," I am struck with pain in my arm. Once again, I feel it getting wrenched back. A heavy hand is clamped on my neck and before I know it, I am immersed in the sensory past, fighting to protect myself. I feel pain and turn my head, trying to face the vivid sensations of the memory. I see that it's an early memory of brutal rape on a young girl—me. And then I roll away, away from the hands that hold me. My heart pounding hard in my chest, I breathe and breathe and breathe. I am safe now. I am safe now. I am safe now. Sweeping my head back and forth, I send the energy of the memory away. Breathing in my own good energy, I let the negative energy of my abuser go.

I Tell Chuck About Jeanne

I calm myself, repeatedly doing the breathing pass, aware that the kids will be home in a little while from their weekend with their dad. I must be ready to receive them. It's been a busy few days for both of them, with the added stress of concert performances, and I expect they'll be tired. I must greet them from my calm center, welcome them home and take care of them. I can take care of myself later, or I can stay calmly centered and take care of all of us, and in so doing firmly establish that in this part of my life I *am* in control.

I have to remember to send the memories away before they overwhelm. I have to remember to maintain the calm inner certainty that I can handle this, remind myself that I'm doing this because it's leading me somewhere new, and that everything will be fine in the end. I must anchor in that certainty, over and over again, even as I get tugged back to that place that no longer exists in this world, the property of the man who abused me. For the truth is, even though that property, as I knew it, only exists in memory now, I exist there as much as I exist in this present world, for when I recapitulate it's a very real place and it sometimes feels like I could die back there. Now wouldn't that present a conundrum!

February 2, 2004

I get up and check on my daughter to find she's not feeling well, having arrived home last night with a fever, probably the same virus my son had a week ago. She'll stay home today. My son still sleeps; he has no school today anyway. I make coffee and climb back into bed, the cats at my feet. I notice a general sense of depression hanging over the house. I sense it's something other than my personal depression, for it has an unfamiliar, impersonal weight to it. My own depression, by contrast, is well known to me. Probably best we all hunker down for the day.

I realize I can allow my spiritual guides to take over all the time now, not just when I'm in the car. Perhaps they show up in the car because I'm distracted, my mind focused on driving, so they can easily take charge. But I've noticed that "someone else" in charge at other times too, not just when I'm in the car. When I'm creating, I get a similar feeling that someone or something, within or without, is running the show, a feeling of being a pure and empty channel with no mental thoughts, some other force moving through me. I easily open to the energy and allow it to flow through me, for there is nothing sinister about it. In fact, I experience and understand these energy flows as something more like divine intervention. I accept the friendly help and try to relax and enjoy the experiences.

It's when I'm in the car that I've had the most profound experiences lately. When I get into the car and put my hands on the steering wheel and start to drive, I sense immediately if someone else is driving. It's such a strong feeling! I could remove my hands from the wheel and the car would stay its course. I'm sure if I tried to go off course, I would feel the other driver pulling the wheel back. I am certain of this. I simply get in the car and begin to move and I sense instantly if someone else is driving. I actually say to myself, "Oh, someone else is driving today." And then, I can't wait to see what happens!

All of this has taught me that I am safe and protected, that I am watched over and taken care of. And, yes, that magic abounds!

I've spent the past few years dismantling myself piece by piece and I'm in the process now of reassembling myself, with newly made and newly adjusted parts, and I don't quite feel that everything fits together yet, or that I fully inhabit this body yet. Some days I feel pretty together, some parts functioning well, while others still shy away from being present and participating in life. I know I need to fully exist within this body in order to be whole and alive, and when fully healed I expect to finally know for certain what it feels like to live inside my own body, without pain, without fear, without a dark fog in my head, but with clear vision and easy, graceful movements, as one entity, all parts co-existing in perfect harmony.

While all this magic has been going on, I've been dealing with this new memory, constantly struggling to get away from the tight grip of my abuser, as I feel him twisting my arm and poking me with what I perceive as his "stick." Locked in a tug of war, I pull away from him toward the light and the magic while he drags me back into the pain and darkness of the memory. It's a physical, mental, and emotional struggle, a fight for my very existence, for my life, for my body, for the life I haven't yet had, and for the life I should have had and am only now realizing I can still have.

I must appreciate the abuser's role in the context of this recapitulation, showing me the memories as only he can. It's funny to think of him as a positive influence, but I can honestly say that he's very dependable, showing up regularly to assist in the process, making sure I don't miss any details. I intend to complete this healing journey, fully recapitulate every memory, and whatever comes to help out in the process is appreciated, so I guess I have to be grateful to him for that!

I do try to focus on all the gifts and help I'm offered as I follow this healing path. And I must constantly remember, as I plod along, and as I go through the scenes and the sensations of the memories, that everything is part of this unfolding journey, that this is my life, and that in the end I will be fine.

February 3, 2004

"We are born as two souls," Chuck says. "One is known, the other unknown, until we rediscover it."

After birth, in the circumstances of our lives, those two souls become separated and live apart. Many people never find this other soul again, but I have rediscovered this other part of myself through the deep inner work I've been doing. In fact, it was this other soul calling out to me so loudly that got me started on this whole recapitulation journey to begin with, a part of myself that I'd been separated from for a long time. I had such a longing to get back to it, though at the time I had no idea what that would entail or what it really meant. I just knew I was missing a big part of myself.

"During recapitulation, along with retrieving memories, you also rediscover this other soul, and now you are in the stage of rejoining with this other self," Chuck says.

"It feels as if I'm in a battle between two separate and distinct forces, each with its own agenda, between light and dark, between male energy and female energy, between life and death."

"Yes, the two parts of you are colliding as they seek to rejoin," says Chuck. "It's the final stage."

"It's a tremendous battle, part recapitulation, part spirit merging, as you indicate, and though I may sometimes be battle weary I have no intention of giving up."

"Of course, you won't," says Chuck, matter of factly.

We stand up and go over the magical pass called *forging the energy body*, a pass I've used in the past to great effect, but this time for a different reason, to help facilitate the process of merging my two souls, the once unknown self, the lost self, with the known self.

Following Chuck, as gracefully as I can, I try to recall the movements. They are immediately calming and centering, which is exactly what I need, as I attempt to keep myself grounded and centered, and as I seek to enter the world in a new way, as a newly integrated and whole self. The movements come easily as I sculpt my new body, breathing and bringing all the parts of myself into energetic alignment, integrating clarity of vision, the sweeping energy of arms, hands, and torso, tapping and stirring up feet, knees and thighs. Stretching and flexing, I create wings of recapitulation and intent. I create a window of clarity through which to see and know. And then I stamp myself firmly into the ground. I am here.

I do these movements several times throughout the day, so often that I lose count. I just do them whenever I feel myself starting to separate and disappear.

The Matrix is on TV again tonight. My new reality really hits home when the Oracle points out that Neo doesn't want to believe in fate because he still wants to believe that he's in control. I too have been in that position, but now I'm really beginning to understand that I am most decidedly *not* in control. Over the past few days, I've discovered just that, as I acquiesce to the power of an energetic presence at the wheel of my car, to my fate, to my destiny, to my other soul self, acknowledging it and letting it take me where I need to go. The other day it took me back to the property of the man who abused me and showed me that everything is gone, changed, that it only exists inside me now. It asks me to confront the truths of the reality of the world that I live in now, the truth that the world of the past has changed, and the truth that I'm changing too. It's time to let things go, time to move on now, with the truth of the past fully exposed. Time to move on without attachment to any of it, though I will carry the truth always inside me, fully known, accepted, and integrated.

The practicalities of life still need attending to and I do pause to wonder if I'm irresponsible for continuing along this intense inner path while I have two children to raise, a business to attend to, bills to pay, and all the other things that must be done to keep afloat. Surely this recapitulation has taken its toll as I have largely been gone, in other worlds for the better part of three years. But I know it's right. It's where I always come back to, to myself and to this deep inner work, for I know that without it I would probably be dead, or at the very least ill with some unexplainable illness, in chronic pain, barely able to function.

Over the past three years, I've discovered that this journey is a journey of heart, for I am discovering peace and love, compassion and kindness, creativity and wholeness, all within myself; everything I need as I journey on. I am melding into a totally new person, already softer and more available. Though I have no idea where I'll end up, I trust this journey to take me forward into new life, and I intend to hang in for the long haul. I really have no choice. In the meantime, I'm being shown every day how life unfolds for the best. I have the energy to work hard and to create, and I'm strong. I have strength and endurance. I have money when I need it, the kids are thriving in so many ways, and we're all growing and changing. How could I not take this journey to its blessed end?

It's been another snowy day and it's expected to keep snowing through the night, a dark and dreary day overall. I sensed a depression hanging over the world earlier this morning, and indeed it sat like a black cloud overhead all day. I tried to ignore it, tried to gain clarity in spite of its attempts to block my view of the truth. I need to find ways to see through it, to come out of it as quickly as I go into it, so I can live a normally functioning life. It's like an old friend I've outgrown, one I'm no longer comfortable around, and as often as I've asked it to leave, it seems reluctant, but it must go, for there is no room for joy and happiness when depression reigns. I do the magical pass again, forging my energy body, merging my two souls, releasing all that no longer belongs to me. Out with the old, in with the new!

Perhaps my dream soul will meet my other soul and take it on a dream journey tonight, and perhaps in the morning, instead of running apart at first light, the two will stay awhile, hand in hand, noticing how good it feels, how right that they be friends and companions on this journey through life. And then I may truly have the peace I so desire. For now, we will sleep curled together, strong and invincible, two peas in a pod.

February 4, 2004

I wake in a panic at six a.m., mind and body vibrating so hard I fear that I'm shattering, breaking apart into a million tiny pieces, turning to dust between the covers of my bed. Why now, when I've worked so hard to bring myself together? I breathe and breathe and breathe, willing myself back together with every breath I take. Pushing the panic away, I remind myself of why I'm doing this recapitulation: for life, for wholeness, for oneness, for the joining of my two souls. And then I remember that I woke in the night in fiery pain! I cried, calling out, "Sorry, sorry, sorry," whimpering as the pain tore through me. Gradually the pain stopped and I fell back to sleep. It was like a bad dream, but it was no dream at all; it was an old memory searing through me.

Why am I still suffering such pain? What is the point of it? And why did I feel I had to apologize? I was the one in pain and yet I felt I had to apologize, and for some crazy reason it worked, it made the pain go away. Now I lie still, just breathing, turning myself over to the safe hands of my guides, knowing that they won't let me die. It's not my time. It's time now to finish this healing journey.

Eventually, I'm able to move my body and get out of bed. If I can just get through the next few days and months, I'll be fine, I tell myself. I make coffee and set my sights on the day ahead. I have a meeting with an outdoor art committee, an article to write, an illustration to do, and a decorative painting job to start, so all of that will keep me busy. The key is to remain busy.

I Tell Chuck About Jeanne

To whom was I apologizing last night? To the abuser? It felt as if I were apologizing to him for killing him off, for having to commit this act of war against him, for we are at war as I seek to take back my energy. Or perhaps I was apologizing to my inner girls because we're leaving those old familiar places of pain and comfort, of fear and depression, where everything is so known and predictable, and so strangely safe. It's striking how pain and comfort are so terribly linked. But the apology worked, the pain eased, and I fell easily back to sleep.

"Something wants you to go back," Chuck said to me yesterday. "Do the movements to counter it. Every time you go through a major shift something wants to pull you back. Fight it."

Everything is shifting and changing now and I'm feeling the full brunt of it, a head-on collision of the old and the new.

February 5, 2004

I wake at five, vibrating, feeling like I'm going to fly into a thousand pieces again. I've slept all night on my left side and now I shift over to the right, knowing I have to equalize, to balance the energy of my two selves. My right side, myself in this world, is no longer feeling as strong as it once was. It struggles, knowing what has to be done, that it has to acquiesce to the left, to the spirit side, but the spirit can't take over totally either. I have to keep them in balance. They have to work together now, my two souls.

I lie still, breathing calmly to bring down the vibration, to bring my body and spirit back together and my energy back into my body and into normal range. I hope for a good day, wish for calmness, peace, and strength to enjoy the day ahead. Work will help.

"*You can do it. Do the moves,*" Jeanne says, "*get yourself back together again.*"

The pain and comfort are so intricately linked, one requires the other, and where there is old pain there is need for old comforts. The comforts that worked before still work, though I'm intent upon dismantling them, like removing the substance of addiction from an addict. When the old pain pops up now, I don't automatically retreat to the old places of comfort, and that shows progress, though the desire for those old comforts is still pretty intense.

I get out of bed and forge my energy body, introducing the vigorous movements as replacements for those old comforts. Yesterday, it worked just fine, and today I'm hoping for equally positive results; for the disappearance of pain in body and spirit, for calmness, for pulling together and staying together.

I've been allowing myself to feel and say things I never would have allowed myself to express before, things that were buried deep inside me, but I refused to acknowledge them, too afraid to allow myself access to them. And I'm finding that they're actually acceptable in certain circumstances, where it's safe to acknowledge a spiritual side, where it's considered not only acceptable but normal.

This recapitulation journey has taken me far, but I'm still in transition, still shifting, still at a place of great change. I feel the collision of the old world and the new in my body, and in the intense reluctance of the old self to move on. I must convince her that we're safe now, that it really is okay to move forward.

It's late at night now. Once I got myself out of the house this morning, I had a fairly good day. The moves kept me together. I didn't do them as often today, but whenever I felt my energy beginning to vibrate, pulled toward disintegration, I used them to bring me back and, magical passes that they are, they quite magically held me together.

Waking up in the morning in that vibratory state has been strange, as if I'm still dreaming, still in spirit form, so preferable, and yet I must return to my body and to this world. It leaves me feeling fragile.

"Don't fall apart," I tell myself, "don't leave your body again. It's not time for that, it's time to be in your body."

So, I keep moving, forming my energy body, bringing myself together, body and spirit. It works like nothing has ever worked before. So magical! I've almost forgotten my troubles.

I Tell Chuck About Jeanne

February 6, 2004

It's another snowy day, no school. I plan on meeting with Chuck nonetheless. I'll be okay traveling in my SAAB, which is heavy and good in the snow.

I tossed and turned all night, with left side/right side struggles, each side more uncomfortable and uncompromising than the other. Every time I started to drop off to sleep, I could feel myself start to vibrate. It would begin with a slow dimming of reality followed by subtle vibratory sensations before I'd disintegrate, shattering and scattering into pieces before jolting wide awake again.

For a long time now I've thought, "Oh God, I'm falling apart. I have to put myself back together again!" And every day I would forget that I'd felt the same way the day before. Every day the feeling was as if a new phenomenon was occurring, but now I don't forget from day to day, now I remember that I live in two distinct worlds. There's the world of human ego, this reality where I am a mother, where I support a family, run a business, earn a wage, and maintain my earthly and creative self. In the other world, there's the spiritual self, my consciousness, psyche, and soul, everything that makes up what is not physical but is equally as real and important as the body. Both of these worlds encompass the past, the present, and the future, in an intertwining journey, all parts and phases of life overlapping, the worlds constantly switching back and forth. Both worlds tug at me to reside fulltime in their reality. They fight to keep my energy to themselves, while I strive to bring them together in a new combined reality.

Once you're aware and realize that you're always on an energetic journey, not just when dreaming, you discover that you're dreaming all the time, that everything is in constant motion and constantly evolving, and on any given day you cross over into many worlds. It just depends on how you choose to look at it. In this new world of energy, I imagine that I'll never actually arrive at a final destination but always be energetically alive, in one sense or another, moving on to new plateaus and new places, always shifting, working my way through each shift to the next, for all eternity.

Dreaming All The Time

It's become increasingly clear to me how important this recapitulation work is and that my decision to stick with it is proving to be life altering and, yes, life shattering. Every day it gets reconfirmed by a quiet knowing that I'm on the right path, that I've always been on the right path, and that if I can just get through the next tough spot and the next month or so I'll be okay. There's a sense of smoother sailing ahead. It's clear to me that all of this is going to come together in that new life I've been working so hard for. In fact, it is coming together. Every day I realize that I *am* doing what I need and should be doing at this moment. I *am* doing what I have long wanted to be doing, and my new life *is* coming together.

I *am* changing, already in the change I've been waiting for, wanting for so long. It's here, now. There's no more waiting for things to happen. They're already happening and I'm already living what once was the future. Along with all the good work I'm doing on myself, I'm also kept going by the goodness of others; support is there. It's like suddenly realizing that the house of my dreams, always in some stage of construction, is finally done, though I've been acting as if it's still unfinished. But in my last house dream, I finally clearly saw that the stairs were done, and that I didn't have to climb around finding new ways to proceed. To stop making everything so hard on myself, I just have to see what's right in front of me. The path I'm on now is the path to take. I don't have to look for another path or wonder where I'm going to end up anymore. I'm already there.

I brave the snow to go see Chuck but am too nervous about the weather to concentrate on inner work. I keep looking out the window and realize I should leave, that the snow is piling up a lot quicker than expected, everything fast disappearing beneath it. I could have waited until Tuesday, but I wanted to come, so much pressing now. Once in Chuck's office, however, the snow proves too distracting.

"I intend to proceed in a positive vein, with a sense that everything's okay and that I'm on the right path," I say, and I tell him about that "someone else" who's been driving my car most of the time lately, and how that seems to be the lesson for me now, to let it happen. In fact, that's how I got to his office, I tell him. The car just took me through the deepening snow, leaving two straight

I Tell Chuck About Jeanne

tracks behind it that I saw disappearing in the rearview mirror as the car drove itself along in a strange silence, while the road ahead appeared blurry, totally unfamiliar in the falling snow. It was as if I were entering territory I'd never experienced before, though I've traveled the same road twice weekly for years now. It appeared foreign, a strange uncharted, unknown country. How I got to his place safe and sound is almost a mystery.

I leave after half a session, promising to call him when I get home. Whoever is driving will get me home safely, that I'm sure of, I tell him. We head out slowly, me and my driver, the only car on the road. As we pull into my driveway, I'm aware that I'll have to shovel the deepening snow later before it turns to rain and becomes a heavy wet mess, as is predicted. I go inside, the kids still asleep, and call Chuck, letting him know I'm safe.

I make a cup of tea and climb back into bed, aware that this process is unfolding by itself, day by day, very methodically, one step at a time, as I put myself together each morning, one part at a time—one thought, one realization, one magical pass at a time—as I put Me together.

February 7, 2004

The days have gotten easier, especially as the week has gone on and I've gotten busy with work. A few more jobs came in; more writing assignments and a new mural to paint. I'm feeling better overall, though I'm still occasionally struck hard by the old feelings. I try to push through anything negative that comes up, while at the same time hold onto the new positive things I've only just begun to tap into. But some days it feels like all the new stuff in my life is far removed from me, as if I'm alone on an island in the sea, unable to reach anything, far removed from reality. Other days, I stay more connected to the new magic and those old states are less intrusive.

I try to keep writing, tapping into the flow of the inner voices as they flow through me, tapping into Jeanne. I've been receiving consistent messages, signs, and inner certainties that I'll be fine, and I'm grateful for that. I'm able to see and hear much better now too—that which is not usually seen and heard, that is!

February 8, 2004

I felt Jeanne's energy in the office the other day when I drove up through the snowstorm to meet with Chuck. I sensed her trying to communicate something, but I wasn't sure if she wanted me to tell him something or if he was supposed to get something on his own. She stood on my right side, pressing against me with what felt like an urgent message, something that was important to her, but I just wasn't getting it. It was a little unsettling, and I think I may have wanted to leave because of her as much as because of the snowstorm. I may bring it up with Chuck, if it feels right. So far, I haven't had the courage, but it's probably time to tell him about my relationship with her. I've been waiting for the right time; perhaps it has come.

I'm feeling and reading my own energy more fully now and this seems to allow me to feel and read the energy of others as well. Sometimes when I'm with Chuck I hear his thoughts, and then he says aloud exactly what I've heard. I could mouth the words as he speaks them, as if they were coming from my mouth and not his.

Also, when I spoke to my Benefactor yesterday, I got a very different feeling about him than at other times. I felt that he was sent to me during a dark time, to let me know that I wasn't totally alone and lost, to let me know that it's possible to reach out to another human being and be responded to in a kindly manner. I acknowledge his presence in my life, and I greet him and treat him well in return, because it's meaningful to be his friend too for this time. I realized this when I discovered that he needs me as much as I need him, that our friendship is mutually beneficial. Yesterday it became clear that I'm getting beyond my desperate dark time now, that things will be better soon and that I'll probably move on from this friendship with him, just as I'll move on from others.

I worked on my writing assignments today, then came home to be with the kids after school. We had a nice dinner together, with lively conversation and everyone in good moods. My son is at a music rehearsal while my daughter has friends over, four lively thirteen-year-old girls bubbling with energy, just the way I feel!

I Tell Chuck About Jeanne

I've been thinking about Jeanne all day, and I realize she was the real force behind my going through the snowstorm to see Chuck. She wanted me to tell him that "someone else is driving the car." That seems to be the message for him as much as for me. Someone else, namely Jeanne, has a hand in more than just my recapitulation. I think *she* drove me through the snowstorm, in order to deliver that message to him. I'm not sure if there's some other more specific message for Chuck, beyond that she is and has been part of this recapitulation process, but I do know that she wants me to tell him that she's been acting on my behalf, that she's been in my life since she left this world. It feels imperative that I share this with him now. I can't keep it to myself any longer.

I think the dream I had of the woman therapist telling me to take off the large black shoulder bag is part of all this, because when I left her office, I saw Chuck in the next dream, standing at the bottom of the stairs in the new house, and I still had that bag with me. There's something happening here that's way beyond my control. I feel like calling him now and telling him, but I think I'd better let him have another peaceful day before I give him this added burden. For it does feel like a burden, a heavy burden, as if that big black shoulder bag that I was so exhausted from carrying in my dream is perhaps holding something that I must pass onto him. I'll wait until I see him on Tuesday. Perhaps by then I'll have greater clarity, and greater courage too!

Jeanne has actually been standing beside me in Chuck's office during my sessions on more than one occasion lately, quietly watching. I've been aware of her presence, but she hasn't said or done anything until now. Why now? Perhaps Chuck will know what it means. I am just the messenger.

February 9, 2004

I go around turning off all the lights in the house after the kids leave for school. And then I stand in mountain pose in the early morning darkness for a few minutes, grounding myself. I do the magical pass, forging my energy body over and over again, further grounding myself in this body and this world. I follow that with a few minutes of breathing exercises. Then I sit on my bed and meditate.

Almost immediately, intense energy pulses through my body, eventually turning into a vision of a large snowplow, its huge blade pushing through deep snow, forging a wide path. I intuit how important it is to forge ahead, to follow the path that's been prepared for me, and to continue using my own strong-as-a-plow spiritual energy to assist and guide me. This has been a difficult journey and without the assistance of the "snowplow," that incredible spirit within me that wants to heal, the magical assistance of Jeanne and my other guides pointing me in the right direction, and Chuck's incredible guidance, who knows where I'd be now. I understand from this vision that the only way forward is the path I'm already on. It's already cleared. I just have to take it. This has been a consistent message.

I must talk to Chuck about my relationship with Jeanne, that's clear from this vision of the snowplow too. I'm aware that as soon as I talk to him about her, something new will appear on the path, a change will be created, and I'll have to accept it, the crucial need for it, and I'll have to prepare myself for all that it will bring. It's not something I can avoid any longer; I get that. If I continue to avoid talking to Chuck about Jeanne the inner tension and anxiety will continue to build. A release is necessary, and in this case the release will come in acknowledging to him my deep connection with Jeanne. It's all about trust, trusting her and trusting the process we've embarked upon together. It's not just about me anymore; I must be open to the needs of others now too.

If I stand still and look around, I see no other path, no other choice. There's nothing to confuse me, no sidetracks, no forks in the road; there's only plowing ahead. I already know what I'm leaving behind and I've already made the choice to go forward into the unknown, it's what I've been doing for the past several years. I also know that I'm being challenged now to go on unafraid, completely trusting that all will be well. To be unafraid, absent of fear, is to conquer fear. Fear has been such a prison and I'm the only one who can unlock that prison door. I'm the only one who can step out onto the path before me and take the next leg of my journey.

I suppose I could stop and stand still for a while longer, but I'd only be postponing the inevitable, perhaps until another lifetime. I know there's no reason for standing still now. I've been training for this moment for a long time and it's time to fearlessly

I Tell Chuck About Jeanne

trek on. That is my challenge now, in this lifetime. It aligns with the fact that someone else is driving my car and the fuller awareness that greets me every day, the knowledge that I'm totally safe and protected. This is the next step and I'm ready.

I feel strong and determined as I make the decision to follow behind that plow and to pass along the messages I get from Jeanne, when appropriate. She tells me that Chuck needs to know this truth about her now, that she communicates, that she made a strong connection with me because I was available and have certain talents that we can work with.

And the path being forged by that giant snowplow in my meditation is very wide, with plenty of room for plenty of people to follow along. We will not be alone.

My yoga teacher stops in at the studio and asks if I would be a "guinea pig" for him. He's looking for someone to work with on a new therapy he's been studying, Embodiment Therapy. I've been wishing for a way to work with him again and here he is offering his services! And, I have indeed been needing a hands-on therapy to complement the recapitulation.

"Yes, I would love to be your guinea pig," I tell him. "I need some anchoring, because I'm floating, just floating. I need to be more grounded in this body and in this world."

February 10, 2004

Today's the big day! I'm going to tell Chuck about Jeanne, how I've seen and felt her, how I communicate with her, and of the guidance she brings me. I don't even know what to call it. I'm not sure there's even a word for what's been happening. Is it channeling? It doesn't seem to be that because there's so much more to my experiences than channeling implies. Jeanne tells me to just trust her, to trust him, and to drop my fears and inhibitions and trust this process too. Laughingly, she says to tell Chuck that I speak with his dead wife, quite regularly, and that she answers back. Yikes!

Dreaming All The Time

I'm nervous driving up to see Chuck, the trip way too short. Too soon I'm in his office, sitting across from him, telling myself over and over again that this is the day, the agreed upon day, and I'm not backing down. Taking a deep breath, I tell him that Jeanne has been helping me ever since she died. I tell him that when I said I had dreamed about her it wasn't always in dreams, but that I was afraid to tell him the truth. I didn't know how he'd react, so I kept it to myself until I felt the time was right, and that time is now.

He's immediately receptive, leaning forward and listening very carefully. I tell him how she appeared to me on an especially pain-filled night, and how he appeared beside her as well. As I tell him the details he nods, his ear cocked toward me so as not to miss a word. I tell him that I see her with my other guides, in an open room with several chairs where they sometimes sit, as if they all resided together in an infinitely tall office tower without walls, rising high into the sky. I tell him that I call up to them when I need them, and one or other of them responds. It's not always Jeanne, but more often than not it is.

"They seem to be joined together," I say, "at least for the duration of this recapitulation, each of them equally intent upon helping me in their own separate way. When I don't need them or ask for anything, I still see them sitting there, calmly waiting, like figures in an old faded black and white photograph, patiently waiting to come back to life."

"Go there and see what transpires," Chuck says, rather abruptly, when I've finished talking.

It's the first thing he's said since I began my recitation. I'm not really surprised by his request, as he rarely beats around the bush. "Go there" is one of his favorite phrases, and so without hesitation I do as he asks. I've never done this before in front of another person and so I'm a little self-conscious, but Jeanne indicates that I should just relax and allow for things to happen.

"*Don't try so hard, be calm,*" she says. "*Trust yourself and trust what you are given. Trust Chuck. It will be okay.*"

I tell Chuck what she instructs, and then, closing my eyes, I take a deep breath and relax on the exhale, letting everything go, all thoughts and discomforts. I let myself be as relaxed and empty as possible with no attachment to anything, not even to Chuck

I Tell Chuck About Jeanne

sitting opposite me, calmly waiting. I just breathe. Then I ask Jeanne to show me something. Almost immediately I go from being me, sitting in a chair with my hands on my knees, to a tiny girl. I feel myself on a cellular level shifting and transforming back into a tiny three-year-old child. I actually feel my legs becoming small and boney beneath my hands, and as the sensations continue, I get scared. I acknowledge the fear but stay with the feelings. Transforming more, I dissociate, leaving my body until I'm a big floating blob of energy.

"Now I'm safe," I think, but it doesn't stop there. I keep going, changing, morphing into new and different energetic forms until I become a small round molecule, nothing more than a small bead of energy, and then I sense that I'm about to disappear, that this is the end, that I can just go if I want to, leave, not come back. But I don't want to go. I want to stay. I'm not done yet.

With great difficulty I force my eyes open and slowly return to the present, to my body, to the room where Chuck sits calmly waiting for me to tell him what I got, where I went, what happened and what was said. I don't know if I have anything for him, just this experience, that's all. I don't have a message for him, which is what I had hoped for, though for me the message is very clear: *Don't be afraid.* Do not fear the experiences you will have. You will survive all the changes, all the forms, and all the permutations of energy and remain whole.

I tell Chuck what happened, that it's how I often feel when I communicate with Jeanne, that I become an amorphous energy being, that my awareness is present but I don't feel my physical body.

"Perhaps she was showing me her own changed state," I say, "beyond a molecule of energy now, a state I pulled back from, pure energy. Are you okay with that?"

"I'm not that fragile," says Chuck. "Jeanne accepted her death without regret when it was clear that it was the only option left to her. As did I. We were always a team, intent on what was right. Always."

"I didn't know if you would have believed me," I say.

"Oh, I would have believed you," he says, "that's the kind of stuff that makes the world so interesting."

I tell him about the incredible calmness, the utter joyous peacefulness, and the intense love I feel when I ask for her help and guidance. He thanks me for sharing with him and I leave, knowing that I have perhaps changed his world forever, just as Jeanne has changed mine.

I learned what I need to do now, to just listen, and to speak of what comes, to share, to not hold back when I have something that might be of service to someone. For I've often felt pressure from Jeanne to speak when I've gotten something that might be valuable or helpful for someone, some information or insight. I've chosen not to interfere in people's lives, so I don't say anything, but maybe I'm supposed to pass on the messages unedited, let them land how they will. It feels like I went through a new kind of training today, and, overall, it was a pretty good experience.

I am, however, a little reluctant to be this new person with this ability to see, know, and hear, but this is the person I really am, finally allowed to emerge and live. This person has always had the gift of knowing, if you can call it that, the person I've always been afraid of being. I need time to get to know her, how she operates, what she needs and wants, and what she can do. I'm being offered a process to shed my fear by facing this person, by being more open and accepting of this new self. In a strange irony, what I've been most afraid of is my deepest self, the very being I've been searching for my entire life.

There was a sense that what I faced today with a certain amount of fear, that moment when the molecule of energy was about to fade away, was a moment not of death but of new life. Why am I so afraid of that?

I face another fear and call a woman who owes me a lot of money. I've caught her just as she's sitting down to write checks, she says, one of which is for me! Instantly, I see myself on that wide, snowplowed road looking back at where I've been. I'm not able to see ahead yet, but I know I must turn forward now and go unafraid into the unseen future, into the unknown. Today clearly marks the beginning of another segment of this fascinating journey on the road to healing.

    I'm so relieved that I talked to Chuck today, that I finally told him the truth about what's been going on behind the scenes. It never felt right to say anything before, but today it was right and I'm glad I finally spoke. As I've gone through this process today, revealing myself to Chuck, my entire body has been aching. I see it as part of the continued transformation, as if I'm physically changing, being restructured, taking on new form, all the morphing and vibration I experienced today being part of my own process too.

    I've been thinking about acceptance today, what it really means, not acceptance of things, like failure or death or anything like that, but acceptance of who I am and who I've always been. I've always felt different from others because of my life, my creativity, my abilities to dissociate, and because of my abilities to know and see things. I always wanted to change those things about myself because they seemed so weird, so abnormal, and yet they are exactly the things I should embrace, the things that make me uniquely me, the things I'm learning to appreciate now, things I must find a way to utilize in good and productive ways. Normalcy was never in the cards; I see that now, though I always longed for a normalcy of sorts. But the truth is that I never really knew myself the way I do now, and what was once abnormal, almost abhorrent, is beginning to feel quite normal after all. Though I've always been reluctant to be who I truly am, I now know that I'm on the verge of total acceptance of who I am.

    Jeanne has long hinted that we're going to be together for a long time, that she's training me for a mission, whatever that may be. Whether I'm reluctant or afraid, whether I'm quaking in my boots, I sense that I'm about to enter brand new territory, so I'd better get on board and go with the flow! And although I have no idea what is to be in the future, I do know that someone else is leading the way, and it may be Jeanne after all.

    She wants me to learn about myself, to accept myself, so I can fully be myself. It all sounds so simple, but it really is the hardest thing in the world to truly be one's self!

February 11, 2004

I wake up early, slightly depressed, my body aching, but it feels as if the aching is from having forged my new self with the magical passes rather than from the old clenching and holding. The depression may be part of the same transformative process, some last wisps of old energy hanging on. I get up slowly and hobble out to the kitchen like a little puppet on a string to make some coffee then return to bed with a steaming cup. I have a little time to myself before I have to get the kids up for school.

The feeling of calmness that I experience with Jeanne is like nothing I've ever felt before in my life. It's a deep knowing calmness that spreads throughout my entire body, enabling me to intuit far into the future and know with certainty that all will be well. Whenever I ask Jeanne for advice, she always tells me that everything is going to be okay, reminding me to be steady and calm, and just let it happen.

"Let the continued unfolding of this incredible journey happen naturally," she tells me, *"just be present and take the journey as it comes."*

I can say that everything already *is* okay, that every day things are better and better. I'm better, more grounded, surer of myself, more able to just be myself. I realize that everything *has* worked out just fine and that yes, I *am* okay. I still have daily challenges to conquer; fears, inertia, and some lingering sadness, but I'm being given new tools to work with all the time, offered gifts, some of which work for me and some that don't. I have new people in my life wishing to help me along the way. I have friends and I have my children. I have my work and my creativity. I have my inner strength and my inner life, my ability to go back into the past, to go deep inside and find places that most people never find, and to work in the realm of spirit as well. I have long had the ability to dissociate, which I now understand is an ability and not the fearful disability I've long interpreted it as. I have many gifts, and I'm daily more aware of how lucky I really am.

The experience I had during my last session with Chuck, as that disappearing little three-year-old girl, seems important. On the one hand, it felt as if Jeanne was showing me a process, perhaps her own dying process, while at the same time it felt like she was taking me back to my own innocence, then even further

I Tell Chuck About Jeanne

back than that, to the infinite realm of non-being, before life in human form began, or after life in human form, which it also felt like—perhaps it's really the same thing. It also felt like I was being shown something about my child self, that I have to go back to her yet again, access the terror that she still carries, find out what it is, for there is still something that haunts her; that I am certain of. I must safely guide her through whatever is unrecapitulated and bring her safely out the other side.

I must remain anchored in this world as I work through these terrors with my child self, keeping a foot in this world as I simultaneously step back into the past. Jeanne seemed to be showing me what it would be like as I accompany my little girl self into the final memory, showing me how we will complete this journey of recapitulation and finally merge together as one. That may have been what that bead of energy was, the final merging of all parts of myself into one of wholeness. I'm in the process now of completing the final stages of my recapitulation and becoming a unified whole, the goal being to have nothing left to inhibit me from fully living life as a healthy, happy adult.

It's about regaining my innocence too, for Jeanne is leading me back to my innocence for some reason, but I still have to do the work, embrace and accept it, and I sense I must understand innocence from a new and deeper perspective now. Initially, I must encounter the child's innocence, but in the long run there's a different kind of innocence that Jeanne seems to be guiding me toward. I must comfort my child-self, even as I must confront the fear that she presents me with if I am to discover what true innocence really is. It's quite a task.

It does seem as if Jeanne is indicating that we're finally nearing the completion of this recapitulation. She reminds me that I still need Chuck's guidance though, that he remains a steadying hand, a trusty anchor in this world.

When I think about how my bones shifted and changed the other day in Chuck's office it blows my mind. I really am changing, and not just on the inside, but physically, on the outside too. It's apparent when I bump into people. They tell me I look different, that they don't recognize me, even good friends. I could feel the three-year-old girl's bones under my fingers. I could feel actual change taking place, as if the molecules in my body were shifting into a new form. Yesterday, the intense pain I felt all day was as if I had someone else's body for a day, as if I'd been stuffed into someone else's form. It wasn't my body. Is that possible, for me to take on someone else's form? I guess anything is possible, things I can imagine and things I can't.

Pain continues to come in fleeting reminders that there's still something to face. Writing helps alleviate the tension of it, relaxing and calming me. The magical passes, along with what Jeanne communicates, work together in the process of reuniting my past with my present, my body with my soul.

February 12, 2004

Letting go. Cleaning out. Releasing. I write these words in my journal during the night, related to a dream I was having in which I was in the old barn where I was often taken by the man who abused me. While there, in that empty barn, I dreamed about letting go, completely releasing, accepting, and trusting everything, including my entire life's journey.

I meditate for a few minutes upon awakening, looking for Jeanne. She seems disturbed, gesturing me away.

"*Don't do it alone,*" she says, "*not without Chuck.*"

And then I understand. It's not the time to transform into my three-year-old self, for that had been my intent. As soon as I realize what she's trying to communicate she calms down and recedes back into that quiet steadiness so characteristic of her. I wonder if that's how she was in real life too, if that was her personality. It's what I hope to achieve myself, that quiet, calm steadiness that seems capable of weathering through anything, hardly a feather ruffled. I have come to rely on her calmness. I wonder if she's there for Chuck in that calm way too. Does she reveal herself to him the way she does to me? Does she watch over her children?

Cosi, our kitten, somehow gets her claw stuck under the refrigerator. I assure everyone that she'll be fine and that we'll get her free. I hunker down on the floor trying to figure out what she's hooked on. My son walks away with a loud groan, unable to deal with the emotional intensity of the squealing cat, my daughter in tears, and my own loud admonitions for everyone to remain calm. I feel under the fridge and discover that her paw is twisted at a weird angle, caught on the edge of the refrigerator frame. Standing up, intending to carefully lift the fridge without hurting her, I am amazed to see her running into the living room, having freed herself. What a relief! And what a strange way to begin the day!

In spite of my anxiety, which on some days can feel off the charts, I've been feeling more contented about everything lately. Work is coming in steady streams now and the next few months are already looking good, with plenty of jobs lining up and other creative things happening. I'm feeling lighter too, for the most part, the sadness slowly lifting. The fear, however, is still present. I deal with it every day, although all the experiences I've had and continue to have with Jeanne help tremendously. I'm gaining a new understanding about life that I couldn't have fathomed before when I was totally controlled by fear and my thicket of defenses. I lived in a different world then, the "matrix," as Chuck would say. Indeed, everything, other than this bright new clarity, is the matrix.

Most of the time we do live in the matrix, an agreement of the world that's constructed on a fixed set of ideas that never change, a fixation on there being only one reality. It's pretty clear to me, at this point in my journey, that most people live their entire lives in that world of set ideas, fixated there, never even realizing it, and never realizing there's another way to be. But I've learned to shift my perspective, intentionally, to be open to the magic that abounds and surrounds us all, to see things differently, and to feel and read energy. I've been learning how to seamlessly navigate back and forth between worlds, that of the magical and that of this reality, dealing with what arises, as it arises. I'm learning to bear the tension and remain calm, no matter what I encounter. And I've been discovering that it's not really that hard to do. The hard part is dismantling an old belief system that limits one's experiences. Breaking through that fixed reality, where everything stays the same and thus nothing new could possibly happen, takes a lot of work. You have to be a daredevil if you really want to change.

I meet with Nicolas, my yoga teacher, for a session of Embodyment Therapy, a gentle manipulation of the sacral bone in the lower back and the large sitz bone at the base of the pelvis. Working first on one side of the body, then the other, allows for a release of stored or stuck energy. I lie on my back on the floor, a thick layer of heavy blankets beneath me, my legs bent over a small stack of folded blankets so that my spine is flat and extended. I'm curious and calm as the process begins. Already used to Nicolas's gentle energy I feel no fear whatsoever as he slides one hand under my lower back, allowing my weight to rest upon his fingertips, and as his other hand presses lightly into my sitz bone. Before long a tingling sensation stirs in my lower spine, followed by a slight clenching, followed by a release of energy that travels up my spine. For the most part it's a relaxing experience, only becoming slightly uncomfortable when my emotions begin to stir, when I feel them rise up my spine too, curls of heat that burn through me, dissipating as I let them go.

As I lie there and release wave after wave of stuck energy, it immediately becomes clear to me that this is the missing component in my work with Chuck. I've known for a long time that I needed some kind of physical therapy to encourage and support a physical release. As a psychotherapist, Chuck is bound by the rules of his profession and cannot touch his clients; he's not licensed to do so. I've been aware that I needed to go outside of his work environment to find the one thing he cannot give, and yet I wasn't sure what that would be. I'd thought of contacting Nicolas many times, aware that he did spiritual counseling and energy work outside of his yoga practice, but I'd been reluctant to speak of what I was dealing with. Today, I am extremely grateful to be lying on the floor of his workspace, receiving the gift of this Embodyment Therapy and discovering that I was right, that touch was indeed the missing component in my work with Chuck, subtle though this touch is. The universe has answered my call, and in yet another safe and supportive environment I am offered exactly what I need.

I soon realize that just as when I work with Chuck, it's not Nicolas doing the work of releasing but my own ability to let myself release, my own ability to accept the gift of healing and do the work that comes with it. I'm not passively lying on the floor; I'm feeling and working through every release that my body presents me with. Nicolas offers a tool to a connection with my own body, but I am totally in control of how far I wish to engage it and how far I wish to take it.

My nighttime dreams, and even Cosi getting her claw stuck under the fridge this morning, all portended my experience with Nicolas, how to relax, how to let go and release. Just as Cosi somehow got herself free from where she was caught, so do I release what's caught inside myself, allowing old stuck energy to burn off, relieving me of its pain. Quite an experience!

I have so much inner work begging to be attended to. I feel inclined to go home and steep myself in it, especially after the Embodyment session, but I heed Jeanne's message to wait until I see Chuck, so I head over to the studio instead. The physical pain is much less today. Perhaps the Embodyment session did the trick, though I feel a slight pull to go back into depression. Nicolas did say that the amount of release achieved in Embodyment may have the same effect as taking about fifteen yoga classes. A warning to be prepared for what may come!

Tired, ready for bed, so grateful for all I've received. Tomorrow I see Chuck. I wonder how it'll go, if it'll be the right day to work on the emerging memory.

"*Yes, that's the way to go,*" Jeanne says, nodding, sitting alongside my other guides in their ethereal tower. They wave, and I see that they're all with me on this.

"*Let's see what happens!*" they say.

February 13, 2004

My whole body is sore, inside and out. Nicolas did warn me that I might feel a lot, emotionally as well as physically, over the next few days. I didn't tell him about my traumatic past, though I know he has always sensed something, and I know I will be telling him before long. In order to fully utilize the healing potential of his therapy, I'll have to be totally open, and then perhaps my body will open more too. Perhaps telling him won't be as hard as I imagine, though I haven't spoken to anyone about the abuse except Chuck. The idea of telling anyone else is just frightening.

Like a child standing at the service window of an ice cream truck, I look expectantly up to my guides, sitting calming in their tower.

"I understand that yesterday was not the day for me to push myself," I say. "It was important for me to wait until I was with Chuck."

They all nod, as if to say, "*You know what you have to do, and now is the time to do it!*" My whole body feels ready, mentally, physically, and emotionally. And my spirit is ready too.

"They want you to reclaim every bit of yourself," Chuck says, when I tell him about my communications with Jeanne and my other guides.

I'm sitting in the pose of the little girl again, my hands on my knees, when all of a sudden, I feel myself speeding back in time, everything rewinding, my cells morphing and changing into her body again, just as happened last week when I was here in Chuck's office, and then the pain comes.

"Come back!" Chuck says, loudly, because as soon as the pain hits, I start to dissociate and he senses it.

"I feel I have to do this for the little girl," I say. "I can do it for her, so we won't feel the pain anymore, so we can move on."

"Yes, of course, but your guides are right," Chuck says, "you don't have to do it all at once. Slow down, breathe, and let yourself be guided."

After meeting with Chuck, I spend the morning at home doing laundry and hanging out with the kids, who are on a school holiday. We go out in the afternoon for a hike across snow-covered fields, the winds warm, the sky clear blue, and all of us in good moods. We stop at the studio afterwards so I can attend to a few things and then I drop the kids at their dad's house for the weekend. Back home, my energy is so depleted I feel like curling up for a while. It's been my desire all day, since I left Chuck's in the morning, to just curl up into a ball in the old way, looking for some

I Tell Chuck About Jeanne

of that old comfort, but it isn't quite there anymore, the comfort, that is. I can't find it, even though I lie down and give it a good try.

Though I'm achy and sad, and somewhat depressed, I know I'll be okay, that this is just another phase I have to pass through, perhaps a combination of the work I did with both Chuck and Nicolas this week. Funny that I've been turning to men for healing. I feel safe with both of them.

I'm really looking forward to a quiet weekend alone. I have something going on each day to get me out of the house, but I'll also have plenty of quiet time.

By the time darkness descends I'm in agony, going into painful places I had no intention of ever going back to again, though I also understand why I'm drawn to revisit them. I'm going where I must, as I take back the energy that's mine, leaving behind that which doesn't belong to me, as I merge my two selves, and as I go through the final phases of this soul retrieval journey. It's quite a cathartic experience, deeply purging and deeply cleansing. I've actually been cruising along pretty well for a few weeks now, less despair and agony, but now it's come back with a vengeance! I look to my guides for help.

"Why am I back in this old state? Did I miss something? Is there something I still need to get? What is it? What!"

"*Just go through it,*" my guides say. "*You'll understand. There's stuff you haven't dealt with yet.*"

It hasn't been this bad in a long time. I find myself back in some memory from a long time ago, spinning with pain and fear, and I can't turn it off. I've been feeling so calm and safe lately, and now I feel like I've fallen back into that dark hole of oblivion again, into the black tunnel of my childhood. The pain comes in waves. After each wave I calm myself down to a manageable level, until the next wave comes.

"Breathe, breathe, breathe," I tell myself. "Calm down. Get back to that good place."

Indeed, I had achieved a good place, a real sense of safety like I've never felt in my life. I've been so calm, feeling so good lately. Now I'm back in a full-fledged recapitulation, bigger and more intense than ever. Desperate for a way to stop it, I reach out and call Chuck.

"This is the physical aspect of the release," he says. "It's a necessary component and exactly what you expected. You have those guides pushing you, but they're also supporting you. It's different. It's not the same as in the past, but it's still intense and very excruciating."

"It's not a visual memory this time, it's physical," I say. "I don't have the usual recall with it, no pictures or smells. I just have the agony of the physical body."

"I'm not surprised by the state you're in," he says. "It's to be expected. The physical aspects need to be dealt with."

"I need to lie down," I say. "I need to try and sleep. I'm so exhausted."

I hang up and beg for sleep, knowing he's right, that I haven't dealt with the physical yet.

February 14, 2004

I dream that I'm in a square room devoid of furniture or ornamentation, an empty cell with a locked door, a food tray on the floor. The walls are periwinkle blue. I'm aware that I've put myself in here in order to go through something that I know I have to go through.

I wake up in the same state of pain as last night, my body clenched and aching, feeling brittle and breakable. I wrench my right arm in the simple act of reaching for a tissue and I'm immediately brought back into the memory that's been hovering for weeks now. I'm a little girl again and my arm is wrenched back, a hand tightly clenches around it, another grips my neck. I'm in great pain. I must somehow unclench the hand from my arm. It's as if my abuser is still holding me captive, dominating me still, after all these years, restricting my every move. Every movement brings more pain. Instinctively, I pull away, trying to free myself, but he clamps down even harder.

"Hang in there," Chuck said last night, and I told him that yes, I would hang in there. What else is there to do, except hang in

I Tell Chuck About Jeanne

there? I'll cry if I have to, feel the pain I need to feel, feel the sadness, all the physical aspects. I can handle it. I have strength of endurance. I'm trying to get back to that safe place of inner calm that I know is inside me. I'm aware that the person in the square room of my dream is my abused self, needing safe shelter and caring, needing quiet space and privacy, needing to be looked after while she goes through this process, but also needing to be rescued from her prison cell.

When I was at my session with Chuck yesterday, I felt a great welling up at one point, a building up of a ball of emotion rising from my belly to my chest, as if I had a huge fire ball of pain inside me that wanted to come out, but I couldn't find a voice for it. Instead, I shook with the intensity of holding it in, and I haven't stopped shaking since.

I realize that my recapitulation process has unfolded in the way that it has needed. In the first year I recalled the majority of the memories, then I went through the varieties of feelings and mental pain associated with those memories. Now I seem to be reaching the deepest physical pain that was buried alongside the memories. That pain is in my body still, so I have to accept that its release is a necessary step. I have to also remember that this is what Nicolas warned me about, the aftereffects of fifteen yoga classes in one fell swoop. OUCH!

I imagine a calm eye in a storm and I try to concentrate on that calm center while the storm swirls around it. I breathe. I am centered and calm, anchored in myself even as the pain and anguish try to destroy me, even as the abuser repeatedly tugs at my arm, trying to pull me back, back to being his slave girl. I was his slave girl once, but only in body. I kept the tiny seed of my spirit hidden from him and now, after all these years, that seed is emerging from long germination, growing, carrying with it my memories and my pain, but also my freedom.

Home after working at the studio all day. I'm depressed, feeling swamped by the sadness and the heavy stuff that's been emerging over the past few days. I continue to imagine calmness, my calm center at the eye of the storm. I painted that today, a small round white circle in the midst of a dark swirling storm. I centered myself in it as I painted, focusing on getting back to calmness with each brush stroke, holding onto the memory of the enduring calmness that I know I hold within myself.

I watch a movie called *Till Human Voices Wake Us*, about a man who confronts his past with the help of an anima figure, who leads him to a painful memory. He uses dissociation to repress his pain as the memory overwhelms him, just as I've always done. As I watch the movie, I realize that dissociation, at the moment of trauma, triggers the forgetting. Forgetting begins even as one is in the midst of the trauma; in leaving the body, one has already forgotten! I understand how I was never aware that anything had happened to me, not cognitively at least, because I was not present in my body during most of the abuse. Repression began immediately, while in the midst of the trauma. During recapitulation I get to relive that which I have no memory of. This is something I've known, but the movie helps me understand it better.

I understand that memory is stored not only in the brain but also buried deeply in the physical body. But now I also understand more clearly how pain and memory are intrinsically linked, encapsulated in each other. The pain I experienced so long ago, at the time of the abuse, was the reason for dissociating in the first place. In order to escape the pain, I dissociated, and yet the memory of what was happening, the sexual abuse itself, was also dissociated from, by default. The memory of it remained behind in the body, encapsulated in the pain. Maybe that's why the pain is the hardest part to remember and to deal with, as it holds so much, yet it also dominates much of life, as pain of unknown origin, until recapitulated. After the shock of trauma recedes, that physical and mental pain of unknown origin sets off an avalanche of other defenses as well, from frequent episodes of dissociation to OCD behaviors, hypersensitivity and hyper-alertness, to fear of life itself. Pain is behind it all.

As this realization goes through me, I become faint. I feel myself physically giving up and I have to lie down. I stop fighting the feelings and my body goes limp. My body feels like it's dying. My body *is* dying; my life energy is leaving me. I feel it seeping out through my fingers, escaping, leaving behind a shaking shell, an empty shell of a girl. I am no longer the adult me but an empty shell of an abused girl, who doesn't know what's happening to her.

I know I have to climb back into that fallen girl and move her, get her up. Even though she's heavy and unsteady, I lift her and get her to move, get her out of there. She can't stay! She has to get up and move! Move! My body takes over the remembering. My body tells me what it felt like to dissociate, then to have to get back into the body that's lying on the ground and how difficult it is to make it move, make it come to life again, how hard it is to breathe, and move, and walk out of there!

I let my body keep remembering, knowing that my little girl self has been holding this pain, and that we have to release it or we'll never stop clenching and being afraid. I tell her that this is the last thing we must do in order to get free: *we must release the physical pain.* That's what has to happen now and, as with the other kinds of releases, once it starts, I have no control over how the process unfolds.

As I sleep and dream now, I hope to forget everything... for just a little while.

February 15, 2004

I dream that I'm sitting at a circular table with some other people. In a large vase on the table incense is burning for the dead. A woman gives me advice on how to deal with death and disappointment. She tells me to "fill up with grief" and to "be prepared for it." I look more closely at the vase of incense and notice that the tall stalks of incense are as large around as cattails. I reach out and touch them, but they are burning hot.

The feeling of heat shifts the dream and suddenly I'm lying on a warm sandy beach, curled up with a man. We're sleepy. I'm very comfortable and feel extremely safe with this man. A busy world goes on around us, but it recedes as we lie there safe and sound in each other's arms.

The first dream appears as a circular mandala. The circular table, at which I'm sitting, has a round vase at the center, out of which the burning incense sends its healing smoke, indicating the burning off of all that once was, what is no longer necessary. It's as if my inner cauldron has been exposed, what was once inside now visible on the outside, the deep work I've done on myself confirming the changes that have taken place. I have to be prepared for the death of the old self, the woman in my dream tells me. I must suffer the burning off of my memories, the pain and anxiety, the fear, and everything else that must burn off from my old life in order for me to resurrect, to reincarnate into new life. Through this recapitulation process I am offered new life without actual dying, but the process is much the same as a real death; there is the sacrifice and pain of transformation, there is the grieving process to go through, and there is the ritual of honoring the dead.

My recapitulation is a circular journey, as I pull into my center all that I am, in the end arriving at my wholeness, the true and completely known self, which the center of a mandala indicates. In the second dream, I lie curled up, safely and comfortably in the arms of a male companion, perhaps an animus figure, the inner masculine counterpart to my inner feminine self. I do know that I'm really the only one who can create and maintain a place of safety for myself, and not another person. My dream is showing me that the end of this process will unite all of my parts, not just my child and adult selves, but all that I am. My future bodes well, as one of peace, wholeness, centering calmness, and love too.

I woke up several times during the night hearing the wind howling as a cold front moved in. It's a chilly twelve degrees this Sunday morning, bitterly cold after the balmy weather we've had for the last few days. It fits right in with how I've been feeling lately, lost in a howling storm, everything swirling around me and I can't seem to touch down, to anchor for very long. My dreams, however, remind me that I have within me the necessary tools to achieve calmness, no matter what's going on inside or outside of me.

To prove that point, I get up and do the magical pass of forging the energy body, followed by some calming breaths. The movements do me good. I warm up and get back to that stable center, that calm place of my dream, and a sense of safety within. I've worked hard for that calm center and yet it's still very new to me, so new that when I get swept away by the past it feels like I may never get back to it again, though eventually I do. And my

I Tell Chuck About Jeanne

dream points out the truth, that it's always available to me because it's inside me. Even just imagining lying on a warm sandy beach is calming.

I head out to meet with Nicolas for an Embodyment session. As I drive over to his office, I decide to be open, to just go with the process and see what happens. No agenda needed, no decisions to make, no preparations to make. The intent to heal was set long ago when the universe received my call and set it in motion. Now, it's just about showing up for the unfolding of the journey and being as fully present as possible.

It doesn't take long for things to happen. I am relaxed and have good results right away. I lie on the blankets and let release after release flow out of me. I clench less than last time. It feels good, as I acquiesce more and more, letting fear flow out of me too, letting pain go easily now, letting myself heal.

Afterwards, I notice that my shoulders have dropped considerably from their usual hunched position. I feel naturally relaxed. I feel myself standing straighter and taller. I'm more present in my body than ever before. I am centered.

"Stand fast and remain united and all will soon be well." - Chief John Ross of the Cherokee nation.

I come upon these words of wisdom, which provide a certain sense of being on the right path, the warrior's path. And I do believe that all will be well. I believe in peace. I believe in my calm center. I believe in my spiritual advisors. I can go to their tower on high whenever I need something, and they always answer me.

"We've had a big day and we have many big days ahead of us, with lots still to come, and you need to be rested," they say. *"Rest now, sleep."*

February 16, 2004

I dream that I'm walking through a dark tunnel of trees. It's nighttime and snowing heavily. I'm following my daughter's footsteps in the snow. She has borrowed my boots. Her footsteps end abruptly and I become worried, wondering where she could have gone. I know she needs me. I hear her move about in the darkness and I can tell she's afraid. I'm afraid too. Then I become lucid; I wake up in my dream and explain to myself that she is not me.

"Things that happened to me won't happen to her. She's a totally different person. She's her own being with her own journey, and this is a dream."

Then I become aware that I'm following the footsteps of my own little girl self, as she takes this recapitulation journey, and not my daughter at all, and I know exactly what happens to me, so no worries!

"Just calm down," I tell myself, as soon as I realize this truth. "Everything will be just fine."

I wake from this dream, sit up in bed, and close my eyes in meditation. Immediately I am drawn into that dark tunnel of trees in my dream.

"Where am I going?"

"*Back to the woods*," Jeanne says.

"Why?"

"*You left something back there.*"

"What?"

"*Yourself. You left yourself back there, your young undeveloped self. Go and get her and bring her out into the light. We'll all take care of her. Okay?*"

I have to get ready for work. If I go into the woods right now, I may not have enough energy for the day. I pull out of the meditation and say goodbye to Jeanne, for now, telling her I'll take it up with Chuck next time we meet.

Thank you, I tell her. Every day you show me how much support I have. Last night's dream is showing me that I do have to go back into the woods, to retrieve the little girl who's waiting for me there. I can hear her crying for me. I'm the only one she wants. I'm able now to understand this. I must find a way to take her with me, to hold her in my arms and comfort her, and take her forward with me into new life too.

February 17, 2004

"I make bad decisions, I'm a complete failure, totally incompetent," these are the words I wake up saying to myself.

Only five in the morning and already I'm hating myself, despising myself. Bad feelings laced with exhaustion and apathy spell out the beginnings of a bad day. I won't accept it. I sit up and turn my eyes upward toward that tower on high and ask my guides for help.

"*Stop struggling so much,*" they say. "*Just let it happen, let the unfolding of the process guide you. Please, just acquiesce. Even if you don't feel like you're fighting it, you are, and that's why you stagnate. When you go against the flow, or try to control the unfolding of the process, everything pools up—pain, emotions, moods—even the recapitulation comes to a standstill. Better to release to the journey. Just go with what the release brings, as it comes. Just flow with it. You won't get hurt.*"

Comforted by their words, I get the kids up, send them off to school and then go see Chuck. I step into his office, sit down, and go right into the woods of my dream. I walk down that dark tunnel of trees that Jeanne and my dream pointed out as the next path on this journey, but I'm reluctant. It's a natural instinct, the urge to pull back, but I remember the message from my guides. I persevere.

I recall the words of the Cherokee Chief as I head into the woods: "*Stand fast and remain united and all will soon be well.*" I hold myself together, even though my heart is beating loudly in my chest, my palms are sweaty, and I'm shaking like a leaf. I sense the little girl leading me deeper into the woods, and yet she goes so slowly, for she knows how deeply painful it is and how far inside the woods the memories and pain dwell. She's willing to take me there and I have to follow her with equal willingness. I must remain united with her as we take this healing journey. I must go once again back into the past with her so she can show me what I missed. And I have to bring her back out with me too. Strong and steady, united we go, but at the same time I'm scared, resistant.

"If you keep breathing you can get through anything," Chuck says.

"I don't want to do this anymore," I whine, pulling out of the woods, "but I know that's not right. I have to go through it again and again until there's nothing left to bother me."

Chuck tells me to leave it for now, to turn it off, to come back to the present and not go there again until we meet on Friday. Friday seems so far away, but I promise myself that I'll try to make the next few days more than just a waiting period, more than just a void. I'll try and make them be important days because important decisions have to be made every day.

"*Stand fast and remain united and all will soon be well,*" I tell myself, slowly re-centering in the calmness within that waits so patiently for me to return to its soothing embrace.

I head to the studio after leaving Chuck, determined to have a good day, but almost immediately I'm in the void. It's like walking into a cloud. Suddenly I can't see or hear. I lose the hand of the little girl. I lose my connection to my inner place of calm and I feel myself spinning in the void. I know I have to keep busy and moving if I am to survive.

I pull out a large canvas that I had originally painted with an abstract design. It had been meaningful at the time I'd painted it, full of the energy of a different time, but I'm ready to sacrifice it. Dumping a mound of white paint onto my palette I begin painting over the old painting, forming large white circles, concentrating on making them as perfectly round and precise as possible. I focus all my attention on this task, but I can't seem to maintain the hard edges I so desire. The circles are not perfect. No matter how intently I try, I keep blurring the edges. It feels as if I'm losing control over my hands and over my ability to paint what I want.

As I work, I realize that I won't be able to achieve what I want because I'm being challenged to change, to let go of my need for perfection. Consciously, and ever so slightly, I begin to soften my body and my intentions, as well as how I hold the brush, how I work the paint, and even my idea of what perfection is. I allow the brush to become an extension of my softening intent. As I soften, I watch the circles grow larger and softer too. I allow that the need for release is now greater and more important than the need for containment and control. Rather than hold in, I must let go, but I must also let in. I must let in something new at the same time I let go of something old, an even exchange, so to speak.

As this idea develops further, through the physical action of painting softly, congealing in both my mind and on the canvas, I ponder the meaning of this "exchange." What am I supposed to be letting in? I soften the edges even more. Is it love? People? The circles grow wider and even more blurred, lighter, easily expanding. I actually feel myself opening up as I paint, but to what? As these thoughts go through me, I consciously leave space for new things to come through on the canvas. I don't completely cover the surface with white circles but leave areas of color showing from the old painting underneath, small openings so that something in the past can still come through, or something in the future.

I open myself even wider as the white circles grow wider too, until they are floating on the canvas. The more I paint, and the more I acknowledge that *opening* is what is important now, the calmer I grow. I am painting the void and painting the void away at the same time, using it to shift, asking it to speak to me, to communicate what it holds and why, asking it to guide me, to show me its secrets, to educate me in why it's so necessary right now. I open to the void.

Then the phone rings and I am jolted out of my creative bubble and everything shifts. All of a sudden there is a hubbub of energy, of activity. People stop in to visit me. There are comings and goings, hellos and goodbyes, and the phone won't stop ringing! I am not going to be left alone to get lost in the void. The void has delivered its message.

In spite of all the friendly activity, I am back in the void by the end of the day. Somehow it just slips back into the studio and wraps its arms around me, like a ghostly companion, and before I know it, I'm in the thick of it again. I finally come out of it while shopping at the grocery store. I'm standing in the cereal aisle, reaching up for a box of cereal when I feel a shift, and suddenly my head clears, the fog lifts; all of a sudden, I see better, breathe better, feel better. And what made it lift? The act of doing a movement similar to painting; a slight turn to the left, my right painting arm extended and raised, the same action as when I was painting this morning. A physical movement caused the shift, much like a magical pass.

I think the void and I actually needed some quality time together. I learned how the void works and how to work with it, how to use it creatively and how to shift out of it. And I've created my own magical pass—a painting pass!

February 18, 2004

I dream of letting go and then plunge into a dizzying spin, aching in my body while I dream. When I wake up, I'm still spinning and my body aches in the same places I dreamed of. I have no control as I swirl downward, my body feeling like it's collapsing in on itself. There's a sense of impending explosion, that something terrible is going to happen. I am like a bomb about to go off; a great hot ball of emotion welling up from deep inside me, seeking a way out.

"It's okay if I cry," I tell myself. "It'll be okay. It'll be good. Don't be afraid. It's okay."

I can't do it! It's too frightening to be alone with the intensity of the emotion. I stop it, pull out of the spin and breathe into my stomach. The anxiety reduces. I turn toward my guides sitting in their great tower in infinity, requesting guidance on what to do, how to approach this great ball of emotion.

"*Go back*," they say. "*It's enough for now.*"

And then I watch as a shift takes place among them. I see them moving around. The three on the right, my relatives, invite Jeanne to join them. She's been standing off to the left, while the others have been clustered on the right. But behind them, for the first time, I clearly see what I had once intuited, a multitude of unknown others, standing with caring looks, gazing down on me, and everyone else in the world too, waiting to help us. But now everyone stands together, united, on a mission: Me. And they all tell me the same thing.

"It's enough for today."

I'm letting the kids sleep late today. I'll drive them into school rather than have them take the bus. They'll get an extra hour of sleep that way and I'll get an early start at the studio. I'd like to stay in bed myself, but I make myself get up. The truth is, I anticipate something good out there for me today. I have no idea what it is, but I'll never find out if I don't go out and meet it.

It's so important that I continue to deal with the painful physical state of my body, though I find I can barely relate to the pain, barely feel compassion for myself. I still push feelings and emotions away, begging them to not get near me. How can I heal if I refuse to accept what happened to me? It's all so disturbing, and so I run from that huge ball of pain welling up inside me. I run from it, knowing that one day soon I will have to turn and face it. It's the only way to make it go away, and I know that once I turn and face it, it will lose its power.

The sun is shining. After writing down my thoughts I feel better about myself, sunnier too, at least for the moment. I'm exhausted though, as if getting over an illness, but I sense I'm healing too, little by little.

I drop the kids off at school and head over to the studio. I pick up my paint brush and begin working over another old painting, one that I'm willing to sacrifice to this unfolding process, as I don't have any new canvases lying around. I notice that I keep getting pulled back into the white void as I paint, and I keep pulling away from it. I also keep having the feeling that I must let that huge ball of emotion rise up on its own and find release. I put my brush down and sit down to meditate instead, asking for help. Jeanne and my three other guides tell me that it's like magic.

"*Don't be afraid of it,*" they say. "*It's good magic.*"

"*Nothing bad will happen to you,*" they say. "*Once you let the magic in then everything will change. It's okay to cry, it's okay to break down. It's okay to need someone. It's okay that you need Chuck to be there to help you. It really is okay.*"

I must take some time for the truth of this to finally sink in. First, that I have Chuck's total support, and secondly, that it did happen to me, that I was sexually abused and tortured as a child. It's as if I haven't realized this before, actually, fully let the truth in. Is this the magic they're talking about—*the truth*?

Suddenly, I'm jolted into heightened awareness. My body begins to vibrate and I feel myself morphing into a child's body, becoming my familiar child self again. I receive a quick download of the truth of my entire life, a life review that fills me to the brim, as if being returned, poured into me from wherever it has been stored all these years.

"*Let the magic happen! Don't be afraid,*" my guides say. "*Trust us. We are all here for you.*"

"Why? Why does anyone care about me? I'm nothing."

"*We care because you are something. You have survived in order to do great things. You have gifts to give to others. You will continue to give, but first you have to depart from the old life and begin the new life, without thinking, without worry, without fear. Leave those things in the old life. There won't be room for them in the new life. You will need room for other things. Magic will take you there. Take Chuck by the hand and go there with him. He is your sponsor. He'll go with you, but really you can do it on your own. Go, go, go! Be unafraid. TRUST. Believe in the magic that's all around you. No one else can see it, but you do. You feel it every day. You know it's there, everywhere. The magic is everywhere.*"

"*This is what you need to do over the next few days: let the magic enter you so you can be transported and taken to the next level, and from there, you will know where to go. Leave reluctance behind with fear and worry. Give all that up. You won't need it. Everything you need will be there when you get there. You don't need to take anything. More than enough awaits you. Open to the magic. Let the pain out and you will have room for the magic.*"

And then I get it. If I stay dissociated from the painful feelings and experiences, keeping them at a distance, I will never merge into oneness. I will never be whole. It's like saying, "Oh, I'll just keep the memories over there, away from me, with that detached little girl. I'll let her deal with everything so I don't have to feel." But that's not fair to her and it will only continue to impact me as powerfully as it has always done. As long as I leave "it" out there, outside of me, even if on the far periphery of life, it can still get me; it can still stalk and haunt me. If I don't deal with it head on, it will always chase me. What do I have to lose? Nothing! And to gain? Everything!

"Take back the child. She doesn't deserve to be out there, detached and alone. Look how horrible it is out there in the void, how lonely, blank and foggy, how unreal it is. Bring her into the clear blue waters and wash off the white void and find a real live person underneath. Wash off the void."

"Tears are okay," they say. *"When that ball of emotion wells up, don't stop it and don't run from it. Let it come. It's okay to let the child come back."*

"She's afraid it won't be for real, that it won't be good," I say, speaking from a place of old fear.

"Trust. You need to give her the gift of trust," they say.

"And then we give each other life!" I say, excited now. "I get it! Trust equals life! They are both equally important gifts. We have to just decide to go for it."

"Just go for it," they say. *"Let it happen."*

And, with that, my guides recede, their words echoing in my ears. Wow! I guess that was the "something good" that I'd anticipated earlier this morning. This is certainly proving to be a good week for shifts, in dreaming and reality. Inside myself too!

Once again, I pick up my brush and begin painting. I let myself step into the whiteness of the void and soon I am swept away by it. Painting furiously, in angry jabs and swipes, I paint the white void. When I step back and raise my eyes and soften my gaze, I find that I have painted my pain.

Home at the end of the day. In spite of my magical morning, I feel needy. I want holding and touching, things I didn't even know I needed. I know everyone does, but I never allowed myself to even desire them. Now I lie on my bed and hug myself, okay with the wanting. I accept my humanness.

It suddenly dawns on me that I'm still so afraid of success that I stop dead in my tracks and find it hard to move forward. That's why I'm in bed right now. It has always been the case, in my work as in my life, but it's especially being pointed out to me as I undergo this pursuit of my total self, as I near the moment of achieving my wholeness. My feelings, in their rise to the surface, are alerting me to the fact that success is imminent, that it is absolutely guaranteed, but I have to get over my refusal to embrace it. I have to push aside my stumbling blocks and my old ideas of myself and let success be mine. Because I will have success. I can make it hard on myself or I can make it easy on myself. Above all, I have to take responsibility to ensure that it happens. I have everything it takes within myself. I must keep listening to my spiritual messengers and follow their guidance. This is not a dream. This is my new reality.

February 19, 2004

I meet with Nicolas and decide to just relax and go with the flow. I'm prepared to accept what comes and to release into it. During the session, I experience tensions flowing out of me in wave after wave until I'm sinking and rising, as if floating on an ocean. The swells and currents take from me what I no longer want or need, sending me farther and farther away from my old self. When I land back on the shores of the present, my body is still flowing, vibrating. When I stand up, it's as if I'm emerging from the ocean, a new person, taller and looser than ever. In total submission to the process of release I have achieved this new body. I am flowing in the universe. I have let it happen.

"*Just relax and let it happen,*" say my guides. "*The magic happens when you open to it.*"

And you know what? I did, and it did! I now know what that really means, and what it actually feels like.

I go to the studio afterwards, feeling blissfully happy and so much lighter, having released a huge inner weight, the pain of carrying it now so noticeably absent. I intend to remain open to more experiences, to magic, to success, to no fear, to allowing for things to happen naturally, to letting go. I'm drawn into inner solitude and quiet, into peaceful expression. I'm not fighting *anything* right now. I'm just flowing!

I've spent my entire life not wanting to be in my body, not feeling like I fit in it, but now I find that I fit very well, that I *am* this body, and I'm conscious of wanting to stay in it, and to rid it of any remaining pains or memories, any bad feelings, any self-deprecating thoughts that may keep me from this body. This is who I am, I realize—I am this body, and it is good.

February 20, 2004

I dream a dark and heavy dream, filled with old tension and despair, then watch as it disappears, like a snake slithering down a hole, the old tension and despair riding away on its tail. I wake up to catch Chuck's face hovering in the air before me.

"Stick with it," he says, calmly and kindly, then he too disappears.

The struggle between body and spirit persists. There is struggle, struggle, struggle as I attempt to stay focused on my intention and desire to release while simultaneously staying fully present in my body. When I give way, especially during my Embodyment sessions, there is endless release and a state of bliss is achieved. But then I return to struggle, struggle, struggle and all I want is that moment of release again. I yearn for that state of bliss too. What goes up must come down, though, for I am far from the bliss state I experienced yesterday. The light has been replaced by the dark. That fiery ball of painful emotions was returned to me in the night as I slept and dreamed, letting me know that it's something I still have to deal with. Somewhere in the future, I suppose, I will be more in balance and more easily able to give way to release and bliss and light, rather than having to deal with the constant ups and downs of this rollercoaster world of recapitulation.

I know I should relinquish my preconceived notions of what or should happen and just go with the flow of life all the time, the goods and bads, the ups and downs. That means being totally open to the process as it unfolds, to whatever is going on inside, and to staying mindfully cognizant of what's happening to me physically, neither forcing nor directing, neither resisting nor controlling, simply allowing. It's a difficult lesson to learn.

I meet with Chuck. The uncomfortable fiery ball of emotions sits lodged firmly in my chest, a hard ball of pain. He suggests I try turning the painful heat into healing heat.

Breathing deeply, I put my attention there. It's easy to imagine healing energy swirling into my chest, going right into the center of that fiery ball. I imagine warmth and relaxation. I imagine gentle waves of heat and calmness. It's so nice. I just want to stay in the calm warmth of it and see what happens.

"What's happening?" Chuck asks.

"A slight release," I tell him. "It feels good."

"Good," he says. "Go back in, go deeper."

I breathe long deep breaths, envision healing heat and warmth, reminding myself to just go with it, to relax and release.

"It's okay, nothing bad will happen," I tell myself. "It's good. This is good."

As I go deeper into the experience, I feel my adult body begin to shift into a smaller body. It jolts me a little, the feeling that I'm losing myself again, but I'm able to pull myself back to the present by focusing on my breathing.

"I am me, breathing into my lungs, feeling the warmth, the healing warmth," I tell myself. "I am me breathing into me, finding me."

Chuck calls to me to come back, but I don't want to. He has to call a few times.

"I'm so full of stuff that I need to release," I say. "I can't let any new stuff in until I get rid of the old stuff. Nothing will happen until I make some room inside myself. I feel absolutely cluttered inside, packed to the hilt, and I want to be rid of it."

"Slow down, be patient," he says.

I Tell Chuck About Jeanne

I go to work, painting a mural in a large freezing cold mansion high on a windy hill, the driveway covered in ice, the housekeeper suspicious when I arrive. She shuts the door in my face, leaving me standing in the icy wind while she calls her employer, who has failed to notify her that I would be coming. When she finally comes back, I grab my stuff and slip in the crack of door she has reluctantly opened before she can shut it again. I notice how edgy I'm feeling, holding everything together inside, only half present as I work, the healing energy of my early morning session with Chuck a distant memory.

I pack up after six hours and let the suspicious housekeeper know that I'll be back in the morning. She nods without saying a word. I drive back to the studio to clean my brushes and spend a few hours painting another white painting, but it doesn't work for me, the white dull and listless now. I start adding color on top of what I've already done, adding warmth and feeling.

"It's the next stage, after the void," I tell myself. "It's what comes next; light, color, and new life."

Back at home I enjoy the quietude of the house, only me and the cats, the kids at their dad's house for the weekend. Anxiety finds a way in though. I breathe deeply and slowly to keep it at bay, like I did this morning with Chuck, sending healing energy deep into my heart. This getting born thing continues to be such a difficult struggle, this seeking of new life, of gaining knowledge, this spiritual journey. It feels like I'm still not getting something right. Why this constant anxiety?

"*Stop trying so hard to figure everything out,*" Jeanne says. "*You know what you must do. Face the fear and expel it by allowing for things to happen. Allow the magic to happen. It's all around you. Be open to it. Listen and you will hear it. Be quiet and still and you will feel it. Go deeper and you will find the answers. Everything you need is inside you.*"

February 21, 2004

I dream of fighting a medieval knight, clad in armor, breaking his fingers and knocking him off his horse. In the end, I apologize for hurting him. He gives up fighting then, knowing I'll always win. Then I'm walking beside an old blind woman, who tells me she can find her way because she has inner vision.

"Watch, and you will see magic happen," she says, as I follow her into an abandoned house where she trips on a phone cord, pulling it from the wall.

"We don't need that to communicate, we have other means," she says. "You already know that."

The blind woman said that even though I'm in the in-between world, not quite in the past nor fully in the future, I can find my way too. Even the present feels nonexistent, for I'm in a world of my own that exists only because of where I am right now. I sense I'm nearing the end of a critical phase though, the last fight with my old staunch defenses taking place, represented by the first dream, while at the same time I'm being introduced to the new me. And even though I feel as blind as the old woman in my dream, she reminds me to just keep going.

"You will find your way," she told me, "even though you can't see where you're going either."

I must ground myself in this world, keep my feet on the ground, ground myself in work, ground myself in planning my day, in driving out to that cold house again and painting the mural. I can ground myself in returning a call to another client who wants me to do some work for her too. I can ground myself in writing and illustrating and painting, unlocking and waking up once again the passion for creative expression.

"Feel your body, feel yourself in your body," Jeanne says. *"This is who you are, a whole person, fully merging and emerging at the same time. You will get through this."*

My turn to sit at the art cooperative that I've been an active member of for several years. It's another bitterly cold night.

Luckily only one lone man comes into the gallery, for I have no inclination to engage in conversation. I'm tired, having worked all day on the mural, coming here directly afterwards. Now, as I sit down, for really the first time today except for being in the car, I realize how tense I've been all day, unable to relax and be in this body that is my home on this earth. In spite of my intent to stay grounded, I floated out-of-body for long stretches today, traveling in and out of that in-between world, going places I can't really remember. It's been a strange day to say the least.

I close the gallery at nine and arrive back home twelve hours after I left in the morning, happy to have gotten through the day in one piece. I'm grateful for my life, but I'm also lonely. I want to be in love and be loved. I don't need a crowd of people around me, I just need one special person, a real partner. But that's not to be yet, though perhaps at some time soon.

Now I just need sleep and I wish to dream, of course! I'll look for answers in that other world, the dream world, for I know it holds all the secrets I seek.

"Remember," Jeanne says, "*you don't need telephones or eyes to communicate and see. You know what you need to do. Conquer the fear.*"

February 22, 2004

I awaken filled with an urgency to stay the course, to do what I need to do. I am aware that as long as I keep working on this recapitulation everything will be fine. Only if I stop, if I give up, will I be in trouble. I must stick with it, as Chuck said in a recent dream. I must continue trusting that everything will work out just fine. This is what my dreams tell me. This is what my guides tell me. Money is not an issue anymore, I am told. The only issue is what I must do to free myself, and the truth is that I'm pursuing that head on, so I know I'll be fine.

"*Don't give up, no matter how strong the urge,*" Jeanne says, "*no matter how deep the despair feels, no matter how far down you get dragged, don't give up. Stay on the path.*"

My dreams and guides are pretty clear in spelling out what I must do as I continue this recapitulation. Stay grounded and keep going. There is no other path to take—this is it!

Looking upward toward the tower in the sky, I wonder if Jeanne and my guides have anything to add. I see them all sitting around looking bored, as if waiting for the show to begin. What show? Are they waiting for me to do something?

I turn from them to meditate. Going deep inside myself, I experience a slight release of tension. I come out of the meditation having received the directive that I must keep at it, that sometimes things slow down for a reason, and that I must be persistent and patient.

"*All will be revealed*," I hear.

I meet with Nicolas. The Embodyment work progresses nicely and I achieve wave after wave of release. At one point, a very comforting warmth spreads throughout my entire body and I feel that huge ball of fire that Chuck and I worked on the other day slowly begin to spin, releasing a little of its warmth too.

"So much more happens when I willingly let go, when I acquiesce," I say. "Release happens at a much deeper level simply because I stop resisting. I've always equated the idea of letting go with disintegration, with death and annihilation, but now I *can* let go, for I know and trust that nothing bad is going to happen. I've had enough experiences now to realize that letting go does not mean disintegration, that I won't die."

"That's a hard lesson to learn," Nicolas says.

"Yes, it is," I say, "but for me it's also a new concept. The idea of feeling safe and trusting hasn't always been true, or even an option, in fact it has never before been either true or an option."

As the waves of release flow through me, meeting and merging with the swelling ocean of my own energetic self, I feel laughter bubbling inside me, the first hints of new life, like the first bubbles of water in a newly struck well, on what previously had only been dry ground. I laugh and laugh, but I know it's only the very beginning of something deeper, that there is pain behind the laughter, and so much more. As soon as I acknowledge that, I feel that huge ball of fire in my chest spinning and spinning and spinning, and I know I'm right.

I've gotten through the weekend mostly intact, with some tiredness, with some feelings of despair, but with a bit more of an even temperament than in the past few weeks. But the battle between the past and the future continues, and present reality still seems more unreal than my other worlds, for I am still someplace else most of the time.

The main challenge right now is to inhabit my body, for perhaps the first time in my life. To actually live in it, to feel that it belongs to me, to feel the past me merging with the present me, in a very physical way. And when my two selves finally merge, perhaps I'll finally really exist. Maybe.

February 23, 2004

I wake up feeling all in parts again, strewn about, unable to piece myself back together. Everything hurts too. Panic rises. Keep it down! Breathe slowly, slowly. I fear that I can't do this merger, that I'll always be a fragmented person. I seem to wake up in pieces most days, and so I have to clear out the crap, especially the bad thoughts about myself, and build my body anew every morning. Before I even get out of bed I have to reorient, ground myself in this body and in this world that I open my eyes to every day, and start over.

Yesterday, when I met with Nicolas, I kept thinking that if I could truly let go of everything, I would let the memories go too, and then I wouldn't have to go back to them. If they were totally released from my body, I wouldn't have them inside me, dragging me down the way they do now. I would get to a new level where they don't exist, and then I'd be okay, more whole.

The kids go to school and I get ready for work. I have another long and busy day ahead of me finishing up the mural at the house on the cold mountain and then onto the studio in the afternoon. I still feel disjointed, but I know it's the process of merging, making room for all those sixteen little girls, one for each year of the abuse, that leaves me feeling this way. Each one of them is a separate being, with separate experiences and separate needs. Each one of them needs me to make room for her alone, to invite her into a safe place within myself that's free of horror and pain. They don't want to come in if the memories are still there, they tell me. They'll only merge with me when there are no horrors there to greet them.

That's it! They want to make sure they aren't going to be ambushed, that *he* isn't lurking in there somewhere, that it will indeed be safe, that we'll all be safe together. Well, they must know that I've been fighting him off for the longest time now, that I've been working like crazy for the past three years on ridding myself of his energy and the things he did to me. They have to trust me when I tell them that I've successfully fought him and his energy off, and that I'm sloughing off the memories of him too, every last vestige. I dreamed last night that they were all dancing happily and I was preparing a special playground for them, a place of psychological and physical healing and safety. So, things really are coming along!

Chuck is my spiritual guide on this journey and Nicolas is my body repair shop. I found my way to Chuck and that led to other things that have helped me immensely: the magical passes and the shaman's world, the *I Ching*, Jeanne, my other guides, and even myself, for I truly do hold the key to everything.

Noon. Finished the mural and drove back to the studio for lunch and an afternoon of invoicing and painting. So far, it's been a pretty good day, mood-wise. I'm feeling more optimistic, light and airy in mind and body, consciously trying to remain aware of not getting pulled back into the worries and darkness, even though they hover nearby.

A few more jobs have lined up, which is encouraging. I'm actually beginning to feel good about the business, feeling successful. It's good to be busy and earning some money. Without the added stress of wondering all the time if I'll be able to pay my bills, I'm free to indulge in creative activities without worry seeping in and telling me I need to get a "real" job. That's not going to happen, as I've always been fully committed to being my own boss.

I Tell Chuck About Jeanne

My horoscope for the month tells me to go with what I know feels right, that it will bring a kind of adulation that I'm not used to, due to my retiring image of myself, but that it's time to allow for a brighter self-image. Okay, I won't say no to that!

I am definitely in changing mode now, in metamorphosis with Butterfly Girl, an image of my young self I've kept in mind as I've taken this changing journey, tracking the stages to wholeness. I wonder what she has to say?

I pick up my paintbrush. Picking out yummy colors, good enough to eat, I squeeze them onto my palette and begin to repaint another of my canvases. I'm in a pretty good mood as I begin painting, but all of a sudden, a rush of emotional pain courses through me, building to such intensity that it punctures my lighthearted mood and, suddenly, I begin painting with hard, furious strokes, large and cumbersome. I can't help whimpering with pain, holding my stomach, clutching my breast, choking on the huge ball of fire searing through my chest and throat. This is what I felt behind the laughter the other day when I was in my session with Nicolas.

In intense pain, and with tears pouring down my face, I paint a huge fiery ball in bright yellows, pinks, and purples. Butterfly colors! When I step back, I see that it's actually quite a lovely thing. And then I finally get it. I get that I have to let the emotions out, but also that I have to "go there." I have to go to them, into them; I have to experience them. Jeanne and my spiritual guides have been hanging around all weekend waiting for me to get this.

I feel lightheaded and more than a little uncertain about how to move my body after this emotional outpouring, for I don't feel like myself anymore. It's almost as if I've removed something from my body, some monstrous tumor I didn't even know I was carrying. I feel clumsy and unfamiliar to myself as I stand back and look at my creation. I'm clumsy as I walk around the studio trying to get a handle on this new feeling of being in a body I don't recognize. I don't feel as if I'll walk or run normally ever again, for I feel heavy, uncoordinated, certainly not that light little Butterfly Girl anymore. I know this for certain because I'm waddling like a duck. This trying to be in my body is surely a strange and whacky thing!

February 24, 2004

I awaken groggy and exhausted. I spent most of the night dreaming that I was hovering above the Earth, tethered to an anchoring point, 130° N 29th — whatever that means! It seemed to be located somewhere off the coast of Maine, high above the ocean, among the stars and planets. My spirit left my body and went there, yet stayed safely attached to my body while it slept undisturbed, getting some much-needed respite from the work of this recapitulation. But now, here I am, back in my body, back in this reality. No more escape. Time to face what I must. Time to release whatever it is that I'm holding onto.

There's still a part of me that refuses to let go, to change anything, an old defense, I gather, while another part is pushing me to open up, to release, to trust that everything will be just fine. That must be the healer inside me, the part of me that really does want to finally see the end of this torment, but the old defense still holds sway, and a lot of power. I know I can't stop what's going to happen, nor do I want to, but that old protector thinks she's helping me, thinks she's keeping me safe, thinks it's best if I don't change, but the rest of me is itching to let go, mind and body, to just go with the flow of this recapitulation.

"*Allow for the merging to happen,*" Jeanne says. "*Allow the dancing girl to come back. Let her in, the playground is prepared.*"

"I am child-ready."

"*No one will harm her. Now is the time for healing, with good caring people. Let her in so she can be a part of it. It isn't fair to block her out. She needs to be a part of the healing too, otherwise it won't be complete. She too must learn to trust and feel safe with these healers. She needs to trust too.*"

That's it, isn't it? I can't do this without the child self. She needs to heal too, and I have to allow her to join in this process more fully. I can't leave her behind, safe in the arms of that protector. She has to come out into the open and be part of this healing, but I also have to open up to her and assure her that all is well now, that we will be fine, that she can trust me.

"Please come and be with me; I'm safe," I whisper to all sixteen of my little girl selves. "Be with me when I meet with Chuck this morning."

Then it hits me: I am the protector! I've been protecting those girls and keeping them safe so nothing bad would happen to them, not letting them play or have fun, keeping them isolated and confined because it's the only safety tactic I know. But everything is different now, and I'm ready for a different approach. I have to let them out to play. We have so much support now. I have to allow the girls to be a part of my life too. It's the only way they'll learn to trust. I'm not really protecting them anymore; I'm hindering them, hindering a major part of myself from being fully alive.

"No more hiding. It's time to come out," I say. "Okay? Nothing bad will happen. The bad stuff is over. It's a new and different world now."

There is no answer from the girls.

"I haven't let them live because it was too dangerous," I tell Jeanne. "It was always way too dangerous. I had to be careful or they'd get hurt. I had to protect them."

"*The child psychologist has prepared the playground now,*" Jeanne says, referring to my dream of the other night. "*It's ready. She wants the children to come play in a safe environment, protected and cared for. Open up and let them come out now, to live and be children. They might be afraid at first, but eventually they will understand that it's safe, that nothing bad will happen. Everything will be okay.*"

"I keep thinking that I must release, release, release, but no release is happening," I tell Chuck.

"Something is stopping you," Chuck says. "Something is holding back. What is it?"

"I'm afraid," I say. "It's the emotional stuff. That fiery lump has moved up from my chest and is now lodged in my throat. It sits there like a huge raw lump and I can't seem to release it."

"Maybe EMDR is too harsh," he says, "maybe the Embodyment Therapy is gentler."

"Yes, in a way it is, but this also feels so necessary," I say, clutching the vibrating EMDR pods. "This helps too."

"Getting to a healthy emotional release is the point now, and everything I'm doing supports that possibility," I tell myself, as I let the vibrating pods soothe and relax me. "Everything is telling me it will be okay to just let go; it will be fine. Chuck is safe. Nicolas is safe. It will be fine." Even though I tell myself these things, I still don't feel safe enough. Clutching the pods like lifelines, I close my eyes and put my head down.

"Stay conscious, you have to be here," Chuck says, rather sternly, and I know he's right. I can't go flying off anymore. I have to stay present. It's the only way to experience all the pent-up emotions. I must release them in full consciousness, fully feel them, and then move forward into new life in full consciousness as well.

I leave Chuck, go home, and get into bed and cry. I agree with him that I have to stay conscious because even though I feel suspended between two worlds I do need to stay present in this reality, because I exist in this world. On the other hand, I would really like to stay curled up here in bed with my cats. It's so quiet and comforting. But who wants it, the little girls? The old me, the protector?

The real truth is, I have to pry myself out of bed every day. Every day, I have to remind myself that I live in the real world. As much as I want to stay in bed all depressed and sad, I have to get up and go have a life, experience what it's like to be me in the real world, even if I'm not totally in it yet. Even if only one foot is in reality, I have to follow it. And I know that even if I take only one little step into reality today, it will bring me one step further along on my journey. And each little step I take will induce a little more consciousness!

Home by four. I did a small patching job this morning and earned twenty bucks. Big deal; gas money. Then I went over to the studio and started painting two more previously painted canvases.

I Tell Chuck About Jeanne

Painting helps release something, the whole-body movement of painting on a large canvas releases tension in the mind, and I felt freer as the day went on, though my lower back has been hurting all day. No amount of movement or exercise has released the pain I carry there. I think it's from tightening up, from my usual routine of holding in and clenching when I don't want to do what I know I'll eventually *have* to do. Maybe it's a memory, but maybe it's just my old defenses acting up, purely out of habit!

The kids and I eat dinner and then I drive my son to an evening rehearsal. Only then do I have a moment to sit and put things into perspective. I realize that this is all part of the process of disassembling and reassembling myself. I've deconstructed myself piece by piece as I've recapitulated, and I'm still trying to figure out how to fit everything back together again. I have to decide where to put all this new information about myself, and how to physically reassemble myself into the whole being that I'm becoming, though nothing quite fits yet. At the same time, I'm challenged to complete the final phase of this recapitulation and dissect the final memories, whatever they may be. All of which involves the ability to trust and let go to the process.

As much as I rationalize, and as much as I feel supported by others, and as often as I hear the voices of my guides urging me onward, it's almost frightening to imagine really letting go, to trust so deeply. It's a bit like flinging myself into the air and hoping that someone really is there to catch me. To be fair to myself, I have been going with the flow of this recapitulation for years now, letting things happen naturally, in my own struggling way to be sure, going with what feels so right and so necessary. But, I admit, I'm afraid to let go in the area where I have the tightest resistance, in the area of trust, in my ability to fully trust another person or, in this case, many persons. I fear being hurt again, so I remain cautious.

"Is this right? Are you guys listening up there?" I ask my guides, aware that, funnily enough, I don't have a problem at all trusting them!

I don't get an answer, but it feels right. It's the answer I keep coming back to within myself; the ability to trust is the key to really trusting life itself. Even though I feel safe in a lot of situations now, I still hold onto vestiges of fear. I know how devastating abuse can be. I know what it does to you. Thus, the caution, but Jeanne is right. As she has told me so often, I must conquer my fear; it's the final frontier, and to do that I must trust that life has me in its loving arms, and that I will arrive at my destination in one piece.

This feels like the final phase and the final lesson in this process. The truth is, I'm afraid to let myself feel safe enough to trust. Is it even possible? I'm afraid to feel successful. I'm afraid to feel brave. I'm afraid to feel confident. Every good and positive attitude gets struck down by that old cautious voice of fear that says: "Don't! It's not safe. It won't last. None of those feelings are going to last. Before you even turn around, you'll wish you had kept everything locked away!"

That old voice is still loud and strong, and it has proven right in the past, but things are different now. I'm no longer a child, and I'm not as lost and afraid as I've been in the past. As I change, the world is changing too. The world I exist in now is a different world because I've worked so hard to change myself. It's time to replace the old world's negative, pessimistic voice with a new positive voice, more in alignment with this new world. I must let it speak new and invigorating words of wisdom and encouragement, gained through all the hard work I've been doing on myself. That old voice of fear no longer works, though it once kept me safe from knowing the truth, from knowing the fullness of what happened to me. Truth is, though it once protected me, it now hinders me.

The thing that's so interesting is that I now know that the old negative voice actually belongs to me, the old me. Deeply rooted in my subconscious, spouting its old depressing beliefs based on my childhood experiences, it has ruled for decades. But I'm disassembling those old beliefs now, the old structures that once protected me, allowing new experiences to guide me now.

February 25, 2004

I dream that everything, every step and every event in life, is a link in an eternal chain of events, unfolding for eternity, that everything evolves and changes, just as the seasons, night and day, life and death, that everything is one long chain of events and I am part of it all. At first, I go with the rapid flow of the dream simply because it's futile to fight, but soon I'm swept along in the unfolding energy of the dream. I tell myself to just go with the energetic momentum and soon an endless chain of speeding, swirling, rolling dreams carry me along, like dominoes falling, and I am part of it all, just a dream in the ribbon of dreams unfolding into each other. I am fully aware that the dreams can't be stopped, that life can't be stopped, and that I'm going with the flow because I must. I give up all idea of control and just flow rapidly along, knowing that any attempts to stop the process, or even trying to slow it down, will only harm me.

"I have to learn to trust everything," I tell myself, as I go rolling along. "I must trust everything."

Those are the words I hear as I wake up, and I know it's not just other people that I must trust, and not just myself and my own decisions, but everything in the universe, because right now everything in the universe is on my side. My recapitulation has been like that roiling, boiling ribbon of dreams, sparked by my spirit's desire for reconnection, and all I have to do is trust it, trust my spirit, trust this unfolding journey, and the universe's part in it too. It's time to finally acquiesce to this journey with a trusting heart, knowing that I'll be okay. I know this deep down inside myself where that little nugget of resistance still sits, held tightly by that little determined waif who decided a very long time ago that she had to stay safe by staying incredibly strong and separate, resistant to all outside influences. Now I'm asking her to release her tight hold, her old ideas of what it means to be safe, and to let go to the unfolding of this journey. I'm asking her to let go of everything that once seemed so right, because it no longer is right.

"It's time for a major change in how we think, feel, and believe," I tell her. "We have to get in alignment with the unfolding of it all, for we are a part of the whole universe, just as it is a part of us."

I get the kids up and off to school and head over to the studio, admitting that I really do feel pretty safe now, though I still get triggered to go back to that old place of comfort. How do I establish a new place of safety and comfort? Do I need one? Yes! Of course, I do; everyone does. I need a place to anchor, to ground. It's necessary to have a place to settle down in and feel safe enough to let the emotions and fears out.

    As if to point out just how ungrounded I can sometimes be, I experience that suspended feeling that is so difficult to describe, as if my spirit has gone back out to that dream point in space, the hard work I've done to bond with her not quite holding up. Sometimes I just can't feel her inside me. I know that's where the safety and comfort are to be found, within myself, within the unity of my body and spirit. That's the final goal, to achieve that unity of spirit-in-body *all the time*, though it's still an elusive thing right now. But I know that if I don't totally let go of the past, I'll remain suspended between the old comforts that are no longer viable and the new comforts yet to be explored. I'll remain separate, an out-of-body being, disconnected from my spirit. She'll be calling to me forever, until I finally find my way back to her again, in some other lifetime.

    As I write, the old pains in my hips come again too, protesting my determination to step out into that unknown, preferring that I stay stuck in this old stuff, in pain, my hips a marker, an anchor digging into the grounding past, reminding me constantly of all that I've been through. But my dreams of last night tell me to let go in order for everything to flow, for one thing to lead to another, for the chain of events to link and grow, for me to evolve. It may be in exploring my creativity that I'll find comfort now, for when I'm creatively working my spirit is with me. Oh yes, she is! She's especially there when I paint, for I'm working with her guiding hand, with her calming mind, letting her express herself with her calm and steady presence. It's then that I feel most unified and whole. As I acquiesce to the creative, allowing it to flow into and through me, I am immediately calm.

    Yesterday, when I met with Chuck I was fighting getting pulled back into that sad little place where I used to feel safe, that tunnel within myself, and where I still sometimes go. I focused on breathing, but I couldn't loosen that hard nugget of holding. When I paint, I feel it loosening. I feel anger and sadness and pain well up. I feel all the long-buried needs welling up too, and I get emotional and I start to cry. There are tears mixed into my paintings. But I know I also have to open my mouth and let it come out there too. I must express verbally.

Anxiety revs up as I straddle the split between worlds, between the old and the new, a hand in each world tugging and pulling. I pull inward, trying to realign, resisting the frantic pushing and pulling, focusing on something else—on painting, on writing, on walking, on breathing, on getting my spirit back into my body. I must push the anxiety away, and not get drawn back into an old place. When all is done, I must stand solid in a new peaceful place.

I must find my way to mature stability, for even though everything is telling me to let go of control, I can't let anxiety control my decisions anymore. For in spite of the great need to release and flow with what comes to guide me, I must still be able to function, and that requires mature, grounded control that's nurturing and sustaining. I concur that it can be difficult to find new places of comfort and safety, but I cry when I paint now, and that's comforting in a way, and thus I find that I *must* paint, for it's being revealed as the perfect outlet and the perfect place of comfort.

Good things are going to happen more frequently now. I feel and know this at a very deep level. I also know that I'll get through this phase. I have so much support, and my wishes have been granted; I have plenty of work and my bills are getting paid. So far so good! I have to admit that I don't really have a money problem. What I have is a spiritual problem, which I displace by turning it into a financial issue, but really my deepest problem is with my fragmented self, and recapitulation is the answer to that!

"*Know that you are doing what you need to do to heal,*" Jeanne says. "*You have to do this. This is your life. It will be fine. Everything will be fine.*"

Eleven PM. I must have fallen asleep, for I am jolted awake by sudden vaginal and anal pain. Breathing deeply, I let it go through me, let myself feel it and accept the fact that there is absolutely no denying the abuse when I experience pain such as this. When in the throes of pain, everything tells me to believe it, though I still want to deny it. But I *know* the truth when such pain comes. I *can't* deny it! I believe it! I want to heal, but how can I heal if I won't let myself go free?

"*Stop blaming, stop blaming,*" I hear.

Yes, I must stop blaming myself and free myself of the old belief that it was my fault, for deep down that's still what I believe. Even after all this time and all this work, that's the truth: I blame myself. I've held that belief forever. It's what's been holding me back. The man who abused me told me that I wanted him to do the things he did, that I made him do them. "It's all your fault," he'd say. He couldn't stop himself because of me. I made him do it. I made him hurt me. I forced him to do it.

It's all my fault. It's all my fault. It's all my fault.

No, it isn't! It was never my fault. No matter how painful, I have to free myself. Free that little girl who's still caught there believing she's bad. Free the little girl caught in a lie, in someone else's lie. I don't care how much it hurts; I'm going to free her.

I realize that the anxiety I've been suffering lately originated in this memory that seeks to make itself known, the pain and the truth of the abuse pushing at me to accept it. I haven't had a memory in such a long time that I've forgotten the tremendous power of it. And this memory, from when I was a three-year-old child, shows me how far back and how deeply embedded the self-blame is, and how much power my abuser exerted. I can't continue to allow him to have that power over me. I have to free myself from it, and from him.

I see my abuser differently in this memory, as disgustingly weak and sick. I see him clearly for who he really was, and I feel deeply my own child's loss of "Self." I've been wandering around looking for that "Self" my entire life.

February 26, 2004

Shaking and still raw from last night's recapitulation, yet elated by the clarity I gained, I now understand more fully how deeply seated is the belief that I am to blame for being abused and that the abuse was essentially my fault, drilled it into me by the man who abused me. So deeply embedded are his words that to this day they are still entwined in my mind and body. I am discovering that to truly free myself I must go through very deep physical releases, letting go of the words he spoke, as well as the pain inflicted, thoroughly clearing my mind and my body of him. I am not to blame; it wasn't my fault.

I head out to an Embodyment session with Nicolas. I decide that I won't think about anything. I'll just lie there and let whatever happens happen. I'll let my body take me where I need to go, through the next step in releasing. Whatever happens, I know I'm safe.

I lie on the floor on top of the thick blankets, my legs bent over a separate stack of folded blankets, my head supported by another blanket, my arms outstretched, palms up. Nicolas piles two folded blankets on top of my torso; the weight of them feels warm and secure. Working first on one side of my spine, his fingers pressing into the specific pressure points of sacral and sitz bones, I begin my ride upon the ocean waves of release. I try to breathe as a swimmer does, counting rhythmically in and out as the releases begin, as the waves wash over me, and as the energy of my own life flows through me.

When I tried to describe this process to Chuck, I told him that I just lie here, but the reality is that I'm not just lying here having someone do something to me. I'm fully present and fully participating. The more I release, the more I work too.

I become aware of my guides in their tower, watching me. I see them looking on with such hope in their eyes, holding their hands clasped before their faces, as if praying, praying for me. And then Jeanne is beside me. I feel her warmth, her energy, and her love.

"Please, help me," I say, and she cups my face in her hands, sending calming energy into me so that I'm able to more easily unclench and release.

"*It's all right,*" she says. "*Just let it go. It wasn't your fault. Allow it to release, release control.*"

I ask her to stay beside me, but she soothes my brow and reminds me to just focus on the Embodyment process.

"*We're right here, Jan, we're right here,*" she says, and then I feel them all inside me, not far up in that tower, but right inside me, all of them.

"Oh! You're inside me!"

"*Yes, we're right here,*" they reply, and then I know I truly am safe and that everything will be okay.

"It was not my fault; I am not to blame."

I repeat this mantra as wave upon wave of old stuff leaves my body, as I relinquish my hold on the old ways and the old beliefs, as I release control and pain and blame, as I let the past go. I ride the waves until the session is over and by then I am ready to stop, my body spent.

I feel safe enough afterwards to tell Nicolas about the abuse. The time is right. I speak about what happened to me and about where I am in my healing process now, and I tell him about what just happened to me as he worked with me. He tells me he loves me and that makes me want to cry. That people love me is a new experience; that they say it, and mean it, is very new. I never allowed it in before.

"Rest, take it easy today," Nicolas says, as I get ready to leave. "You may feel some exhaustion, feel a little tentative."

"Yes, I do already, and a new kind of energy too."

"Yes, making room."

"Thank you, Jeanne, for being there," I say as I walk to my car. "Why did you choose to help me?"

"*Because I understand you,*" she says, "*and because of Chuck. I can work with both of you.*"

February 27, 2004

I dream that I'm walking with many little girls on snow-covered roads, across snow-covered fields and into snowy woods. The little girls are telling me silly jokes, but I don't get them. I can't see very well either. I roll over in bed to clear the crust that's covering my eyes, but it keeps forming again, like ice. Then I'm walking alone. It's a grey day, snowing heavily, and the air feels cold, damp, and heavy. Someone went off the road into the woods, taking a short cut, for I see footsteps in the snow, trailing into the woods, and I know it's a bad idea. I know the terrain well, for I've been that way before, and although it seems like a short cut, it is in fact an extremely difficult route of cliffs, steep ridges, and dense forests.

"A bad idea," I think, "better to stick to the road; it may take longer, but at least I will eventually get there safely."

The kids have left to catch the bus and I'm getting ready to see Chuck. I feel raw and open. Open! Yes, for perhaps the first time in a long time, or the first time ever.

"It's okay," Jeanne says, "you'll be fine with Chuck. Stay open, don't close down; stay soft, vulnerable and open for once."

As soon as I step into Chuck's office, I notice that he has new chairs. I don't like them; they're too big and my feet don't touch the floor, but I tell him it's okay. I should try to sit in what he presents, force myself to change, accept what is. He gets me a footstool and I sit there with my feet propped up.

Feeling shy, vulnerable and open, I fill him in on my recent experiences with Jeanne and my guides. He suggests I go to the tower to communicate with her. I close my eyes, breathe, and find her easily. She tries to show me something, but I can't see what it is, the image hazy and unclear, like trying to see through the crust covering my eyes in last night's dream. Finally, I see what she's pointing out, a clay pot lying on the ground. She very pointedly directs me to look inside. Looking into the pot, I see a fat baby struggling to get out. Jeanne tells me that I must get the baby out of the clay pot and that Chuck can help me, but I alone must break through the final barrier of fear.

"Trust Chuck," she says, "he knows what he's doing. He can help pick away at the pieces of the pot, the dismantling of it. Once you dismantle the pot you can free the baby. Let the baby come forth, let the last bit of control go. Trust Chuck, trust him."

I relay the message, describing the baby in the pot, describing how I "see" things, as if looking at a movie screen or into a pool of images that float before me. Some things might appear very clear while others fade into the background. I usually decide what to look at by how clear it appears. The baby in the pot was very clear. Chuck nods. Turning to the shelf behind him, he picks something up and hands it to me. It's a tiny red clay pot, punctured with holes, about as small around as my index finger.

"Here, take this with you," he says. "It was Jeanne's."

"It has holes in it; the baby can breathe in there," I say.

He nods again, and we end the session.

"I'd like to sit in *that* next time," I say, pointing to my old black chair in the corner of the room. "It's my spaceship, my time capsule. Don't get rid of it just yet."

"I won't," he says. "You can sit in it on Tuesday."

I head over to the studio still feeling raw and open, chilled to the bone, the tiny red clay pot tucked carefully into the pocket of my coat. I touch it and imagine Jeanne touching it too, picking it up and holding it in the palm of her hand too. The clay grows warm at my touch and I imagine the baby inside getting warmed too, knowing I'm here, preparing to free her.

I try to work but feel so raw and vulnerable all I can do is curl up on the studio sofa and cry, hiding under the knitted blanket I keep handy for such moments, rolled up with my fear and my pain. Why would I want to hold onto something that hurts me so much? The truth is, I'm afraid to let it go, while at the same time, I am urged to release. Release seems the thing to focus on and the only thing that will get me through this. I get up with intent and do the sword movement, a magical pass I'd learned a couple of years ago. I cut through the urge to go home and crawl into bed. I walk around the studio cutting and slicing and moving until I'm in a better mood, knowing that rather than going home and crawling into bed it's much better for me to stay at the studio and face what I must. The end is surely in sight.

"No more mysteries," I say to Jeanne. "Don't leave me having to figure out what you're trying to show me, because it takes me too long. Please just give it to me straight, like you finally did when showing me the baby in the pot today. I got it because it was a clear picture, but what I don't always get, or what takes me a long time to figure out, are the fluctuating blurry pictures that speed

I Tell Chuck About Jeanne

across my vision. I can't figure most of those out. Please just make your visual messages clear and to the point. I want direction; and you know I can handle bluntness."

I must go forward without fear now. I must look forward to fulfillment. I must look forward to the newborn baby, fat and happy breaking out of the pot.

"*Yes,*" Jeanne says. "*Focus on the good; release and make room for the good.*"

My dreams last night pretty much prepared me for the unfolding of the day, the bleak winter landscapes and the crust-covered eyes predicting my inability to get grounded and clear, but then I was able to acknowledge that it was better to take the long road, that no shorts cuts would work. And that's pretty much where I am right now, trying to find my way on the long road to healing. I know I must listen to my own heart, for though I look to others for guidance, it's really there, in my own heart, that I'll find the answers I seek. Whatever happens, I have to keep going, keeping in mind that everything is meaningful and every day is another step on the journey.

On good days I float and have expectations; on bad days I hide and expect nothing except pain and betrayal, but even a bad day must be accepted for what it is, without judgment, as part of the journey. Perhaps a bad day just means that it's time to lay low, to not act but to look ahead, remembering that tomorrow is another day with new possibilities, new energy, and new opportunities. It's often hard to hold onto such a perspective when in the throes of a bad day or a bad memory, but I must remember that all of these bad moments will pass and all the memories will fade away. Just as each day passes into night and night back into day, so too will terror and pain and fear all pass.

Part of me doesn't want the baby to come out of the pot. Part of me knows it's not safe, that she should stay hidden away. I'm afraid she's too innocent, that she'll get hurt, and all the happiness and innocence of new life will be stolen away in the cruel world we inhabit. I imagine her innocent and happy and then I see her stunned by the violent assaults made on her baby body, and then I hate myself for letting her out of the pot. I blame myself for subjecting her to the terrible abuse I know is waiting for her; I know because it happened to me.

February 28, 2004

Except for a very brief time I have never been without fear. Once I was like the happy baby in the clay pot, but my innocence was taken from me so early that the recollection of it is but a mere hint of delight, vague and swift, like a sweet scent barely sensed on a summer's breeze. To put aside all fears and to find and own that moment of delight again is a monumental challenge, but I know its memory lives somewhere inside me and that if I am to fully heal, I must find it again, no matter how difficult, and really grab ahold of it and bring it back into my life.

Today, I'm better, not in the void, more able to see and think clearly, not clouded by pain and anguish, aware of life's gifts and possibilities again. I dreamed of children performing, as in the concert I attended last night that my kids were in, talented young musicians, but I know that in my dream they were my little selves daring to be free, to express themselves, unafraid. Little by little I dare to be free too, in my dreams and in my waking life. But the truth is, fear is big. When fear takes over, fear rules. I deal with it every day. Even today, I'm drawn to stay in bed and lick my wounds, but that just leads to stagnation. I must find the strength to move beyond the confines of the bedcovers if I am to experience what life has in store for me. Sometimes I do need to indulge, but not today. I have to get the kids up and take them to their dad's house for the weekend, and then I have to get to the studio.

Evening. I had a much better day today. My studio partner spent part of the day working at the studio so I wasn't alone; no solitary time for fear and sadness to creep in. I'm much more optimistic than I've been in a long time too. The sun was shining and it was warm and springlike today. I even washed the car in the driveway when I got home.

My energy is surprisingly good, even now, not as dark and moody as yesterday, which I think was a result of the deepening work with both Nicolas and Chuck, which stirred up a lot of emotional pain. I have great ability to easily "go there" in both therapies, which can present difficulties when returning to reality, though it makes for some very unusual experiences, to say the least! Once I got out of bed today, however, I was okay, determined to shift myself into a better mood, and I just kept moving. Tonight, I'm going to my son's jazz concert, so I'll be out again, which is good.

When I told Chuck that I had finally confided in Nicolas regarding my recapitulation work and my childhood abuse, he said, "That's wonderful!"

"Why is that wonderful?" I asked.

"It's wonderful that you've been able to talk to someone about it," he said.

Do I need to talk about it? Is it really that important?

February 29, 2004

I dream that I walk into a wine store and go right up to a clerk and hand her fifty dollars. She looks with astonishment at the money in her hands.

"Oh, yes," I say, "I have to pick out some wine!"

The shelves are practically empty and there are no fine wines left, only cheap sweet wines. I wander around but find nothing I want. I leave the wine shop, telling the clerk I'll be back later. I walk into a salon next door. The hairdresser announces that she'll cut my hair short and hands me water to sip while she works. Each time she fills my cup she mumbles something over the water, a prayer or chant, before handing it back to me. The cup is always filled with plain seltzer water. When my hair is half cut, I get up and go back to the wine shop where there is now an abundance of wine. I pick out two bottles of wine and take them to the counter. When I look at the receipt, I see that it takes into account the fifty dollars I'd handed the clerk earlier and that I now have a credit. On the way out of the shop I grab a jar of maple syrup and a jar of honey. I stuff them into my wine bag, deciding they will adequately cover the credit. I feel like a thief because I just take them. I have to pass by a security guard standing by the door, but he didn't see me take the jars nor does he notice me as I walk by.

As soon as I'm outside, I begin running. I glide along effortlessly, physically and emotionally light and happy. I realize I should go back to the hairdresser's because only half of my hair is done, but when I turn to where the shop had been a moment before, I stop short in surprise, for the brick-and-mortar city I had been in is gone. Disoriented, I try to figure out what just happened. To my left is a row of trees and behind them some buildings glow golden in the sunlight. As I turn my head to the right an entire golden city appears, shimmering in the sunlight. Turreted and domed buildings made of real gold sparkle in the light. It's magical, the most beautiful place I've ever seen. The air is warm, the temperature is perfect, and I am utterly calm and at peace in this beautiful city.

I am awoken at nine by the cats whining for food and I realize I've slept really well, for I am normally awake before dawn! I feed the cats and while waiting for the coffee to brew I ponder how deeply ingrained memories are; like bad habits they repetitively make us believe things about ourselves that aren't true; telling us that we're bad, that we've done things wrong, that everything is our fault. It's time now to think new thoughts, to let the old voices go, to let go of the things that don't work anymore, that are not helping us advance. As I've learned during this recapitulation, it's okay to change.

My dream of the golden city, with its religiously symbolic water and wine, portends a transformative process. The haircut seems to suggest making an image change or perhaps that the changes I've experienced on the inside should be reflected on the outside. The golden city was of heavenly majesty, constructed of real gold, sparkling clean, and glistening in the incredible light. The trees and fields surrounding and leading up to the city were a brilliant spring green color, verdant, suggesting an abundance of new life. The splendid city appeared both distant and close, stretching far off into the horizon and yet I stood in the midst of it as well.

In contrast to the golden city, the buildings that housed the hair salon and the wine shop were made of red brick and the rooms inside were painted a dark red and were heavily draped in red velvet, with an almost Victorian atmosphere, like a swank hotel with fancy carpets and plush drapery, quiet, with porters and guards, steeped in an old-world flavor. I stepped out of its old-world atmosphere and into a shiny, rich new world of a totally different sort, from the world of the body to the world of the spirit.

The wine store, which had been nearly empty, was overflowing with wine by the end of the dream, the counters loaded with bottles. I held the two bottles of wine close to my chest in their brown paper bag as I left the shop. I could feel the small jar of maple syrup I'd shoved down in the bag and see the label of the honey jar on top. I tried to cover my act of thievery as I left the store, but no one noticed me. It was thrilling to get away with the theft undetected, but at the same time I felt justified in taking what I felt was due. Perhaps it's finally time to claim what's rightfully mine in life, in the world of the body, embrace all that's offered, accept my place in the flow of a life that's now destined to be different, naturally sweeter and more fulfilling, and to engage in the pleasures that life offers, pleasures and successes I have long denied myself, having felt unworthy. I'm certainly ready for that!

In contrast, the golden city offers a view of spirit. When I saw that beautiful city, I was amazed, astounded at its beauty, like nothing I have ever seen or imagined, everything sparkling, so clean and perfect, a heavenly kingdom to be sure. I was in awe that a city like that could actually exist, for it was so real! It was absolutely mindboggling to imagine that any city that large, with so many buildings, could be so beautiful and so spotlessly clean. I knew that if I got closer it would remain so. There was no ugliness or pain in that city, nothing bad. As far as I could see there was only peace and tranquil beauty there—a holy city, a place of spiritual fulfillment.

I meet with Nicolas for an Embodiment session, open to whatever occurs, wondering what to do if nothing happens. Of course, things start happening right away. To begin with, I feel myself fill with fear, which is immediately followed by an urgent need to dispel it, to rid myself of the memories that cause the fear, letting them go through me.

"Go, go, go," I say to the fear. "I don't want you. I don't know why you persist."

Waves of energy ripple through me and suddenly I am floating on that familiar ocean of energy, my spine undulating in the waves. I become aware that everything I have ever been and done lies encased in my spinal column. It's my personal library of all that I am, everything that makes up me, my personal Akashic Record. As the energy moves up and down my spine, my spine opens like a file drawer and everything there is to know about myself is revealed. In a matter of seconds, my past, my present, my previous lives, my future lives, all flash before my eyes; things that haven't happened yet, things that will happen today, tomorrow, next week, all in the blink of an eye. I see that I'm a living, walking catalog and that my spine is the container of all that I have ever been and will ever be.

Everything I've already recapitulated scrolls before me as the life review continues. I see things that are currently in my life, decisions I have to make about things that are pending, things I haven't decided how to handle. I see what will happen as I proceed through this time in my life and how things will play out over the next couple of days and weeks and years. I see everything that happened to me in the past and everything that will happen to me in the future and yet it all flicks by so quickly, gone in an instant, though I do hold onto some of it. Some of the images stay with me, as a deep knowing, that yes, yes, yes, that is how it was and that is how it will be, but the details are gone as quickly as they appeared, and then the whole thing explodes, and all the files go flying off into the cosmos like a deck of cards thrown to the wind, and with them goes the fear, and along with the fear go the memories.

"Go, go, go!" I say, as I watch them go spinning off. "I don't want you here!"

I stay in the tension of the releasing process, breathing through it without dissociating, not even needing to call on my gang of four in the tower, though I know they're with me through it all, inside me. An image of my abuser's daughter appears and I get rid of her too, along with my abuser himself. I must release them over and over again, for they keep returning.

"Go, go, go," I tell them. "I don't want you. Don't you get it? I made the decision to get rid of you, to make a change, to rid

I Tell Chuck About Jeanne

myself of you and the fear that accompanies everything about you. I'm too far along now for you to draw me back. Go!"

I experience some vaginal and anal pain as I encounter the images of this man and his daughter, which doesn't really surprise me, but I release that too, as many times as necessary, sending it off into the universe along with everything else, until I am free of pain.

Nicolas, sensing the intensity of my releases, lays a heavy folded blanket over my chest and it immediately comforts me, anchoring me in my body and to the earth. Without speaking, we let the healing process proceed uninterrupted. The only difficulty I have is in how to allow for such kindness.

"Oh, don't. I don't deserve that," I think, when I feel the weight of the blanket, for there is loving attention in the gesture.

"It's not good to be kind and loving toward me," I think. "It isn't good. I don't deserve it, please don't waste it on me."

But I want to be loved. I want kindness in my life. I want to achieve a place for sweetness in my life, for that golden city of my dreams and all it revealed to me, but there is so much still blocking the way, keeping the sweetness of loving kindness at bay. Pain, self-doubt, and fear still clog the many rooms inside me. Passageways are blocked and guards still stand at every door, keeping good things out, sentinels thinking they must protect me still, though in reality they are blocking me from my wholeness.

The kids arrive home after the weekend with their dad, both sick, needing sleep and some tenderness from their mom. We're all tucked into bed by ten, ready to sleep, and perhaps to dream. I wonder if I'll dream of that golden city again. I thought I was going to be lost for sure when I came out of the wine shop and was suddenly disoriented, but once I saw that magnificent city, I realized I was home at last.

Chapter 3

Apprenticeship

March 1, 2004

My body is in such pain, my dreams tell me, because it still has so much stuff stored in it that needs to be released. I wake often during the night, trying to release, as I am instructed to do in my dreams. In the morning the pain is still with me and I can barely get out of bed and walk into the bathroom. The mornings are always hard, as I step out of the dream world and back into present day reality, as I fight negative feelings, as I seek to reassemble my disassembled self.

Lara, an energy healer and fellow artist, from the country of Georgia, comes to see me at the studio. She has been reading my energy for a long time now, sensing that something difficult is going on, and has frequently offered to help. She was diagnosed with a brain tumor when she was nineteen and taken to doctors in Moscow, at which time it was discovered that she had "big" energy. They taught her how to release stuck energy, which resulted in her curing herself, and she later learned how to use her big energy to heal others.

"I want you to come and see what I do," she says. "I think I can help you. You come for free; I won't charge you."

I accept her offer. How can I not? People keep coming to me, healers offering themselves, gifts from the universe. I am open and ready to receive what comes to me.

"I love you," she says. "I want to help you."

As I work on issues and release old energy, I make space for new energy. It actually feels as if I'm retrieving what I lost a long time ago, some familiar part of myself that I've been searching for. There's emotional pain in this healing process as I let go of old ideas and old perceptions of myself, and there's physical pain too. It's as if I'm forming a new body, inside and out, and I feel every nuance of the process. I'm not quite used to this new physicality, for it does indeed feel as if I'm in a new and different body. I have to figure out how it works, how it thinks and feels, what it likes, and how it moves. Even just walking feels different now. I feel heavier and my feet are more rooted to the earth. I'm not floating as much as I used to. I'm learning to accept that every day is different now and that I'm different too. I'm changing rapidly now.

March 2, 2004

In a dream, I sit in a courtroom with a group of children who are testifying before a judge. I'm not sure what I'm going to say, just that I want my turn to speak too. Other girls talk about what men did to them. A few boys are present and they too speak of being abused. I wait for my turn, listening to their stories, looking for signs of disbelief on the judge's face, gauging whether or not it's safe to talk.

I wake feeling achy, stuffy. I've been trying to stave off a virus the kids have, a cold going around that lingers, I've heard. But I won't accept sickness, only wellness and health now. And yet I feel brittle and fragile, sad, and I'm tired, having woken several times in the night. I dreamed also of being a wild child, living alone in the wild, safe for the most part because I was away from humans, but occasionally I had to fight off a solitary wolf.

It's rainy today, the atmosphere gloomy, and fear raises its ugly head again. It always gets me when I'm feeling low, sneaks right in when it detects a chance, circling around me like the wolf of my dreams.

I meet with Chuck. He put my chair back. I sit in it and within moments I'm back in my dream, nervous about speaking about my own abuse in court, wondering if it's safe. I breathe, calming myself.

"Take the pressure off, just observe," Chuck says. "Notice what's happening. If you don't like what's happening shift away."

As soon as he says that, I shift right out of the courthouse and into the wilds of nature. And then I am the wild child in my other dream, tracking the energy around me, aligning and realigning when something doesn't feel right, using my heart to decide what's right, using my own heartfelt sense of what's right in this moment to guide me, using it to judge what's happening outside of myself. Suddenly, I realize it doesn't matter if the judges in the dream believe the stories of abuse. It doesn't matter if anyone believes them, because it's not about anyone else believing, it's about tracking the energy that's taking me where I need to go because it's important and right *for me*. My life's unfolding has offered me the path of recapitulation and I have elected to take it, because it does feel right to do so, and thus I have recapitulated the facts of abuse in my childhood, what I lived through and what I repressed. This journey has never been about anyone else, nor about their believing me or not; it's my own journey of retracing my childhood, what happened to me and what affected me. This recapitulation is about going where my inner road leads, and healing the invisible wounds within.

I realize that I have indeed been going where the inner road suggests I go, shining a light on my past as only I can do. I've been tracking my own past and my own life, taking an extremely private and solitary journey to experiences that only I had, that only I lived through in the past, and that only I can re-experience now.

As these revelations arise, I encounter those sentinels within again, judges standing guard at every turn, blocking me, questioning my beliefs, suggesting denial still, assuming they are protecting me. Once they were important, keeping the memories secret for me, keeping the memories hidden away so I could grow up, but now they interfere in the flow of my healing journey. As I encounter these sentinels now, I also realize that the wolf in my dream did not come to threaten but to show me how to track the energy of the journey. With its nose to the ground, it was showing me how to sniff out what's right, and where to go next. It's not time to fight off the wolf, as I did in my dream, but to allow it to show me how it's done.

"I'm tracking," I say, at session's end. "I'm following the guidance of the wolf."

March 3, 2004

This week is for healing, I dream. I am told that this time has been set aside for healing, for tending to my sick children and the damaged child within myself too.

"Just go with that," I am told, "and don't be too hard on yourself, or them. You all need healing."

I wake in the night, full of inner pain and turmoil in spite of this healing time, but even in my drowsy state I am aware to not let the old voices depress me or pull me back. I strive to connect with the new voices, to listen to the calming words they speak, and to follow where the healing energy takes me.

"Go with the flow," I hear.

My guides look down on me so kindly, telling me that it's impossible to be perfect. I feel Jeanne crawl into bed and lie next to me, wrapping her arms around me, soothing me and telling me that everything will be okay, to just let everything go.

"We can only do what we are capable of at the moment," she says. *"When we are in the kind of pain that you are in, and pulled back and forth, then we should be happy for small accomplishments. Leave the big ones for later."*

"Take each moment, each challenge, as it comes," she says, *"one at a time, and do the best you can. Don't judge yourself. Don't injure yourself further. You are healing and sometimes healing takes on a back and forth feeling, as if you are swinging and unable to stop the motion, but that means that things are happening. You are not stagnant and decaying. You are growing each day, adding new layers of health, and you are breathing in fresh air. You will be fine. You will be fine. Let the cool hands of spring bathe you in freshness. Let the warm hands of healers comfort you. Take these gifts that are given and incorporate them into your new life. You deserve them. Let people be kind to you. Let new life spring up in you."*

"Don't be afraid," she says. *"Is the daffodil afraid as it pushes through the cold earth? Is the bluebird afraid as it busily builds its new nest? Shed your fears like a heavy winter coat that you no longer need. The air is warm now. The days are lighter.*

Apprenticeship

The sounds are clearer. Listen closely and hear these words of comfort."

Thank you. I hear the words. I understand the messages. I will seek to drop the fear. It's the main thing holding me back, the biggest and longest lasting remnant of my old life. Why does it remain so powerful? Even at this very moment, embraced by all the encouraging and calming messages I have received from Jeanne, I could just roll up under the covers and let the old voices smother me with their negativity. But then I remember to shift away from the fear and the negativity, to realign, as the wolf of my dream shows me to do.

"Realign yourself with all the new positive things you are learning," Chuck said yesterday. "You don't need the fear, it needs you. Its energy is dying and so it tries to feed off you. Let it die."

"Let the old stuff die. Let new life begin," Jeanne says. *"Wake up to a new spring day every day of your life. Wake up to new energy and new friends. Wake up to all that is there for you. Track it as it appears. Follow the scent. Put your foot into the imprint in front of you and once you do that you will see where the next foot goes."*

"It's your journey now. It's where you should go."

"Don't go into the past right now, stay away from it," Lara says, when I meet with her. "It's not good for you. If it comes up, go and do something else right away, move away from it. Emotionally, you are very stressed and the emotional stress is blocking you."

I notice that it's the same advice from Chuck and Jeanne. They too have been encouraging me to shift away from the past and realign in my new self. I haven't said anything to Lara about what I'm going through. I arrived at her house open and ready to receive, curious about what she does and what she might intuit on her own. Right from the beginning she hits the mark. I don't have to say a thing. She reads my energy with her hands, with an inner knowing, decisively flicking away that which is unhealthy and unneeded, gently pouring new and refreshed, healing energy into me.

"Stay away from dairy foods and drink lots of water. You will feel lighter. Maybe tears will flow and you may be depressed, but then it will go, it will release."

"Don't go into the past," she repeats several times. "It is dangerous for you."

"Water is important to you. Take sea salt baths. Do your art. I often feel that you are not there; you are not in your body. Sometimes I would see you and talk to you and I would think, 'oh, she's not here, she's not in her body.' You need to come back to the body and get grounded. One day you will be grounded. Your two feet will be on the ground then. You are so sensitive right now; your nerves and emotions are right on the surface. Your outlet is blocked in the chest and shoulders and neck, the chakras are not open there yet."

I know this. Nicolas and I have been working on opening the lower chakras, and I am well aware that my upper chakras are blocking the flow of energy. I feel it.

She touches me lightly and I feel the warmth from her hands, and even when she doesn't touch me, I feel pressure. I feel immediately lighter, a sensation of tingling and floating, like after working with Nicolas. Her style of energy work is certainly along the same lines of what I've been doing in yoga and meditation, and in my work with Chuck and Nicolas.

"Everything is right in front of you," she says. "You just can't see it. Your vision will be clearer and you will see."

She speaks of tracking, of putting one foot in front of the other, staying focused on the path forward, one thing leading to another, staying focused forward. I am amazed how all my worlds are coming together, speaking the same healing words, setting the same healing intentions!

"Don't look back now. Looking back is so bad for you now. You need to look only forward. Take one step at a time and look down at your feet instead of back. You are done with the past. Maybe some time in the future you can look back and it will be easy, but now you can't. Stay focused forward."

I too have been feeling that the past has had its say; I've been shouting at it to go away. Without knowing a thing about me, Lara senses how the past takes my energy.

"You will feel something over the next few days, then you will begin to be better," she says. "You will open and come out, like a butterfly."

"Water is important to you," she says again. "Listen to water, bathe in water, drink water. Trees are your sacred icons."

Everything she says strikes true. She feels everything I've been experiencing and learning.

"You will get better," she says, as we finish. "You will be in your body, with your feet grounded."

March 4, 2004

When I sat down in the old black chair the other day at Chuck's office it felt too low, almost uncomfortable. I nestled into it, but saw that it didn't fit the room anymore, nor did it really fit me. It was like going back into an old position, to an old place I can't relate to anymore, to an old vehicle that no longer fits the changing me. The truth is, I *can't* go back anymore, only forward. Everyone, and everything, is telling me the same thing.

At the center of each of my latest paintings I have painted a new core strength. New light and new energy spring forth from this new strong center, and as I paint, I know that this is who I am now, that this light is my own light, glowing within me. My paintings now are illumined by the work I've done on myself. They are transformational works, reflective of my deep inner process of self-transformation, depicting all that I've been experiencing over the past few months, the culmination of my years of recapitulation. They represent my need to express myself visually too, and they speak volumes about who I am and what I'm going through, though perhaps only to me.

I meet with Nicolas for an Embodyment session. As soon as the session begins, I discover that I am no bigger than a tiny marble rolling down the spiral ramp of the Guggenheim Museum in New York City.

"You are just a marble rolling, nothing can stop you," I tell myself, "just go, just roll. You can't get hurt and you won't go too fast, just roll and tumble all the way down, like an innocent, happy kid. Enjoy it! Let it happen! And don't forget to look at all the artwork on the way!"

I hold onto that easy and fun image, letting go and rolling like a marble for the rest of the day, letting myself repeatedly experience the sensation of rolling down the Guggenheim ramp. Each time I do, I am able to breathe a little deeper and achieve a deeper sense of calmness within myself. That calmness only lasts about a minute at a time, but I know that it's inside me and that it's accessible again at any time. My intent to follow the wolf, to keep tracking, to accept what's presented to me, each small and each large gift, is well underway.

I tell myself: "Take one step at a time."

Nicolas said: "The future doesn't matter, just focus on the small daily movements."

Lara said: "Just one step and then another."

Chuck said: "Tracking."

Jeanne said: "Follow the scent."

This moment is where I am right now, and this moment is all that matters. What is behind me doesn't matter. What is in front of me doesn't matter. Even all that old stuff still hovering around me, waiting to be revealed, waiting to be released does not matter. Only now matters. Only looking down at my feet matters. And so, over and over, I look down at my feet and stay focused on now.

March 5, 2004

I woke at four with anal pain and tried to ignore it. I didn't attach to it and it didn't get any worse like it normally would have, but it didn't go away either. Eventually, I fell back to sleep and right into a dream where an artist friend was leaving me notes around the studio. Upon each note was written the same question: *When do you want me to quit?*

Apprenticeship

  This may reflect my turmoil regarding the expenses of the studio and as I contemplate letting it go. As hard as that would be, it seems like the practical thing to do, as I fear getting into debt if I hold onto it much longer. It's been my workspace and my sanctuary, such a big part of my life for years now, and yet there comes a time when it's appropriate for things to end, even good things.

  Business is steady, but the expenses of the studio eat up a good deal of my profit, which I'd rather keep in my own pocket. I could use my garage for a studio, especially in good weather, and perhaps weatherproof it and put in a woodstove for year-round use. A part of me considers this a good plan, but the stubborn part of me wants to keep the studio, hold out for a bit longer, even though my dream poses the real question at hand: *When* do I call it quits? For that seems to be the real issue here and now, not *if* but *when*. Every month I wonder if I'm going to make enough to cover my studio expenses, along with everything else, and every month I barely squeeze by. I keep telling myself I can't give it up, that I'd be giving up on myself, but that's not really true, for I am more than the space I work in. My dream is telling me it's time to finally make a decision.

  It's been a strange and unusual week, even a tremendous week, I tell Chuck, when we meet. I explain how Jeanne came and soothed me in the night, telling me it was a week for healing, telling me it would be okay to let go of things that no longer work, that no longer provide or sustain me or my life. It has indeed turned out to be a week of healing and I am certainly being challenged to let go of that which no longer serves me.

  I'll survive without my studio, I tell him. I have loved it and needed it, but if I didn't have it, I'd be okay, I'd still be me. Change is good. And in all practicality, I can't really afford it. If I let it go, I'll also be letting go of so many restrictions I've placed upon myself, for in a sense I've kept myself boxed in by the idea that I can't survive without it, when in reality I can't survive *with* it. The idea of letting the studio go is freeing, I tell Chuck.

  I'm trying to take my dreams seriously, I tell him, for I believe they are guiding me in a most honest and practical way, showing me that I need to pull my head up out of the fog and take this next step very consciously, not just blundering along in an old way, but daring to intentionally make and act upon a decision that will drastically change my life. I'm trying to stay focused on where I am now and not worry about what will come later. Even so, I'm fully aware that this move will lead to real and lasting transformation.

By the end of the session, I am able to admit that the old me is very comfortable in staying on at the studio but the new me would rather move on. With that said, I go home and call my studio partner to discuss moving out of the studio, facing the ending of a place that has been so important to both of us. We've both gone through so many changes over the years we've spent there together. I'm not surprised when she agrees that it's time, even saying that it's been on her mind as well. We agree to meet soon to discuss a moving date that's agreeable to both of us. We'll notify the landlord as soon as we've made that final decision.

I hang up the phone, my heart pounding. I'm going to do this, take the next big step. I feel bold and fearless. I look up and see my gang of four cheering me on. Am I getting it right?

"*Yes! Finally!*" they say, clearly relieved.

I understand that as I release the pain and fear inside, my greater creative potential breaks through. This has resulted in my ability to channel. As I continue to sever old ties and release myself from old contracts, within and without, I make myself more available to the magic of the greater universe. I'm often given too much information when I channel, too much to write down, too much to keep in mind, though I know that it's readily available inside me now too, firmly planted knowledge that I can tap into when I'm ready.

I've learned from Jeanne that the generations of women currently alive are being asked to carry forth messages of healing, ancient and otherwise. Women are naturally receptive, she told me, and connection is being sought for the good of all human beings. I myself am holding a backlog of words at bay. I could sit and write all day. I need merely select an opening time and my whole being floods with Jeanne's energy as she speaks through me, as I allow her to speak. For centuries there was no place for these words, I have been told. Spirit beings have been waiting for channels to open. It's a form of possession perhaps, though to me it feels so natural, more like a form of release, of emptying, a form of real spiritual connection and expression, all with a sudden urgency to it. I sense other sentient beings, like Jeanne, waiting for human beings, especially women, to discover them and, like me, be willing to channel them. They tell me they have long been silent, unable to speak, but that it's okay now. Times have changed and they are safe in this world now. They are needed and will become more acceptable as time goes on. They are seeking communion, waiting patiently, but at the same time there's much to do and thus they are eager for connection with ready and willing partners. I feel so lucky, so deeply grateful to be part of this evolutionary process.

    I spoke to Chuck today about riding parallel to the pain as it comes upon me, staying alongside it rather than crossing over into it; not getting too close, but not backing off either, staying with the tension of it, but not falling into its devastating qualities. I've practiced this new method on and off for several days now. It worked well last night and even at this very moment the pain is trying to intrude, to take over, to pull me back into despair, but I've made the transition away from it now, having already gone through many transformational stages. There's no going back, no turning away from the next step forward. Though I'm still drawn back on occasion, and drawn to look back too, I won't. I will stand and look at my feet and ground myself in the here and now. I will look forward now. This is where I am.

    I know that as long as I continue to have Jeanne in my life, I will be successful. She is like me; I sense her essence like mine. We are similar in spirit and perhaps that's why she has selected me to be her channel, for there is resonance between us. I recognize her energy as if it were my own. And I know that as she teaches me, and as I let her speak through me, I will be successful in everything I do; as partners we will be successful.

March 6, 2004

    As I lay down to sleep last night, I became aware of my guides swirling in the air above my bed, their energy come to watch over and support me through the night, happy wisps of light barely discernable in the darkness, but I could see them nonetheless, the air so alive, their energy in constant flickering motion. I could feel it like tiny puffs of breath against my skin. It felt as if everyone was cheering me on, happy that I've navigated onto the right path.

And then I dreamed of helping people, of being available for healings and other things. As people came to see me, asking me to help them, I painted their pain onto canvases. I told them I would do what I could for them. I protected the little children especially, because I knew they had no one else. There was a boy afraid of bullets and a girl with no sweater in the cold desert air. I knew, as I dreamed, that this was my future, and that somehow, I would become a healer. I have no idea how this future will come to fruition, but I sense that I am being prepared for it every day now, for I sense that everything is already decided and all I have to do is say, "Yes!"

So yes, I accept the challenge. I will begin today to more fully accept and embrace that evolved person that I will one day become. I know already that I can channel, that I can help people by translating the messages I receive, especially the message that we are all safe and protected. If we accept that we are guided and guarded during our lifetime on earth, and as we open up to communicating with the spirit world, we will discover all that is now hidden. We will access a higher consciousness and have the opportunity to save ourselves from our ignorance and from our destructive tendencies. This is a force that is available to all of us, if we can open up to it and let it in. It's an energy force in constant motion, alert and alive, just waiting to be recognized and embraced. Do other people see and feel this energy too?

I must live with my decisions and find support within myself as I take this path, as I stay focused on what's right. I know I am cared for and supported by my spirit guides, and that really helps. Knowing that, I feel that I can let the baby out of the clay pot now. It's time to do as Jeanne suggested. I will follow where she leads, knowing that nothing bad can happen now. Okay, baby! Time for you to come out of the clay pot. We shall see where we end up!

Apprenticeship

I see the full moon from my window, shining brightly behind the trees, and suddenly I know that I must embrace the changes I am being challenged with or I will go nowhere in the end. I must embrace the new me and the new ideas that enter me on the gentle breezes of those who whisper in my ear, on the cool fresh breaths of air that brush my cheek in the darkness. I must embrace my own spirit within myself and live from her now.

"*Yes, yes, yes, this is you!*" I hear Jeanne saying. "*This is the you that has waited for a long time. Come out, come out, come out now! Come out of the pot and see where you are, where you have landed. Life is here waiting. Something good and new is here. Let it happen, let it happen.*"

"*You were off the track,*" she whispers, "*but now you have come back. You have realigned with us; you are part of the universe now. It blows a gentle breeze at your cheek so you don't get lost, so you won't get lost again. The way will not be easy, but you can go forward to clear the path so the baby may crawl through unharmed. Keep the baby safe, the innocent one; protect her and you too will be fine as well.*"

"*Don't get lost. You were so happy! Remember how happy you were. Remember last night when we danced above you and showed you the way. You just need to follow the breath. Follow the breath.*"

I feel that gentle breath on my face now, reminding me to write about all the things I've learned, and to not be afraid to speak of them. There are other people who want to know, who will benefit from knowing what I've learned.

"*People are waiting.*"

I seem to need constant reminders of this in dreams, in mystical visions, and in spiritual experiences. I need reminders so that my reluctant old self will be brave enough to finally leave her old life behind, for good, and step away into new life, as unafraid as the innocent baby crawling out of the pot.

"Please keep pushing me, Jeanne. Keep reminding me to embrace the spiritual being that I am, to listen to my inner voices all the time, to fully trust them. I know that all of my guides believe in me, support me, encourage me, and love me. I need you to help me stay on this healing path, as much as you need me to be your voice on Earth. I want to be that spiritually connected person for myself, as much as I want to be it for you and our sustained connection. I want to remain spiritually connected for my own sanity and growth. It's all that matters to me. So yes, I will align with you in this process and pick up my pen and write your words of wisdom. My pen is my magic wand, my means of spiritual survival."

March 7, 2004

The most important legacy is *the truth*, and there are a thousand truths waiting to be told, on a personal level and in the world too. Our world will only be a better place when the secrets are exposed. Keeping those secrets is so damaging to us, the human race, and damaging to all that we aspire to be. Cover-ups, lies, conspiracies, judgments, racism, sexism, hatred and fear, all these things keep us knotted in the past. The only thing that will free us to a new level of humanness is to expose the lies and cover-ups so that future generations may be freed to make better decisions. It begins with each of us being able to face our own secrets and determine our own truths. It's not about blaming and getting even, it's about transformation. It's not about getting or giving forgiveness, it's about evolution. It's about change that is real and meaningful, lasting change that will catapult us all into a new world of equality, respect, and fairness for all, where what matters is the truth, and where truth will rule.

As an artist, I painted the tensions and neuroses of my own deeply buried truths into everything I ever worked on, but when the pains of those truths pushed to the surface and into my physical reality, I could no longer ignore them. Those pains hid the truth of who I really was, of my fuller potential. Now I'm grateful for that pain, for it has led to my healing.

I've shed the old armor I once used to protect myself and found that underneath I am alive, really alive. Like that tiny baby in that tiny pot, I am whole and real. I am telling the truth about myself now because I finally know it, and because I can. On top of everything else, I've discovered such tremendous support, from the entire universe. As I continue to do this recapitulation, I will let my guides continue to do their work. They have been waiting a long

Apprenticeship

time for this, they tell me, and I believe that. They have been waiting for me to say, okay, I trust you. But of course, the time had to be right, a whole series of events had to line up and be right, and then I had to open the door.

I'm changing all the time now, and with each transition more creative energy emerges. I tap into it, into the flow of it, and let my guides show me how to use it, where to go next, and how to remain open and trusting. It's what they want me to do, what they've been waiting for, to take me forward into new life. They've been waiting for me forever, they say, in order to do this for me. They're teaching me how to be an outlet for energy, they say, for their energy to flow through me, and for words to flow. I've discovered that I can do this and I'm allowing for it to happen. When I channel, I feel no pain. It's as if in allowing their energy to flow through me I am afforded a healing balm, a celestial cure. I am accepting the challenge because it feels so right. I'm not directing it, nor do I feel that it's being imposed upon me, for I am fully choosing to participate and be part of this process. Someone else *is* driving the car, and I *like* it. The driver's name is TRUTH!

I do some grocery shopping, take my son and two other boys to a band rehearsal, then take a walk with my daughter. Crossing a field, we stop and stare as something flies past us, glistening in the sunlight, something tiny and slender, with a wide wingspan. It does a circular flip in the air in front of us, then lands on a dried stalk of grass, bending it. It perches there for a few seconds before flinging itself up into the air again, doing another flip and landing on another stalk, bending that one too. Then it flies off and joins a second winged creature that has been mirroring its own movements. We stand absolutely still, in awe, surrounded by tingling vibrations as this plays out before us, the air crackling with energy, aware that something otherworldly is happening.

"What is it?" I ask, knowing that reason cannot help us here, for what we are seeing is incomprehensible by normal standard, the movements so quick and light, the creatures not of the insect variety, their weight on the stalks of grass too heavy for insects, and yet there is no denying that we are seeing something highly unusual.

"Fairies?" my daughter says.

"Probably," I say. "There really is magic all around us!"

We walk on, excited and grateful for what we've just witnessed. We make promises to stay open to the magic, to always allow it into our lives, to not get so jaded that we forget that magic really does exist. We talk about being artists, and pledge to always remember to follow our creative spirits.

March 8, 2004

I dream that I'm in my art studio. Only a few painted things are left behind because I'm moving out. Two women sit in front of an open window. One of them is large, smiling and happy, Abundance. The other is emaciated and pinched, dressed in a dark business suit, Saleswoman. Saleswoman, pointing at my artwork, says: "You could make so much money with this stuff!" I know the phrase so well; it's one I've heard far too often. Abundance gets up and leaves the studio as soon as she hears this. The window they were sitting in front of opens onto a rooftop. I see a child out there, drawing. When I look again, she's gone, but her papers are left behind, the wind blowing them away, so I climb out the window and get them. I explain to Saleswoman that rather than painting I'm going to be writing now, but my voice is so soft I can barely hear myself. Then I shout, loud and clear: *I am going to do something else now!*

The dream shifts then. Now I'm in the home of a family, a mother, father and three sons. The mother is the same large and happy woman from the previous dream, Abundance. The family is hanging out in the living room, reading, laughing and joking. There are piles of fresh bread in the kitchen, some loaves just baked, still warm from the oven. No one offers me anything to eat, but I know it's the kind of home where you are welcome to go into the kitchen and get something to eat whenever you want, but even so, I'm embarrassed and shy about taking anything.

I notice that the door to the refrigerator is wide open and food is spilling out. I shove and push things around inside the fridge until I can close the door. Eventually, I do take two slices of warm bread and smear them with butter, but I still feel shy. I'm just about to sneak out of the kitchen before anyone sees me, when

Apprenticeship

I hear someone come in. It's Abundance. She's humming a happy tune.

"A mother who hums!" I think, quite surprised. She smiles at me and nods, happy to see that I've helped myself to something to eat. Relieved, I go outside and sit in a chair by the back door. I eat my bread, enjoying the sunshine, looking out over rolling green hills. I see other people basking in the warm sunshine too, lazing about like sleepy animals, just enjoying life. I am utterly calm, contented, and happy.

Good dreams! All about making new choices, accepting what life offers, being open to abundance and happiness. There was no life left in the studio of the dream, no happiness. It really is time to leave my own studio behind, to seek happiness and fulfillment elsewhere. Abundance showed me the way, with her relaxed happy home and an abundance of nurturing food and laughter. When I realized it was not only permissible to enjoy it but expected, I was able to relax. The dream was about making new, positive, healthy choices; pointing out that it really is okay to embrace happiness, and to enjoy the simple pleasures in life too, which are totally natural and totally acceptable.

I know the changes brought about by this recapitulation are more than good for me, that I really need them. Old stubborn me has to realize that I can change, and that change is natural and good. It's happening all the time, even if you can't see it. Today, the daffodils are emerging even though the ground is covered with snow. Happy spring is not far off. Mother Nature allows for continuous change. I must also allow for change and try to flow with it more easily. I'm learning. I'm happier every day, as I see more clearly, as I turn away from the old boring voices, as I allow the baby out of the pot, as I allow myself to feel good and happy. I'm still cautious, but definitely more firmly rooted in embracing life and all it has to offer.

I like Abundance and would like to be more like her, rather than solemn and stiff like Saleswoman. Abundance is so happy and contented, not afraid to enjoy life. That's what I'm looking for too, happy contentment. I'm shy about it though, shy about acknowledging what I really want, but I did cut myself a few slices of bread, slathered them thick with butter, and ate them! Abundance didn't care; she expected that I would take what I wanted; there was plenty, and it was there to be eaten.

I'm not used to taking for myself, but I'm learning that if I don't take a little of what's offered every day, like that bread in the dream, it will just go to waste, that many opportunities will simply pass me by if I don't reach out and partake of them. I sensed this in the dream. As I cut those two pieces of bread, I knew that someone had to eat it or it would spoil. It was okay, I reasoned, for me to have some of it too. Why should I forego the opportunities that others so easily enjoy?

I'm not used to feeling worthy, and even the generosity of Abundance was a little overwhelming, but there was a genuine feeling of warmth and happiness in her and in her home. It was expected that, naturally, I would go into the kitchen and take what I wanted. No one showed me around or offered anything; it was expected that I would find my way around and simply help myself. My dream points out that we are not *invited* to partake in life but *expected* to partake of what is offered. Life is meant to be lived and enjoyed and we are all part of it. So, partake and enjoy!

Such is life too. No one tells you how to live; you have to figure it out and make your own decisions; you have to take what you can get. In recapitulating, I'm learning to let go of old inhibitions and ideas that have kept me from fully partaking in the bounty of life. I'm learning that I really am as worthy as the next person. In the dream, I had to get beyond my old shyness and bad feelings about myself and take what was so freely placed before me. I finally did, and sitting in the sunlight, I was flooded with the joys of contentment! It felt so good! Time to enjoy the abundance of real life now too!

Today, I intend to send out messages to the universe that I'm looking for more writing work, that I'm making a change, the same change I mentioned in the dream. Just as the child in my dream let her papers be taken by the wind, so do I send my intentions on the winds of change.

I stayed distant from the old stuff today, though I felt it hovering, waiting for me to slip up and put it on like a pair of comfortable old shoes. I decided I would be happy today instead, that I would stay focused on my dream of the mountains of fresh bread and the jolly woman, that I would be happy and contented too, and that I would embrace abundance.

It's ten at night now and the old pains have been nudging at me, almost constantly, over the last several hours, but I have refused them. I've stayed in the present today, and the past has grown a little dimmer as a result.

March 9, 2004

I meet with Chuck and tell him of my experiences of energy, how I see the air full of wispy dragonfly energy. I tell him about my experience with my daughter in the field and about Jeanne, who flies right up to me, her ballerina dress twirling in the darkness, her feet tied up in toe shoes, and the ribbons of light that flare out from her as she twirls. I notice his look of surprise when I say that Jeanne dances before me like a dragonfly ballerina. He reveals that the image of a dragonfly comes up repeatedly around people's experiences of Jeanne since she died. He also reveals that she was a dancer, did ballet as a child and teenager, that dance was her passion, that she was an impeccable dancer.

"She is definitely here," I say, gesturing, "on my left."

"Why there?"

"I don't know, but it's where I can always find her. She's definitely with me. It doesn't surprise me anymore; it fascinates me. I'm not afraid or freaked out by it. I'm trying to accept her, the visions and insights, the unfolding of this amazing process of connection with someone who's dead."

It was a strange day. The magical got interrupted by worry and stress; the old world interrupting the new. I know I'm supposed to trust that everything will be fine, but I started to stress again about possibly not having enough work, when the truth is, I have plenty of work right now. I can't seem to just go with the flow. I'm supposed to relax and see what happens, but that's still hard to do. But I certainly don't want Jeanne to stop sending me any amazing thing she wants. I really need it!

"Why do you have anything to do with me?" I ask.

"*Just accept it*," she says.

Maybe it doesn't matter, but I think everything matters.

March 10, 2004

I wake up at five, legs stiff and painful, bleeding heavily for the first time in months. I thought I was done with that! I have no optimism at all today; I just feel stressed. But I know that stress can either be productive or it can be destructive. There has to be balance. And that's what I'm looking for, balance.

I have plenty of spiritual help, and as I daily track my journey, things continually confirm that I am indeed on the right path, but I wish to see more signs of actually getting somewhere. I need to see some results in my daily situation, which still often remains stressful. It's so hard not to worry!

March 11, 2004

"*Exposure brings out lots of life—exposure to knowing and then being able to act on all you know—trusting. Trust in all the gifts you are given.*"

Jeanne spoke the above words to me in a dream and I wrote them down while still dreaming. I saw her energy, her white dragonfly spirit, fluttering and flitting about as I prepared to sleep. She settled in the corner on the right side of my room. I ended up lying on my right/fight side, watching her until I fell asleep. Whenever I opened my eyes she was there in the same spot, her dragonfly energy flickering, calming me. She stayed with me all through the night. I sensed her watching over me.

"Why are you doing this?" I asked.

And she answered that she understood that I needed the kind of support that most people are given as children, taken for granted that they are cared for and safe, and she assured me that I was being taken care of and that I'm safe. I was so grateful, I cried as a child would, and every time I opened my eyes she was still there, flickering. She came so close that I could feel her enveloping me with tremendous love. Such a small fluttering spirit, yet I could feel the weight of her love blanketing me. I understood that she was giving me something I had never felt, and I knew I was safe and protected, and that I was loved. Every time I felt the need to open my eyes and check to see if she was there, I felt like a child desperately needing to feel safe, but, more than anything, wanting to trust another person.

"*Trust in all the gifts you are given,*" she said, and she gave me the gift of unconditional love, the very basic gift that a child so naturally takes for granted.

I was not alone last night. Alone is where I have always been, so I know it well, but last night was different.

As the dream words say: *exposure brings out lots of life.* I've exposed myself to all that's available to me, exposed myself to healers, allowed myself to trust them, and to trust that in so doing I'm on the right path. I trust Jeanne and her presence in my life. Little by little I'm learning to trust that my experiences are real and meaningful, as they show me things I could never have dreamed of. Indeed, they are guiding me into a bright new future I could never have dreamed of either.

I see Jeanne best at night, in the dark; her small, bright, fluttering energy like a white moth, butterfly or dragonfly. I ask her about Chuck, but I don't get a clear answer. Maybe I'm not asking the right questions.

"*Trust him, you know you can trust him,*" is the only response I get.

I ask if she has a message for him.

"*He will know what to do,*" she says. "*Each day he too becomes more aware. As your needs arise, he will know what to do to guide you.*"

When I lie in bed at night I become like a little child. I think to myself: "I know this is childish, but I'm going to open my eyes just one more time and if you, Jeanne, are there then I will believe everything you are telling me." And she allows me to be that child, and she teaches me to trust her by being there every time I test her. She doesn't desert me the way my child self was deserted. She doesn't care how many times I need to open my eyes. If I need to do it a hundred times in order to feel safe and trusting then that's fine with her. She's going to be there every time I look because she's giving me what I need, the one thing I have no memory of: being able to trust, and that means being able to feel safe, like an innocent child, trusting that no harm will come to me.

I feel a gentle breeze against my cheek as I write these words, and I know she's here. I feel her presence on my left, up close, pressing against my arm, leaning into me, guiding me with her love, calming me. I must carry that safety and trust into my waking day, into every part of my life, so I can become who I have the potential to become. I'm learning what it means to fully *trust in all the gifts I am given*, and to let them guide me, as I also let Chuck and Jeanne guide me.

I understand from my group of spiritual advisors that we are given helpers as we need them, and as we allow for them. I have a strong core group that is solidly here for me. It includes the recent addition of my three known relatives, but also includes many others who have been present throughout my entire life, and lifetimes too, like a personal Soul Support Group. Jeanne has joined them more recently. They brought her in as a specialist, and because she can work with Chuck too. For a time, she sat on the side and observed, taking in the process the others were engaged in with me. She knew when the time was right to step in. She came on board to assist more intimately, to become a key player in this recapitulation process. She complements and enhances the work I'm doing with Chuck, working beside him, supporting me when he can't. Quite a team!

A sudden and violent memory comes out of nowhere and I am momentarily frozen. I listen to the voices that emerge from the memory. One voice in particular distinguishes itself from the others, speaking very clearly. It is the voice of Truth; the voice of my innocent child self, finally being given the opportunity to speak the truth about the reality of the sexual abuse. And I am finally here to listen and believe every word she speaks. I feel her pain. I hold her gently in my heart and tell her that everything is okay now, that she's safe, that nothing bad will ever happen to her again, that I'm with her now, that we're safe. She tells me that she trusts me. And when the voice finishes speaking, I step back in wonder. WOW!

    I am so grateful for Jeanne's compassionate regard of me and the process I've been exploring with her, as well as our potential long-term connection, which she has hinted at. And yet another part of me really wants to know what's going on. Why me? Why am I in touch with her in this deep way and not someone else? Apparently, she's decided I have something to offer. I know she has plenty to offer me! At the same time, for some reason, it feels as if I'm entering new territory with Jeanne, and with Chuck, and that scares the heck out of me! At the same time, I have grown to trust her implicitly.

    She's here with me now as I write. She'll watch over me while I sleep, and she'll still be here in the morning when I wake up too. It's just the way it is now.

March 12, 2004

    "Jeanne has been urging me to speak with you of my experiences with her," I tell Chuck, when we meet. "She says they are extensions of the work you and I do together. She implies that your own awareness will grow and become keener as you are made aware of my experiences. I'm not sure what this means, but it seems to be related to your shamanic work and especially this process of recapitulation that we've been engaged in. Frankly, I'm a little confused as to why I'm in this role."

    "Your direct connection with Jeanne is made possible," he says, "because of the experiences you've had your whole life."

    "Perhaps that's the reason," I say. "It feels almost as if I've been selected for a task, though I have no clear idea what the task is, but I'm agreeing to take it on, to see where it leads."

    "I must trust this channeling process," I say, "which I've been practicing, trying to figure out how it works, writing down what comes, not censoring or editing anything but trusting that what comes through me is right. The hardest part of doing this is getting totally out of the way so that my own thoughts don't intrude and so I can decipher the images and words that come, without ego interference, as honestly and accurately as possible. My intention is to purely express what comes through from Jeanne, making sure that her meaning and intent are clearly stated and expressed in her own eloquent language, as I hear it and see it."

As I speak, I begin to feel dizzy, my head buzzes and my body tingles. What's happening? What's going on in my body?

Chuck sits looking down, his gaze on his knees. It looks as if he's thinking deeply. Suddenly, I am overwhelmed with intense desire for him to look up, to look directly at my face.

"Look up," I silently scream. "Look up!"

I am vibrating and buzzing with intense energy, but he doesn't look up. And then I know I am not me anymore, that I am Jeanne at this moment and she wants him to look at her, but I am unable to hold onto her energy or to speak the words she's shouting in my head. It's as if I'm paralyzed. And then, just as suddenly as it started, it passes, and I come out of it still dizzy, vibrating and buzzing with Jeanne's energy. Unable to explain or fully grasp what just happened in those few seconds, I don't say anything. I need to think about it and what it might mean. I don't want to jump to conclusions or say something that's not true.

When Chuck finally looks up, it's too late. I really do think he just missed an encounter with Jeanne, yet it almost feels like it doesn't matter, that maybe it was more for me than him. But it was so weird!

This is about me, about me discovering my true self, who I really am, what I'm capable of, and finding my true place in the world as a spiritual being. As the process unfolds, I get things revealed to me; I learn. Being connected to Jeanne and learning to channel is about healing and being healed.

It's as if I've opened a door I could never quite identify before but always knew was there, a door to seeing clearly beyond the veils that normally shield us from the great unknown. I've always known it was somehow possible to intentionally access that great beyond. Now I've opened the door, and all that's been waiting behind it is finally being released and revealed.

Apprenticeship

I find channeling both difficult and exhilarating. When I'm doing it, I shift into an altered state of consciousness. The world around me disappears, becomes muffled, and my vision shifts inward. My attention is focused, one hundred percent, on what's happening behind the veils, so to speak. I can hold that altered state for a pretty long time, an hour or even longer. As the channeling ends, it's as if I'm plunked back down in this reality, feeling slightly dizzy, vibrating, all my energy having gone into it, kind of like what happened today in Chuck's office, but at the same time I return so energized, totally cleansed and invigorated by it. When I read what I've written during that time away, I'm blown away by how deep and wise it is, how completely comprehensive, how much sense it makes. If I weren't doing it myself, I'm not sure I'd believe it was possible. At the same time, it has a strange quality to it, an eloquence of language, other worldly, and not one word needs to be changed or edited. It's perfectly delivered and written. The only quirky thing is that it seems she prefers speaking in metaphors, and trying to figure them out can be a challenge.

I know I've been terribly hurt in my life, but even so, I've never felt like a victim. The funny thing is, I now realize that this abused life is working out quite well for me, allowing me to experience things I otherwise would never have known about. Thank you for this life. Thank you for the gifts.

"*Trust them. Trust what you know.*"

March 13, 2004

I dream of visiting a large country estate, the grounds of which are beautiful, with expansive green lawns. I'm standing next to two sets of twins, a set of twin sisters and a set of twin brothers, around my own age. Suddenly, the earth shakes and shifts violently beneath our feet, the once solid earth now rolling in waves of energy. If feels as if we might flip over, the entire world turn upside down. Just as suddenly, the shaking stops, though the Earth remains rolling for a long time afterwards. My companions and I cling to whatever we can grab onto and wait for the undulations to settle down.

As my dream indicates, something is going to shake my world, turn it upside down. What better symbol could there be than an earthquake? My world *is* going through a shake up; a shift *is* happening! It's directly related to my connection with Jeanne and what she's teaching me about being a channel, but in the end, all will be well. At least according to my dream! The twin couples, male and female, perhaps indicate all the parts of myself joining me on this journey, as I dare myself to take on the task of learning from and collaborating with Jeanne.

Last night, as usual, Jeanne reminded me to trust what I know, to trust my abilities, and to not be afraid.

"Trust in the gifts you are given."

March 14, 2004

I dream that I'm inside a house that's loaded with small electric transformers and tiny computer components that make everything run and function properly. There are rows and rows of computer chips and I'm trying to figure out which ones need replacing. I'm reading numbers and words, using my finger as a guide, running it down rows and rows of switches and components, searching for something. There are so many words and numbers, so many tiny details that must not be overlooked. Obsessively checking and rechecking, I make sure nothing is missing, that no component is burnt out, that everything is in proper working order.

This is the only dream I remember clearly, so it must be significant. This represents my careful attention to detail, my checking for truth, making sure that everything works as a whole, and that nothing is missing when I channel. Every day I set myself the task of tuning in with Jeanne and writing down what comes, practicing this new skill. Am I getting things right, hearing her correctly? These are the questions that plague me and scare me the most as I learn to channel, as I try to decipher meaning out of pictures and images, as I listen closely to the words I hear. But I'm also learning about who I really am. I'm learning about my place in the world, discovering where I'm going, who I'm going to be, and the possibilities that lie ahead as I accept this channeling gift and figure out how to use it. The more I do it the more I really am

Apprenticeship

learning to trust it. And I'm aware that it won't help anyone, including myself, if I keep it to myself. Jeanne tells me that at some point I will be prompted to use it for good.

I've also discovered that if I hold back, if I refuse to channel, I become depressed, mentally and physically fraught with pain that spreads throughout my entire body, and then all my old demons come back to feast upon the old tasty energy of fear and anxiety. In some strange way, channeling offers a spiritual release of sorts. Sometimes, when I begin to hear things, I become dizzy, almost overwhelmed with a lightheadedness as my body reacts to what's coming through. As I tap into what I'm getting, accepting it in some way, by writing it down for instance, my physical, mental, and emotional distresses simultaneously release as well. I'm beginning to believe that this is how Jeanne teaches me, alerting me that there's something to channel.

I wondered how Chuck would react the other day when I brought up my channeling experiences. He's already shown how very receptive he is. Everything I've ever said to him has been accepted, absorbed, and reacted to in a most thoughtful and honest manner. When you say things to some people, you can feel your words reverberate against them, as if they're falling heavily against a steel barrier, dropping to the floor in a heap at their feet, untouched, spurned, judged, but Chuck is like a soft pillow. Your words get absorbed into him, gently, and once there, he ponders and weighs and treats them with quiet respect before he reacts. You know that what you are saying is being considered very thoughtfully, deeply, that he's listening intently to you, and that he'll find the real meaning in what you're trying to relay. He'll discover the importance of your communication and he'll return your trust in speaking so openly to him with utter respect for you as a person.

The kids arrive home after a weekend with their dad, my daughter covered from head to toe in a rash of small red spots with one eye swollen shut. It looks like a food allergy. I give her an antihistamine and it immediately starts to clear up. My son is in a great mood and gets right to work finishing up a big stash of homework. By eleven they are both in bed. As I prepare to sleep too, I ask again for any dream or message that might be helpful.

March 15, 2004

"Plug in and copy what you receive. It's the true message. Go with the flow."

The message is clear, no editing. I am to channel exactly what comes through, even if it isn't clear to me. Another channeling lesson delivered! As I write, I feel Jeanne next to me. I can tell she's very excited, because she's so energetic, her energy VERY ALIVE. I know that's a funny way to express it, considering she's dead, but that's how it feels!

March 16, 2004

I dream that I'm clearing woods of underbrush. When I'm done, I step back and look upon my work. The woods are totally cleared, just the trees are left standing, tall and straight. Clarity is achieved.

Then the dream shifts and I'm sitting at a square table with three other women. I sit opposite an energy healer. I hand her an envelope with a check inside and watch as she writes me a check for a greater amount.

Can't see the forest for the trees? This saying comes to me as I ponder my dreams. As I cleared the forest, I felt that I was doing the groundwork, preparing for what comes next, gaining clarity as I worked. The second dream seems to underscore that I'm going to be exchanging healing energy, and that I'll receive an abundance of energy in return, as has been my experience when channeling Jeanne. I am fully prepared for what comes next.

The schools are closing early, due to an approaching snowstorm expected to drop a foot of snow later today. The kids are happy for this unexpected opportunity for play and relaxation. I'm grateful for the opportunity the snowstorm offers to pull inward, to get into a peaceful place within myself, to step back from my own life, look at it from a different perspective, and find

Apprenticeship

clarity, just as I did in my forest clearing dream. I also have to begin plans to move the studio, begin the packing and move on.

I know that if I stand still long enough, I'll find and hear what I need. I know that there are so many other things at work behind the scenes, and if I center in my heart, in stillness, the truth will eventually be revealed. I have to remember that everything may not be as it appears. As I prepare for more change, I must stand still and get a clear picture of what I should do next. My realities are shifting all the time.

My mother calls. My father is dying, but my mother lies to herself, refuses to accept the inevitable. He can't drive straight, she tells me, can't point the car and stay in his own lane, but she props him up, straps him in, points him in the right direction, saying, "now go, just go, keep moving, keep moving." She doesn't drive herself, or very badly at best, so she relies on him, even in his diminished state.

"He's a danger!" I say. "He shouldn't be driving! How can you send him out like that? He may hurt someone; kill someone. He's a weapon and you load him in!"

She just laughs when I say this. It doesn't really surprise me; she's never been very good at accepting reality. As her own child, I accept this about her. I have to find a way to accept her for who she really is, not wish she were someone else, and not be so offended by her either, nor take her so personally. She's not going to change. I have to accept that too. And for my own healing I have to forgive her, look deep within myself and find a way to forgive her. And to love her too.

Jeanne, you have shown me my gifts, my own true gifts, but I need more from you. I need so much more. Where do I go from here?

"Write it all down."

"Write it all down? That's it?"

"Write out the pain and sadness. Write out the hatred you feel for someone you think you are supposed to love. Let her do

what she does. It isn't your fault. You can't stop her, you can't change her, or them, your parents; it's her life and his life, not your own. Let them self-destruct, but it's not your fault. You, Jan, owe them nothing. And when you finally realize that you want nothing from them, because you don't want what they have, then you will be free. They never could and never will be able to give you what you need. Don't look to them for anything. They don't even deserve a second glance when you think about how terribly you have been treated. You don't want anything from them; they don't have what you need."

"*Look to your spiritual support. Look to me, who is with you, supporting you. I am here for you the way no one in your past life was ever there. That's right: your past life. You have a new life now. You have new friends who love you simply because you are you. They want nothing from you. They offer themselves to you because they see you need them. They say they love you because they do love you. Trust in it.*"

"New life, that's what I need to focus on, that's what the Holocaust survivors focused on too, new life."

"*Forget the past. Forgive, without attachment, without need, simply forgive, so that you can heal, so that you can allow your healers to prepare you for your new life.*"

She's instructing me to break my old attachments, one of the most challenging of shamanic practices. This is where I need to go next.

March 17, 2004

I dream that I'm interviewing for a faculty position in the art department of a prestigious college. Some drawings and linocuts I had sent in five years previously are spread out before the selection committee.

"Has your work changed?" they ask.

"Oh yes, that's from a long time ago. I'm changing all the time," I say.

I wake depressed, with a large lump stuck in my chest, right around my heart chakra. It's painful. I've done well for several weeks now, gone with the flow of things, felt a change, made decisions, but now I feel stuck again. I've reverted to old methods of protection, gathering my pain close to me, curling around it, wanting to disappear, to hide; old reactions to life's challenges. I have to find new ways to deal with the feelings and stresses that are arising as I seek to settle into my new position as a channel, for as enthusiastic as I am about it, I'm also feeling the weight of what I'm being challenged with, to become a go-between, between one world and another. It's a delicate position. One I take extremely seriously.

Breathing slowly and deeply, I unseat the blockage. With each breath, I feel it slowly moving up out of the chest area until it lands in my throat, where it firmly lodges, a painful lump. I know it signifies getting used to speaking the words that come through, finding my voice as this channel that I'm being trained to be, Jeanne's channel. I send love from my heart center with every breath, intending that my throat be open, intending that only true words come forth, so that everything that comes through me is right. That's what concerns me, that I get it right, that no one gets hurt, that only good comes of this.

Last night, Jeanne's dragonfly energy was in my room again. I was crying, but she didn't go away. She showed herself to me, very clearly, a small white-winged, fluttering being.

"Why are you asking this of me. I'm so tired, exhausted from all the stress of the recapitulation," I said. "Please, go away and leave me alone."

But she stayed with me, making sure I knew she was there. And she had me sleep on my right side, my strong side, rather than on my curling up left side where I hid from her at first, telling her to go away. By the time I fell asleep I knew she cared deeply about me, that she was not asking the impossible of me but only to tap more deeply into the spiritual. She showed me this by filling the space above my bed with a thousand fluttering, white-winged beings.

"Okay, I get it!" I said. "I see you and I see all the support I have. Thank you! Now go away and let me sleep!"

But why this new pain? Maybe this is what healing feels like, the pain of growing new skin over old wounds, the pain of new growth, the pain of making room for something new.

Jeanne told me to stay with what I know. In the peace and stillness within myself I expect I will also find the clarity I need to understand my gifts, find where my new talents truly lie, and discover what I'm really supposed to do with them. On the flip side, I also have to find ways to deal with the struggles and challenges of a life in transition, for this is a time of transition into new life. I sense it ahead of me, just over the horizon.

I seem to have clear answers for everyone else, but not so much for myself. How did I know that a friend should pursue her art, something she had never really intended doing? She's come so far in a year, after my encouragement, getting into national shows, being tapped as a new young talent, someone being closely watched. How did I know another woman would be the perfect fit for a certain job? It was one I would have liked for myself, though I lacked the confidence to pursue it, too afraid that my computing skills were inadequate, though her skills were really no better than mine. I seem to have such clarity where others are concerned, yet my own situation is difficult to perceive and gain clarity on. Maybe I'm helping myself by helping others achieve their goals. Maybe my strengths really are as a guide, as a channel, as Jeanne implies.

I meet with Lara. She tells me I'm very open now, taking in her energy so easily and, indeed, I feel it sinking into me.

"I could always feel your pain," she says. "I felt such anger in you and you didn't even know why it was there."

"Just be open," she says. "Forget about hurrying and needing to get things done. Slow down, because if you rush you clench up and get tight, and then the energy won't flow. You need to stay open in order to be able to release and then to be able to receive. Allow for openness. Breathe. Drink plenty of water, and stay away from sugar."

I look out her window and into the field across the street where I had previously seen a tree, a tree I visualized very clearly. I see now that it doesn't exist, not in reality at least. I could have sworn it was there, that I hadn't imagined it, but now I realize it only exists in my own reality, my personal vision, a clear image of my own power and my own desires, an image of who I am. On my last visit, we were talking about my tree paintings when I began to see it and when I left, I had that image implanted in my mind's eye, a small sturdy tree perched on top of a small round hill, seen through a window, the window to my soul. I see it again. The window is open, gauzy white curtains billowing in the wind, and there's the tree.

I feel the old crotch pain, very slightly, while Lara works on me. And then I feel it seep out of me, a slow trickle of pain, the final reluctant vestiges of a memory. "You don't belong here, you can't stay here anymore," I tell it, and it leaves me.

I leave Lara, pick up coffee and a bagel and go to the studio. I work all day on a mural, settling into a more contented state as the day progresses.

Home at nine. It's been a long but successful day. I felt somewhat depressed after I left Lara's, but as I worked, I got lighter and better and everything became easier. I also found that talking was easier than it has been. That lump in my throat was obviously affected by the energy work she did today. "You need to talk," she said, "it's very good for you." And it did feel that way. Words flowed today. I'm finding a voice, both a speaking voice and a writing voice. I feel safer now, bolder too.

People keep saying they love me. It's a new experience, to hear those words coming from friends, from colleagues, from healers, and to know they mean it. I find that I'm sorting through the people I know and settling on those whom I feel a strong connection with, where I feel safe, loved, and accepted. This feels like an important part of my transition. I'm beginning to feel more secure that everything will work out just fine, as Jeanne has always stressed to me, that everything will happen as it should and that in the end all will be well.

March 18, 2004

I awaken to heavy snow falling and a two-hour school delay. I slept in a funny position and awaken with a sore neck and shoulder. I scrunched up as I tried to get comfortable last night, perhaps sensing and guarding against the approaching storm and the coldness of the night. Adjusting the pillow, I noticed that I was trying to get into an old position, but I'm different now and the old positions don't feel right. I don't fit into them, nor do they offer any comfort.

I saw a big group of white dragonfly energy on the left side of my room last night, so I decided to fall asleep on that side, to allow for dreams about myself to come through. And I did have dreams about caring for myself, and the clear message that giving and receiving are the most important things I can do for myself now. Giving and receiving are this week's theme, accepting and allowing, allowing for love.

I truly am connected to such generous people with beautiful souls; I feel such love coming from them. I'm finding that my little world can be a very different place from what I'm used to. It all depends on how I decide to perceive it. The pain is melting away week by week, the cold hard anger and fear too, and my own heart is softening.

This week my car has been acting much the way I feel, unbalanced, off kilter, unstable, trying to find middle ground, the temperature gauge fluctuating wildly, from hot to cold, while trying to settle somewhere in the middle, only succeeding for short periods at a time. I've been watching it carefully, talking to it soothingly, lovingly urging it on, but it's time now to take it to an expert. I'm taking myself to an expert too. First, I'm going to Nicolas for a much-needed adjustment, and then I'll be getting my car fixed.

Nicolas greets me with his usual calmness. As soon as we begin, I go into recapitulation mode and suddenly realize that the pains I had experienced while working with Lara yesterday were a precursor to and not the end of a memory, as I had surmised. And then I realize that the sore neck I woke up with is part of it too, for as the first wave of release flows through me I suddenly feel the familiar hand of my abuser curling around my neck. As soon as I identify his presence, my arm begins to ache too, and then I know that I'm in for a confrontation with the physical pain of a terrible day, an early rape that I have yet to fully recapitulate.

I am three years old at the time of the rape, and yet I can feel my right side, my guarding side, my strong side even then, trying to fight off my abuser, trying to focus away from the other pains in my vagina and anus. As I lie on the floor in Nicolas's office, I let the old pains go in release after release, in waves that pass through my body, as if I'm lying in the ocean's surf. My left side holds all the emotions, and they too flow out of me as the waves of release spill out of me.

Yesterday, at Lara's, I released the pain I was feeling, thinking it was the end of it, unaware that the remainder was still in my body, waiting for me to release it as well. The Embodyment Therapy goes deep, finally allowing for release of this memory that has stayed in my body since I was three year's old, long after my mind had found a way to deal with the trauma, long after I forgot. All of this helps explain my feelings yesterday and why I had such a need to stay busy all day too. Perhaps this very difficult memory is finished. When we're done, Nicolas asks me how I'm feeling.

"My arm hurts," I say.

"No," he says, very gently, "I mean your inner feelings, how are they?"

"Empty," I say, "I feel empty."

March 19, 2004

Another snowy day. Another day of waking up in pain. So, what else is new? I sleep in pain and wake in pain, my neck, shoulders and legs aching, for the old leg pains that I haven't felt in a while have returned. What does this mean? Are there more memories still to come? Have they been loosened as a result of all this energy work? It certainly makes sense, and both Nicolas and Lara warned me to go easy, to be prepared for things to arise in the first few days after a session. Indeed, I feel like crying but fear that if I start, I won't be able to stop. That last memory is still moving through me. Lara's work helped unplugged it, Nicolas's work unleashed the flow of it, and Chuck will help me understand it, but really, I know it's all my own doing, my own intent to heal showing me the next step on this journey.

The pain of release is a most necessary healing step, as it gets to every tiny increment of memory stored inside the body. Nicolas said that memory stays in the body, deeply hidden, and the longer it's been there the harder it may be to release it. The memories that I have stored inside for fifty years are going to take some time to release, and they may not come all at once, he said, even though I may wish them to.

I meet with Chuck and immediately express my shock at discovering that I still have more memories to work through. I update him on my most recent meetings with Lara and Nicolas, and how things are working through me, leaving me feeling quite untethered at the moment. Ultimately, I must find the stability I seek within myself, and that it will only come as a result of completing this recapitulation, I tell him, and that means facing all the memories as they arrive, expected or not.

I mention the burden of responsibility I feel regarding my connection with Jeanne, but that I've reconciled with that and accepted the fact that she's training me, though for what, I'm not really sure.

"This seems to be part of what I'm supposed to be doing with my life now," I tell him, "learning something new from her, for use in the future. I'm a little uncertain about all of this, but it feels safe enough, not scary or frightening, just a little unusual, to say the least. I sense I'm just going to have to figure it out as I go along."

As I'm leaving, something makes me say: "I always knew you, Chuck Ketchel. Even before I met you, I knew you."

Jeanne is not in human form; she is spirit energy, the energy of love and compassion. She no longer exists in the human experience, but I can ask for her guidance and support anyway. The other spirit guides I'm in contact with have nothing to do with the human beings I knew them as, the bodies they last inhabited as grandparents and brother, but I know they are the spirits who dwelled in those human bodies and lived the lives that I'm familiar with. Jeanne says that her opinion isn't that important but what happens *now* is, in the experiences of those of us who are here. I feel that she's offering some advice and some resolution for living that goes beyond our normal thinking, to include the spiritual realms. She offers herself as a guide to those of us still in human experience, and encourages that we find a way to make contact with those on the other side. Learning to allow spirit guides to communicate with us, while we're here in this human form, is a challenge we all face, not that easy to feel comfortable doing or talking about.

As we work through conflicts that arise and challenges that present us with our life's lessons, we must also be ready to constantly shift if we are to evolve. Our human experiences constantly need reevaluation in terms of our personal growth and our spirit's awakening, all part of the journey of our greater Soul. These are some of the things I've learned as I channel, that we are all on a Soul journey, not just a human journey. They are intricately interwoven, as we are many-faceted beings, comprised of so much more than we normally intuit ourselves to be.

Things flow through me rather easily once I begin to relax and listen. If I'm quiet and still, I hear clearly. Once I open the channel, I hear someone else speaking through me. This is the experience I have when Jeanne speaks through me, as if her voice is speaking. In fact, I hear what I believe *is* her voice, without words actually being spoken, yet I hear her. I guess it's telepathic communication; she simply downloads her words into me. The same thing happens when I paint; some spirit energy flows through me and I, Jan, cease to exist. I am merely an instrument for creative and spiritual expression.

I seek to accept all of this without fear and conflict, to be open to it, to trust the process, to learn to trust that what I receive is true. But I want, above all, the fine spirit that dwells within this human body, within me, to be allowed to come forth and live in the outer world too. I have not only my own connection to spirit to reckon with but also the voices of the other spirits, those in the spirit realm whom have told me they are looking for people to connect with. I seem to be open to all of them, an open channel, and yet I do not fall prey to any of them. It's been clearly established that I am already taken, as Jeanne's channel, and so I'm not bombarded with too much, though they have told me to let people know they are waiting, that people only need ask and they will respond. This is something they remind me of often, but otherwise they leave me alone.

Is this real? That is the question I ask myself every day, even as I so clearly hear Jeanne speaking words of wisdom to me. And every day I confront how wonderful and incredible this is and could be. The possibilities are endless. I feel that I must continue to express myself in all the ways I know how, to be open to channeling what comes through, directing it where it needs to go. I believe that I will somehow find a way to use this, that these channeling gifts are going to be part of my future. And I think the standard message to me, to stand still and get to a place of peacefulness within, to a deep stillness of being, is teaching me how to hear true words being spoken, that which will challenge me to act. This is what I'm learning, how to act on the messages I receive. They are guiding me, showing me where I too need to go.

I know I haven't been ready to accept these truths about myself until now. I recall the dream message I received not long ago, to copy down what I receive and pass it along. Thank you, Jeanne, for trusting me.

March 20, 2004

The inner spirit, once allowed voice, is stronger than the human voice. It is, in fact, the true voice inside us all. The spirit within, a separate and individual entity, acts on its own, without boundaries, without judgment, only with love and compassion, in alignment with what is right and good. My own spirit is full of knowing and compassion, and she is good. She guides the human me. The first part of my life was full of encounters with evil, and my spirit was able to guide me through all those encounters so I could end up here, today, in this place of growing awareness, learning what it means to be an evolving being.

I've been lucky enough to encounter the spirit of Jeanne as a personal guide. She leads me through this time of learning, teaching me how to trust, sending me daily encouragement and support, training me to eventually open my mouth and speak the words that come through. In order to facilitate the training, I'm also being asked to let go of the last grip on my past, to my last inhibitions, fears, defenses, and denials. I know there isn't really anything to hold onto. I've already been working independently of the past for a long time now, but I am clearly being instructed to leave behind all bits and pieces of an old self that have no meaning or relevance now. They just interfere. Furthermore, I realize that I'm no longer seeking meaning in my life, it's not what I need now. I'm seeking quiet. Everything waits in the quiet; all the answers are there. Meaning will come later, out of acting upon the answers I receive from the place of quiet within. From that place of peacefulness within myself, I seem to know exactly what I'm supposed to do, for in that place of quiet everything is clear.

Anyone can do this. Anyone can go to the place of quiet within and listen for the voice of truth; truth, not reason. This is what Jeanne teaches me, how to get to the place within where listening to the truth is everything. Truth is knowing. The hard part is separating the human self from the spirit self and listening only to the spirit self, the true self, shutting down the mind and listening to the heart. Only each person can hear their own true words; no one else should tell another person what to do. We must all discover how to make decisions based on our own truths, on our own heart-centered knowing. Only we can hear our own truths, only we can realize and choose to act upon those truths or not. And if we do not allow our spirit to speak the truth, if we continue to shut it down, we will continue to remain in conflict, in pain, in turmoil. In denial of spirit, we remain lost in a life without meaning. My whole journey of recapitulation began because I could no longer avoid or deny my spirit's call. Jan, the spirit, is very strong now and Jan the human, the wounded child/woman, is learning to trust that spirit implicitly. It's not so much about finding Jeanne, she's an added bonus, it's about finding me.

Emptiness is required before we can fully access the voices of truth. We might hear them occasionally, but it's pretty hard to stay connected when the mind slings in its doubts and fears, when reason comes knocking, asking us to come back to it, for only it has the answers, only it can bring us the stability we seek! My recapitulation has been an emptying process of all attachment to my human experiences, to letting go of everything I have ever believed or been taught, including what reason tries to convince me of. It has been a process of losing self-importance and ego and trusting spirit.

My world is changing and becoming a very new place as I accept a different perspective, as I change, deeply, at my core, and as I learn to let go of old attachments and ideas. As I let go, I am learning that I won't collapse, my world won't collapse. In fact, I know that if I can totally let go, I will find that I am standing firmly on my own, completely supported by a new core strength and stability, filled with my own energy, filled with the wisdom of my own inner voice of truth within, but also having established open access to my spiritual guides as well, and even far beyond them. For spreading outward from that strong core self are layers and layers of spiritual support. I am encased in support. I have experienced this support firsthand and I know that nothing bad can happen to me now, nothing can hurt me.

I also know that I'm not fully done yet, for there is still a small shred of fear left to face, to reckon with, to detach from. Fear ties me to the human experience. In letting go of the human experiences of my childhood, in entering the new spiritual experiences that I'm offered every day, I shed the last vestiges of fear. This fear is the last shred that I still cling to, for it's not tied to me but rather I cling to it! I am well aware that I hang onto fear as a *known*, rather than taking the last and final leap into the frightening *unknown*.

Starting today, I am going to let go of that last shred of fear. Whenever it pops up, I intend to consciously let it go. If I cling to anything, it will be to listening to true words from within. And my new job is to speak about what I'm learning and hearing. The human experience has to be put aside in order for that to happen, to have full access to inner truth. I have to step outside of the mess of my human self so I can hear and know what to do next. I can't hear clearly if I'm bombarded by human worries or desires. It's the message to all humans, to stop trying to figure everything out mentally, to stop the mind and just stand still and get quiet, and then listen to the deepest voice you hear. Shed the human experience. That's really the key to all of this, the answer to everything—shed the human experience, shed the ego.

Apprenticeship

What comes after recapitulation? A journey of heart-centered listening, another journey to take and another process to master. It's also necessary to maintain balance between worlds, to constantly shift back and forth between the world of spirit and human reality, for we are in human form and this human experience must not be neglected. We always have to take responsibility for our own life and where we decide to take it.

It's clear to me that it's just as important to remain connected to the human experience as it is to stay attuned to the spiritual, but to do so as an evolved being, in an evolved manner, knowing the deeper truth. Ego has its place, but it must not become the sole energy behind this human experience. But I also know, during this point in my training, that I must take care to stay more rooted in the spiritual, the inner realm, at least until it becomes more familiar and I am more fluid in how it works. It's also the place where I am most whole and knowing. It's also becoming clearer every day that this is what I've been working toward in my recapitulation, that it's where my future lies, as Jeanne told me, at least in this lifetime!

When we encounter the wrong people, or the wrong energy, we can easily lose access to that inner realm that is so important, as we are usurped of our energy, compromised by that which is outside of us. We need to train ourselves to be aware of the energy that approaches us, learn to distinguish whether or not it's good or bad for us. I find that mechanism is working quite well inside me now, as I am better able to read energy as it approaches me. I can feel if it's compatible, if it's off balance, if it's angry, sad, tired, etc., and I'm not at all afraid to refuse it if it makes me feel uncomfortable. My outer numbness is gone now, my shields have been shed, so I'm able to do this.

I understand how incredibly lucky I am to be where I am now, taking this inner journey. A whole new world has opened up for me; I really feel that I'm part of some bigger energy now. But I'm also discovering my own way in that world, my own voice, my own energy, my own connection to a world I had forgotten about, deep inside myself.

I'm choosing to go ever more deeply into this process of learning, not only rediscovering a lost self but being offered a whole new direction, like nothing I ever imagined.

March 21, 2004

I dream that I am a seeker on a journey that never ends. I have to protect and take care of others, and I have to lead them. I have no choice in this, though I go willingly, eagerly allowing for and accepting each part of the process. I must deal constantly with making the right choices, listening always for truth to guide me. The most important aspect is to protect the children and make sure they are always safe. I never lose a sense of awe at the role I find myself in.

In spite of my positive dream, the human in me is still a little reluctant to accept the role as Jeanne's channel, the part of the process I'm in now. I'm not jumping for joy but taking it very seriously. Jeanne constantly reminds me to just trust the process. TRUST. She says I'm in training and at some point, I have to learn to apply what I'm being taught.

When I channel, I become *enlightened*. I use that word because that's what it feels like to channel, to be filled with inner light. When I receive a message about myself and my own life, I interact with it by asking how it applies to me now, to choices I must make, perhaps about my studio work, my inner work, or just life in general. As a question-and-answer process unfolds, I become involved in an exchange of ideas. I write everything down. The writing has a life of its own. I don't stop to mentally think or piece anything together; my brain is basically asleep, but my awareness, my consciousness is fully alert. I receive images and put into words what I get, letting the story unfold. The messages come through me; my job is to copy everything down.

I'm a little daunted by the responsibility this might one day present, but I've also been feeling very strongly, for years, that I needed to find a way to help others, that my mission in life is to be of service to others in some form that's meaningful to me. It has to be through the skills that come most naturally to me, through my art and writing, and my ability to listen to the wise words that flow so easily through me. The ultimate purpose and goal of all this is *truth*, to get to the truth. Words imply speaking and writing. Words imply communication. Words imply paper and books and reading. People have to be able to receive the messages in some readable form. In a recent dream, I was told to plug in and copy down what I receive. So, I plug in and wait for the download. And when it comes through me, I know that I am hearing the truth.

I can't keep the words inside me. If I do, I begin to feel pain and anxiety, and a strong awareness that my body contains something foreign, an element that does not belong to me. I know I have to release it, whatever it is, because I can't physically hold it in without getting anxious and suffering some kind of pain. In training my body to participate in this process, I have asked it to alert me when it's time to channel, to remind me that if I don't, I will suffer.

My old protective shell is breaking off and falling away as I learn to channel, as I let go of old ideas and inhibitions, old rules and old beliefs, old protective measures that just don't fit my new role in life. I'm learning that I have a spiritual voice and I'm learning what that means and how to use it.

As I become more and more involved in this channeling process, I begin to understand and experience what true love might be, for a new sense of love and loving energy comes with doing this work, love as a universal essence that permeates all things. I'm aware that we need only wake up to this essence to experience it, like the Buddhist concept of loving kindness and compassion. I feel this when I channel, an all-encompassing love, highly impersonal, and yet fully enjoyable personally, though I experience no special attachment to it. There is no desire for ownership or feelings of neediness attached to it. It's simply very loving energy, and it's a beautiful feeling.

When I channel, I separate from my physical identity. I am no longer a human self but instead a receptor, an open channel. When I achieve that place of quiet emptiness within, things begin to flow. It's only then that I'm able to hear the truth and know that I'm not controlling what's happening, that the knowing ability that I experience comes from someplace else. I don't edit, or rewrite. I am not the originator. I am just the messenger, and my job, as I understand it, is to listen very carefully and intently, and to make sure that every word I hear and write is the truth. I must totally dissolve myself in order to do this. I must submerge my own thoughts, observations, feelings and fears, lose my ego, and be empty in order to dip beyond the self and find a clear and glowing message, untouched by human ego.

But I know that I could not do this if I had not learned about and experienced complete trust, if I had not tested the give and take of trusting another human being with the deep spiritual needs of my soul, and if I had not done the deep work on myself that my spirit demanded of me. I could not do this if I had not gotten to such a deep place of inner knowing and calmness within myself during this recapitulation, if I had not become so empty of my old self. Perhaps some people get to this place by one stroke of enlightenment, but for me this has taken years of work. It's through hard work that I've gained a new level of understanding, along with an inner certainty that this is where I belong. Though I still struggle with where I've landed, I have no doubt that I won't be departing from this new place of trust and knowing anytime soon.

This is an incredible journey. My life has changed. I am no longer buried under painful memories, stagnated by their threats, or frightened and haunted by them. Instead, I have loosened the old bindings that held me down and become not only free but something I never imagined possible, an open channel. I am like a new baby, pure and true, and everything is possible. Nothing in this new world has been tried before, at least by me; it's all new to me! So, nothing has fear attached to it, nothing is judged, criticized, or ridiculed. And everything is new and available for exploration in this new world, and I too am open and interested in exploring this new world I find myself in. I am open to everything. Perhaps I'm experiencing the innocence that Jeanne spoke about, true innocence, like that of a child. The baby has crawled out of the pot at last!

My old wounds and scars have almost healed over now and the last little bit of reluctance in my throat and jaw is releasing as I heal, as I talk, and as I channel. This is my training, as Jeanne told me, and I am full of hope and wonder at this new life I am stepping into. Wow!

March 22, 2004

"Trust, Jan, trust everything."

That's easy for you to say, Jeanne, but I still don't want to be in this role. Am I nuts? Wouldn't most people be thrilled to find that they're psychic? I, on the other hand, just want to say, "Don't make me do this! Don't burden me with this!"

The tide seems to have turned. Yesterday I was blown away by the changes in my life and today I wake up having the greatest difficulty accepting the gifts I've been given. I also know that nothing really matters right now, except that I continue on the path laid before me, taking one step at a time, doing what needs to be done. Challenges appear at every step. It's the way life unfolds, and the thing to do is accept those challenges and do the very best with them. And apparently, being psychic is my next challenge to face and to do the very best with.

The depression I feel today, laced with a good amount of fear, presents the truth of imbalance. As I seek equilibrium, I am tossed up one day and pulled down the next. Jeanne would tell me it's part of my training, and I know that it'll probably even out after a while, that I won't always feel this way. The depression pulls me back under the covers. "Just stay here," it whispers, but I know that would be disastrous, feeding my fear. It can't have that much power anymore. Remember, I have a new life now!

"So, go live that new life," Jeanne says. *"Trust in it and all the gifts you are given. This is a new day, a better day. Go embrace life. Don't run from it. Go live!"*

I work at the studio for most of the day, attempting to focus, but my mind won't shut down. I am bombarded by psychic revelations, by thoughts and feelings, by insights that I write down, as instructed. Writing actually calms me and releases the busy back and forth energy in my head.

When in a calmer state, I realize I'm going through a new stage now, not only learning to be a channel but also shifting my focus and energy away from others, bringing it back into myself. This is good. I'm making a conscious decision to do things for myself now, after so many years of giving my energy to others, being involved in every art event in the area in some way, being called upon to participate, to help out, to volunteer. The truth is that I know how to accomplish things, to do the seemingly unachievable, and people come to me seeking advice all the time. They turn to me with all kinds of questions, and I know exactly what they should do. The other day the head of the county arts council asked me something, and I said, "Oh, I know how to do that!" And a fire got lit and suddenly we were off and running with ideas. It was exciting, but I stopped myself, because I don't have the energy anymore. I have to save it for myself now.

March 23, 2004

I dream that I'm walking in snow, following wolf tracks leading into a house. I step inside the house, which is owned by an artist, still following the wolf tracks because the inside of the house is full of snow too. I follow the tracks into the artist's studio where she has painted an enormous mural that stretches beyond the studio, onto all the walls in the downstairs part of the house. The wolf I've been following is the artist's pet, I see. That explains the tracks leading into the house. I stand for a long time and look at the mural, which is painted in very healing tones, greens and blues, very detailed and impressive in its scope and beauty and coloring. I wander around the house, which is very large, with a lot of rooms. I encounter noisy, bubbly activity, vibrant energy and vibrant life in this artist's home. The rooms are full of people, visitors exuding warmth and gaiety, human bodies pressing against each other in the crowded rooms, people interacting and having fun.

I have a room upstairs in this artist's house. It's cold and dark upstairs, and I'm the only one who ever goes up there. I'm slightly afraid of what I encounter downstairs; so much life and warmth and interaction, so many bodies, everyone alive and close, too close for comfort. At this point, my ex-husband comes into the house. I'm aware that my dreaming self has conjured him up, simply because he offers an old familiar kind of comfort, but almost immediately I tell him it's not what I want now, and I apologize for calling him to me. I'm nervous about all the strangers in the house, all the joys of life, but at the same time I know I'm done with the old. I'm trying to get myself somewhere new, but it's a struggle. I communicate this to my ex-husband, but I see that he doesn't care. Kindly, with compassion, I ask him to leave. He turns

Apprenticeship

away abruptly, without saying goodbye. I stand at the door and watch as he walks to his car. I notice that it's spring now.

This dream is all about new life, creative and vibrant, just what I'm seeking, and yet it stirs up old fear, fear of the unknown, fear of getting too close to people, fear of new life bursting forth, some of the same feelings I experienced in the home of Abundance in a previous dream. The wolf appears again, yet here it's a tame wolf, the wildness toned down. This is all about time passing and things evolving; that which I fear now will one day be commonplace. If I am to move from the dark and dreary upper floors of the house and partake of new life, I must follow the spirit of the wolf, conquering and taming my fears of the unknown. It's time for new life, and being open to the joys and happinesses, the human qualities of it. It's just life, after all!

Though I am reluctant to take on this channeling life too, I hear Jeanne reminding me that I am just the messenger, the fax machine delivering the messages.

"*Copy it as you hear it,*" she says.

She assures me that this is my time of learning, as I find out who I am, as I find my place in this new world, and learn to trust. It always comes back to trust, to trusting what you know to be true, finding the truth in everything, learning that the truth is a very powerful message.

I realize that Jeanne has been teaching me to get more comfortable with being a channel, as I work at perfecting my communication skills with her. It's like having to first learn a foreign language, unscrambling a strange mix of images, words, and feelings, and then translating it all into English. If I don't capture her meaning right away, she persists, continuing to feed me data until I understand what she's trying to convey. Upon finally figuring out what she's getting at, the tension of her energy immediately subsides into a gentler presence. I prove this to myself every day as I channel. Sometimes I protest and beg her to go away and leave me alone, telling her that I don't want to do this, but in the end, when I finally understand what she's trying to say, I feel so relieved and happy that I've been able to solve the mystery. It really is quite invigorating!

I receive a new channeling lesson every day, sometimes more than one. The challenge is to not reject but to go with the flow of what is presented. Jeanne is an excellent teacher, and I'm learning something new every step of the way. Each time our communicate process is successful I feel rejuvenated, lighter and happier. I feel my own new energy accumulating rapidly. I feel physically, mentally, and emotionally lighter and brighter. I can actually feel my own new stash of energy building, like money accumulating in a bank, as we work together. I'm beginning to see how this process works, and I'm learning to trust it as it unfolds. As I see how it affects me, I feel how very beneficial it is for me. I'm going to stay open. And maybe I'll find a way to use this ability in the future.

March 24, 2004

In a dream, I'm standing beside Chuck. Jeanne stands in front of us, facing us, holding our hands clasped together in hers.

"*Get rid of the demons so you can trust what I tell you,*" she says, looking right into our eyes. "*Clear everything away, all doubt, and open up to inner silence. Listen with inner peace.*"

"Okay, I accept," I say. "I know that what I hear is true. No matter what else it is, it's true." Calmness enters me as I let go of all struggle, as I let Jeanne's energy in, as I open to hear the words that come in my place of inner peace and silence. I feel this same inner peace and calmness emanating from Chuck, and I feel that Jeanne is satisfied with how we are reacting.

I remember that when Jeanne first told me I would be taking a three-year-long journey, laying out the plan of my upcoming recapitulation and the aftermath, she also intimated that something unusual would happen. Perhaps that time is now, as I learn to be her channel. I sense a culmination of events and feelings, all I've been going through and learning coming together, consolidating into some kind of wholeness, some kind of greater understanding.

March 25, 2004

Jeanne shows up at my Embodiment session. She kneels on the floor and holds my head cupped between her hands.

"*Let the bad out,*" she says, cradling my head. "*Keep only the good, only the essentials.*"

I ask her why she's doing this for me. She says that she was asked by my spiritual advisors to step in and be my guide. They feel she can do a better job and that I'll feel easier with her than any of them, that the relationship that will develop between us will be better for me. She says she'll never leave me, that she'll be with me forever.

While Nicolas works on my right side, I ask Jeanne about the time she had gone away to Southeast Asia. It was during the first year of my recapitulation. She says she had to go there on personal business. What she needed to do took quite a while to accomplish, but her business there was now complete. She says that when she first came into my life, she came to give me what I needed in order to get started on the road to trusting Chuck, so that I could begin my recapitulation in earnest, then she took off to go take care of that other business. When she returned, she took some time to observe me before beginning to develop our deeper connection. This work with me is her job now, she tells me, and she will be my forever-guide.

"Why?" I ask.

She feels a strong connection because of Chuck, she tells me, and because she knows she can help me through everything I have to go through. She stood on the side for a while, she says, observing and studying me, making sure it was the right thing to do, before more actively stepping in. When the time was right, she moved in and made herself more known to me.

As Nicolas works, I feel strong energy in my right side. I hear Jeanne's message coming through, to let go of the bad, and I feel it rushing out, going reluctantly, but going nonetheless, and I feel that the good and the essential will stay and grow. Releases move up into my throat, the center of speech, where I've been daring myself to be more open, and Jeanne instructs me to concentrate on this chakra.

While Nicolas works on my left side, I feel release in a more emotional way. I feel the immense holding-in that I've done my whole life, and the huge blockages that have formed as a result. I feel certain that I'm on the right path, that what I've been seeking to do will happen. All of my experiences and feelings seem to roll together and form inside my body, and I can feel the strength and conviction of them for the first time, in a real way. I have a physical body now and all the stuff that makes up who I am lives here in this body. I'm not scattered and afraid anymore. I'm not in bits and pieces anymore. I'm entering and residing in this body now. I am real.

As these pieces come together inside me, I feel all my thoughts and wishes, my art and my writing, my actions and my decisions, and all of my future works, actions, and decisions already inside me! This blows me away! All the words I have yet to write, all the paintings I'm going to paint, all the choices I'm going to make are inside me, right now, just waiting for me to release them at the right moment. I contain everything. I am whole, more whole than I could ever imagine. I see all of this, my life shown to me in a thirty second flipbook, and I understand *everything*.

I know I still have many obstacles to overcome. As Nicolas works on my left, sensitive, vulnerable side, I realize that I *need* to be vulnerable, that it isn't a negative quality, that it may be the only way I'll have access to some of the things I need to learn. The biggest obstacle is overcoming fear, which absolutely hinders growth.

Embodyment Therapy is really incredible. I knew I had to find a way to work individually with Nicolas, but even so, I had to be ready for this great outpouring. I had to be ready to handle these intense physical releases related to my recapitulation. My work with Chuck has brought me to this point where I not only allow and trust such a process, but where I can actually acquiesce to it, where I experience the wholeness of everything—myself included. I accept everything now, without judgment or denial, but only as utterly necessary and meaningful.

Encountering Jeanne during the Embodyment session today made me realize that she too is part of this body that I'm building, and that I have to continue to be open to whatever she has to offer me. When something comes through from Jeanne, I know more strongly now that it's coming from a source that cares deeply about me and wants me to continue learning and growing.

My Benefactor comes into the studio for a visit. "How are you?" he asks, and before I can even answer, he answers for me: "You're fine," and the quiet voice inside says: *He doesn't really want to know how you are, he's here for himself.* I accept that.

Maybe I'm starting to "feel" things the way Lara feels: *energetically.* It's a little sad that I don't really feel a connection with him anymore, no resonance whatsoever. The original connection, whether it ever existed or not, is now cut, leaving him out there at a distance, in a foreign land almost. I don't like to deal from such an energetic distance, it's difficult and exhausting. This is how I've learned to weed out the people whose energy doesn't feel good to me. In the past I might have simply gone numb and tolerated such energy, but now I'm learning to recognize and discriminate, and even choose whether I'll interact with those I don't feel anything energetically positive or likeable about. If I'm uncomfortable with energy, I now know there is a lack of resonance. This is a big concept for me to grasp. It not only explains a lot about how I've acted in the past, but spurs a process of detachment that's so valuable as I move forward into my new life.

When my Benefactor leaves, I instinctively brush away his energy that I feel has attached to me, wicking it off, and I recognize the gesture as one I've been doing a lot lately, unconsciously, whenever I'm in the presence of non-resonant or disturbing energy. Something inside me has taught me to do this, a gesture of self-preservation that has become so natural now that I don't even think about it, but I find myself doing it quite often, a protective measure that's become second nature. It's another sign that what I've been learning about energy is sinking in at a deeper, more instinctual level.

Jeanne says that learning to trust is the most important lesson and the most important issue in any relationship, and when it's lacking there's no growth. That certainly includes my relationship with her!

"*Trust all things. You are safe now, Jan. I am watching out for you,*" she says.

March 26, 2004

In a dream, I attend to a small girl of about three years old, delicate and beautiful, who is recuperating from having been terribly sexually abused. I'm helping her through the healing process. She constantly looks to me for approval and to ascertain if a situation is safe or not. I give her a nod if it's okay. She's not used to being near other people or being touched. An older woman invites her to sit on her lap, and I see her decide on her own that it's okay to accept the invitation. As I watch her sitting on this woman's lap, I feel so proud of her because I know how much courage it takes for her to do this. I feel her developing her own sense of trust.

At this point in the dream, I look at my watch and realize I missed my appointment with Chuck, but then I see that my watch is upside down and that I actually have ten minutes to get there. I can still make it. Suddenly, I collapse. I can't take the stress anymore. A doctor comes and tells me that I must not strain myself in any way, that I must take everything slowly now. "Okay," I say, and at the same moment I see that I still have time to get to Chuck's, but when I try to leave, the stairs inside the house collapse, preventing my exit, but I climb down a metal fire escape instead. My daughter, frustrated, watching me from below, says: "You're not supposed to be doing stuff like that!" And the doctor says: "Can't you live downstairs for a while, just until you recover? You really need to take care of yourself!" Then I wonder where the little girl went, the one I was taking care of.

I wake up feeling exhausted, as if I didn't sleep at all. I should listen to the advice of that doctor! The first part of the dream is about accepting all that I've learned from Jeanne about trust. This work with her has been about learning to trust not only her, but other situations I find myself in. The little child in my dream, my inner child, is learning what trust is too, as I've parented, protected, and taught her during this journey of recapitulation. We're making good progress, my inner child and I. Like the little girl in the dream, I too have to trust that I'll be okay as I venture out into the world.

But, as the second dream indicates, I also need to take care of my physical self, for indeed, I am quite exhausted. I've given so much energy to my inner work, and to my inner child, that my physical body has really suffered from all the stress and anxiety, and even from all the healing modalities I've put it through. It really is time for me to tend to myself in a different way, just relaxing for a change perhaps, eating better, sleeping more, and taking it easy on myself. The intensity of this recapitulation journey has taken its toll.

I go to my real appointment with Chuck, on time. I mention that Jeanne showed up at my last Embodiment session and explained how she came into my life. She told me that she got called in by my team of guides to help teach me the importance of caring for the self, the thing I probably need the most.

"I intend to stay focused on this healing journey more than anything else," I say.

"Yes, stay focused on that," he says. "It's what matters."

Chuck remains my guide in this world, and will be until I don't need him anymore. One day I will be done, my journey of recapitulation will be completed. It's up to me to decide when that time comes, for only I will know for certain.

Jeanne, I ask you to allow me completion of my recapitulation with your love, protection and guidance, but I'm not ready for more than that, at least not yet. Be with me with your calm voice that guides, encourages, and tells me everything is going to be fine. Our other work, the channeling, will have to wait until I'm more physically replenished.

March 27, 2004

In a dream, I crawl along on all fours, like a cockroach, my bones clicking the way a cockroach's feet skitter and click as it walks. I am only a skeleton, with no flesh or muscle, no skin, no organs, no warm beating heart. I am just stiff bones that creak and rub and chafe against each other, and I am in constant pain as a result. I have to lay out a path for myself. I have to figure out, with only so much pathway material available to me, how to get from the skeleton to the warm body that is waiting for me far, far away. I am given bits and pieces of tattered woven cloth to make the path. I lay them out, trying to figure out the best plan for achieving my goal: my real human body.

There are teachers along the way who give me advice, but it's usually in metaphor or code, dense messages that I have to figure out. Gradually, as I work my way along, constructing my path and deciphering the messages from the teachers, flesh begins to build on my bones. I see others struggling on their own paths and once or twice I meet with others for a moment of respite and celebration as we travel through our human stages of growth. Someone makes a comment about another traveler, an old woman whose body is grey and withered.

"Yes," I say, "she's pretty old on the outside, but inside is a beautiful woman waiting to emerge."

I know it's a cliché, but I also know it's true. Eventually, as I work my way along my path, I begin to stand up and walk hunched over. More time passes and I become a normal human being, standing and walking tall and erect. At one point, I am suddenly no longer in pain! After a while, I realize that even though I haven't reached the end of my path yet, I have nonetheless transformed from an ugly creature into a beautiful person. I am real!

I sleep until nine in the morning, though I wake up feeling a little depressed and sad. Perhaps I need a break from the work I'm doing with Chuck? Maybe a few weeks off will help me to re-center and get into calmer balance. I feel like I've gotten off track, been forced to travel trackless through wild terrain, and for what purpose? I want to stay on my path of heart, my path of change. I know that I'm still full of fear, that I have further work to do, and that I'm still vulnerable to the old fears, and some new ones as well. I also find that I'm gaining in strength, that I have plenty of self-protective energy, and plenty of inner knowledge.

Apprenticeship

I've also discovered my life already inside me, waiting to be lived. I only have to begin the unfolding journey. I know that I must track the signs in my life, become aware of the many choices being offered, and keep moving forward, one small step, one decision at a time. My dream showed me this process very succinctly, life as an evolutionary journey, how we change and evolve over time. And I must keep in mind that I've been given so many gifts, and that I'm not alone, even when I may feel that I am. Even when I'm suffering from the deepest feelings of sadness and loneliness, I can reach out and find help. That's very important to remember. It's something I'm learning, something the new voice inside me reminds me of when the old voices come back to haunt. I try to ignore the old voices when they come. Instead, I search around inside until I hear the new voice reminding me of my true path.

"Stay on the path you are on," the new voice says, *"stay on the path you are on. You have come this far, so far, and you are going to keep going because this is the path. You have left the past behind you. Some of those old voices are very loud and they reach onto this new path, but you just focus forward and listen for the new voices and they will become stronger and stronger. It may still seem bleak at times, seem like you haven't gotten far enough, but if you don't look back you won't get pulled back. Never look back. It is gone; it is done. The only things left back there are pockets of black air, spinning vortexes, like black holes. If you get too close, they will suck you in and you will have a hell of a time getting out again."*

"Keep focused on the bright edge of light on the horizon. A new day is dawning ahead and that is where you are headed. Don't stop. Don't ever stop. Keep going through this difficult time and you will get to the next level and your past will be even further behind and your burden lighter. At every forward step, no matter how slow, your burden will lighten."

The teachers on that bleak path in my dream sit on chairs surrounded by books and trinkets, and they toss you something as you pass by, a bone, for instance, no sustenance, just a dry bone that has some meaning you have to figure out. Maybe the bone is meant as a crutch, or maybe it's a metaphor for the brittle feelings you need to release, or maybe it's your job to find the rest of the skeleton, etc.

The meaning is always unclear at first, but eventually you figure out what it is, and just as you are feeling good about yourself, and you have figured that bone out, you meet another teacher and are given another bone. That's what I feel like I'm dealing with now; I'm being given task after task, with no respite in between, except perhaps the healings I receive along the way.

As I step into the healing rooms of Chuck, Nicolas, and Lara, I receive healing and renewal of energy so that I can tackle the next assignment. But I'm exhausted. I need more strength to continue, but I plod along nonetheless, seeking rest, calmness, and the means to persevere, wherever I am.

I seem to be extremely sensitive to all outside energy today. First, I started to develop a pain in my left side this morning. It got worse and worse as the day went on. Finally, at around two, when it got really bad, I suddenly thought: "This is not my pain, this is someone else's. I have to get rid of it. I can't keep it anymore. I'm sorry, you have to take it back." And I lay down on the couch in the studio for a few minutes until it went away. It was so excruciating for the last hour that I could barely breathe. Whoever it belongs to, I hope they survive it.

Then, at about noon my Benefactor called and invited me around to his house. When I arrived, I met his wife, daughter and grandson, who were all sitting in a circle in the living room. I was at the edge of the circle, talking to them, when I was suddenly awash in their personal miseries, overwhelmed by all the pain the entire family carries. I felt that my Benefactor, for some unconscious reason, had brought us all together.

"I'm uncomfortable with this," I said, silently, pleading with Jeanne for an explanation as to why this was happening. "I don't want to get involved."

I knew I needed to get out of there and, as gracefully and politely as possible, I said I had to get back for a meeting and I left. Since then, every time I think of this episode, I know I don't want to be burdened with the pain of others.

Apprenticeship

This was a gift. I was being shown something about myself and I was also learning something new. I realize that I'm opening up to feeling more, and to reading the emotional energy of others, but I have to protect myself too. It doesn't feel safe to be so open. My immediate reaction was to run from the energy, from the sucking quality of it, and that was a correct reaction, purely self-protective. There was no way I was going to accept it, just as I didn't want to continue accepting the pain that I'd felt in my side for most of the earlier part of the day. It seems I'm being trained in many aspects of being an energetic channel. Even though I asked Jeanne to hold off for a while, I'm still in a learning phase.

I've named such energetic insights *mystical downloads*. Though I'm not thrilled about receiving them, I really am trying to open up to learning what they mean. I know I must follow my path as it's laid out, as I lay it out myself, trying to fit together all the pieces that will lead me to what I already know is there, as if trying to remember how to do something that I once knew a long time ago, as if I'd already done it, because I knew instinctively, in my skeleton dream, how to go about it. It wasn't a mysterious path, though it was bleak and terrible, full of pain at times, as my early childhood had been, but I felt I knew all that transpired and knew what was in store long before I got very far at all.

I must learn about these undercurrents of pain and desperation from others, why I feel them so intensely, and what I'm supposed to do with them. Is it to test my ability to refuse that which is not energetically productive or enhancing? Maybe I'm being presented with a few examples so I'll begin to notice how easily it comes to me, how fairly quickly I interpret and read people's energy. But being in a roomful of strangers and feeling their pain is quite unnerving, and I don't really want to know or feel such things. After all, I'm still trying to feel my own pain. I already know that being burdened with other people's pain will drive me to exhaustion. I can't live like that.

"*Let the demons go, let them all go. Trust what you hear.*" As usual, the messages from Jeanne are always about being receptive.

March 28, 2004

When I think about not meeting with Chuck for a few weeks I feel generally lighter, the heaviness that's been weighing over me lifts as I anticipate letting Jeanne go for a while too. I think about concentrating on other things, getting my priorities in order, of working and sleeping and eating like a normal person. I think I need to take some time away from the intensity of our work, and the work with Jeanne too, take a spring break, perhaps two weeks off. My energy has been drained and my enthusiasm for life has gone with it.

I call Chuck and tell him about the mystical downloads and he says: "Listen to me. You tell it to stop, with intent!" And then he agrees with me that it seems the right decision to take a break, to shift, to gain surefootedness, to get grounded again.

"I'm still here," he says. "If you need me, you can call."

He's as understanding as always. I'll miss him, but I'll be okay. I intend to stay busy, occupied, and be open to let good things happen. With that, I release myself. No more knowing, no more feeling, no more messages, no more mystical downloads, at least not now. I want only to know and feel things about *myself* now. I need to heal.

After I hang up the phone, I take the tiny clay pot out of my sweater pocket where I've been carrying it ever since Chuck gave it to me. I could feel it anytime I wanted and remind myself to stay open. Now I don't want to be so open. I've already let the baby out, the innocent part of myself that has become a channel; she has joined me on this journey in such an unexpected way. That was the goal, to teach her to trust and then to free her so we could travel on together in new ways, our innocence free to journey on too. That has been accomplished.

I put the pot into a small plastic bag and I step on it. I smash it into fine terracotta dust, with the aid of a rock. As I pound away at it, I explain to Jeanne that I can't be this open anymore, that I'm not ready for it yet, that I can't accept the channeling work until I'm stronger. At this point, it simply drains too much of my energy. I'm exhausted from the recapitulation and need time to rest now.

Apprenticeship

"I'm grateful for the glimpse into this gift," I say, "but I need distance from it now, for a little while."

I'm not really sure what to do with the small bag of red pottery dust. I don't want to throw it away. It's a gift, and it represents my own gifts, but I don't want to walk around with it in my pocket anymore either. I bury the dust in my garden where it can nurture and grow; perhaps one day soon I'll be strong enough to use it. Jeanne thinks I'm ready, but I know I'm not. I feel very calm, certain that I've done the right thing, as I plant the red dust, working it into the soil in my flowerbed. It feels like the right place for it.

When I meet for a session with Nicolas I feel, for the first time, that I am very much one being, my mind not separate from my body. I flow. No theme today, I tell myself, just go with the flow, and I have a totally new and different experience. I feel my lower spine expand and catch fire, like I am being ironed out with a hot iron. As the heat rises and spreads outward and upward, all parts of me iron out too, flattening and melting together. There is no shut off between body and mind, no sense of them as separate entities; everything fuses together. I sense the heat of my own energy flowing up to the top of my head and back down to my feet again. I don't experience anything terrible or frightening, nor do I have any great revelations, but for the first time I feel whole, complete. I definitely left the past behind during the last Embodiment session and have been moving on to a new place ever since, to discovering and owning my own body.

When I get to the studio my computer won't start; a system failure of some sort. I go home and get my son, my technical genius, and we spend several hours booting it back up and reinstalling everything, eventually getting it working again. It seems to offer the perfect opportunity to bring it home, something I've been contemplating doing for several weeks now, a first step in the move out of the studio. I can spend the mornings at home working on writing assignments and the afternoons at the studio, until I finally close it up for good.

March 29, 2004

I wake at five and cannot return to sleep. I agonize over my decision to bring my writing center home, though I know it's the right thing to do. It will allow me more separate writing time, but it really marks the beginning of the end of the studio. As soon as I take that first step and bring my computer home, it will be a reality, and that scares me.

I really am feeling more optimistic these days, so I don't understand why I'm experiencing this fear. If my decisions are scaring me then they really must be the right ones. It's been my experience that if I'm afraid, it must be because I'm allowing for waves of change, which is certainly scary. If I wasn't changing, my decisions wouldn't be having an impact; stagnation does not produce any waves.

I send the kids off to school and head over to the studio. In spite of being in a fairly good mood, a deep undercurrent of panic sets in, an old fear that I can't do this life, that I can't take on what this life is asking me to do. I wonder why I'm feeling like this when I have, in fact, come so far and done so well. One day I feel very together and mellow, the next I'm splintering again and life becomes too much to handle. Sadness comes creeping in and I doubt my decision to take a break from Chuck. It's a difficult position to be in. The only remedy I come up with is to keep busy, so I don't have to think about it or lapse into regret.

At the end of the day, I pack up my computer and my writing files, my printer, and my chair and, feeling like I've made a momentous and frightening decision, I take them home. My son very sweetly sets everything up for me in my bedroom. Tomorrow morning, I begin a new writing job.

Later, I sit on my bed wondering why the sight of my computer in my room is so frightening! I feel as if I've hit rock bottom, that I can go no lower mentally, physically, emotionally, and financially. There is the danger that I might totally CRASH, like my computer did. Luckily my spirit is strong. Some glimmer of hope keeps me hanging onto the belief that things will get better soon. At the same time, I wonder why I'm so afraid of changing even something as minor as the place I keep my computer. I know I must stick to the plan, dare to keep changing. It's the only way.

I must follow in the tracks of the wolf, the path marked by that creature of ritual and wildness. The wolf shows me where to go and how to create a new life, urges me to go inward, to discover once again my creative, innocent, spiritual self. It doesn't matter that I can't see very far into the future, it only matters that I keep going. The next step is enough.

March 30, 2004

I wake before dawn, conscious of still being in fearful CRASH mode, like an airplane in a nosedive, heading straight down, in a panic because I can't pull out of it. It feels like so many of my dreams in the past, the moment of impact looming frighteningly before me, imminent, but this time for real. What is wrong with me!

I remind myself that I'm strong, safe, and capable. I've seen my future and it looks good. Why then am I so afraid? What do I actually fear? Fear has always lived inside me, and it's still festering after all these years. I send it away, the way I sent the pain in my side away the other day. I refuse it. It does not belong to me. It's not mine. I no longer accept it.

The truth is that the crumbling structures of the old me are going, everything I've been and counted on up until this point in my life. I *am* crashing, in a sense, losing the old self as I face a new, unknown future. It's the future that's so frightening. I must withstand the pressure, hold onto the core of myself as I go through this process. I must not let fear rule. I must embrace life in a new way. The truth is that a part of me still resists life. But what do I think is going to happen? Life will unfold anyway. I have to remember that only good will happen now!

I do realize that the Embodyment therapy is causing many of these emotional and deeply rooted issues to re-emerge, and that the intensity of the past few weeks, taking a break from Chuck, and stepping back from the intense connection with Jeanne have all contributed to how I'm feeling. I know I'm on the verge of real change now, real transformation. So much has been revealed. I just have to hold on a little bit longer, heal myself, and maintain my confidence that everything will work out. As Jeanne always tells me, "*Follow your spirit.*"

I struggle to decipher the electronic files sent by the publisher, but eventually figure out what is expected of me for this new writing job and how to do it. By noon I head over to the studio for a meeting and then back home where I work on the writing job again. By the end of the day, I realize I hate the job. I find it tedious and energy draining. The entire project absolutely bores me. This is definitely an important lesson to learn, so reminiscent of being confronted by a painfully boring homework assignment as a child and deciding to get it done as quickly as possible, simply because I hate it. I realized the same thing the other day when I was at a painting job; it was not something I wanted to be doing. So, I'm learning some new things about myself this week, what I *don't* want in my future life.

I realize that moving the computer out of the studio has taken the sacred resting place of my bedroom refuge from me; it no longer serves as my inner sanctum but has now become infused with the energy of the outside world.

As I took my things out of the studio the other day, I kept telling myself that I was just changing the location where I make a living. "Change is good!" I kept telling myself. But I still wonder why it was so frightening a move, and why I have the feeling that I'm going off onto the biggest adventure of my life? Perhaps I am. Perhaps this is just the first step in my next big adventure, in my post-recapitulation life. It sure feels momentous, huge in fact, and I'm scared as hell at having taken that first step, because I am certain that more and bigger changes are soon to follow, and that's scary.

March 31, 2004

"Today will be different from yesterday; it's a new day. Today will be good," I tell myself when I wake at four, full of my usual anxiety and uncertainty.

Apprenticeship

I'll finish the boring painting job I started the other day and forget about everything else for now. I'll stay on my strong side, get myself pumped up for new life. At the same time, I must face that I'm at the end of a long stretch of intense work and it makes sense that it's time for a different experience, a time for rest and recuperation rather than keeping up the good fight. It's time to soften. The truth is, I'm so exhausted I can barely lift my head. I'm too tired to even point myself in the right direction.

I miss Chuck and Jeanne. It's only been a few days, but it feels as if I've started a long trek across the desert and have said goodbye to my dearest friends. I'm alone now with my rawness and my pain, trying to figure out where to go from here. There are no road signs out here, no paths, no tracks in the dry desert sand. It feels very much like the nightmarish dream I had of being a skeleton, crawling along a barren path, meeting teachers along the way and having to figure out the metaphors, the puzzles I was presented with, in order to know where to go next. I continue to put one foot in front of the other, trying to get myself into a better place mentally, so I can be physically strong.

"You are watched over and cared for and supported, even if you don't think so."

Jeanne, please help me get through today!

And with that, I head off to work, intent upon staying focused on the future, intent upon keeping my mind open and my soul lighting the way. I will not turn back to look at the dark nightmare behind me. I am only available to embrace what lies before me.

I hold my own during the day, but when the teenage son of the homeowner comes home after school and starts blasting music on his electric guitar, I hightail it home. By the time I get home I'm in crash mode again. Plunging into a hot bath, I suddenly realize what this is all about; the truth! The truth that things are changing now and changing more rapidly than ever, and yes, more changes are imminent, and all I want to do is avoid them. Why am I so fucking scared? To top it off, my studio partner told me she gave notice to the landlord that we'll be moved out by June first, without first consulting me. That's two months away, which sounds like a lot of time, but there's a heck of a lot of stuff to pack up and get moved, as well as prepare my garage to accept it all.

Moving my computer home did mark the beginning of this next change, the ending of my time at the studio, which I've seen coming for a long time, and the beginning of something truly new. This is just the first phase though, for I feel an even bigger change coming. What it will be is still unknown, but I sense something happening soon. And so, naturally, I'm scared, but maybe it will be good. I just have to get myself into alignment with the flow of this thing and find the energy to actually do what needs to be done!

Chapter 4

Stalking a New Self

April 1, 2004

Stress invades, seeping into every fiber of my body until I'm vibrating with worry. I don't know what to do with all my studio equipment and supplies, or how I'll make a living with my studio and gallery gone. I meditate, breathe, and do some relaxation poses, but I cannot stem the rising tide of anxiety.

I call Chuck and arrange to meet with him tomorrow morning. I feel as if I've been single-handedly holding up a structure for a long time, I tell him, and the whole thing has finally collapsed.

"I guess it wasn't a very good structure to begin with," I say. "Inevitably it had to go, but I'm left standing in the debris of it, feeling negative and self-demolishing, suffering aftershocks that will not cease, and my old defenses are trying like heck to reestablish their supremacy."

"Yes, the old sees an opening and goes for it," he says. "Hang in there; we'll talk soon."

I have never, ever been this physically exhausted or felt so defeated. I don't have the reliable old blocking and numbing mechanisms any more. I don't have the old deadness to keep feelings out. I am totally raw and exposed now. The final straw was my studio partner's blunt announcement that she'd already given the landlord notice. I wasn't expecting it, even though I had instigated it! I thought I'd have a longer time to figure things out, but my studio partner doesn't work that way. She makes a decision on her own and announces it, while I normally sit with an idea for a long time before I finally receive the signal that it's time to make a move. I can stay in what looks like stagnancy for a long time, but inside I'm churning away, planning, making decisions, waiting for the right time, looking for the sign that says the time for action has finally arrived. Well, whether I'm ready or not, that time has arrived. I'm learning that the universe does not work on my schedule.

"Jan, you are trying to do too much," says Jeanne, very clearly. "You just need to make a living, that's all."

Easy enough. Sometimes the best move is to give up, to declare it quits and then start anew. In the long run, I know that everything will be okay. The known structures of my life will change, but my life will go on.

I meet with Nicolas for an Embodyment session. Once again, my experience is intense, lots of heat spreading upward, beginning very low in my spine, until I feel like I'm on fire. My team of spiritual guides come to support me. Funny, that as soon as I contact Chuck, Jeanne is right there again too. I've given my permission. I need them both.

"*Do you remember the lessons I've taught you about trust?*" Jeanne asks me, at one point.

"Yes," I say.

"*Trust me,*" she says. "*Give me your hand and I'll guide you. It will be okay.*"

"Am I dying?" I ask, because it feels like I'm lying on a burning funeral pyre.

"*No, you're not dying.*"

"What's happening then?"

"*It's okay, it's called change. Things are changing.*"

And as I let go, relaxing my body in increments, the hot energy flows upward and my tight throat muscles begin to relax. Slowly and gradually, my throat opens enough for some small whimpers and sighs to escape. I notice, when Nicolas moves over to work on my left side, that I've become even more open, and the releases come in a constant stream. Soon they're almost jumping out of me. My left shoulder jerks back repeatedly, as pent-up energy whips out of me and into the blankets beneath me. My chest reacts to the battery of releases too, expanding outwardly, popping open like a flower.

I head off to work, painting a mural. I think about how I've been trying to uphold an old untenable dream, for my studio was always my dream, and yet now I must face the financial burdensomeness of it and let it go. At the same time, I have plenty of work lining up, another mural and a faux painting job next week. I acknowledge, as well, how I tend to feel responsible for others more than for myself; for my studio partner, for the artists in the cooperative, etc., and that now I feel I've disappointed them all in my inability to sustain my dream. I feel I must carry the burden of everyone else's problems, that I must take care of them over myself, that if they are hurt or angry then I must fix it. I realize I must find solitude within myself, find the answers for what I must do for myself alone now. Time to go totally solo.

After dinner, while the kids do homework, I attend a contributor's meeting at a local newspaper that I often write and illustrate for. The room is crowded. Looking around, I once again realize that I'm trying to do too much. I had decided that I would not turn down any work, that I would take whatever came along, but now here I am struggling, trying to figure out who I really am and what I *should* be doing. It's even a struggle to introduce myself to the group. I don't even know who I am anymore and it feels as if I'm talking about someone else. I realize that I need to build a new structure that is completely my own now.

"You still have bones, and your muscles are still here. You have *that* structure to begin with," Nicolas said today. Yes, I still have my own body. I can begin with that.

April 2, 2004

Anxiety lives inside me. It has invaded every tiny muscle, seeped into my bloodstream and built-up pressure. I'm like a shaken bottle of champagne, ready to explode, unable to flatten back down into calmness. I've gone from stoically holding everything together my entire life to suddenly losing it. This is not my usual demeanor. I never lose it; I hold myself together at all costs. Now though, without my old props of numbness and dissociation, I *feel*. I have *feelings* now, and I have to figure out how to deal with them.

On top of that, my physical body is a wreck. I am barely creeping along at this point, in pain all the time. I need a vacation, from everything, but the truth is I never give myself more than a few hours break. I haven't had a real vacation in years. In fact, I use work to define my day, to help me get through it. I admit, it would be nice to be whisked away for a few months of rest, but as in my dreary nightmare, I must trudge onward. I'm beyond the skeletal stage now, but I don't want more puzzles to figure out, I want clearly stated directions. For the first time in my life, I want someone to tell me what to do.

I make a list of ten outside projects that I'm currently involved in that give me no reward. They offer me nothing; they are only energy drains. I remember what Jeanne said to me in the Embodyment session yesterday. *"Take my hand, everything will be fine,"* she'd said, and with that in mind, I go for my meeting with Chuck.

It's nice to see him again. I've missed his company. We spend most of the session working on strategies for dealing with the anxiety. He teaches me the lifesaving magical pass, to protect my energy by creating a barrier around myself. It's easy enough to do, holding the arms slightly out from the body, turning the shoulders and swinging the arms in a protective arc, essentially drawing a boundary line around the body to keep outside energy out. We practice it a few times. Chuck reminds me that I have so many tools at hand. I forget about most of them when stress strikes, but this one should be easy enough to remember.

April 3, 2004

I dream that I'm in a large, ramshackle Victorian house. Things have deteriorated badly; the plumbing is clogged, the structure falling apart. A family of little orphan girls lives in the house. The oldest girl is taking care of everyone, worrying about the house as it falls apart around her. She feeds the children bread and water and cucumbers, which is all there is. I'm aware that she's exhausted and needs special care, but I'm also aware that she's me, and that I need care too. She glares at me angrily when I try to help and things don't go as planned. My father shows up, wandering around the house in his bathrobe, ill, unbothered by the deterioration. The girl is disgusted by all the adults who fail to attend to things properly, including me.

The dream shifts and I'm running in sand, not getting anywhere. I fall down and get up again. I run some more, fall down, get up. Eventually, I get out of the sand, but now I'm in a jungle, running, getting whipped by branches and prickly palm fronds, having to push my way through dense undergrowth. No matter which way I choose, all of the passages are difficult ones. I decide to ask Jeanne for help.

"What should I do?"

"*Let it happen. Trust,*" she tells me.

"Okay," I say, "but if something good is coming my way then make it happen fast, please. Make it now!"

I need a vacation. Time to slow down and destress, time for self-nurturing so that I might energetically preserve myself for me, and all those needy little girls I still have inside me too, the orphans in my dream. When the oldest girl looked at me with anger and disgust, I recognized it as the same look I often gave my parents when their handling of things irked me. My father wandering around in a daze was pretty accurate. I realized that I'm not taking care of myself well enough either, that I'm still too concerned about everyone else. I will begin this new process of self-care by starting to pack up the studio, a little bit at a time, so it won't be too overwhelming. It'll be a good time to expunge, to only keep what's right and useful.

At the same time that I look forward to this move, I'm also worried about too much solitude, that I'll retreat too far from life, from interaction with others, as I've done in the past. But I know I'm not the same person anymore. I think I'll handle things differently now. I've learned how to be in the world now and I'm not so afraid of it. I won't be retreating to hide this time, but only to conserve my energy and complete my healing.

Change is always frightening. I know that, and to go on this journey alone, admittedly with lots of helpers, but ultimately alone, is the biggest challenge of my entire life. One minute I feel like I can't handle it and the next I get angry for feeling that way.

"Stay focused," I command myself, "just stay focused."

And with that in mind, I spend the day at the studio beginning the packing process. I make a nice pile of money when I sell one of my painted children's table and chair sets. A couple stops in to chat about a painting job, and I talk with a friend about some possible writing work. I stay focused on paring down the number of things I'm attempting to accomplish and be involved in, careful to take on only what feels right. I know I must stick only with the two things that are beneficial to me right now, my painting work and my writing. In the evening, I head home for a quick bite to eat, to shower, and change my clothes before heading out again to work at the gallery, which has an opening tonight. I'm home again by ten.

As I lie in bed, quite exhausted, I realize how relieved I am about giving up the studio. Whenever I spoke to anyone about it at the opening tonight, I felt as if an immense weight had dropped from my shoulders.

April 4, 2004

I dream that I'm back in the old neighborhood where I grew up. I'm with my childhood best friend, standing on the road outside her house, noticing how everything has changed. The road has been rerouted and widened, trees are gone, landscaping that her parents had worked so hard on is gone. There's a gigantic porch on the front of the house where before there had been a modest porch. There is new decking and a swimming pool on the side. We hate it. We wish for it to be as we remember. At the same time, I'm aware that *everything changes*, nothing stays the same, *especially if we want it to.*

This week has involved my acceptance of change, the fact that it's inevitable, and that I have the power to make change work *for* me, rather than against me. I must remember to keep focusing on myself; no more doing for others. People have gotten used to me being available, but it's time for me to step back now and to slowly construct a new life, a simple and contented life.

"Let everyone else go for a while," Jeanne says. "Say no. You won't lose anything. You have already proven yourself, to *everyone, even to yourself. If you look deep enough you will already see that you have proven everything you need to know about yourself. Now take all that knowledge and make your new life. There is nothing more to prove. Accept change. Make room for you. Build a new life."*

During my Embodyment session with Nicolas, I relax and allow for deep releases. Jeanne is with me again, helping to pull old "ghosts" out of me, like tissues out of a box.

"*Remember, I told you, it's all about change,*" Jeanne reminds me, "*getting rid of the old that you have no use for, making room for the new.*"

My body responds to the expulsions, reacts to the sound that each ghost makes as it leaves, just like the tearing sound of a tissue being pulled from its slot in a tissue box. It's quite painful.

"*Take my hand,*" Jeanne says. "*I'll take you where you need to go. You aren't dying, it's just a removal of old dead stuff that you don't need, dead issues, all the leftover memories and feelings that will bother you if left behind.*"

It's like having surgery, for it feels as if something is actually being yanked out of me. I see the horrors of my life with my own eyes, every horrible aspect of the past as it gets pulled out and dragged away. In the blink of an eye, everything that I've recapitulated gets pulled out and leaves my body. The process is quick and yet wrenchingly painful, but I go with it; I let it happen. I try to follow, to see where the ghosts go, but I'm not allowed to. I'm forced to stay in my body and experience the removal. When the session is over, I can't move or speak. I feel physically tender, and raw, as if I have indeed had major surgery.

"Breathe," says Nicolas, "be conscious of your breath; try to breathe deeply, down into your stomach, deep and steady."

April 5, 2004

I wake feeling stressed, tired, and sad. I want to call Chuck for another appointment, but I'm pushing myself to do without. I'll keep busy with work. I'm unhappy where I am right now. My life is not fulfilling enough, but I'm trying to accept that things are the way they are now for a reason, that I'm being led to where I need to go next, and that more than one good spirit is helping me. I've been trying on dozens of hats over the past several years and none of them fit well, and I've also been giving myself dozens of labels, but I've also discovered that I don't need a hat or a label; I just need to be me.

Hopefully, the process of learning to trust will carry me beyond just this inner work and this recapitulation, out of my inner world into the real world in a totally new way. If I can feel solid and safe in the world that I create for myself, will that be enough? Can I ward off outside fears simply by being strong internally? I hope so. Someday, I will achieve the right balance.

I call Chuck, feeling like a wimp, but so what. We set up an appointment for tomorrow. I still feel the old pull and that worries me. I'm confused as to whether it's the old stuff pulling me back or the truth pulling me forward. Or perhaps a little of both? I need clarity.

The reality is that I still have inner work to do. Even as the recapitulated memories leave, I still have the scars to deal with. I understand that as a young child I was subjected to so much pain and I found the only way I could to protect myself, totally shutting off all feeling and all connection to my body. Knowing this changes everything; it changes me. I'm different, but I still have to deal with the old voices. As I turn from them, they scold me, shrieking at me to not leave them. I get pulled in two directions, forward to the new me and all the possibilities that new life offers, and backwards to the old me and the old habits. In this middle ground that I now inhabit, I am the object of a virtual tug of war.

April 6, 2004

I must take care of the sixteen-year-old girl inside me now, that emotionally blocked and starved child, so like the girl taking care of the orphans in my dream. It's time to begin tackling the huge emotional aspect of all of this, with her as key player, for she does hold the key to the next phase of healing. She has all the answers; she remembers everything. It's time to give her an outlet. Her needs are deep. She needs love, caring, and understanding.

She needs to be listened to and encouraged to speak as well. And she needs to be told, over and over again, that it was not her fault.

"What do you think she needs?" Chuck asks, when I tell him where I am with my sixteen-year-old self.

"EVERYTHING!" I say. "She needs, first of all, to know that she's safe, that she's cared for, and that she matters. It's difficult to approach her because she's so closed up and quiet, so shut down and far away, but I feel her need to communicate. I remember that need. She was always looking for a sign that it would be all right to try to get close to someone. She sometimes dared to imagine getting close to an adult, imagined asking for help, but mostly she felt how isolated the adults around her were, how they too were distant and cut off from their own feelings."

"I'm beginning to understand that a merger with her can only happen now because we're both ready. Denial of the abuse is no longer blocking us, and the false beliefs that it was my fault and that I was to blame have also been removed. With those obstacles dismantled, I think we'll be able to connect, and for her to accept that she's not alone anymore, for her to believe me when I tell her that she's safe and that she can trust me. We have each other now."

I go back to my sixteen-year-old self, the girl in the dream, throughout the day, letting her know that I'm here for her. Simultaneously, my own twelve-year-old daughter is angry with me. I gently hold her and kiss her, letting her cry. After a while she feels better, anger released. In the evening, I send the kids off to their dad's house for the week of spring break, my fifteen-year-old son under great protest; another synchronicity.

I now have the next six days completely to myself. My own sixteen-year-old self is waiting for me, waiting for her dreams to be fulfilled. She has been unable to live the life she wanted because of the enormity of what happened to her. I know this. I was there too. She's in such pain, sad and afraid. She needs so much, but mostly she needs me, just as my own daughter did. I don't think I could have survived had it not been for her. I'm grateful to her for her stoicism, for withstanding the trauma so strongly, and for the fact that her suppression of the memories kept us alive. But now that I'm able to accept everything, and understand it completely, I also know that I'm the only one who can give her what she needs, which is everything that I need too. I give and I receive. Her dreams were never fulfilled and I am the vehicle to fulfilling them now. She wanted to become a writer; I remember that now. Choosing art was easier, safer. It fed her creative urge, but deep down were all those words she never spoke, buried under the memories.

This time of solitude is appealing. It will give us time to get to know each other. I want to reacquaint myself with that strong girl, try to break through her silence. Things are so deeply buried, and I'm aware that it'll take some time, but eventually we'll succeed. To begin with, I feel her emotions. When I breathe, I feel them. When I imagine them, I see them; raw, red and tender, painful to the touch. I feel them deep inside, kept down and out of sight for all those years but now beginning to creep up into my throat, words forming, sounds emerging.

April 7, 2004

I dream that I'm sitting at my computer, searching on the Internet, going where it takes me, clicking on whatever pops up next, going with the flow of it, letting it happen. Nothing disturbs me. I just accept the journey as it unfolds.

I don't know where I'm going next, but I'm taking the hand of that sixteen-year-old girl and we're going together. She's often unapproachable, distant in a lot of ways, isolated and shy, but I trust that I can bring her out of her darkness. She's awake, alert, and listening, so I think she's ready. We'll work on some things together, begin by drawing and writing together. I tell her I love her, that I care about her. I need her as much as she needs me, I tell her. We are incomplete without each other. I know how much she hurts. I know how terrible her situation was. I know how frightened she is. I tell her that I won't let anything bad happen to her again.

I head out for a healing session with Lara.

"Think green," she suggests, "eat better, eat protein, eat more often, small portions, stay away from sugar. And drink lots of water."

As instructed, I lie on her sofa for a few minutes after she works on me and "think green." Green leaves, green grass, green money. Green is prosperity, calmness, nature flowing through me. Green is acceptance. Green is quiet. Green is solitude. Peace is green. Love is green. I am green grass and green leaves. I am flowing, part of nature. I am green.

"Change leads to good things," Lara says, as I leave, "allow for it. Accept it. Don't stop it. Let it happen; it can only lead to good things."

I'm learning how to connect with my sixteen-year-old self, how to begin a dialogue. I allow her to learn and receive from me. I have a safe home for her. I offer stability and security, food, love, and nurturance so she can feel safe, and perhaps begin to develop the talents that have been waiting all these years to be explored. I'm open to hearing her voice, to hearing her speak the words that have been so deeply buried. I too am learning that there are good people and safe places in the world. I too am going with the flow of this process, like in my dream, journeying onward as the next sign comes along to guide me. I am *trusting*.

My body is beginning to release the blockages and the pain. My legs don't hurt anymore at night or when I wake up. I am truly healing. I've been in such pain for years and now I find it has decreased significantly, only a slight hint every now and then. When I'm stressed it ratchets right up to the old intensity, but otherwise I'm much better.

I really am trying to take better care of myself, but I don't always do a good job. I don't always eat enough, I don't sleep much, and I don't cry.

April 8, 2004

I dreamed all night of holding back, of *not* letting go. It made me realize how much I still compartmentalize, how I keep my emotions and needs separate, still under my control. In order to heal, everything must emerge and merge. I have to accept all parts of myself, and acknowledge that everything I hold inside is part of me too, including all those needs and emotions. All my memories are connected to what I'm struggling with right now; everything is interconnected. My entire life has been leading up to this point of final release.

I don't have to ask why anymore. I don't have to ask what's wrong with me anymore, or why I'm always so sad and afraid, or why everything hurts. I know now. I've been granted the gift of knowledge about myself, the unblocking of everything during this recapitulation journey. Slowly, I've learned about myself, and slowly I'm learning how to totally reconcile it all, inside and out. I'd like to someday enjoy this life, take some pleasure in it, and in who I am. It's time to get started on the next phase of this adventure, all parts merged as one. It feels like coming home, like being alive, like being encompassed by love.

So, don't be afraid, my sixteen-year-old self. That is my advice to both of us, don't be afraid. I'm here for you. I'm walking into the woods where you've been with all those horrible memories, with all the pain and all the things you couldn't say, and I'm taking your hand and asking you to please trust me, to trust me and all of our helpers and guides. I'm putting my arms around you and holding you, and telling you that everything is all right now. It's over. Okay? It's finally over. I feel you holding back, reluctant to accept my hugs. You're stiff and distant, but, gradually, as you understand the true meaning of what's happening, you'll soften and accept what I offer, for you'll understand that I really do know everything now.

I feel the truth pour out of you the way I have felt it pour out of me. A huge river of pain pours out of us both, as we step out of that horror chamber in the woods, as we leave the woods, the barn, and all the horrible places behind. We leave them to drown in that river of truth and pain, but we save ourselves. We're starting over now, you and I. We have my adult knowledge of how to fulfill our dreams. We have new guides in our life. Trust and love surround us.

I'm not going to worry about love, about finding it or not. Right now, I have to understand that it's all around me, being offered to me in many different forms. In fact, I really am surrounded by it. I only have to reach out and I can touch it. So now, I'm teaching my sixteen-year-old self that trust is key to this whole process. She's healing within me. I'm conscious of her now being within me, not standing off to the side, not looking at me angrily for leaving her behind to deal with the memories all alone. I had to get to this point, to this place of acceptance, without denial, in order to go back and find her. Whenever I tried before, denial blocked me. Now I can see and feel and hear her again, my younger self, without a hint of doubt or denial.

I remember some of her deepest desires and I'm working on convincing her that I've found my way to some of them. Right now, in the safety of Chuck's office, and in myself, I've found some of the things she always longed for. I've found someone she can talk to. I've found someone she can trust. I've found a place where she is accepted without judgment, appreciated for herself. I've found a place where she can express every fear and every dream without being laughed at, ridiculed, or abused; a place where it's safe to just be.

By learning to trust, I've found my way back to the greater supportive universe, to the voices and guides who have been protecting and guiding me my whole life. In the process, I discover that I am indeed surrounded by love, in all its many forms. I've learned to stay open; even if it hurts, I know I must stay open. I may not ever experience romantic love again, but I understand that I am surrounded by love. I understand what that means now. I *feel* it.

April 9, 2004

I dream of skiing down a long hill, enjoying the freedom of gliding and flying effortlessly down a steep snow-covered hill. As soon as I reach the bottom, I am instantly back at the top of the hill again, heading down once again, experiencing the same level of exhilaration. I do this over and over again until the dream suddenly shifts.

Now I'm at the corner of a very busy intersection, digging in the dirt beneath a white rail fence, extracting dirty paint rags, which I hang in a row along the fence. I do this over and over again, digging up the rags and laying them out on the fence, coming back to the intersection, to the same spot, to do the same thing many times. Cars speed by as I kneel in the dirt, but I ignore them, even though I know some of the people driving them, and I know they must wonder what I'm up to, but I don't care. The final time I come to the intersection, I remove all the rags from the fence and walk down the street with them. I'm on my way to give a lecture. I'm feeling extremely self-confident, knowing that I've accomplished something important. As I walk, I acknowledge to myself that I've never cared what people think of me, I just do what I have to do, and that's the most important thing in the world to me, to do what I know I must do. So, it doesn't bother me that one minute I may be seen digging in the dirt beside the road and the next giving a lecture to a huge crowd of people. It's just who I am, and I'm perfectly contented with being who I am.

On my way to see Chuck. I invite Jeanne and my sixteen-year-old self to accompany me. It's important that we all be there together because we have to finish this, trust the process, and take it to a new level. My first dream portends effortless fun activity, smooth sailing ahead. And the second dream indicates that the two aspects of myself, my inner seeker, my spirit, and my outer presenter-self, my ego, will soon be merging in a good way. I look forward to experiencing that serene self-confidence!

When I arrive for my meeting with Chuck, I notice that he's unusually quiet. I don't attach. Instead, I talk a lot. How unusual! Am I making up for his lack of energy? He says that I seem to be on the right track. He feels that I certainly will be writing soon, and I know he's right.

"Yes," I say, "in fact, I think I already am."

And we leave it at that.

I spend the day at the studio then rush home to clean up, dress, and grab a bite to eat before heading off to work the evening shift at the gallery. There's not much activity and I have time to sit and jot down my thoughts. There's a labyrinth painted on the floor, large enough to walk, so I periodically get up and walk it, making my way slowly to the center. As I walk, I think about how tired I am of being sad and gloomy, and after I've walked the labyrinth for a while, I notice that I'm snapping out of my gloom, that my intent to change is working. When people come into the gallery I stop and greet them, invite them to see the show, and to walk the labyrinth as well.

I'm thinking about getting drunk. If I get drunk, I'll be able to cry, I surmise. It might help with releasing. It might enact a shift into a new frame of mind, one I so desperately want and need. I have to find a way to aggressively participate in this change that I'm going through, rather than constantly dragging my feet, saying that I don't want to. I do want to! And I think the young girl inside me finally wants to be active as well.

Whenever I need some energy, I get up and walk the labyrinth again. Each time I walk I gain new insight and clarity. The sun is out, the evening is nice, though there are not too many people out and about. I have the gallery door open and the fresh spring air is invigorating. As I walk the labyrinth, I make a firm commitment to more actively participate in this changing time in my life. I have to help things along. I have to be proactive. I can't just wait for things to happen; I have to help them happen.

Maybe I should start skipping, I think, it might make me feel better, and so I try skipping around the labyrinth, to jolt myself into a new place, to shake up my energy and shift my *assemblage point*, as Chuck calls it, the energetic ball of personal energy that shifts into heightened awareness when least expected, though he's also taught me that I can shift it volitionally. And so, I skip, trying to jolt my energy into a new state of being. And just as in my dream last night, I don't care if anyone sees me!

By the time nine o'clock rolls around, I've walked and skipped the labyrinth dozens of times. I close the gallery, go home, and watch a movie until midnight, but I'm not really tired. I get up and walk around, worry brewing inside me, not letting me settle for the night. I've been making some decisions tonight, repeatedly stating my intent to change, to willingly participate more fully in life and my own process, to accept the guidance I receive, to more fully become who I truly am. I've come to conclusions that have long waited to be realized, and so, of course, worry lifts its ugly head, wondering if it needs to jump in, just like the faithful old dog it is!

I tell it to go back to sleep, for I don't need it now. I'm on a new journey now, searching for a broader and more sacred understanding of who I am.

April 10, 2004

It's time to finish the recapitulation, to go back into the woods and dig in the forest floor one last time, unearthing the final hopes, dreams, and memories of my sixteen-year-old self, moving them out of the darkness into the light. My dream of digging up the old rags was showing me this. I can go back there now without the old horror attacking me, without fear disabling me, for I have become detached enough now that there are no energetic strings binding me to that old world. I know everything there is to know. When I go back there now, I find that younger self waiting, and I know what to do for her, how to approach her and what to say to her. I know exactly what she needs.

After working all day, I make a conscious decision to get drunk. At first, nothing happens. I can't seem to get even tipsy. I'm looking for a shift, for something to happen, but nothing is happening. Now after a whole bottle of wine, I am suddenly drunk. So, what have I learned? Nothing, except that I can let go and get drunk! But it did not facilitate the shift I desired.

April 11, 2004

I wake in pain like I have not felt in a few weeks, my hips hurting, tightly clenched, bemoaning the fact that I drank that whole bottle of wine. Did I get release? Nope, not even that. I was looking for an opening to some other kind of experience, but I've ended up back in an old place. I guess that's not the way to shift.

Shift will happen on its own, when the time is right. I should know that by now.

I spend most of the day reading in bed trying to feel my way out of my dark muddle, depressed, a bit hungover. I should get up and move around. I should rearrange my room and make space for my drawing table, which I'll be bringing home from the studio, but try as I might I cannot muster the energy to do even that. Where is my desire for life? Don't I have any? No, right now I have absolutely none. And where does that leave me? It's a deadly state to be in, for I don't care about anything.

Luckily, the kids will be coming home tonight so I'll have to be attentive to them. In the meantime, old thoughts of running away pop up, my old reaction to being stuck and frustrated. It's time to take the bull by the horns and do what I need to do in order to survive, to more than survive, because mere survival is what I want least. I want to FULLY LIVE. And how do I find desire for life again when I feel only exhaustion? I've been wallowing in self-pity all day, and that doesn't get me anywhere.

"I hate my life!" I shout, to no one in particular.

"*So? Do something about it!*" I hear, very clearly spoken, and I wonder who said it, for it sounded as if it came from outside my window.

April 12, 2004

It was a failed experiment with the wine. I didn't get the results I wanted. Steeped in self-pity and self-hatred, I effectively wasted a perfectly good day when I could have been productive and creative. I lost all contact with my spiritual helpers too. I did something out of character and it didn't sit well anywhere, with them or me.

"*Okay,*" Jeanne says, "*get back on track. It was not a good idea, Jan. Don't do it again. All you did was try to numb the pain and it doesn't really work that way. It just adds a heaviness to it, a suffocating depression.*"

I must get something accomplished today. The best thing is to just plod on, staying in touch with the important things, like learning to trust that all will be well, and tracking the ups and downs of this adventurous spiritual journey without losing my sense of place and focus. I must overcome my fears, and concentrate once again on putting one foot in front of the other, listening to my inner voice, and my guides. Please remain with me. Please help me. I need you.

By the end of the day, I feel better, and things are looking better too. I even have a couple of good painting jobs lined up for the week.

April 13, 2004

I dreamed last night of being trapped by arms wearing long black gloves, arms that seemed to pull me off my path. They held me so tightly I couldn't move. At first, I was afraid of them and thought they were evil arms, but then I began to think they were there to support and steady me, for they calmed me down and made me feel safe.

I woke up feeling grateful. At the same time, I was afraid I had to start all over again, that I did get off my path, but then I realized that those arms in my dream were actually reminding me to reset myself every day, to remember why I exist, and what I'm doing, to refocus my attention and my energy on my path of heart, and to drum up a little enthusiasm for myself. They were reminding me that every step of my journey is supported.

"*Get back on track! Get back on track!*" they said. "*Stay on track and you'll be fine!*"

I meet with Chuck and talk about my lack of energy and enthusiasm, as nothing else matters at the moment.

"It's called depression and they make pills for it," Chuck says.

"No, no more pills. I'll just deal with it," I say. "I'll find a way to stay focused. I'll make lists and look forward to the day with tasks, with organization! It seems to be the only way to proceed right now, to point myself forward and to tackle one thing at a time. Right now, even getting gas for my car seems like an incredibly monumental project."

Stalking A New Self

Strange things are happening again! I go to Staple's to return a batch of faulty printer ink. I bring it to the return desk and after I explain how it didn't print any yellow color, the woman behind the counter says: "You thought it was just you, didn't you?"

"Of course, I did, it's always me!"

"Not this time, Honey, they do that all the time," she says, referring to the ink cartridges.

I buy a bunch of other stuff, approximately forty dollars' worth of paper and other items, and I get a new ink cartridge as well. I am poised, ready to write a check for my purchases when the cashier gives me a cash refund card.

"I don't get it," I say, totally confused. "Don't I owe for all this?"

"Just accept it; take it, and be happy," says the cashier, whose name is Jeanne. "Don't even think about it! Take it and enjoy your day!"

From there I head to a session with Nicolas.

"What have you been doing?" he asks. "You're a mess!"

"I know," I say. "I couldn't handle the openness, so I shut down and retreated back to an old posture."

"You got to the precipice, looked down, and said, I'm not ready yet. It happens. When you are ready you won't run."

As the session progresses, I experience extreme distress. Something is trying to work its way out of me, something that wants out, now, immediately! It claws at my ribs, digging for an exit, something alien, something foreign that doesn't belong. It feels like a small monster ripping my flesh, tearing at my bones. I hear it growling and gnashing its teeth. I feel how desperately it wants to escape. It's not being helped, pulled out like those tissue ghosts, but fighting to get out on its own. It knows it doesn't belong there, and I don't want it in me either.

"There's something ancient," I say, "something alien and evil, something very bad thrashing around inside me."

"When do you see Chuck next?"

"Friday."

"Good. When that thing is ready to come out, it will come," says Nicolas. "I think you're just afraid, but you'll see that there really isn't any reason for it."

"Do shavasana and breathe," he says.

"Nicolas is right, nothing bad will happen," I tell myself, but I fight its release anyway. I want it to go, but I'm so afraid of losing a part of myself with it, a known part. But I actually saw it, ugly and hideous, reeking of evil. How could I want to keep that! How could I want it in me? Even it knows it doesn't belong. Why won't it just leave? Why weren't you there, pulling it out, Jeanne? Where were you?

"*It's your fear, Jan,*" she replies. "*You have to work on that by yourself. That one is yours alone, because if you don't let it out, it will stay inside you. Only you know exactly what it is and how it feels; only you can truly recognize it. So only you can release it.*"

April 14, 2004

I slept in an old position and wake with legs and hips cramping again, depressed and out of sorts. I wish Chuck hadn't spoken the word *depression*. I was better off thinking I could fix it somehow myself, with wine, for instance. Now I know I don't have control over it, that it's something real, whereas before it was just some amorphous energy. Without a name it wasn't real.

Back home, after a day spent painting. Next week I'll be painting doors, about twenty or so, in my garage. I need to make room so I can begin to work there. At least I can breathe a little easier in the work and money department now, as work is flowing in and all the bills are getting paid.

I realize I can't stop the depression, the sadness, the pain, the lack of motivation or the exhaustion. They seem to be physical manifestations of the inner issues and nothing I seem to do alleviates them. I don't want drugs. Coffee helps while the caffeine effects are present, and so does physical exercise; temporary fixes, but better than nothing. I also realize that my symptoms are to be expected, as I really am exhausted, and I have to respect them, for they are, in a sense, asking me to slow down and take care of myself properly.

It's really the old self who's so exhausted. Her work is done. She's taken good care of me, but now it's time for her to retire and for a new self to take over, the new self who knows everything and has no need to protect old secrets. The old self is so stoic and dedicated that exhaustion really is the only way she'll be forced into giving up her guardianship ways.

As I drove home tonight, my car overheated again and I had to pull off the road, shut off the engine, and let it cool down. This has been going on for weeks now, but it always operates just fine after an initial overheating. The thermostat returns to normal again if I take a minute to let it cool down. I suspect there is some blockage that's working its way out, or perhaps a faulty thermostat. The mechanic will look at it tomorrow.

By ten o'clock at night I'm fighting the old stuff again, my shoulders hunched and clenched, and I can't see well. I know it's partially because I'm exhausted, but I also know my old demons so well.

"I'm tired, I'm going to bed," I say to the kids. "Can you guys do quiet stuff now."

"Well, that's too bad, too bad for you!" my son yells. "You're always tired!"

"Yes, I am," I say, "and I'm working on it. In the meantime, please, just be a little respectful."

I go into my room and pray to Jeanne for help. Please help me deal with life, please help me be a good mother, even when I feel so miserable and incapable.

April 15, 2004

I dream that I'm in my studio, very slowly removing paint from a painting on a glass panel, peeling and scraping it away in tiny increments. I scrape with a razor blade or my fingernail, slowly and methodically removing tiny flecks of paint from the picture, which is a self-portrait, me sitting cross-legged, in meditation. I work on this peeling process for a long time. Days, weeks, months, years go by and I am not done yet. One day, a shaman walks into my studio. He walks right up to the painting and starts ripping away huge strips of paint. Quickly, he totally removes the remains of the picture.

At first, I'm upset, because he's not doing it the way I want it done, but then I think, "Oh, what the heck, it's done." He tells me to start over now, to make a new self. I think about the fact that change happens in spite of my efforts to slow it down. I notice that the shaman is familiar in some way. I know I have some deeper connection with him, but I can't remember what it is, or how I know him. I look directly into his eyes, trying to remember how we're connected, but then I realize he may not know it yet, and that it's not the right time to mention it.

Last night, before I fell asleep, I was thinking about the sixteen-year-old girl. I felt my body being pulled back to its old clenching mode, as I thought about her, to the old posture of curled and hunched shoulders, to her fear. I realized that the fear itself is what I fear, for it's the embodiment of everything. It's the memories, the pain, the sadness, and the loss. It's the depression too, both physical and mental. When fear takes over it certainly rules! The Embodyment Therapy with Nicolas is bringing it to the surface, the next thing to tackle. My child's body is so used to having it there; she clings to it. How do I oust one and keep the other? How do I release the fear but keep the girl?

"*Accept, and allow it to just happen,*" Jeanne says. "*Let everything happen. Let go totally and allow it to happen. Continue to trust. Don't forget about everything I've taught you about trust. Don't forget about trusting in Chuck, he's there for you. He's offering his services. He too loves you. You know that don't you?*"

"I guess I do, but why can't I see? My eyes are not functioning properly."

"*Relax, allow, trust. Let everything happen, Jan.*"

"How? How do I do that? I don't know how."

My still automatic response to all this opening and releasing work has been to withdraw inside myself, to re-enter the old body, still there, not so completely changed yet that I can't slip into it, still accessible when I want it. But once there, once enclosed, dissociated, and distant from the outer world, it doesn't really feel that good. It doesn't offer the solitude and protection it once did; in fact, it feels pretty terrible. As soon as I get there all the old voices speak up, all the old pains return, and I feel stuck in a foreign body, no longer my own. Then hatred for myself arises for allowing this reprise of old habits. I must find a way to turn this whole process around. If I can allow myself to get pulled back to an old bad place so easily, I can surely allow myself to get pulled forward to a new good place!

Please, Jeanne, I need your help.

By mid-afternoon I am barely muddling through the day, walking around in a daze. People come in and out of the studio and it's hard for me to speak and connect with them, and I still can't see clearly. I feel distant and only peripherally present. I promised myself that if the mechanic can finally figure out what's wrong with my car's radiator then I will finally be able to fix my own internal blockage. When he calls to tell me that a hose had collapsed in on itself, I know I must find a way to fulfill my promise to open my own blockage, to finally let things release, especially the pain and fear, those monsters that want to get out of me as much as I want them out.

By the end of the day, I have enough energy to move my drawing table home. I set it up in my room alongside my writing desk. It feels right, it works. I generate a little energy during the activity and the depression lifts a little. I lie in shavasana before sleep and try to breathe myself into calmness. Eventually, my lower spine opens, tingling, and I get some relief.

Thank you to *everyone* for helping me!

April 16, 2004

In a dream, I sit cross-legged, naked, dipping pieces of paper into glue and applying them to my body where they stick and eventually harden. Each piece of paper has a different word on it. I apply layer upon layer of pieces of paper, each meaningful word representing me and my past, representing my situation and the circumstances of my abuse. I work until I am completely covered in words, in a hardened cast, creating a piece of artwork on my own body. I call it: *Words of Pain*.

I wake up with my legs completely cramping, in pain, sad and depressed all over again. I not only dreamed this second self-portrait dream, encasing myself in a hard shell, but also about a sixteen-year-old girl coming into my body and taking over! I totally feel her in me! This is definitely an old place, one I thought I was free of. What's happening?

When I meet with Chuck, he immediately hands me the EMDR pods. I clutch them tightly, my little lifesavers.

"Breathe," he says, "just breathe... Breathe... Keep an open passage... Realign... keep realigning... When you get out of alignment then realign immediately. You know how to do it."

"Let go. All signs point to letting go. Just let go and the tension will release. The pain is in the holding, in the resistance," he says. "Relax, do all the relaxing techniques you know."

He reminds me that I promised that if my car got fixed, I would fix this, so now is the time.

"Go to work," he says. "Stay calm and relaxed and allow for release. And keep breathing."

Everything will be all right, I remind myself. *Everything*. Remember that. Stop torturing yourself, everything will be fine.

I meet with some women friends for lunch. We're all a little unhappy for our own reasons, but still excited about life and the possibilities that lie before us. I find that the more I talk about this change I'm going through the more I feel that it's good. I get inspired and decide that I'll finally clean the garage this weekend and really begin to move the studio.

    I talk myself through the rest of the day, reminding myself that everything will be fine, giving myself calming and reassuring words of support. I'm trying to not think of myself as two separate individuals, as the adult me and my sixteen-year-old self. We both have needs, but we have, in fact, the same basic need right now: to let go of the fear. If I think of us as one, then I can deal with this better, because we both need the same release.

    In the late afternoon I'm feeling more alive and it feels good. I head out to pick up the kids at school and discover that the car isn't repaired after all. It overheats and spews antifreeze, as usual. I drive back to the mechanic's shop. They see me drive up and I feel their collective sigh before I even get out of the car. They decide it must be the thermostat after all, since nothing else seems to be the problem. I'll bring it back on Monday.

    This merging thing is hard. I remind myself that I'm an adult and that, as such, I know everything will be fine, but my sixteen-year-old self still carries such fear that my immediate reaction is to protect, to withdraw with her into some old familiar place where we're at a safe distance from everything that makes us uncomfortable. Am I really regressing to the age of sixteen? I have to admit, I strongly feel the need to retreat, want only to be alone. It's a really familiar place. How do I fight the real fear that she, the sixteen-year-old self, still carries?

    "Align and re-align," Chuck said today, "and remember that everything *is* okay, and everything *will be* okay."

    I know this, but I feel as if I'm being drawn back, that the sixteen-year-old is pulling me back, rather than me pulling her forward, and that has to change. I have to be in control. If she pulls me back, I'll be in big trouble.

April 17, 2004

I dream of letting go and letting things happen, of not holding in, clamping down, or denying anything. I dream of needs, wants and desires, and ultimately of trusting, of trusting *everything*. In spite of these dreams, I wake up feeling achy and sad. There's a big family gathering tomorrow that I don't want to go to and I suspect my body is protesting, agreeing heartily with me. It doesn't want to chitchat, put on a happy face, or pretend that it's happy to be there.

I have such a strong desire to create my own little world, to live outside the expectations of family and society, and my old self too. As I withdraw from the bustle of the studio, and retreat into my writing corner, I will create what I want, the life I've always envisioned myself living, going about my work, living simply and quietly in the world, but also quietly apart, by choice, and for the right reasons, not out of fear. That's what's changing now. As I lose my habitual fears, I allow myself access to a new vision of myself. I can no longer do this life as it is, and as it has been; I have to change it.

"Don't be afraid of withdrawal," Jeanne says. *"Don't be afraid of the needs of that sixteen-year-old girl. She's finding her way, learning to let go of all the troubles she's been surrounded by, all the misconceptions that her life has given her. She too is seeking truth. She's listening for clarity. She's allowing for love too; first allowing it by slowly letting it in, then accepting it more fully. It will be what it will be. And it will be right. It can only be right."*

Leaving the studio is really the first step toward creating a new world that I can really live and thrive in, be happy in; far different from the world I live in now, still so full of turmoil and pain. The transition began a long time ago. I must accept it as a fact, but also as my deepest need. I can't hear Jeanne's voice, or any others, when I'm pressured by trying to live a life that doesn't fit me. That, I think, is what I've been trying to do my whole life, live a life that doesn't fit.

Something's going to happen, something that will change my life forever. I can't see what it is, though I sense its approach.

I know things I couldn't possibly know and I realize this is how Jeanne is teaching me to trust her. This is my learning process, my apprenticeship, and I must trust the process if I am to be able to accept the messages and gifts that I receive from her. Learning to trust everything, as it comes, is part of this process. It's *magnetic*. At least that's how I experience it, that I am magnetically drawn to know things. I feel something in my body and I have knowing, intuition. I guess that's what psychic channeling is.

I spend the morning running errands, depressed as usual, with little energy. When I get home, I curl up in bed with my boots on. There are lots of people like me, unable to cope in the real world, wracked by depression, traumatic or otherwise. The way the human mind and body are, they work both against us and for us. We have to grasp that, if we are to change anything. We have to decide what's good for us and what isn't. And only we really know what that means. No one else can decide for us.

I realize that Jeanne has been teaching me about letting go of what I've worked so hard and so long to maintain—my studio—and it's not only my attachment to my studio but a whole life that I've built around the studio that I must let go of. It's been like keeping a body alive by doing all the right things and having, in the end, to face that it isn't tenable anymore. It's time to let the studio go, to face its death, and let it die, just as if it were a body. You have to leave a known form behind as you change and transform, just as Jeanne did when she passed from this life. This is what I must face as I let go of the studio—and it's a major change. No wonder I'm depressed.

For the rest of the day, I clean and rearrange the house, trying to make the place more pleasant and able to handle the influx of things from the studio. I run out of steam at around four. I lie down then and try to relax. Internally, I am quiet and calm, but also depressed. I'm trying to not get anxious about money and work, old worries that come so easily, even when there's no true need. Even though I know I'm changing this life into something I really do desire, the transition itself is like being in a dark tunnel, constantly in motion in the darkness, unable to gain a sense of balance or true direction. Where is this leading me? I just know I'm going for it, taking the leap, following my spirit, but everything else is a complete mystery.

I ask Jeanne for guidance.

"*Continue to trust the magic, the truth, all that you are given,*" she says. "*All the signs are important.*"

"Anything can happen," a friend said today. "Anything."

April 18, 2004

I have the same dream over and over again. My body is an image on a computer screen and I try to fix it by choosing "select all" and then "change all," which are the only options. I do this hundreds of times, but the changes are so incremental it doesn't seem as if anything is really changing at all.

I wake up early, my three cats meowing loudly, clawing and climbing up the screen of the open window above my head. It's another perfectly beautiful, warm spring day and they are drawn to be outside. The birds are chirping, the sun shining, but I am unable to lift my foot and take the next step. I'm off track again, lost in a desert. Agitated, I feel this loss of direction physically, in my body. My hands are numb, my shoulders tight. I can't seem to see either. Where do I put my foot? What is wrong with me! My self-esteem plummets; anger wells. The real truth is, I don't want to go to the family gathering, but I also know I should get out of myself for a while.

Somehow, I will focus, breathe, and get calm. Somehow, I will regain my sense of security in the world, my sense of safety within, and my own knowing that guides me. I have seen my future and it's all light. I should take the next step. I know the path is right here, even though I can't see it.

I meditate, get the kids up, take my son to a music rehearsal, and then my daughter and I head off to the family event. I still don't want to attend, but, as my mother said: "You have to come! *Everyone* will be here!" I don't really care. My daughter, however, will enjoy seeing her cousins.

Staying detached was the only way to get through the party, though I literally vibrated the whole time I was there.

My mother was her usual cold self, bundled up tightly in her matching sweater set and pearls, her steel gray hair cut in a hard helmet that says, I can't stand myself. I know because cutting off my hair has always been my own mark of self-hatred. I'm softer now, my hair long and flowing again. I'm allowing for prettiness, allowing myself to be feminine, and I look at myself now and say, "Hey, I'm pretty; I look good today." I like the way I look now. In that sense, I'm happy with myself. I realize I need to let everything flow now, not just my hair, but also my body, my thoughts, my feelings, my life.

April 19, 2004

"It's got to be you, Jan," the mechanic says, when I drop my car off.

"Yup, you're right, it's probably me," I say.

I walk over to the studio. As soon as I climb the stairs and close the door behind me, I am immediately overtaken by a rush of feelings and emotions. Everything that could possibly be inside me races around—needs, desires, anger, fear. Everything I've ever wanted churns inside me too, but I feel stuck in an empty desert, lost, unable to point myself in a direction that will lead me out of this muddle, unable to find a point on the horizon that looks promising, for nothing I see outside of me beckons.

"Okay, in that case," I tell myself, "just look down. Look down at your feet and begin to move. Take one step. Put one foot in front of the other and just walk, one step at a time, one second, one minute, one hour at a time, one day at a time. Forget about going anywhere right now, just focus on moving forward and staying in alignment with the intent of this journey. Keeping in alignment with each moment, as it comes, is enough for now."

I sense that if I stop, I'll die. I will die in this desert. So, I keep moving, keep walking; nothing must stop me. Stopping means death. Stopping is lying down in the sand and being buried and not having the strength to get up or dig myself out. Stopping is the end of everything. You always told me to be patient, Jeanne. You always told me that when I was ready, good things would happen. Am I ready?

"Trust," says Jeanne. "*You need to trust and you will be fine. Everything will be fine. Letting go is part of life, releasing something that doesn't exist anymore in reality.*"

I know it's just a matter of time before the changes I long for will arrive. But why must everything take so fucking long!

I pick up my car at the end of the day and the mechanic tells me it's fine now, that it worked just fine for him.

"Well, just wait until she drives it!" the other mechanic jokingly says.

Back at home, I mull over the possibility of finding a smaller space to rent in the same building where the studio is now, just for a painting studio, a place to retreat to and do my art. But I know that with rent, insurance, and utilities I would be stuck in the same place, a lot of overhead again, and for what reason? In the meantime, I need to put some energy into getting the garage habitable as a workspace. Maybe I can afford to insulate it and put in a woodstove before winter.

I've been tired and cranky, near tears all day, and my body is constantly tense. Maybe I need to start running again, do more yoga, get into a routine that focuses on my physical self. But I've been so depressed lately I can barely get this physical body to do anything. Instead of trying to whip it into a shape that just doesn't fit it anymore, maybe I should pay attention to what it's trying to tell me. Like my car, there's something not right. I've been doing so much inner work that it makes sense that my outer body will change as well, no longer feel right. It doesn't have the same stuff inside, nor does it need to keep stuff hidden anymore. It's changing, along with the rest of me.

I've been trying to find out what the sixteen-year-old girl inside me needs, thinking it was all about her, but I know that in reality we're the same person with the same needs. I'm not made up of separate parts; I am one person and all my needs are the same. They are longings and deep yearnings that go back all the way to infancy. They are things I have not allowed to be known or fulfilled. I mostly kept needs and desires out of my life, because I didn't believe they'd ever be met. Now, suddenly, I find myself a different character, opening up to so much. In this new person that I have become, I find that I want to understand myself more deeply. I want to know and understand what those needs are and how to fulfill them. They are important, and only in accepting the fact of their existence, and allowing them to be expressed, will I evolve. For I must evolve physically, mentally, and emotionally, as well as spiritually, if I am to gain equanimity and real balance.

In the past, I was able to securely suppress that which I did not want in my life, long enough to forget it was there. I'm good at keeping things from getting out, but now I've learned that if something doesn't come out, I will suffer. I don't want to suffer in that way anymore.

My two worlds are clashing, the old and the new, and I'm caught between them, learning how to navigate through this time of shift and change. Making decisions about how to use my energy is a key element of this transition time, selecting who I want in my life, and who I don't want. I'm conscious of the need to use my energy for what's most right for me now. I'm learning that I have the power to control my energy by making decisions that are energetically beneficial to me.

April 20, 2004

I dream that I am just a pile of rocks. I piece myself together and try to stand up but I just fall apart again, back into a heap of rocks. I'm aware that I'm being too hard on myself, trying to get through this period by ignoring the real issue.

I can't hold the old self together any more. I can't hold myself in the new alignment either. I'm so tired of the old me and I'm not fully my new self yet either. I'm stuck in this in-between place, just a pile of inert rocks. The metaphor is apt.

I continue to encounter the huge ball of pain, the orange ball of anger and frustration. I don't want to admit it really exists because then I have to deal with it, all the emotional pain the sixteen-year-old girl has been carrying. It's why I've had such a difficult time merging with her, because I keep bumping up against that huge, fiery ball of pain. If I admit it exists then I'll have to tackle it; I'll have to let it out.

I meet with Chuck and, unable to bear the tension of the big orange ball of pain, I leave after a few minutes.

"I can't stay, I need to get out of here, go for a walk."

"Would you like me to accompany you?" he asks, gently.

"No, I want to go home first," I say.

"I understand," he says.

I drive home, barely taking in the road ahead of me. I go into the house, into my bedroom, and crawl under the covers with all my clothing on. After a while, I get up and go for a walk. I walk in a daze, for perhaps an hour, walking fast, attempting to run off the fire, away from the orange ball of pain lodged in my chest. Back home again, I call Chuck and leave him a message, telling him that I walked, that I know I can't keep running from it, this pain, but that's all I want to do. I hang up and crawl back into bed, needing some kind of comfort.

After a while I get up to pee, take off my outerwear, my shoes and jeans, and crawl back into bed. I'm aware that it's time to finally deal with this. Maybe when I see Nicolas this afternoon.

And my car is not fixed! It's spewing again! The mechanics swear it's me. I know they're right. It's all about me and my own need to spew my guts, to relieve myself of this inner pain, to totally let go of all I've been holding in for so long, the orange ball of pain, and the blackness encapsulated in it.

Chuck calls me back. He says that walking is good, and suggests that I keep moving, and find a way to deal with it. He reminds me of all the tools I have at my disposal, but I'm so depressed that I have difficulty talking to him, and nothing he says penetrates my depression. In the end, even telling myself that I'm depressed really doesn't help. It explains how I feel, but it doesn't help.

During my Embodyment session, the sixteen-year-old girl appears. She tells me she always needed a mother, but never found one. She's carrying this humiliating secret, along with the ball of pain. What she always wanted was a mother to love her, talk to her, make her feel safe and protected; a mother she could tell things to. At first, my adult self doesn't feel equipped to handle her emotional pain, having so much of my own, but I realize we have both been pushing the same pain away, not wanting to deal with it, not wanting to admit that it even exists.

As the session progresses, the pain at first appears to be an evil force, that small monster I felt a few weeks ago. Fueled by the idea of escape, it wants only to get out, at all costs and as fast as possible. It's really only still inside me because I've held it in. It wants out so badly that it tries again to break out through flesh and bone during the session, appearing to be evil, when in reality I know it's only desperate. I do experience a small amount of release, and a small upward movement, during the session. My ears and jaw begin to pop and I suddenly have the thought, "Oh, of course, it's because of the altitude," meaning that as it rises upward it's gaining in altitude, causing ears to pop, as if I'm Sisyphus pushing a big boulder up a steep mountainside.

"It's getting there," Nicolas says.

The sixteen-year-old confides again that from the very beginning she has felt the lack of a real mother. Even now, as an adult, I feel the lack of a mother too. I feel that girl's tremendous sense of loss and her tremendous need, especially since there *was* a mother in reality. She was always right there, but she was totally unavailable, even though she was needed in a most tragic way. I understand that I must be the mother figure now, for both of us, because I too could still use some mothering. I tell my sixteen-year-old self that, yes, it was a painful life, that we are full of pain, but we can continue to release it.

"I am our mother and I am a good mother; I have a lot of practice," I tell her. "We *will* be happy together."

I notice that my right side is holding tightly to the orange ball of pain, while my left side attempts to push it out. I struggle with these two opposing forces, the one attempting to hold onto the familiar pain, while the other tries with all its might to push it out. In the end, a sort of calm acquiescence is achieved as the two forces drop back, as if on cue, letting the ball sit there between them. With a truce called, the two sides agree to disagree, at least for now.

Today was indeed a different day. I feel a change in my body, in my muscles, and in the exhaustion. I was so depressed in the early part of the day; I could think of nothing that was good. I was totally lost, but then, in the session with Nicolas, I found a part of myself that did indeed want things to be different. I held hands with that young girl self and felt our mutual sadness and pain, and yes, our deep humiliation at wanting something from a mother who could never supply what we needed and desired most. Our new desire to connect and change has allowed us to slightly shift that huge ball of pain, still lodged so deeply inside us, but movement has begun.

April 21, 2004

I wake up from a dream where I'm telling Chuck that I'm okay today. I went to bed earlier than usual last night and slept really well. My dream is right, I do feel better today!

I'm still having difficulty confronting the needs of my sixteen-year-old self. She's so angry! She's especially angry at her mother, a woman who completely alienated herself from her child, abandoning her to a fate that she herself allowed. She enjoyed her own pleasures while sacrificing her own child to a monster, and then cut herself off from that child, as if she, the child, were responsible and at fault. It was always the child's fault. Luckily, the child forgot. The mother counted on that; she counted on a child's ability to forget. But even so, the child encapsulated the abuse and the neglect, storing it away inside her. In some of the deepest caverns of her body and mind she hid them, where they lay buried for nearly fifty years. Now it has all resurfaced, like a murdered child's body being uncovered by time, wind, and erosion. And with exposure comes memory, pain, anger, fear, and sadness.

This recapitulation has been a haunting experience, to say the least. Now I stand before my sixteen-year-old self. I see her so clearly, that great bundle of anger and pain, full of such incredible suffering, and so needy still, yet also so strong. Spiritually she was always strong and resilient, capable of so much more than just mere survival.

To mother myself is indeed my biggest challenge—to become the mother I always needed. It was the biggest loss and greatest lack in my childhood, and I know that trying to fulfill that need is now the most important next step. So, how to do it? Creating a comfortable home is one important step, a safe haven; a place I want to come home to and enjoy being in. To find some peace here in my little house is a good beginning. To provide the basics, such as food, clothing, and enough financial security to live comfortably is the next thing.

Dealing with depression, picking myself up every day and going to work, is possibly the hardest thing right now. The need to constantly withdraw from life is intense, for indeed, I am in the process of recapitulating the needs of my sixteen-year-old self, especially her need to retreat in order to save and protect herself. This recapitulation takes over every single day. How do I recapitulate and still go to work?

"*Stop clenching your jaw,*" Jeanne says. "*Paint, breathe! Work intensely on yourself. Take advantage of all the gifts that are given to you. Trust in everything you are given.*"

Okay! Thank you!

I go to the studio and paint the big orange ball, mostly with my left, nondominant hand, which Nicolas suggested I do. It's definitely a therapeutic experiment. In the middle of this, I get a call from a reporter with the New York Times who says he's writing a story on the arts in the area. I tell him about the old factory where I have my studio and the art gallery I exhibit with. We set up an appointment for him to visit this week. Last week I was interviewed by a local newspaper about my mural paintings, making me wonder why I'm leaving my studio. Is this really the right time to shut it down, when there's so much stirring? After that I get a phone call from an artist friend who's ticked off about some stuff going on at the gallery. I talk him down to a cooler state. I send out an email to the other artists in the gallery, trying to drum up a little enthusiasm for the place, which is losing its energy and focus. I don't like to think it has anything to do with me withdrawing my energy from it, but to be honest it certainly looks like it. "What will we do without you?" someone moaned to me the other day. "You'll be fine," I said, as I talked of leaving, of putting my energy elsewhere in the coming months.

A friend asks me if I would like to share her small studio in the building for a modest monthly fee. I tell her I'll think about it and meanwhile she should decide what she might charge me. It would be quiet and private, and a lot cheaper than what I'm paying now. But am I really worth it, and do I really need it?

"Stop putting yourself down so much," Jeanne says. *"Lift that girl up and tell her, face to face, that she is worthy and deserving of everything good that comes her way; that she is capable, smart, and talented. Tell her she has everything she needs inside to make a very interesting and productive life for herself."*

April 22, 2004

Even though I slept fairly well, I awaken exhausted. I'm so tired of this struggle, of not resolving my internal and external conflicts, of being in a position where the old stuff can still get me and knock me out for a few days. Why can't I resolve this? Why is this recapitulation taking so long, and taking so much of my energy?

I go to the studio to try and forget about everything for a while. As I drive over, I wonder if I should sell the house, rent an apartment, get out of debt and move on. Do I stay because this is the safe haven I need now? Do I give everything up and just get any kind of job? Where is clarity?

The morning at the studio has been extremely busy. Several people stopped in, encouraging me not to let things get me down, to keep going, sure that clarity will come over time. I know I have to be careful before I take action, that I have to step back and be sure that my decisions feel right, for all parts of myself.

My friend with the small studio upstairs stops in and proposes that I pay her $150 a month to rent half of her studio, no extra charges. I tell her that I'll seriously consider it. And with that, I'm able to acknowledge to myself that I've been afraid to completely withdraw from the building, from the other artists and the energy here. I'm afraid to isolate myself too much, afraid I'll just sink into deeper depressive torment and despair. I really am making good progress, but I find it so hard to get my body to let go of this old stuff. I'm able to acknowledge that lingering attachments to the past are really all that keep me locked in this terrible no man's land.

I constantly pull myself back on track, to the place where I've begun to feel comfortable and happy with my life. I know who I am when I get there, and it's a good place to be. And from there, the future does indeed look bright.

I ponder the dilemma of my sixteen-year-old self. I struggle to find a way to mother that girl, but she scares me because her needs are so great, and she's so angry, and so quiet. I see her standing beside me, yet unable to accept anything from me. I try, but as usual she just presents me with that fiery orange ball of pain and emotion, everything she's held inside her for the past thirty-five years. And for now, it's way too much to handle.

I fled from her pain because it was such a nightmare to begin with, and now here I am reencountering that nightmare, hating it all over again. She's extremely withdrawn, so quiet, her body rigid and tense, with such heightened vigilance, alert to anyone coming too close. Her life is completely ruled by trying to protect herself. She's on alert all the time, ready to run. She's physically restricted because of the incredible tension in her body. I feel it now in my own body; the hunched shoulders, the clenched stomach, the constricted hips, tight jaw and throat. I feel her seriousness, experience her emotional withdrawal. She's full of painful memories. I'll have to go through it all with her. We'll have to dissect her life, recapitulate and relive again all the fear and anger, address the pain, and learn to speak about it.

"It's all over," I whisper to her. "It's over, it's finally over. Sleep now. We'll talk more tomorrow and you can give me the big orange ball to hold."

April 23, 2004

I notice immediately that my mood is better today. I'm not as raw and edgy as I was yesterday. My talk with the sixteen-year-old seems to have paid off.

I've reached a decision to accept the studio share, the offer too incredible to refuse. I feel good about it; I'll still have a painting studio. Today I meet with the reporter from the New York Times; that should be interesting.

And how is my sixteen-year-old alter ego doing? I went back and took a good look at her from my adult perspective last night. I saw that frightened girl trying to protect herself as best she could, keeping everything inside, intent only on survival. I'm aware that she constantly wanted escape from her life, and she wanted magic, and real rescue too, but rescue only came in the form of escape, first in creative escape, then in physical escape, in finally finishing high school and going away to college. She never really escaped the lasting horror of it though, all that lay deeply embedded inside her body and memory. Only now am I finding ways to remove it, like in my dream of chipping away at the painted self-portrait, when that shaman came in and scraped it all away and told me to start over, to create a new me. Well, I'm starting over, stalking a new me. This time around I'm armed with awareness, freeing myself of the last stronghold, that tough little sixteen-year-old self.

Doing the recapitulation breath, I go back to her. I find her standing in the woods, holding that big fiery orange ball. I try to convince her to put it down on the ground between us, telling her that if she does, it'll roll away and destroy itself, that it'll burn and melt away into nothing. I explain to her that holding onto it is the same as fueling it, and at the same time it's draining her life force, taking her energy. The longer she holds onto it, the longer it will cause her great harm.

"Put it down," I say. "I know you want to. You've been calling to me all week, telling me that you're ready, that you want to release it. I'm sorry it took me so long to get here. I couldn't find my way back to you. I didn't understand what was needed, but now I clearly understand what we both need. In order to merge and go on from here, we need to put down the ball of fire."

"It's nothing but pain to us. We must hold onto the truth that, in its consuming of itself, we will be free of the evil control it has over us. It has been stealing our energy in order to keep itself alive, stealing our breath away for its own sustenance, and that's why we've been so exhausted lately, so tired. If we don't put it down, we *will* die. It's it or us."

"You are my inner child, my other self, the one I thought was surely dead, but you aren't dead at all. You've simply been a captive in time, in memory, caught in those by-gone years, living in the dark woods, burdened with holding onto that ball of fire. That's what he told you to do, didn't he? He told you that you would die if you put that down, right? But I tell you, you will live if you put it down!"

"Please, for your sake and mine, put it down. It's over. The abuse is over now. Put it down. I see you standing there with that burning orange ball in your bare hands, scorching hot and blistering, hurting you still, after all these years, consuming your strength. If you just put it down for a minute you will feel your strength grow. It won't be flowing out of you anymore, wasted, but will stay within, giving you the strength to finally defy him. After a lifetime of carrying his awful burden, you will be free. This is our story, our true story, and we are going to write the end of it now. Do you understand? We are going to end this trauma together, now. Now is the time."

"We'll work on it all weekend. We'll release it somehow. It doesn't belong to us. It isn't a natural part of us; it was placed there by that evil man. Think now about putting it down, while I get ready for our day. Find one last ounce of strength to put it down. It's rainy today, and that will help. The rain will put out the fire, and cleanse and soothe our wounds. Then we'll rest, give ourselves time for our strength to fully return. Without the fire to tend, it will return much quicker than you think, and we'll have great creative powers instead of draining energy."

"It's over now. Keep that in mind as we go through this process. It really is over now. Life is coming. Breath is coming. Strength and energy are coming. It's all over now. It's over."

"And remember, my little one, you will know me by my teeth. See my teeth? They are your teeth. Feel them. Everything else has changed but not our teeth; those poor battered teeth are still the same. You can feel them. You know it's true. I *am* you."

"I feel you wanting to disappear, but you can't, you have to stay and take that first breath of freedom. Only you can do that. It will be easier after that. That first breath is always the hardest. This is going to be challenging, but we can do it. We have help and protection, and we are surrounded by love, incredible love. Come on, just take one good deep breath."

"See how easy that was, just one deep breath? Now take another. Yes, it hurts, but it's easier than the first breath and it will get easier and easier. That's all for now. It's time for me to go have my day in the real world, but I'll check in with you often to see how you're making out. Okay? It's going to be okay. We're going to have an incredible experience. Keep breathing. I love you. Remember that. I love you. It's all we need, love and breath. Keep the breath moving."

It's pouring rain. I'm at the studio, a little nervous, waiting for the New York Times reporter, but I'm happier and more energetic that I've felt in a long time too. It was that breath we took. I know it was. As soon as we took that first breath, I could feel a new beginning finally taking hold.

This process of putting down the ball of fire is going to be difficult and I suspect there will be a struggle. The abuser's energy will try, with all its might, to reassert control; it's his job as a petty tyrant to continue to pester. But I've already begun to free myself of him; I've begun to breathe. And having discovered that breathing means release, and life, and energy, I know I'll be okay. I just have to keep the sixteen-year-old girl focused on the task too. Once I went back and really took a look at her last night, I remembered what I was up against. I also realized that I did have to leave her behind and forget about her in order to move on, to learn some valuable lessons, and be able to return one day, when the time was right, and that time is now.

I found my way back and she was still there, holding that ball of fire, afraid to put it down under penalty of death. As soon as I went back to her, I was back on track, my path clear once again. I knew immediately that it was exactly where I needed to be, recapitulating my sixteen-year-old self. She needs rescue now more than ever. I do have to be the mother, in spite of all the needs I myself still have.

"Look, Jan, you are the adult," I told myself, "and only you can save this girl, and save yourself at the same time. Just go do it. Go back and face what's so frightening. Find out what it is that keeps you stuck."

And then I revisited her and knew it was time to free her. I know now that it's over, that he can't kill me anymore, that my own mother is never going to rescue me, that there's no one except me and my sixteen-year-old girl. I have to stop fearing the burden she's been carrying for me all these years. I have to face it too, dismantle it, and show her that it isn't necessary to carry it anymore. We're working on it, one little breath at a time.

It's eleven a.m. now and I'm still waiting for the reporter. I've been working through this process while I wait; a task terrible and wonderful in equal measure. In fighting off the abuser's energy, it literally feels like I'm physically fighting him, fighting his intrusions into my energy field. I do this by breathing and calming myself, by reminding myself of who I am, what I'm doing this for, and why. With a breath, I shake him off and reset myself. The sixteen-year-old girl is counting on me. She needs me. We need each other. No one else can do this for us.

Whenever I look for the girl, she's still standing there in the woods, still holding the orange ball of fire. I keep reminding myself, and her, that we have to keep moving forward, let go of the ball of fire, let it die. We won't die. We will live.

This is a major battle.

The reporter from the Times calls to say that it'll be another forty-five minutes before he finally gets here. At least it's stopped raining, but I'm tired now, my enthusiasm for his visit at about nil. Some of the other artists in the building are also getting tired of waiting for him. I had alerted them of his coming, in hopes of introducing him to them and the work they're doing.

He finally arrives, a quiet, shy guy, who seems nervous and vaguely confused, as if he's not sure why he's here. He says he doesn't drive often and had borrowed a friend's car to get here. I'm starving by now and wonder if he'll suggest we go out to lunch. I think about several places we might go, where it's quiet and we could talk. He looks around the studio and asks me some bland questions. I begin to get the feeling that he's interested in something besides this, that I'm just a supplier of sorts. I get the sense that he wants something from me and that he didn't really come to interview me. I take him around to see a couple of the other artist's studios. He's very sweet to everyone, but he shows little interest. I detect that he's not even interested in art. So why is he here? Even the building, an old factory, doesn't pique his interest. I ask him what he's planning on doing in the area. He doesn't really have an agenda, he says, which I think is pretty darned strange.

"Okay," I say, to get things moving, "I can show you the gallery in the next town up."

I expect him to drive, but he makes an excuse about not liking to drive, so I drive, even though I'm a little nervous. I'm not feeling threatened by him, but definitely starting to feel used by him, and I'm worried about my car, since it's been overheating so much lately.

As we drive, it becomes clear that indeed, he has no real agenda, that he's expecting to be taken care of, and this pisses me off, but his vagueness immediately places me in a position of control. I try to think of things to talk about, try sparking a conversation, but he's perhaps uncomfortable, or not interested in talking, since he makes no attempt to respond. He seems very depressed. He just sits next to me in the passenger seat, despondent, looking out the window, giving nothing more than a grunt every now and then. I get angrier and angrier as we drive, wondering how I got myself into this. I can't help wondering how he could be doing his job with so little energy, no plan, and nothing of interest to talk about. I wonder what the heck he's doing here, and why I'm showing him around? I'm hungry, bored to death and fuming by the time we pull up to the main crossroad in the little town where the gallery is. As I brake at the stop sign, my car shakes violently, rattling and shuttering with a loud groan. I fear that it has finally died.

"Did you hear that!" I exclaim, my anger suddenly gone, as now I'm worried about my car.

"No," he says, "I didn't hear anything."

And now, I really think he must be pretty dim to not have noticed or felt my poor car shaking to death. I give the car some gas and it shakily hobbles through the intersection. I pull into a parking spot hoping that it'll restart when we come out again. I even say a little prayer: "Please start when I come back, please get me out of this!"

He looks around the gallery a bit, showing absolutely no interest, and once again I wonder what he's doing here. Maybe he didn't want to come. I suggest that I take him back to his car and send him on his way. This is fine with him, though I sense his reluctance to be sent on his way so soon. He hints at some other places he would like to see, but I'm now more concerned about the state of my car than his New York Times credentials; I refuse to baby him or be his tour guide. I'm ready to dump him!

Luckily, my car starts right up and we drive back in silence, for I have totally given up trying to entice him to talk. Back at the studio parking lot, I give him directions to the other places that he's interested in visiting, if "interested" is even the appropriate word in this case, since I still can't figure him out. He has no engaging personality, no spark of interest in anything, and I still get the feeling he came for something other than what he originally said was his reason for visiting the area. He asks me if there's a place he can get something to eat, not too expensive, "like a few dollars," he says, "a sandwich or something." I give him directions to the bagel place and watch as he drives off, so happy to see him go!

I go inside and eat the lunch I had prepared for myself earlier in the morning, on the off-chance he might not take me out to lunch. And then I drive over to my mechanic. He very gently and kindly tells me it's time to take it to a dealer. He's at a loss as to what it needs. The only SAAB dealer for miles around is notorious for being very expensive, but I call and make an appointment for Monday.

During the afternoon, I get several phone calls from people thanking me for being so thoughtful in bringing the reporter to meet them. They all wonder what he'll write about them, but after my exhausting time with him I am not too hopeful that it will amount to anything. I get a call from a member of the gallery Steering Committee, thanking me on behalf of the gallery too.

"I'm happy to do it," I say.

"You are really the right person for it," she says, "no one would have been more appropriate."

"We've all been talking about you," she says, and I realize I must have heard that phrase spoken a dozen times this week. I am in people's consciousnesses. Several people had wondered how the guy from the New York Times had gotten my name.

"I don't know," I said, "my name is out there in the arts communities."

I get home by six. Tired, I do some breathing exercises and then relax into shavasana for a while. It's hard to unwind, though I know I'm back on track, the recapitulation energized, unfolding again, as it should. The old energy of the abuser pulled me off track, confusing me, keeping me in a state of high anxiety for days, but in the end it's all part of the process. I know it'll be back, but for the time being I keep it at bay by watching some comedy shows. By nine o'clock, I turn the television off and focus again on my experiences with the girl, my sixteen-year-old self. It's what I have the weekend for. The kids are away and I feel that I can handle it now.

This recapitulation process happens, for the most part, in another dimension, but it's a dimension where I am as alive and real as I am right now in this reality. I feel the sixteen-year-old girl inspecting my teeth, running her small cold fingers along the inside of my mouth, making sure I really am who I say I am.

"You will know me by my teeth," I had said. "Yes, it really is me. There's that bad tooth, the one that had the root canal at sixteen."

Rare for a sixteen-year-old to have a root canal, the dentist had said, but I know I was so stressed out by then that I had to erupt somewhere, and that was where it happened.

We meet in the woods, my sixteen-year-old self and I. We stand and face each other. As usual, she's holding her globe-sized ball of orange fire. I tell her that she doesn't have to hold it anymore. She wants me to take it, but I tell her that neither of us want it, that it's draining the life from us, stealing our energy, and that she should put it down. If she puts it down, it will burn out, I tell her.

"It can't survive without your energy," I say. "It's like a parasite. It feeds off you. You've been giving it the energy that we need for ourselves," but she's afraid that if she puts it down, she will also die.

"That's the lie he told you: I'll kill you! I'll kill you! If you ever tell, I'll kill you! It's the same lie your mother told you: You will never, *ever* speak of this!"

She is definitely afraid that it will take on a life of its own if she puts it down, that it will swirl up like a whirling dervish and encompass her in its ball of fire. I continue to soothe her, telling her that there's nothing to fear, that she won't die. In fact, she will gain life, and her life's breath will go to herself now and not to the lies and fabrications of an evil man.

"You can't be harmed anymore," I tell her.

She tries to give it to me again. She would rather pass it off to me, let me be the one to put it down, but something makes me reject it. Instinct, I guess, instinct that I shouldn't even touch it, that if I take it, I'll be in the same position she is, that we will not have solved anything, simply passed the ball to a new energy source for him to suck off. My energy is already so low that, luckily, I cannot even bear the thought of taking it off her hands. I refuse. I can't deal with it now, and the harder she pushes it toward me the harder I close off, guarding my energy.

I see that she regards me as her savior, so, of course, it's instinctual to say, "here, you take it, your turn to hold it." But, really, she needs to act alone. I'm not here to save her, but to facilitate a healing, ensure that we both reclaim our energy, and take the right steps toward new life. She needs to be the one to get the ball rolling, so to speak.

"It doesn't belong to either of us," I say, "and without the connection to your energy it can't remain alive. As soon as you drop it, we'll be free, and every breath we take will belong only to us now, to us alone."

"It's over now, honey," I say. "It's over now. It isn't going to hurt you anymore. None of it will hurt. He can't hurt you. He can't hurt me. He can't touch us. It's over. It's finally over."

In holding the fiery orange ball, she thinks she's in control of it, that her intent and focus keep it contained, and thus she's safe, but really, she's wasting her time and energy on it. It has no power of its own; it only has the power it has stolen from her. It's a parasite, and if she doesn't let it go, it will suck her energy for eternity.

The belief that it was hers to carry was placed there by him; the belief that it was her fault, that everything was her fault, and that she had to suffer as a result. If she can only let it go, she'll see that it has no life of its own. It's the power of that man in her memory that keeps her holding onto it. We'll just have to keep wearing down the memories so they no longer have power either, because it really is over now. There's nothing to control, there are just old memories. There's no real threat anymore, there's just the memory of threat.

"Drop it," I encourage her. "I see the path it will take. It will fall to the ground and roll under that bush over there and burn out."

Suddenly, she drops the big orange ball of fire. As we watch it roll away, I wonder if I too will be able to release the tightness of the holding. Will this act relieve my pain as well, my own very real physical pain?

"Look at your hands, they're fine," I say. "They aren't even burned! Everything is okay. Now breathe and make room inside you. Just breathe a little every day, just enough new breath to feel real and alive. I know it hurts to breathe now, but you'll get used to the fresh breath of new life entering your body."

We embrace. With that big ball out of the way now, we can begin the final leg of this healing journey.

"It's over, it's over now," I tell her. "The whole thing is over. Breathe deeply, and slowly let new life in. Let the old stuff burn out. Let the memories go. He can't hurt you. It's over."

She needs so much care, but she'll be all right. She'll learn to trust, and someday she'll feel safe.

I'm tired now. It's time to sleep, to let it all go, to rest and to dream; to dream of happiness, truth, love, and kindness.

Thank you, Jeanne. You guide me every day to what I should do, and every day I do it. I trust you. I trust that I will have enough money to pay my bills and take care of my family, that love and life are out there, waiting for me, that I will have trust and truth in my life. You have taught me well. Thank you.

April 24, 2004

I slept well and wake up feeling like I'm still on track. I go back in active imagination to where I left things last night, back to the woods. She's still there holding the ball of orange fire! Even though we successfully worked through the process of release last night, she's still standing there, puzzling over everything we talked about, trying to make the right decision on her own. She's as slow to make a decision as I often am!

The ball needs to be put down, there's no doubt about that, but I also understand the difficulties involved in doing that, and the incredible sense of loss and emptiness that comes when something you have held onto for so long is finally let go of, even something horrific. There are bound to be repercussions. I have to keep reminding myself, and her, that it's over now, that the whole terrible thing is over.

"It will only continue to hurt if you hold on. It will drain all your energy in order to feed its own power. Without your energy it has no power. It has the power it steals from you. It's a true parasite and it has been kept alive by feeding off you and your memories. Let it go."

"How? Just drop it?"

"Yes, just drop it."

She tries to drop it, but it doesn't leave her hands.

"Shake it off. Toss it. Fling it as hard as you can."

"I can't help myself while I hold it," she says. "I can't use my hands and arms while it occupies them."

"Put your arms down and it will fall to the ground. Hold your breath as long as you can and let it go on an exhale. Exhale, and drop it. Exhale, exhale. You've already rejected it mentally; that was step one. Now step two is to physically drop it."

"You don't need it," I remind my sixteen-year-old self, for the umpteenth time. "You don't need it. Let it go. It doesn't belong to you. It's alien energy. It's evil. It's consuming you and destroying your life. You don't want it or need it. Drop it, and let it roll away. Exhale it, exhale, exhale!"

"Trust the process. Trust yourself. Trust all the gifts you are given. Everything is working out fine. Don't be afraid. Drop that parasite. You don't need it or want it. It needs you in order to survive. Without you, it will die. If you're worried that you're killing something that could possibly deserve to live, don't. This thing has survived way beyond its necessary lifetime. Let it go."

"It needs to be annihilated and only you can do that. You hate to kill even the ugliest of bugs, but if that bug were attacking you, you would step on it, even if it would sicken you to do so. You know you can do such a thing. This is like a wild boar attacking you and it's time to fight back. You won't lose anything. The memories belong to you, but his evil draining of your energy doesn't. This is the last of his control. This is the final phase of all that brainwashing and slavery and numbing control. If you hold onto this, he wins again. It wasn't ever your fault, but now you have the power to stop it!"

"There may still be stuff to work on after this phase, some memories, but you will have the power to deal with them once his energy has been disconnected from yours. You don't want this large mass of fear and control to block you anymore. Let it go. And then go wash your hands of it. Wash your face with all those tears that never fell. Cleanse yourself, body and soul, and then breathe in the life that belongs to you alone. He can't have you anymore. He doesn't deserve you. He doesn't own you. It's over, honey. It's over now."

"Shall we do this together?" I ask.

"Aren't you afraid to touch me?" she asks.

"No, I'm not afraid to touch you. Your hands are cold even though you're holding this burning ball. Okay, ready? On the count of three… one, two, three! Throw it away! See it under the bush? It flares up and dies. It dies now. It can't live without you. It's over."

"Hold me. Someone, hold me," she says.

"Breathe now, easy slow breaths, just breathe," I say.

With my arms around her, I feel her struggling to breathe, my own chest and lungs laboring. After five minutes of short gulping breaths, I feel her calming down.

"You're safe now," I say. "You are safe," and then I feel her crawl inside me, where she knows it truly is safe, inside this adult body that belongs to her now too, that *is* her.

Finally, it is done.

She's safe inside me, curled up, sleeping like a tiny, quiet fetus. And that is enough for now. I'm going to help her evolve, and under Chuck's continued tutelage I'll learn what that truly means. But, for now, she needs rest, safe and peaceful rest.

I can already feel my own energy returning. No one is stealing it from me anymore. And I feel only great contentment myself, mission accomplished.

I spend the rest of the day at the studio. A few people come in, and I lock in another commission, painting a china cabinet. I think about the events of the past week, of that other reality I spent a lot of time in, and the process of establishing balance between my two distinct worlds. I revisit the rescue of my sixteen-year-old self and the calmness I now feel, knowing that she's safely inside me, part of me, that she's home at last. I must guard and care for her, help her recuperate and heal, help us both stay focused and on track, as we bring this recapitulation to its completion.

I will keep writing and learning about who I am. I will let my guides teach me and help me, and I will trust that everything will work out just fine. This whole recapitulation process has unraveled like a fantasy novel, or perhaps a horror story, but it's my true reality, the story of my two worlds and the process of rediscovering and merging them. Both are equally real, equally difficult to deal with, and equally full of magic.

I have successfully merged with my child self, the sixteen-year-old girl, who carried the burden of the past for all the other little girl selves. I am utterly grateful that the worlds have finally merged, and all the parts finally integrated. I've landed in a new reality today, a third world, the merged one.

Things are already happening to underscore that the old world has broken down and a new world is forming. My car, my vehicle from the old world, is breaking down. Bills are beginning to pile up again and I have no money, though so many promises of money to come. I'm emerging from the old world like a penniless wanderer who, having traveled for decades, traversing many worlds, is finally home.

Thank you, Jeanne, for helping me get where I am today; it's been a long journey. Thank you, to both you and Chuck.

April 25, 2004

I wake up in this new land, depressed but determined. I have to get the car fixed tomorrow, get out the lawn mower and see if I can get it working again. I have to paint the peeling trim along the top of the house and solve the cat problem. One of them keeps pooping in the house.

"Just do one thing at a time," Jeanne says.

I face that although I have no money at the moment, absolutely none, I will be able to pay the bills next month because I have enough work coming in, but I have nothing extra. I have no food for the kids' lunches tomorrow, except what I can scrape together from what's in the fridge.

I can't fall apart now, when I'm just on the verge of success! I have to keep it all together. I've gotten through the really tough parts, now I just have to figure out how this new world is going to work, and to do that I have to stay organized and focused, working on one problem at a time. Everything is a challenge to be met and overcome, but everything is possible too.

When my father calls and asks if I have a new husband lined up yet, someone to support me, I get furious at his assumption that I can't take care of myself, which leads to my own old assumptions arising and attacking, all based on what I was taught, that girls don't work, girls don't earn a real living, girls get married. My old low self-esteem issues kick me right in the gut, of course.

"You will never make it," my father says. "Get married."

I tell him to shut up, but then I still have to shut down his negative voice in my head, the one that says I don't deserve, that I'm not worthy of a job and earning a living. I don't want to constantly be apologizing for working and wanting to be paid for what I do. I have to turn up my own positive voice instead, the one that reminds me of how talented I am, how hard I work, how good I am at what I do, how worthy I am and that I'll be just fine.

While that little girl sleeps inside me, curled up and safe, I have to learn how to take care of me now. I've finally rescued her, and maybe that's all she needs, but now I must rescue myself. I feel calm when I think of her. Maybe she won't wake up. Maybe all she needs is to be there. With her safe and secure, I can begin to work on the adult me. How do I get myself to feel safe and secure too, full of healthy self-awareness and self-respect? I saved her, so I ought to be able to save myself now too.

I have faced my demons; I know my enemies. I must face the final demon, the one inside me. The reward is full ownership of self.

FUCK! The washing machine just broke! I am so sick of everything breaking, and yet I know it's just another wakeup call, telling me to get my act together and take ownership of my life in a strong and empowering way. I must not get defeated by life, even though I'm sick of the stress and the worry, and not having enough money. I hear my father's voice again, saying: "You'll never make it." Well, fuck that! I *will* make it. *I can do anything.*

I head out for a session with Nicolas. As soon as I arrive, I announce that I don't want to talk.

"Let's just get to it," I say.

"Okay," he says, "that's fine," and we set up and he gets right to work on my left, emotional side.

The sixteen-year-old girl starts to wake up and I know she's bringing up some disturbing issue. Suddenly, I'm caught in a nightmare. A rush of cold salty water enters my nose, smacking into my brain with a thud of such pressure that my eyes hurt. I'm drowning, my head about to explode. A memory comes of being caught in a wave at sixteen, at a beach on the New Jersey shore, of being dragged out to sea by a powerful undercurrent. My survival instinct kicks in.

"You're okay," I say, "you know how to swim, don't let it drag you under. Swim to the surface. Don't fight it; just swim to the surface."

I struggle to swim, the weight of the water tremendous, the undertow holding me down. I look up and see the surface of the water far above me. I see light streaming down through the water, fingers of light reaching down to me, and then Jeanne comes to me.

"*Don't fight,*" she says, "*just let it flow, let it out. If you fight, it hurts too much.*"

These gentle words guide me until I'm ready to give up the fight, until, finally, I acquiesce. As soon as I give up the fight, I'm on the surface of the water, floating on my back. Every now and then a wave comes along and stirs me. Other than that, I achieve a certain degree of calmness.

"No more fighting. I'm just open to this experience of my body," I tell myself.

"*You are surrounded by kindness,*" Jeanne reminds me, "*just go with that thought.*"

And that's what I do, saying it over and over again: I am surrounded by kindness, I am surrounded by kindness.

I stay in this calm place, peacefully floating on top of the water, gently buffeted by the waves as Nicolas works on me. At the same time that I can allow for this relaxing calmness, my nerves are on edge, and every time the electric radiator in Nicolas's office clicks on, I jolt. Whenever I jolt, a big wave simultaneously crashes over me, but I'm able to recede back into gentle, shushing waves again, until the next click of the radiator.

When the session is over, I can't move; I don't want to get up. Eventually, Nicolas suggests I sit up very slowly. He does Reiki over my heart chakra. He wonders if I want to talk now.

"No, I don't feel like talking," I say, and I leave, feeling so ungrounded that all I want is for someone to lie down on top of me, to press their body against mine, human to human, the heavy weight of them pressing me back into the physical, so I can feel real in my body, grounded in this world again.

The old demons are pulling at me. They're angry because I have her now. They're out to get us, prepared to destroy everything I have in this life to get me to relinquish our newly merged energy. Am I crazy?! But that's what it feels like, a life and death battle between me and some alien energy, but energy I know so well. It wants me back.

April 26, 2004

The kids go off to the bus and I spend a few minutes trying to return to the peacefulness I felt yesterday, the floating on the ocean calmness. Maybe I'm just feeling sorry for myself, but everything seems to be breaking down; the car, the lawn mower, the washing machine, my stability. My old dreams of collapse and destruction are coming true. I feel like bad luck itself, and I want to tell people to stay away from me. When I get like this, I get angry and hard on myself, which really only makes matters worse. What I really need is inner calmness and steadiness, minus the drama. I remind myself that making any decisions in the midst of drama is always a bad idea, to wait a week and see how things unfold. Let go; don't take things so personally. Life will change; it always does. Remember, I am surrounded by kindness, I am surrounded by kindness, I am surrounded by kindness.

"Keep breathing," Nicolas reminded me yesterday, "you can't survive unless you breathe."

The final battle between worlds has begun. The old world tugs at me, infusing me with vaginal and anal pain, but I stay focused on what I'm doing in the moment and on where I'm going today. I do believe there's a lot going on in my favor, behind the scenes, and that it will all come right in the end; that my guides are lining things up for me; that this desperate time will conclude at some point, and I will be a wiser and better person as a result. In the meantime, I have to keep my head above water, not drown in the old stuff, but turn on my back and just float, calmly and serenely, as I did during my Embodiment session yesterday. It's the best I can do right now. I must strive to maintain that calmness without going numb, staying even-tempered and accepting, even when I need and want things to hurry up and get done. I must practice patience.

I don't want to wake up the sleeping girl. Perhaps if I concentrate on my intention to keep her in slumberland a little bit longer, the calmness I desire will be more easily achievable. It's important that she stay safely asleep. It doesn't mean I can't talk or cry or feel. It doesn't mean I can't get upset; it just means I need to return to calmness often, reminding myself of where I am now, and of all that still lies ahead. I must pursue rest and calmness, before the next storm, because I do believe the biggest battle still lies ahead.

I see a bleak, Lord of the Rings type landscape laid out before me, my path of life a Middle Earth scene, with armies gathering on the horizon in full battle gear, while I and my small band of supporters remain focused on our daily tasks, not ignoring the gathering storm, but dealing with each single thing as it arises, one step and one day at a time. Otherwise, just the sight of what is to come would destroy us. If I look ahead, panic sets in, and the sure knowledge that this journey of change is far from over. I have to deal with the first contingent of warriors to arrive, the pain bearers, who come sneaking up on me as I go about my tasks. I deal with them methodically now, one at a time. I protect the girl. They can't have her, she's with me now, and I will protect her at all costs.

She's safe, and that's all that matters. It's where I find the good in all of this, the main purpose of this recapitulation, the return of my child self to her rightful place inside me, an integrated part. Now that I have her, I have to keep her. In spite of all the setbacks, all the onslaughts, from the physical and the mental to the emotional, and in spite of all the self-doubt and seemingly destructive tendencies that I continue to confront, I have, in fact, done what I set out to do. And not only is she safe, but she trusts me.

Every now and then, I feel her inspecting my teeth again, her small cool fingers feeling around in my mouth for the familiar lie of the tongue, the shape of the teeth, the fillings, as if she's reaching out in her sleep to make sure I'm still here, and that it isn't just a dream, that we are one.

"It's okay," I whisper to her, "I'm here. You're okay now; you're safe," the same way I whispered to my own children when they were small and needed me to just be there for them, unconditionally, to just hold them.

I have to be strong and protective, reassure her, when all I really want is to feel safe and secure myself. I also know that each day brings change and that each changing day brings me one step closer to achieving my own perfect world. Each day, anything can happen.

In the meantime, I keep tracking. I watch for signs, take note of dreams, synchronicities, triggers and sensations. And I listen. I continue to listen to the inner voices, now more than ever, the calm voices of reason within that tell me I'm on the right track. I listen for guidance from outside of me too, resonating with what I already know on the inside, trusting that I'm on the right track, with my own spirit leading me.

If I get pulled off track, I know I'll find my way back, that it's probably just a minor slip-up, or even a bit of trickery, but no matter, it's only a temporary misstep. There's always a way back. I'm attuned to the cosmos these days too, in alignment with the stars and planets, connected to the spiritual entities that care for and protect me. My whole body and soul are available for intuition and guidance. I am open and willing to receive from a higher consciousness. And I am grateful.

At the SAAB dealer, I get such bad news that I am stunned. I just don't know what to say when they tell me that the repair will cost a minimum of $1500 and two days in the shop. I stand there, tears welling up, involuntarily falling down my cheeks. I can't speak for such a long time that the guy who delivers this news to me just stands and stares, as if no one has ever reacted in this manner before.

"Do you need to call someone?" he finally asks.

"There is no one to call," I say, a little too sharply. "Just leave me alone for a minute while I collect my thoughts."

I sit down, shaking, and stare at the mute television screen, faces talking, no words reaching me. They will not help me here. I decide that my credit card will have to take this hit, since it's the only way to handle it, and after a few minutes the guy tiptoes back into the waiting room and asks if I've made a decision. I ask if it's okay for me to drive the car until tomorrow morning.

"Yes," he says, hesitantly. "But I suggest you drive as little as possible."

"I have some things I have to take care of," I say, and I make an appointment to return the next morning at nine. I drive home and the first thing I do is call Chuck to change the time of our morning appointment. Then I call my Benefactor to find out if he can pick me up at the car dealership, after I drop off the car.

"Finally, I get to be useful!" he says, heartily, and I can just about hear him clicking his heels in delight.

I call my ex-husband and arrange for him to do child transport over the next few days for our busy children, with their afterschool activities, performances and rehearsals to attend. I postpone a couple of other job-related appointments until Friday, including the delivery of some painted furniture that would have produced a much-needed check. The money situation is so bad that I had to scrounge around looking for loose change to pay for the dollar toll over the bridge this morning. The kids even chipped in a few coins.

This is just a minor setback, I tell myself, stressful as it is. I know I need to calm down, though it feels like everything is blowing up in my face, literally, as far as the car is concerned, because it looks like the head gasket went. That was probably the great shaking that occurred when I was driving the New York Times reporter around. Synchronistically speaking, it was exactly what I felt like doing while in his company. With these kinds of occurrences, however, I tend to blame myself, to get angry rather than acquiesce to the inevitability of such things happening for a reason. It must be my fault. I always feel that I should know better, be a better car owner, take better care, that I should, at all times keep everything in tiptop shape. I have to stop beating myself up and remember that it's all impersonal.

A few weeks ago, when the car began running rough, I had the thought, "Oh a valve job, it needs a valve job, and I don't even know what that is!" But my intuition was right because they told me the car actually does need one. I'm just beginning to learn how to pay more attention to intuition and act upon it too. I think I'll be heeding its warnings much more often in the future!

I pull into my driveway and see a newspaper lying on the ground. Something makes me open it rather than toss it into the recycling bucket, as I normally would. Almost immediately, I see an ad for an interesting job at a local environmental research center. I take it as another sign, not to be missed. I update my resumé and write a good strong letter, taking my mind off my worries by focusing on taking positive action. I send off an email application for the job. Twenty-five minutes later, I get a phone call from a woman at the center, asking if I can come in for an interview on Friday morning!

"Yes," I say immediately, "I would be delighted."

Something is happening behind the scenes, something else is lining up. I have no idea what it is, but I can feel it, supporting and preparing me for whatever is to come, firmly guiding me to stay the course. I feel dual energies at play, as well, the magical and the evil, the light and the dark, parallel forces working for me and against me, the old and the new. The big battle I sensed coming is now being played out, on so many levels, and in more than one world! This *is* the final battle, and it's already well underway.

Meanwhile, the girl sleeps soundly. I find her easily now. I go to her and feel her calmness. I breathe in and exhale long calming breaths with her. I intend to keep her safe and protected while my battle for my own place in the world is being fought, even as the evil energy still attempts to sabotage everything I do. It has gotten into the machinery I rely on, but it will not get back into me.

My child self will sleep through the battles to come, so deeply asleep is she. Occasionally, I feel her reaching to see that I'm still here, that I'm who I say I am; I feel my teeth being checked. Meanwhile, I constantly get messages to remember that I am surrounded by kindness, to take advantage of it, to reach out for it, and even to ask for it. Those are the messages I received today when I sat in the waiting room of the car dealership and cried over the cost of the repair. When I said that there was no one to call, I realized that in fact there are lots of people I can call. I am surrounded by people. I am open enough now to accept that there are people who really mean it when they say they want to help. I had called a woman to ask if I could put her down as a reference on my resumé and she immediately blurted out, "you'll get a great reference from me!"

I am certainly surrounded by kindness, and it's only because I've allowed myself exposure to the world. I've allowed myself to become part of life, to reach out, to join in, and I've been receiving such gifts in return! I remember what Jeanne told me a few months ago, *"Exposure brings out lots of life—exposure to knowing and then being able to act on all you know—trusting. Trust in all the gifts you are given."* I certainly have allowed for exposure, and I have learned to trust all the gifts I am given. Jeanne's words set me on a new course. I opened up to so much more healing and I'm able to more easily acquiesce to the unfolding of this journey.

I clearly hear the voices of firm evolutionary intent guiding me now, and I know what to do. This time of struggle has a purpose, even if only to get me to the fed-up point, alerting me to the fact that I'm done with the struggling, that I really do want to get beyond it. I've put out my intention for getting more jobs, for making a better living, and although nothing is really steady enough to my liking yet, I see the slow beginnings of something growing here. At this point, more than anything, what I need is a more stable financial situation. Getting to a safe place within myself enhances the prospect of achieving that.

April 27, 2004

I dream that I'm in an old building with a bunch of old women, sorting through old stuff. I'm aware that renovations are coming soon.

"Keep the destination in mind," the women say.

I can't wait to see Chuck this morning. It feels like I've been holding back a dam all week. This has been a week of natural disasters, as if all the stars and planets lined up for attack, an astrological week full of turmoil. And yes, it is actually a time of eclipses, full of big changes and strange phenomena, posing decisions and conflict, coupled with tremendous pressure. I have felt and experienced it all.

I fill Chuck in on everything that's been happening. He reminds me that the abuser's energy, what little is still embedded inside me, will try to take my energy back, and that he'll use fear to do so, it being his main weapon. But Chuck reminds me also that it will be an attempt of short duration now, for I'm aware of him and his techniques, and I've learned how to fight back. I've also learned how to protect my own energy and not let him control it, with fear or anything else.

"He's a sprinter, he takes short jabs at you," Chuck says. "His attacks will always be surprise attacks. He'll sneak up on you when you least expect him. It's how he operates. He doesn't change, but knowing that, you can outsmart him."

I must keep my head clear, at the same time that I must stay focused on staying on track, on my new path of heart. If I sense his energy, I must immediately shift away, fool him. I must be smarter and trickier than he is, or ever was. I must destroy his energetic attachment by totally detaching my own energy from the past where he lingers, and will forever, unless I completely recapitulate every aspect of him. Anything that still lies inside me, whether in memory, in energy, or tightly clenched in the very muscles and sinews of my body must be eradicated.

"He can't get you because you believe that he can't, and that is your weapon," says Chuck.

At this point in my recapitulation, my own stability is paramount, and so I must stay alert to what comes at me, both the negative and the positive, fight off the negative while being open to investigating the positive for what it might potentially have to offer.

"The job you are interviewing for may be the right one, or it might not be," Chuck says, "but it may offer a jumping-off point, an opportunity to shift."

"Come on Friday morning, and we'll prime you for the interview," he suggests.

"Okay," I say, "that sounds like a good idea. I haven't been on an interview since 1983!"

"And remember," he says, "disasters aren't just endings; they are the ending of something no longer viable and the beginning of something new."

The battle will continue until I totally let go of all attachments to the past. It's no longer feasible or healthy to compromise or compensate, either within myself or projected upon animate or inanimate objects. My car quite conveniently reflected what was happening in my life, took on the whole mounting tension of the past few weeks and suffered a major blow on my behalf. In the process, it actually showed me what was going on inside my own body. Had I suffered that blow physically, it would have killed me. My car loves me! Thank you! And Jeanne, thank you again for keeping me sane and safe, and thank you for reminding me that I am surrounded by loving kindness.

I know that I'm winning the battle against the abuser's attempts to steal back my energy because I snap away from him much quicker and more easily whenever he lays that heavy guilt over me, when he attempts to tug at my old feelings of being at fault for what happened, when he seeks to laden me with shame and blame. Chuck warned that he will continue to try to steal my energy, but I've already noticed he can't hold me as long and as deeply as he used to. He wants my energy bad enough so he'll keep trying, but eventually he'll give up, because he won't be getting anything in return. Only then will he stop.

"A sprinter of short bursts will give up after a while, but the long-distance runner, that would be you, will head off into the sunset," Chuck said.

I know this, and I am prepared. I don't really care what he throws at me now. What could possibly make me want to go back? All of this is metaphorical, on the one hand, a means of stepping outside of the actual feelings and emotions in order to handle them. But, on the other hand, within my body and in the many different worlds that I enter as I recapitulate, this is very real. It actually feels like this is what's happening to me, that I am going to battle in a very real sense, no less real than meeting him in the woods as a child and being raped.

Depression is definitely a difficult place to be, but it's losing its comforting aspects for me now, as I no longer desire or need the kinds of comforts it offers. I want to create my own stable life where I can be happy, secure, and unafraid to personally accomplish whatever I wish. I don't want to be afraid of success anymore. In my newly forming stable life, the challenges that will arise will be nothing compared to what I've already been through. I will easily flow with what comes rather than automatically rail and fight against it. I will enjoy life and all that it brings.

I think I'm going to be okay.

I drop my car at the repair shop and wait only a few minutes before my Benefactor pulls up. He's so happy to see me; a big smile stretches from ear to ear, and he's thrilled to finally be useful. He repeats that this is his greatest wish, to be helpful. We have a pleasant ride home and I thank him for his help. We agree that he'll come get me tomorrow, when my car's ready to be picked up in the afternoon.

I'm amazed when I feel the pull to return to the old world. There's such a strong desire for the comforts of hiding under the covers, where I know the abuser lurks, where my energy ebbs so easily out of me as I fall into the darkness, where I am so vulnerable. This is a test. Or am I just really tired? The events of the past week have been so depleting and I didn't sleep well last night. I woke at five, all keyed-up, my mind racing. I'm just tired. I have to stay strong. If I get weak, I become a target. His energy won't leave if I don't take care of myself. He'll just hang around waiting for moments like this, and then he'll sweep in and take what he wants. I can't permit myself to fall into a weakened state of exhaustion.

I have two things to keep me focused while homebound. I have an article to write and the job interview to prepare for. I must, as Chuck said: rest, eat, take care of my body, breathe, and remember that I am surrounded by kindness and love. I have been preparing for this moment for a long time, my whole life in fact. This is the moment when I open the windows and let in the light, when I permit myself to trust, feel safe, and prepare for real growth. So, what do I really want, and what's stopping me from achieving it? What am I prepared to give up in order to get it?

Fear stops me. Fear is his tool, as Chuck mentioned today, and it's also his means of getting to me energetically. Once I'm caught in the headlights, so to speak, he easily swoops in, like the predator that he is, and energetically takes advantage of me, just as he did when I was a tiny child. It doesn't matter that it's an energetic reenactment of an old physical attack; the fact is that he still holds the power to stop me in my tracks because of mind-numbing, body-numbing fear. Fear is alien energy; I see that now. It has to be denied access, captured and picked through, dismantled into the raw energy that it truly is and redistributed in a new way. No fear is allowed, whether from inside or outside. Once I've conquered that, my energy will fully be my own.

What then do I seek in life?

The main thing I desire, at this very moment, is to have a steady income so I don't have to deal with so much fear and anxiety, the two alien energies that rule over me at the moment. I need stability and a sense of security within myself, with the only open door being the one I myself open, when appropriate and desirable to do so.

Creatively, my greatest desire is to write this story that is so ready to pour out of me, the story of this recapitulation, the journey into my own darkness, into the depths of my soul where everything has been sitting and waiting for fifty years for me to rediscover it, to break the old seals of silence, and reveal the truths of my life. I've been going into that inner darkness for years now, recapitulating for the three years that Jeanne told me it would take. They are almost over.

I'm not totally out of the woods yet. I sense I'm going to be dealing with the repercussions of this fact-finding journey for a while yet, but I'm ready to let the old stuff go. At this point, however, I still can't imagine ever having a normal relationship, getting so close to another person that I would have sex again. I can't imagine that sex will be okay, that I will feel comfortable engaging in it. Or is that just fear talking again?

"*Don't worry about that now,*" Jeanne advises. "*When it comes it will be right, the person will be right and the circumstances will be right. Until then, try not to think about it.*"

I *am* ready for new life, though feeling slightly stunned at the moment, as if waking up in a totally unfamiliar bed, in an unfamiliar bedroom, in an unfamiliar house. I'm aware that I do need new gifts of self, new powers of self-esteem, and I also know I won't find them sitting at home in my shell, as comfortable and comforting as it may be. I will only find new aspects of self by interacting with others, receiving feedback and reflection, by feeling resonance, and by opening the long boarded up avenues of trust. Mixed with the air of fresh new life, I must simply trust in life itself to provide.

"The time has come," Chuck said today, "to just believe. The signs are all there; everything is lined up in your worlds and working for you. Positive aspects are all working quietly on your behalf. Your worlds are prepared for the next step. Now there is only *believing.*"

"But beware of the fear," he went on, "it will reach out and try to get you. All you have to do is step away, outrun it, outlast it, outsmart it. It can't get you for long. You can't let it have the power. And the sooner it realizes it can't get you, the sooner it will give up."

I can't let it win. I can't let it get me in the old way. I've come too far and fought too long. I must take everything slowly and cautiously in order to stay safe and protected. *Believe.* That's the stage I'm at now, believing that I am exactly in alignment with where I should be, knowing that this is my path of heart, my true destiny. And so, what will be will come to pass, whatever it may be.

April 28, 2004

He sneaks in at night while I sleep, attempting to drag me back to his territory. I talk myself through the encounter: "It's okay, you're strong, nothing can hurt you now; you're safe. *Believe.* You are Neo, and the bullets can't hurt you. He is a wimp for coming in the night, for sneaking in like this. It just shows how desperate he is. He can't get you. You'll be fine. Just ignore him.

He's trying to wear you down, but he won't win. Move now! Shift! Get up! Don't let him near you. You'll be fine. You *are* fine. You are strong. It's confusing now because neither world feels right, but you are safe. Trust that. This will pass."

I wake in the morning in a panic, but I know it doesn't rightly belong to me. He's trying desperately to regain control.

"Breathe and remain calm," I instruct myself.

I am strong and independent. I don't belong to him. He needs me for survival, but I don't need him. He's parasitic, attempting to steal my energy in order to survive. The more I withdraw, the more desperate he gets.

"It's naïve to think he won't come back," Chuck said.

"Yes, I know that. I have no doubt at all that he will come back, he always has," I replied.

All night long, I tried to find a strong position to sleep in, where I could fight him off, where I wouldn't be caught off guard. I shifted, tossing and turning all night. I felt his presence in my bed, as real as another human being, trying to force me back to his place, back to his territory, into the embrace of his evil energy and the dark woods.

I remind myself that I really am that confident person who applied for that job, that smart and in-control woman. The more I change, the better I will be, and the more I'll be available to flow with what comes to guide me, though at the moment I'm still not fully comfortable in that new, flowing world yet. I'm still between worlds, in flux, in a tug-of-war, pulled back and forth. One side seeks to consume me and the other to set me free, out of the darkness and into the light.

There will be no rest for a while longer. In fact, rest is almost impossible since that is when he finds the opportunity to attack. I woke in the night feeling that I was being dragged from my bed, back into the past, into the woods, and I grabbed onto the new me, onto my new strengths, and kicked him out of bed.

"I am Neo," I said, "nothing can touch me. Believe!"

I can't continue allowing my car to do the work for me; it's too expensive! Instead, I must note what it's been trying to teach me, learn to read the signs of guidance in the objects in my world that I rely upon every day. I must no longer wallow in inertia but keep shifting.

With that thought I get up. Then I get the kids up and send them off to school, the whole time wondering how I'll ever be able to break through this seemingly endless war zone.

Seven in the morning and I can barely breathe, on the verge of panic. I remind myself that I'm doing okay, that these few days at home are good for me. I also remind myself that if I remain calm, I win. That's how I have to handle this. If I panic or begin to show signs of weakness or fear then the abuser's energy has his foot in the door again. But if I can breathe, do the sweeping recapitulation breath, I can breathe him out and breathe in calmness. I will remain calm and show him that he can't get me, that he can't affect me, and then I'll be safe. If I do not allow him entry, I win every battle and thwart every attack on my energy. Once he understands that I'm not available anymore, then my energy can refocus on my own needs. I do feel that things are going to keep coming together now more rapidly. The next week is crucial.

I told my sixteen-year-old self that it was over, that the war was over, and she has trusted me. She continues to sleep soundly through all of this, and I'm thankful for that. It's not her battle now but my own inner battle against the forces of the past, the final remnants of what was left deeply embedded in my body, and in the darkest of forgotten memories. I know that one day she will wake up, and then we will have to deal with her emotions too. But for now, while she sleeps, I have time to get us into a safer place, where we can experience a stable sense of reality, where our basic survival needs are met. We can tackle the rest later, because I know there's more to come, that deep down there's lots more.

I spend the day writing an article about an upcoming arts festival, interviewing people involved in the planning of it. I sit in bed with my notebook, making phone calls. One minute I'm suffering from incredible panic, unable to breathe, in the next shifting out of it and calling someone, questions at the ready, able to speak and be in control. Then I hang up the phone and dive back under the covers until I get enough energy to make the next call. I stay in bed for hours doing this, until I've contacted everyone on my long list of names.

This is an excruciating process for me, and would be even on the best of days. I am solidly introverted and this is a most unlikely undertaking for someone of my character, but, as the day wears on, I begin to feel like I'm partaking in life, that I'm entering and finding my way through a new world, and I'm pretty good at it. About a month ago, I had a dream of starting a new job and feeling the stress of learning something new, but knowing that I would be fine once I got the hang of it, that it would be all right in the end. That's how I feel now, still in transition but knowing that everything will be fine. It's pretty clear that things have been lining up for me now for a long time. Even the old abuser is being confronted by the changing of the guard that I feel inside myself, and that I feel in the good angel warriors working alongside me, guiding me to prepare for the end of this long battle.

I've been so stressed lately that everything has become a huge mountain. Every day I open the front door and am greeted by that mountain. I can't even get to my car without climbing over it. In reality, however, I know that most issues are only small problems, that things happen; cars need fixing, washing machines break, mowers need to be repaired. It's just that when they happen while I'm in a low position, they appear as impossibly steep mountains and everything becomes cloaked in heavy depression. When I'm standing at the bottom of the daily mountain of problems, I can't see anything except its ugly reality. It can take all day to get to the top, where my perspective changes, where I can breathe easier and see a lot clearer.

At the same time, I'm more aware of endless troves of untapped self-respect and self-esteem inside me, blocked by what's going on outside of me, patiently waiting for me to dig down deep enough to really discover it more fully. As I ponder the idea of working at a full-time job, as opposed to the freelance life I now live, I am drawn to the stability of it, the busyness of it, the contact with people. Yet, I know I need to more than survive; I need to thrive. I like being needed and useful, but I also need to love and care for myself, for my kids, to give us not only financial stability, but openness to new life, to accessing what's truly right. As regards the job interview tomorrow, I must listen to my heart.

The auto repair shop calls in the middle of the afternoon to report that my car is ready. I call my Benefactor and he comes right over to pick me up, assuring me again that he's available any time, that he really wants to be helpful.

"I realized I had to find a way so you aren't afraid of me," he says, "I knew I just had to wait."

And when he says this, I am struck by the truth of it, that I don't feel safe, not just with him but anywhere, with anyone. I note how his intention to help me, good though it may be, runs parallel to the abuser's desire to siphon energy from me, and although my Benefactor's offer is genuine, it still feels slightly predatory and a little creepy, though not in a sexual way. He's returning from death's door, having suffered recently with cancer. His energy actually feels depleted, so he naturally seeks younger energy, and specifically feminine energy, which makes me wonder why he's shown up in my life when I'm in the process of closing all energy drains. What am I supposed to learn from this relationship, and what might it really mean? Is it a test too?

I do feel a little safer each time we interact, more at ease and less frightened in an old sense, less like a sixteen-year-old girl confronted by memories of a sexual predator. I am fully aware, however, that I do not want my own energy encroached upon by anyone now. Not even by someone nice.

I thank him for the ride and after placing the burden of the repairs on my credit card, I get into my car and start it up. It actually *purrs*. It purrs all the way to my appointment with Nicolas, which, luckily, I didn't have to cancel.

I fall asleep a few times during the session, floating on a body of water, waves gently buffeting me. It's nice, easy to lie there, just floating, as Nicolas works. I feel something shift and leave my body.

"Ah," he says, noticing it too, "something releasing," and then I am very open, fluid like water, the clutching tension gone.

When I leave it's almost five o'clock and I am truly exhausted. I want only rest and sleep. I go home and lie down but immediately begin clenching and tightening up, especially when I lie on my left side. Finally, I get comfortable enough to doze off, lying on my right side. I dream of letting everything go. Every muscle in my body has something it needs to release, I am told, even my mind with all its preconceived ideas, beliefs, wants, and desires.

"Let go; let everything go, everything," a voice calmly tells me.

I must release it all, I am told. In order to truly be on a new path, I must begin with a clean slate; everything old must go. As I dream, I feel myself releasing and releasing, going deeper and deeper, as if falling out of myself, falling out of the old me. I am falling and falling, and when I wake up, I see that it's seven o'clock. I didn't just nap but really slept!

When I sit up, I feel different. The shift that began in my Embodyment session continued in the dream, manifesting more deeply. It really does feel as if I've slipped out of the old me. I really am, incrementally, making a complete change. If I dwell on the process, I become fearful, full of old fears, for I do have to acknowledge how frightening it is to allow for this changing self to materialize. I am still so full of such basic needs for stability in life, for love, for creative outlets, but I know I must let even these unfulfilled desires go if I am to truly change. I must become empty of all desires. In order to be open to the universe, which I know is just waiting for me, I must become nothing.

Even though I have no appetite I make something to eat because I promised Chuck I would. I'm still exhausted, though no longer carrying around that huge orange ball of fire and anger, no longer fighting the old demon abuser, just plain exhausted.

It's been important for me to understand the victim mentality, how it has played out in my life, to fully examine it and accept it, which has been hard. In the beginning, my ego would not even accept that I was a victim; no way, not me! I never let anything bother me; I was always strong, always in charge. I was never a victim! But I must not carry forth any attachments to the old self anymore, even the strong and stoic self; she does not get to rule anymore. I must soften and accept reality. I must empty out of this body everything related to the old self as I stalk the new self, allowing only the realities of the new self to emerge. I must believe, in *every* part of her.

I really am getting better. I feel it now as a real distinct physical difference, no longer just a possibility but a reality, as if I am recovering from a long and potentially fatal illness. One day, I will be fully healed and fully free. This I know for certain now.

Thank you, everyone, for another quite wonderful day!

April 29, 2004

I wake early, at 5 a.m., having slept much better than usual. I didn't fight the fear so intensely during the night, and I awaken in a state of peacefulness.

I'm pulling in all my separate selves now, forming a strong unit, not looking outside for everything I might need. I understand what it really means to look deep inside the self and find anchors there. I'm learning to believe in myself, and I'm beginning to allow life to come to me. I now understand the kinds of people I need to surround myself with, the kind of intimacy I seek, and the deepest desire inside of me, which is to continue to grow.

I feel a new form of love and tenderness for others now. The words, *I love you*, sit on the tip of my tongue, easier to say to people who are important in my life. Many people are saying it to me now too. I feel a new sense of calmness, as I recognize that I am, indeed, achieving a new sense of stability inside myself that I only had glimpses of before. I *can* do this life. I *can* handle everything that needs to be handled and, eventually, I *will be* centered and whole within myself. These things I know. I am my own mother and my own father now, and I have given birth to myself. I know who I am.

I am no longer afraid of life, but eagerly seek it now. Its many paths intrigue me, and I'm discovering, as I journey, where I should go next, looking for the next truth, the next means of finding calmness, balance, and peace. I seek that place within myself where I sit quietly and listen to the words spoken by the inner voice, the voice of spirit. The inner voice is my true guide, a voice of inner knowing and clear choice. There is no doubt in that voice, no question of what to do; only truth is spoken there. I'm learning to really listen to it, to pay attention to what it says.

The truth is, I had warnings from it about my car and my washing machine months ago, but I questioned the messages I received. How can I know things? How can I know that my car needs a valve repair or that my washing machine is going to break down, but on both accounts the inner voice was right! Rather than address what I was being told, I ignored the advice, until things got worse. But I *made* the decision to ignore, to *deny* the truth of my inner voice. It's time now to pay attention.

I'm discovering that when I allow myself to be open, I receive. When I put walls up and let fear stop me from being open, I go nowhere, no one approaches, and I am alone. Now I am open to receiving, so I receive. I am open to being loved and I am loved. I am open to being guided and I receive guidance. I have discovered the universe, and it is full of gifts. I am allowing myself to accept them as they come. I am open to giving and receiving at all times, to keep a constant flow going. And I do understand that I am safe now.

My relationship with my children is becoming less stressful now too, as I find ways to reduce the stress in my own life. The past few months have been incredibly stressful, in all aspects, for all of us, thus the blowing of the head gasket was not unusual. Something was bound to go! With reduced stress, the acceptance of my need for stability, and my being able to allow myself to receive, as well as give, has slowly turned me into a new person. I have worked so hard all these years to find this person, this softer self, and I like her. I like who she is and where she's headed. I trust her and the people she's choosing to surround herself with.

I feel incredibly lucky, capable, smart, and beautiful now, things that once seemed so foreign, that belonged only to others. I feel love all around me and I'm not afraid of it. Perhaps that's the biggest change; I'm not afraid of love having a place in my life. I'm rich now because I've allowed people in. I now know how important it is to trust others.

Stalking A New Self

I go to the studio, still in a state of peacefulness. I had no idea it was even possible for me, but here I find myself immersed in a deep pool of calmness, just being me. It's partly a real feeling and partly a feeling of wonder. Is this bliss? Whatever it is, I like it. It happened because I allowed it to happen. I get that now. Over the past few weeks, I was caught in a tornado of stress, spinning with frustration and confusion, unable to find my footing, having left the old world and unable to find anchor in the new one. Now I've been spat out, released from the old self, and I find myself in a new world. The storm has passed. It has left my vicinity. I am safe now.

Everything I need is right here. I just needed to open my eyes, my heart, and my arms. I needed to change how I perceived the world, and how I lived in it. I live in a new world now, because I accept it as such; it's that easy. But, oh, the journey has been rough! Every strength and every character trait in me have been put to the test. I don't think anything will ever shake this peacefulness out of me, at least not for long, and certainly not permanently. Everything was inside me all along. I just had to allow for a shift big enough so I could tap into it. I've changed. I know I'm going to be fine, absolutely fine.

I struggle to remain connected to these new insights, to remain at peace as the day goes on, so, of course, *it* attacks! I was full of quiet peacefulness for a long stretch, so of course the old voices came taunting.

"Do you really think this will last? How dare you feel happy? How dare you imagine any such thing!"

They laid it on pretty heavily, but I was ready for them, and I handled them quickly and efficiently. As Chuck says, when something advances, something else pulls back, it's just the way it works. But I like this peacefulness, and I expect to have a lot more of it now. Everything is coming together now. My time has arrived.

I realize that my energy level is still unstable. I felt exhaustion creeping in at midday. I drank a lot of water, which helped, but I skipped having coffee in the afternoon so I didn't get my usual boost of energy from that reliable source. Without it, I notice the ebbing of my own energy, the effect that the trauma has had on it. The energy devouring stress, and the equally consuming fear have had me as a steady source of energy, as I've lived the life of a traumatized being. Now I understand that the peace I experienced today is my own energy, my true energy slowly replenishing, as I recover it from my traumatized past, but it's not fully recovered and operational yet, and I must protect what I've retrieved. I must learn how it works, what it feels like, where and how to spend it, and how to keep nurturing it, so it continues to grow and flourish after the stressful years of depletion.

Tomorrow, I have the job interview. I'm looking forward to it. I must look pretty good on paper, though there's a lot I didn't include; teaching experience, my published books, and the articles I've written. I intend to be calm and optimistic. I'd like to be as serene and sure of myself, as full of belief in my abilities as I felt today. I want to be full of love too.

April 30, 2004

I wake at 3 a.m. and spend the next few hours tossing and turning. I'm aware of two of my cats nestled at my feet, of the little one curled up by my head, and all the noises the house makes at night. Finally, unable to sleep again, I sit up and meditate on the interview, on establishing a good, positive attitude. Seeking peace and calmness within, I push the old voices as far away as possible. Peace, I want only peace.

I contemplate my good traits: stellar organizational skills and habits, my tenacity, persistence, memory for detail, excellent communication skills, nurturing skills. I am an idea person; I take the initiative and run with it. I love working independently. My bad traits: reluctance to call it quits, tendency to overwork, giving way too much of myself.

I have a calm session with Chuck. He suggests that I take time to reassess where I am and what my energy feels like throughout the day, at least three or four times during the day.

"Check your alignment," he says, "readjust into the new pose, the new posture, the new position, or whatever is it that makes you feel safe and at peace."

"The old habits will always be there," he says. "It's all about the physical. The old physical postures bring it all back, so you must reassess and realign often, bring yourself out of the old postures and into new positive ones. It's the only way out, by creating new physical habits. Begin with lowering the shoulders, opening the chest, and breathing. Maintain equilibrium."

I see Jeanne come into the room, but I look away from her. Afterwards, I wonder if maybe she just showed up to support me, as I'd asked her to do last night. Maybe she just wanted me to know that she's with me.

After the session, I go home and get ready for the interview. I feel extremely calm about it. I do some breathing and get myself dressed. I don't want to appear depressed. Quiet is okay, but I need to be able to talk. I need to get my head into a good conversational place. I'm staying away from coffee today, focusing on maintaining the place I'm in right now. Too much cockiness can get me into trouble, take me away from the new true me, and make me vulnerable. I know Chuck is right, that calm and steady refocusing during the day will be necessary.

Listen to your heart, I chant repeatedly, as I head out to the interview. I knock on the locked door of a temporary looking building clinging to the banks of the Hudson River. I am invited into a tiny, overcrowded space.

The woman interviewer's energy is low and gray in color. She shakes my hand and asks me to sit at a large cluttered table piled high with books and file folders. The table sits in the middle of a crowded room, surrounded by tall file cabinets, also piled high with books, folders and papers. The room also serves as a passageway and people pass through every now and then as we sit at a corner of the table and talk.

"Oh man, this job is so totally not me," I say to myself, as soon as the interview begins, for it is immediately apparent that I would have to hide all my new true personality traits—my sensitivities and intuitions that I'm just learning to trust, my emerging energetic self—and put my old armor back on.

The position includes dealing with the organization's nonprofit Board of Directors, supervising student interns, planning fundraisers, coordinating large events, setting up catering, hiring musicians, sending out invitations, press releases, etc., the list is endlessly ridiculous. Just listening to the job requirements stresses me out, and I begin to feel my energy ebbing, going gray too. I feel as if I've stepped into an alien environment. I notice that every inch of the building is crammed to the max. There is, in fact, the woman says, no office for this new staff person to work out of. All my flags go up.

"You already decided you don't want to do something like this," I tell myself. "Yes, you have a lot of the necessary skills, but this is just way off track, far from who you are now."

With only enough money in the budget to make a six-month commitment to whomever they hire, it seems utterly laughable when the woman tells me that the job also includes having to hire an assistant. I stop the poor woman, cutting the interview short by telling her, quite honestly, that we should not waste any more time, that it's not for me. I'm a creative person, I say, it's far too administrative. She understands perfectly. I thank her for having considered me, and wish her luck in her search.

As soon as I leave the building, I take a deep and grateful breath and immediately feel my alignment click back into place, as if I'm resetting a clock, moving the hands to the correct time.

"This is the right alignment; now remember that," I hear. *"This is what it feels like."*

Feeling much more like my new self, I practically skip down the rutty dirt road to my car, my energy returning, happy to have gotten away.

"I listened to my heart, I listened to my heart," I say, looking up at the trees, and they sway in the breeze, responding, acknowledging me and my spirit.

"Yes, you listened to your heart! You listened to your heart! Hurray!"

"You know," I say to myself, as I drive away, "you're really happy doing what you're doing. It's creative; it has great potential, and you are your own boss. You're free! You don't have to deal with difficult people, which was apparently a real issue with that job. If anything, perhaps this experience is helping me more acutely focus on what is truly most important and meaningful for me. I don't want to be someone I'm not. My job now is to stay in alignment."

"Stick to the plan," I say. "Write, paint, be open to possibility and the work that is coming. People are helping me get through this tough time. I'll be fine. I'll get through this."

When I get home, the first thing I do is read my horoscope, which basically states what I already know, that I've been doing such careful planning and should keep focused on what seems to have come to a halt. In reality it's just coming into clearer focus, and a considerable amount of energy is gathering around it.

I am amazed! This is in perfect alignment with what I keep coming back to, that I need to stay focused on what's important, in spite of other stuff that tries to tell me otherwise. It underscores that although I applied for that job because I want stability, I have failed to give myself credit for the fact that I've been building, albeit slowly, my own stable base, that I've been planning and persisting and hanging in there for years. Why would I give it all up now, when I'm so close to achieving what I've always envisioned? It really does feel like just a matter of time. It's a clear message to stay the course, to be patient a little longer, and to realize that I'm almost there. Each day offers something new; I have to remember that. I'm not stuck! The reality is that I'm constantly changing and shifting. And to top it off, I'm thoroughly enjoying this new calmness!

There's a message on the studio answering machine from a local arts council director letting me know that the *New York Times* article we were all interviewed for will be in the paper next Friday. I let everyone know, so they can stop worrying about it, and then try to get some work done.

As I work, I am able to accept that the place I've been preparing myself for is the place I'm in right now. This moment, this new state of calmness, this contentedness is what I've been yearning for. I felt so relieved when I came out of that interview, changed back into my comfortable jeans, and called a client to discuss a painting job. It made me wonder why I keep trying to mess this up, this life I really do enjoy. I would certainly like to speed up the financial stability and slow down the emotional instability though!

"Stay the course; don't feel so lost, Jan," Jeanne says. *"You really are found; you've found your place."*

I take a long walk around the neighborhood in the early evening, the weather balmy and breezy. I accept that I do actually have a nice little life. I haven't been making near enough money yet, but I just snagged another big painting job and it will bring in a nice amount over the next two months.

I've had enough *disassembling*. It's time for *assembling* now. It's time to pick up the pieces and build something really stable and nurturing.

Chapter 5

War

May 1, 2004

I sleep most of the night on my back, dreaming many dreams. In one dream, Chuck repeatedly tries to give me a backpack. It contains happiness. I keep refusing it, saying I'm not ready for it yet. I don't trust it.

I'm still in the process of taking back my own energy from all the places where it's been ensnared. I'm still learning to protect it, making sure I have enough each day to keep me going. I need sleep, food, and calmness as I recover from the intensity of my recapitulation. I need self-care, nurturing and compassion for myself, but I also need to be a good mother to my own children. Thus, my energy expenditures are limited. Most of all I need calmness, the place I got to this past week, where I felt utterly whole and safe, strong and secure. In that place, I knew I could handle anything. In that state, I am more able to *hear* and *see*. I'm not sure I should be doing more than that. Even taking on happiness seems like too much at this point.

"*Jan, you are happy doing what you are doing,*" Jeanne says. "*You've been planning for so long, getting everything set up and ready to go. You've been building a structure and stability; a place for yourself in the world, the World of Jan, where you are safe and nurtured and surrounded.*"

"*Life is finding you,*" she continues, her words crystal clear, "*because you are open to it. It is coming to you. The whole universe is watching you and rooting for you. You are important. You have an important voice. You speak the truth. You have an innate knowledge of truth and are beginning to accept that. People need you to be open and loving. This is your life. This is the life you have been striving for. You are there now, living it. Remember that.*"

"Stop worrying about where you're going and open up to all that is around you," she goes on, "including the channeling ability. It will bring you richness, purpose, and a greater understanding of the universe. Yes, you do need to allow for it. It will give you confidence. Open up to it and you will begin to strengthen. You need to add strength to that calm center, a new kind of strength and confidence, and then you will have a more stable base."

Oh, I get it: the stability is inside me, not outside. It's not in money and job security and having things in this world, but in a strong core of *knowing*, which allows me to function in the real world while also connected to the greater universe. It's this new self-awareness that gives me a firm base. I have an ability that I will just have to open up to, without fear and anxiety. And that's the main thing, to not be afraid of being psychic.

"*Let go of anxiety and allow for truth. Listen. Open up to truth.*"

A channeling ability isn't meant to cause harm, it's only meant to present the truth, to give guidance. I understand now that it has to be used and presented in a safe way. I must find out how to use it. I understand that what we do with it is up to each of us, to those who practice it, but I feel strongly that it has to be used properly, given as freely as it is received. It doesn't belong to me; I am only its conduit. But a good conduit has to be strong and stable, in alignment with good energy. If I'm not stable in my own life, what good am I to others?

The reality of this world is just as important as the spirit realm, and I must deal with my broken washer and lawn mower, the bills for my car repairs, paying my mortgage, and keeping my home life going. All these things need to be taken care of, but at the same time, I need to be available to the messages that are coming to me, listen to the truths I hear, whether I feel ready or not. Jeanne is teaching me and I have to teach myself how to act upon what I learn from her. I feel that I must make changes immediately, so I can proceed along these lines in the right way, as her conduit, her channel, if that is indeed the right thing to do.

I'm not sure how all of this will unfold, but I do know that I must stay tuned in, connected, and in alignment with my truths. And, without fear, I must listen when spirit calls.

I feel different inside my body now, like I'm beginning to belong in it. I feel safer in it now too. I walk easier, with less awkwardness, flow a little more smoothly. I'm not thinking so much ahead of time about how to move. I'm not walking as quickly, looking as if I don't belong here. I'm realigning, as instructed by Chuck, but much more often than three or four times a day because I find that my shoulders are constantly hunched unless I'm exceptionally calm. It helps that I've cut down on coffee. I want my body cleansed, as well as my mind and memory. I need to stay focused and centered, my eyes on the path. I don't have to look any farther ahead than my next step. This seems to be the best method, otherwise life, both old life and new life, are too stressful to deal with. In the midst of it all, I'm gaining a better sense of who I am and what my place in the world might be.

When I look back, I realize the tremendous amount of work I've done on myself. I've spent years working toward creating a new self and a new good life for myself, wondering when I'll finally be there. Perhaps the time really is near.

May 2, 2004

I was tired and dropped right off at about 11:30 last night, but worry seeped in and woke me shortly afterward and then continued to rouse me often, insistently whining, mostly about money. Then heavy depression snuck in alongside it, and then a pile of self-doubt took up the space that was left. I tossed and turned with those old partners for the rest of the night, constantly shifting my attention and my posture, but in the end, the old fiends won out.

"Really, I feel like just giving up on myself," the old voice prodded.

Yesterday, I decided that my life was okay, that I don't really have money problems anymore, just a few bills to pay, and BAM! Today, I wake up and hate where I am. Chuck would say it's the old stuff making a last-ditch effort. It's a clingy predator, an energy-sucking parasite that loves depleting my self-esteem and anything else it can get in the bargain.

I shift my thinking to a more positive agenda. I have to be as insistent in my maneuvers as the old stuff is in its, staying one step ahead of it, constantly readjusting to a more positive frame of mind, to a positive attitude about myself and this new life I've been creating.

I take my daughter to a voice lesson and then deliver her to a friend's house before I head over for an appointment with Nicolas. During the session I focus on trying to find a way around the clenching, which arises the minute I feel a release coming; I immediately clench in anticipation, right up to my throat. I don't like it. There has to be a way to break the habit.

I breathe deeper so that as a wave of release approaches, I am full of breath, puffed up like a balloon, and that makes it more difficult for the clench to tighten. As I exhale into the clench, it loses its grip. The more I breathe in this manner, the more I notice that my right, guarding side becomes a lot looser, that my shoulder relaxes, that I have literally *let my guard down*. I suddenly realize I don't need it anymore; the old guardian has done her duty. The right side seems to be the most relaxed, while the left, emotional side, is still in check, still being held in, and in spite of the great need and desire to release I still cut it off for some reason. At one point, I think I'm going to start crying and that I won't be able to stop.

During the session, a very clear picture of Chuck's face appears, as if he's right in front of me. He looks very serious, pondering something in his characteristic, thoughtful manner, almost as if he's listening to someone.

"*What does this mean?*" I ask Jeanne.

She tells me to let go and be open to receive, to *allow*. Her message brings back the dream I had the other night, when Chuck offered me the backpack of happiness, which I rejected. I rejected happiness! Who does that!

"*Just be open and be you,*" she tells me.

By the end of the session, I'm very calm. I've been in this calm state at least three times now, so I know it really exists. It's a low-centered calmness, but it soon moves up to where all the trouble lies, into the chest, throat, and head. As it rises, it smooths out the rough edges, and all discomfort rides away.

At the laundromat. I sit in one of the hard, orange plastic seats along the perimeter of the room while my laundry chugs away in the machine. The place is empty and I'm alone, even though it's a Saturday. I've been running around, doing errands; time to rest for a few minutes.

Part of me wonders if it might be a good idea for me to get out of myself a little, away from so much inner searching, but the seeker in me realizes I'll only be a better person for all my work, and that it has to be this intense. If I'm not constantly learning I fear that I'll stagnate and that life will become routine again. I eagerly anticipate the work now, because I'm on a new leg of the journey, and I really am happy now, even though I'm not quite done recapitulating. I still have much to discover about myself, but when I'm finally done, I know that my life will fully belong to me; I will be free.

The old stuff is definitely putting up a fierce fight and I have no doubt that it will continue to do so for a while to come. It can be exceedingly loud, complex, and even tricky, the past intruding into the present, triggering time overlaps, glitches in the folds of the day, the veils parting when I least expect it. I can be driving down the road, or walking in the woods, and suddenly the world before me rips open and I see something so frightening that I want to run from it. The truth is, however, that what I see is something so familiar that sooner or later I know I'll go back to it. I'll step through that rip and face what's there, extricating my own long-lost energy from it. Experience has taught me that I'm finally finished recapitulating something when it no longer drags me back, when there's nothing left to hook or trigger me. Only then am I truly free.

May 3, 2004

I forge my way back to that new place of calmness, slow everything down, and take a look within. From there, I have a sense of everything being right, and a certainty that all the answers lie within. All my mantras and intentions culminate there, not somewhere outside of myself, and I have a sense of achieving the impossible. I get a glimpse and feel of something like bliss, and I want it again, and again. It's a place of perfect synergy; body, mind, and spirit in perfect harmony, no fragmentation, no unsettled tensions. It's utterly quiet in there. And the demons are gone.

My goal now is to get there as often as possible, and that entails completely letting go of expectations, desires, needs, controls, thoughts; a complete emptying of the usual baggage that has defined me. I feel like a traveler lightening her load as she hikes along her path, freeing herself of heavy burdens until she has given everything away, traveling onward with nothing except complete trust, believing and knowing that she will be provided with what she needs. This feels like the truth of my journey at this moment. I am truly traveling alone, believing in myself, feeling strongly that this is the right journey to be on. Though perhaps I have to let go of even that idea? Perhaps I must have absolute and total emptiness, even of my newfound self-esteem and confidence, even of my belief in myself and the trust I've gained as I've taken this journey. Is that possibly the ultimate goal? Total emptiness?

I simply cannot control what happens in my life. I can't control calamity, and neither can I control abundance, but I can acquiesce to what comes, making choices based on what arises, allowing and accepting what comes as necessary for the moment. Even though I may not be traveling along an easy road at this time, I continue to hold close to my heart the key that keeps me going. That is, trusting that I am on the right path.

Last week, when calamity struck in the form of mechanical breakdown, I tried to get control by looking for a job, seeking a remedy in an old thought pattern, thinking that I had to do something to reassert myself back in a familiar world. *Find a job* was the first old idea that came to mind. How often have I heard my father suggest that all of my problems would immediately diminish if only I would find a *real* job? Or a husband! But, in truth, I need to go with the flow of what comes to me, even if it's unnerving, because this is the path that I've carved for myself. It's taking me out of the old world and into a new one where nothing is exactly how it appears. In this new world anything can happen.

My physical body must learn to move with me into new life too, because I won't be able get myself to a new place if I can't get my body to shift away from the old postures and routines. If I can't get my body to try out something different in reaction to depression, sadness, and crisis, then I will not evolve. If I can't get myself out of bed, nothing will ever change either!

I do like this new life I'm creating. What I'm giving up are the structures of an old world that no longer suit me. I'm aware that even if I had greater financial security, my inner journey would be the same. I'm choosing spirit over security, as I've always done, even though I seek security above all else. However, it's not security by an old definition that I seek now, but a kind that exists deeply inside, a spiritual security, an inner knowing, as I listen to the language of my heart, as it tells me each day what I must do and where I must go next. It's a new sense of security in knowing that I can totally trust myself.

In climbing out of the darkness of my own soul, I've gained a higher level of acceptance and understanding, and I find that I climb out of the dark pit of depression much quicker now too. All of this is making me a better, more loving, open, and accepting person. My anger has dissipated to almost nothing and my judgments of others and myself are dissolving, as I find myself entering a new world. By working so hard on myself, by confronting my fears, I become a better mother, a better person, a better me. I'm changing, and I like it.

I don't really want to live alone, without a partner, but I realize I have to be very strongly anchored within myself, to know myself thoroughly, to understand how I operate before I enter into another relationship. To be available for a truly honest relationship I must continue to push myself, to evolve into the person I still only have glimpses of.

Every day I understand better and more fully what this recapitulation journey is all about, as I discover that life is so much broader than the mind can perceive, encompassing incredible expanses of energy and awareness that with the old blinders on I just couldn't see. I'm so much more than I ever imagined I was. I struggle to live more fully in this new world of energy and awareness now, to more fully see and experience everything from a different perspective. I work incredibly hard to maintain balance and stay aligned within these new parameters, within a greater, more expansive, interconnected universe.

I'm in a pretty depressed mood most of the day, with low energy and a low level of motivation in spite of my early morning insights and intentions. I end up having a cup of coffee in the afternoon, in spite of my desire to quit, seeking the temporary lift it offers. By evening I'm fighting the old battles again, the anal and vaginal pain, the self-doubt, and I'm so tired I can barely move out of the fetal position I curl into to alleviate the pain. I realize this is the same old boring routine all over again, where the terror arises, pulling me back. Once in the old posture the energy-feeding frenzy begins, but I don't stay there. I roll out of bed, force myself to get up and do some magical passes, some breathing, anything to institute a shift. Afterwards, I lie on the floor in shavasana, the pain lingering, wondering if it will always be this way.

May 4, 2004

I wake at 2 a.m., my hips burning in pain, taut as boards. I'm hot, can't get back to sleep, caught in a vise. Eventually, I fall asleep, still locked in the vise.

Ugh! It came in the night and got me, locking me in its embrace and I struggled to get away all night. As I awaken, my body is being released from the vise grip. Residual pain runs across my hips, and I'm totally swamped by depression, my energy stolen. Part of me knows something is up, more memories to recapitulate no doubt, but they sure are taking their slow time coming! I have a busy day, so there's nothing to do but get up and find my way to some energy reserves. Today is the feast of Beltane, with a full moon lunar eclipse, though not visible where I live. Apparently, it's an exciting astrological turning point. There should be a noticeable shift. Let's hope!

First, I see Chuck. Then I have a meeting with the art studio tour committee, then I have to finish writing the article about the art's festival, which is due soon, as well as finish up some illustration work. Then I have to clean the garage. I need to find some energy within myself, but first I'll go for the kind that comes from a cup of coffee!

"It's war all the time," I tell Chuck. "But maybe that's just the way my life is going to be. I just have to learn to deal with it, accept what comes and do the best I can. When this old stuff strikes, I write my way through it, waking in the night even, jotting everything down. It helps diffuse it."

I also mention the undercurrents of emotion and energy that come riding toward me on waves from others. I'm affected by walking into a room, able to read everyone's emotional state, suddenly knowing their deepest and most vulnerable secrets. This person is unhappy in her marriage; that one is struggling with loneliness; that person feels abandoned by his mother, that person wants to be taken care of like a little baby.

"Maybe I'm supposed to discover something in it," I say. "I've always been sensitive, but I used to shut it down in order to remain sane. Now I'm more concerned about staying grounded and in alignment. Maybe this is an ability I'm supposed to cultivate, though I'm not sure how or what to do with it. But I'm not afraid to open up to what the universe wants to show me about myself either."

I tell Chuck about a woman I've been dealing with, who can't make up her mind about anything—she can't choose a paint color or decide on a design motif—and how she makes me feel so sane and functional.

"Stay around her!" he exclaims.

"I'm okay," I say, "I'm doing okay," and as I say it, I know it's finally true.

I feel my demons sitting on the edge of the bed, waiting to creep in under the covers with me, and I cringe at the thought. I need sleep tonight.

May 5, 2004

"You are such a failure, totally incapable of life! You can't do life! You don't have what it takes to earn a living. You are a complete failure!"

I wake in a grumpy mood, the old voices taunting loudly.

"SHUT UP! Just shut up!" I say. "I know what you're trying to do; you're trying to suck me back. You're trying to own me. Well, you can't. I won't let you. I'm perfectly capable of life. I'm perfectly capable of earning a living. I am totally functional and responsible. I just need to get away from you!"

If I were not so sure of myself, I might consider myself crazy for talking this way, but for the past three years I've learned the hard way that such voices are terribly real, and that they also have real power, and so I take them seriously.

"Get back on the path, back on the path," I tell myself.

It's a daily struggle, the scent of the woods like a drug, a scent so strong that it takes tremendous cunning and strength to not be drawn by it; its heavy pungency overpowering, even from a great distance. Its scent reaches me over all these years and I begin to drift toward it, catching myself over and over again; don't go back, don't go back, stay on the new path, focus on putting one foot in front of the other. At times like these, the new path becomes a desert, hot, dry, and unbearable, the pull to the shady woods so enticing. But I re-anchor my feet on the new path, visualizing myself plodding along, focused on seeking new direction, new purpose, looking forward to the next step, for I can go no further than one step at a time.

I sit still for long periods of time, just being quiet, trying to find calmness in my inner world. I remind myself that I function just fine, that the things I need in life are here, just waiting for me; I just need to reach out. Even though I have new struggles to encounter each day, I also have new gifts. I wake up each day and know, for certain, that I am in a new world now. I look around and I don't quite recognize where I am, or who I am, and though it's unsettling, it's also fascinating, and my curiosity is stirred like a cat's.

I have a session with Lara. I immediately melt under her touch, accepting what she offers.

"When you first came here," she says, "your energy was so incredibly heavy, you can't imagine, but now I feel that you are much lighter, light and beautiful. You can't really understand how I work until you make some progress and gain knowledge and understanding; only then do things make sense. When the time is right, you discover how open you have become."

She expresses shock when I tell her I had applied for a fulltime job.

"Oh no, that would be terrible! Stay doing what you are doing," she says, much relieved when I tell her I got up and left in the middle of the interview.

"Whew! Don't let those anxieties get to you. You have to find a way to let them all go. Put them in a box somewhere; get rid of them. Stay focused, one step at a time, and don't panic. That kind of job would be so bad for you. You need to be free. You are getting better and better; you can't go back. Stay focused, even if it's only looking down at your feet. Stay in the moment. Fight the battles as they come and then move on, but stay on the path, stay on track. It is essential."

"You must keep painting," she says. "That is your inner voice speaking. You have to do it; it is where you are strong and beautiful. Having a painting studio still will be the best thing for you, you'll see. Turn your rawness into art by being creative; allow it to be expressed rather than building up inside."

She says I can eat everything now, except sugar.

"You are healing and getting better and the sugar will stop that growth and healing; it's not good, stay away from it."

I feel as if I floated into her house and floated out again, like a happy little butterfly, but I also feel weighed down by sadness, even though I fully acknowledge that things are good right now. I think I'm feeling the loss of the old me. She's going now and I know she needs to go, but I also feel such compassion for her, and sadness too as I watch her leave, and as I look back at all we've been through together.

I know I'll get what I need when I need it. I must be careful to not get too wrapped up in desiring anything, but simply state my intent and then forget about it. But I have lately learned that I must be out in the world in order to be available to receive. I must be in the right alignment with my intent, and active in the new world I'm creating for myself in order to find out what it has to offer me.

I could not clearly see or understand the life inside me until I met Chuck. When I first met him, I felt that I was dying, but he helped me to see and understand what was really happening in my inner world, that I was not dying but being pulled to transformation, and that I still had so much life inside me. Ever since that first encounter, I've been creating a whole new life.

Lately, people have been telling me I should write a book because they think I have an interesting life. Do I really have something to offer? I'm a real person having a real experience, learning to throw myself out into the world, off the ship into the ocean, to sink or swim, learning how to survive with nothing, how to catch a wave and ride it, how to find the energy to survive when survival seems impossible. I'm just having a human experience.

I am learning to trust the universe though, even while I scramble to stay afloat on that wide ocean. I know I'm not alone. Even if no one is near, a desperate plea will always be heard; that much I've learned. Every request for help I've thrown out to the universe has been responded to in some fashion, though sometimes it has taken me quite a while to understand the answer. It does not often come in the form I wish, the easy way, simply dropped in my lap. I've had to challenge myself to be in a position to accept the help that arrives, no matter its form. But I've also had to learn that it's up to me to empower myself and figure out how best to save myself. I've learned that no one else can do it for me, that there is no rescue.

May 6, 2004

In a dream, I get a large grant to produce a body of artwork. The grant makes me really happy but I'm also full of fear, certain I can't handle the commitment. "Every day you handle commitments just fine," someone says, contradicting my thoughts about myself. But I still feel like a fake, that I couldn't possibly be considered worthy of such a large monetary prize.

The truth is that I'm as worthy as anyone else! I have to remember that; I am as worthy and deserving as the next person. The old voice, as usual, has other ideas.

"You don't deserve anything!" it says.

My demons are a tenacious bunch, big bullies constantly abusing, harassing, and picking on me. Give me a break!

I do the sweeping recapitulation breath, clearing my head. I have to be careful about letting down my guard; can't let the old stuff creep in. It's so familiar and sneaky, I often don't notice it's there until it's firmly in place.

This I know: if I admit to defeat, and keep saying that my life sucks, then it does suck.

I sense Jeanne trying to tell me something, but I can't understand what she's saying. I relax into meditation, going deeper and deeper, and then it's as if I've suddenly opened a door and she's standing right in front of me.

"Just let it happen, unclench and let it happen," she says, holding my face in her hands.

"All things good will happen, all good will come to you. Time and patience and being open are the answers."

"If you don't open to what will come then it will not come. You have to let it in. You have to finish emptying the old to make room for the new."

I go to an Embodyment session. I lie on the blankets and we begin. Working on the left, emotional side, burning pinpoints of pain spread up my back until they meet the frustration I feel and the need to release, but also the impossibility of doing so. It's as if I've hit a wall. The physical release only seems to go so far.

I try different methods of breathing, try to find what works best for getting fuller releases. I breathe through my mouth, then through my nose. I concentrate on keeping my throat as open as possible. By breathing out on the releases they flow better, but there are so many of them I can't keep up. I become lightheaded.

"So, it hurts," I think, as I feel the pain, "accept it; let it out and it'll be gone and you won't feel it again. Then the next wave of pain will go through you and it will be gone too, and it will no longer bother you either, and so on. Eventually, all the pain will be gone and you'll be fine. Let the pain go."

When Nicolas begins working on my right, fighting side, I've pretty much figured out the breathing pattern that works best, and I exhale on the releases on this side too.

By the time we're done I'm so shaky and lightheaded I can't get up. It's only then that I acknowledge how painful the emotions are, hard and brittle, and hard to deal with as well.

"Sometimes you don't even know what they're about," Nicolas says, "but they want to release anyway."

I know that's true, because although I may have an inkling about what the emotions might refer to, I have no specific feelings about just these emotions; just that they're deep, have been long unattended, and that they need to be released. Many are lodged high up in my chest and throat, having worked their way up from deep inside, close to finally making their escape. Their ultimate goal is freedom, the same as mine.

After the session I feel like going home and crawling into bed for the rest of the day, wanting to hide with the emotions, but I know it's not a good idea, and besides I have work to do. So instead, I head right over to the studio to pick up the supplies I'll be needing for the day. I have to remember who I am and where I'm going. I also have to keep in mind how well I'm doing and just how far I've come.

For the rest of the day, I work at a client's house, painting a decorative floor. I let myself in with the key she's left me and bask in the quietude of an empty house, keeping my thoughts on the positive aspects of my healing process, and on the new life I'm creating for myself. I realize how important this new life really is, how much I want and need it. I stay in the moment, even when the moment is taken up with fighting my demons. I fight them and then I move on. I do what's necessary, but I don't get caught. The old life is done, gone, no longer in existence. Life now is only what lies ahead of me.

When I call the client to tell her that I'm letting things dry and I'll return in the morning, she says that she's been walking around in circles all day, her own antique business slow, but my phone call, my voice, really grounds her, she says, gives her focus. I'm glad I was able to help another person.

I walk into the house to the ringing of the telephone. I pick up the receiver and am greeted by glowing feedback on the article I'd written for the arts festival and for the accompanying illustration. I'd dropped it all off at the publisher's office on my way to work today, slipping it under the door. He's just picked it up and is very pleased, says he's going to make it be the frontpage lead article. Nice to hear! I'm grateful for the positive feedback.

Every day another thing falls into place for me, another puzzle piece clarifies who I am, another problem resolves. Today, I got notice that I'm eligible for the state health insurance at no cost. I have not had health insurance in many years. This is good.

May 7, 2004

I wake up at five with my period again, only twelve days since the last one, my knees achy after yesterday's work on the floor painting. Worry immediately sets in, but I push it away, focusing instead on how well things are going, how the work situation is definitely looking up, a lot of jobs lining up, which means a constant stream of money too. I promise myself I'll not worry so much, it's a useless pastime.

I sit in bed with a cup of hot coffee, planning the next steps of the floor painting, first finishing the decorative work and then doing the varnishing, at least three coats, with a day's drying time in between each. I felt confident and capable yesterday while I worked; I need to stay connected to those positive feelings. I've gotten good at changing my mood lately, shifting away from old depressive tendencies by breathing, imagining new life entering me. I notice that old emotions tend to stir when I do this, as if reacting to my progress, trying to reassert themselves with negativity and sadness. But I know they're moving out as I continue to change, and that, as with everything else that hates to give up its place, they are apt to make last ditch efforts to stay in my life. I'm focusing on maintaining good balance now, staying physically grounded in new physical postures—head up, shoulders back—maintaining a calm center and a new energetic awareness, while also using my new psychic connection more consciously.

Today's lesson from my session with Chuck is to step outside of myself and to look closely at myself from a different perspective, as if I am a third person viewing my situation. Who is she, what does she want, and what does she need?

I spend the day working on the floor again, then head over to the studio to answer phone messages and clean my brushes. The owner of the building comes in to show someone the space. He introduces me as, "rock solid, steady as they come." Where'd he get that from? Maybe I can help myself by writing down all this stuff that people say about me, until I believe it!

By the time I head out it's late in the day. My son needs a pickup at school and then he and his sister head over to their dad's house for the weekend. My own weekend intention is to be nice to myself, though I have to put in four hours at my own gallery on Saturday and four hours at the art cooperative gallery on Sunday. The rest of the time, however, is mine.

It's beautiful weather today. I stretch the day as long as possible, staying outside in the sun, planting some lemon balm, taking a walk. Then I eat and watch a movie; all efforts to keep the demons away.

May 8, 2004

I wake at 4 a.m., aching all over, with blood pouring out of me. I panic momentarily and get pulled into worry. During my visit with Lara the other day, she told me about a woman who came to her with tumors. She worked on her for five days and then the woman bled the tumors out. Am I bleeding out all this old stuff?

If I separate out the real me, the one who's been doing her recapitulation, and look at her from a different perspective, as instructed by Chuck, I can barely stand her pain. If she were a stranger, I'd be horrified at such a story. I'd want to shower her with everything; she would deserve everything. Why can't I do that for myself? Why is it so painfully difficult to receive?

"*Just let it go,*" Jeanne suggests. "*Just let it happen. Chuck is there to help you. He cares.*"

I know that. I know he really cares, and I know he's there for me, every step of the way, but this is my journey. I'm the one who has to take it, revealing every aspect of the lost memories to myself, bearing the tension of them, and feeling the rawness of my locked emotional self. I feel mentally, physically, spiritually, and emotionally much stronger now than I did a few years ago. Progress is happening, a little bit more every day, slow going though it is.

I must get up now, eat, and get ready for a busy day. I have a job being delivered to the garage this morning, a solid amount of work for the next month or so, and good pay, and then I have to get over to the studio.

Late in the day, I'm confronted by the sad self again. I hate having to confront this self, having to push her along to do something other than just whining about everything. On top of this, I feel a new inner issue arising. Something is coming and I can't stop it. I have no idea what it is, but the amount of anxiety I'm feeling reminds me that I'm not done with my recapitulation yet. I'll just have to wait it out, but in the meantime, I must keep going forward. I can't stop life from unfolding; I have to accept what comes. I'm certain there's a reason for everything, and equally certain that this time of struggle will not last forever.

I acknowledge that the negative voice I've always heard has been a true voice as well, as true as the positive voice. By acknowledging the truth of that negative voice something gets clarified; after all, it is another part of me. I acknowledge its realness and its unique strength, and the power it has held over me. That doesn't mean I have to do what it says, nor do I have to believe it, but I do acknowledge how real and powerful it has always been. I'm giving it its due, but it's still my nemesis.

I just want to get through this weekend without beating myself up too much. I feel the crashing of my two worlds as they collide and as I piece myself together, as I pick through what's important to keep. Whether I'm clashing or merging, pulling apart or reuniting, it's a painful process. And I must also keep remembering that crying is good for me; finding my emotional self is good, being real is good, feeling is good. I will learn how to love. I will learn how to care about myself. I will learn how to give myself exactly what I need. And Jeanne will help me. She knows I need her, and my team of other guides too—I need them all.

"Help me find my way. I feel so lost and alone. I can't think positively. I can't find anything good to focus on, just the next step, one step at a time. Please help me."

"*Relinquish control. It may not work the way you want it to work, but it will work. Like at the art gallery; you want things to be perfect, but you can't do it alone. Step back and let the group function as a group. The group will take over because that's how a cooperative works. Relinquish control in order to allow. Allow for it to work by stepping back out of the way and let it happen. It will all go the way it should go.*"

"I must let my own group take over because I can't do it alone?" I ask.

"*No one can: teamwork! You have already proven that you are tough and can get through anything. What are you doing now that gets you through this phase? How do you tap into your strengths? How do you keep going? Where does it come from? Everything you need is inside you.*"

May 9, 2004

It's Mother's Day, a blustery, cold and cloudy day. I've always preferred to spend Mother's Day alone, just doing things I like, like taking a long walk, but unless it warms up later it won't be a day for walking. The kids call and wish me a happy Mother's Day. I'll see them when they get home later in the evening.

I feel a little crazy, but I know it's the emotional stuff coming to the surface. I dreamed about it during the night, telling myself over and over again that it's a necessary part of the healing process; that I have to access my emotions, that they can't stay buried, that they're good, that I'm just afraid of their intensity and because they're so numerous.

How can I heal if I can't get to the core of my own anger and sadness? How will I change if I don't allow myself access to my deepest fears and feelings? I must continue confronting my issues, find ways to release myself from them, and then allow for new life. That's what Mother's Day should be about, new life; bringing new life into the world in some shape or form, not necessarily children, though I did that twice. And now I must do it again, but this time completely within myself.

I spend the afternoon working at the artists' gallery. The hours seem endless; the weather is terrible and there are few visitors. I pace and pace, trying to get out of my head, away from the incessant internal dialogue that threatens to swamp me. The negativity demons are loud, very loud, but when I step outside of myself, as Chuck suggested I do, and look at myself from afar, I see a woman who has had an awful lot to deal with lately, and she is, in fact, doing quite well. She must learn to accept that she's only human, after all, and humans have desires and wants and needs and emotions. She has to allow for all those things. She has to stop pushing them away.

The kids are home, both of them in great moods. We spend some time together in lively chatter. I hear all about their busy weekend and then we all head off to bed.

May 10, 2004

I dream that I'm standing next to a man who slowly darkens, becoming mean and evil. He tells me how he's going to torture me, what he'll do with his tools. Then I recognize him; it's the man who abused me. I run from him, down crowded streets and into a tiny restaurant where I sit down at a small round table with three little girls. I know that I am these girls, that they are parts of myself. We hold hands. "*I love you*," I say, surprised when I say it, as if I've just realized that it's true, that I do love them. Someone is missing, but I say that I love her too.

I dreamed this dream repeatedly all through the night. I understand that this dream is showing me this important and meaningful truth, that indeed I do love myself, all parts, even the absent and unknown parts. The dream image is a mandala, the round circle of the table with the four figures creating the corners of a square, a circle in a square, a symbol of wholeness. This feels right; I am gaining my wholeness at last.

I feel like I spent the entire weekend getting knocked down by waves of negativity, a victim of my own mind. What happened to floating on the water, gently buffeted by the waves? I lost sight of everything. I lost myself as the emotions hit and as I got pulled back to old places. I hated the process, but it's part of my journey, and I know I must face *everything*. I also know that I must access every emotion if I am to finally heal. I learned a lot about myself over the weekend. I realized that this is where I'm supposed to be right now, dealing with the realities of life, struggling to establish myself as an independent woman, on her own, raising her kids. I want to more than just survive though; I want to prosper. A fuller positive life experience will only come with learning to wholly trust in myself. And that is where this recapitulation is leading me; I'm learning what it means to trust.

I lie in bed for a while before getting the kids up for school, just letting things go—my judgments and fears, and the craziness—letting them all seep out of me, leaving them behind beneath the covers, like a shed cocoon. By the time I get up, I know that I'll manage okay, that I'll be able to do another day.

I jump into the morning routine with a renewed attitude and good energy; getting the kids up, making breakfasts and lunches. After ensuring that they have their music, instruments, homework, and lunches, I send them off to the school bus.

I go out to the job I'm working on, the painted floor. I sit for a while and talk with the client before getting to work. She's in a similar situation and we realize we'd both panicked last week, thinking that the only solution to our problems was to run, to sell our houses and move somewhere, and then, we'd both come to the same conclusion that it wasn't a good idea, that it's better to stay put and not let life beat us down. That's the way I feel today, that I'm not going to let reality get the better of me. I have to reside in it, so I'd better figure out how I'm going to do that while still being the new me, the softer me, the person who has been emerging over these past few years, a woman whom I desperately need to claim as myself.

Later in the day, I drive over to the studio to pack up some more stuff. I load up the car and then unpack it into the garage when I get home. I put some new oil and gas into the lawn mower and give it a good kick. When I pull the cord, it starts immediately. Hallelujah! I mow the front yard and then tackle some issues regarding the artists' gallery that I've been putting off. The kids arrive home from school and we catch up on their day. Then I work on an estimate for a new job and talk to another woman about some work I'll be doing for her. It's been a full day indeed.

As I lie in bed, trying to fall asleep, I feel everything seep out of me, all tiredness and all resistance, like I felt in my session with Nicolas last week, after exhaling for so long that resistance became futile. *Resistance is futile.* No more holding in. There is no need, the need is gone; it's only habit now.

May 11, 2004

"*There is nothing to be afraid of. Fear is just habit too,*" Jeanne says. "*There is no need to hold onto it anymore. Trust the process, trust Chuck, trust yourself. Trust that you know what poor little Jan needs. She's so stoic, but why does she have to be?*"

"*Strong and capable Jan emerged yesterday and took over for a few hours,*" Jeanne continues. "*She wasn't afraid, so you know it's possible. You know everything will be okay. Help her. Today is the day. This is what it has all been about, getting to a point of total trust. And please, just let it happen.*"

"*Don't hate yourself. Please don't. Poor little Jan needs you to set her free. Once you begin the process, she'll take it up. She's desperate to let the fear go. She just needs to feel that it truly is safe to do so. No one is going to yell at her. No one is going to humiliate her, but she needs to see it to believe it. Help her. She can't do it alone; she shouldn't have to be alone.*"

Okay, I'm going to see Chuck and I'm bringing my child self with me.

"Think of a high, calm plateau, a high mesa where the wind blows away all the negative thoughts and all the bad voices," says Chuck, handing me the EMDR pods.

"I'm there," I say, almost immediately.

"Good," he says, leaving me there for a few minutes.

"Now go back to the girls in the dream, sitting at the table, and tell them you love them."

I go back into the dream. I feel calm as I go to these places, first to the high mesa and then back into the dream.

"What's happening?" he asks, his voice far away.

"They aren't listening to me," I say. "I keep saying I love you, over and over again, because I know how important it is, but they aren't paying any attention to me."

"Keep going there," he says. "Keep doing that during the day and see what happens. Don't give up."

"I love you," I say, over and over again, throughout the day. I am determined to keep saying it until the girls hear me. I seek the calm emptiness I felt during my session with Chuck, knowing that there, in the emptiness of my own body and soul, I will reconnect with the girls and find my emotions waiting for me at the next leg of this recapitulation journey.

By five o'clock I'm exhausted after working on the floor painting all day, angry at myself because I ended up feeling sorry for the woman and lowered my price. What an idiot I am! Why do I do that! Now I'll get paid less than I should, and on top of that it's utterly exhausting work. I don't feel very good right now. I know that being exhausted isn't good, as it can potentially lead to depression.

I told Chuck today that every day I wake up and wonder how I'll get through the day.

"And, how do you?" he asked.

"I do what I can, that's all," I said.

I'm so exhausted, but I have to keep going. Tomorrow my son has a concert in the evening, and the next night I have an art gallery meeting. Then on Friday an art opening, on Saturday the art studio tours, which I'm participating in, and that night I have to sit at the gallery opening. Oh well, at least I'll be busy.

I cook dinner, eat with the kids, and then finish mowing the lawn. The mower runs out of gas just as I finish. Totally exhausted, and dripping with sweat, my neck, shoulders and hips cramping, I put the mower away and head for the bath. I lie in the hot water, envisioning no end to this difficult time. But on a lighter note, I realize that tomorrow is another day, a different day. So, I have that to look forward to; a totally different day!

May 12, 2004

I wake at 3:30, coming out of swirling dreams, unable to fall asleep again. Stop thinking! Stop thinking! Just don't think anymore! For the remainder of the sleepless night, that becomes my only thought, to NOT think.

After the kids head off to school, I put out my yoga mat and do some yoga. Afterwards, I sit quietly and do breathing exercises, each breath bumping up against the lump of pain in my throat. What was once deep down inside my belly has risen gradually higher, seeking escape.

"Release will eventually come, just keep breathing," I tell myself.

A half hour of breathing and I feel calmer. Something *has* released. I sense the capable me emerging again, and I feel more optimistic too. It's spring now, a time of new beginnings, a time of cleansing, of clearing out the old and looking forward to new life emerging. My recapitulation also points toward a similar cleansing, as I seek to release the old fears, and the sadness too. I look forward to beginning anew. What am I so afraid of? The sound of my own pain pouring out of me?

I'm not home until eleven, exhausted but in a good mood. I made sure to have a cup of coffee in the afternoon to keep me going. My son's jazz concert was excellent, the music uplifting, and although I still feel panic lingering just below the surface it feels good to not be so depressed. I'm feeling a bit more optimistic because of new jobs lining up and steady work on the horizon too. I'm trying to go with the flow of things, not turn to old obsessions and panic.

If I concentrate on Jeanne, I get guidance; things that were hidden before suddenly become clear. It feels as if she's glad when I come to her, that she likes the connection. The feeling is mutual. I wonder where it will lead, and why? Why do I have such a strong sense of her right now? Is she calling to me? Does she want to tell me something, guide me perhaps?

May 13, 2004

I spent the whole night tossing and turning. I've trained myself to turn over in my sleep when I'm in an old position, and now it appears that when I dream something negative, I also turn. All night long I commanded myself to turn in my dreams, and I'd turn, but also wake up each time!

I have to realize that things have changed and that life is not dangerous and evil anymore, that I won't get hurt. I don't have to live in constant fear anymore that something terrible will happen. I realize that although life is full of surprises, and though they may often be challenging, they are also meaningful in some way. Thus, there's always something to learn. I'm open to new adventures and challenges in spite of the old fear that wells up, asking me to turn back and keep it company in the old way.

Strong emotional energy courses through me during an Embodyment session, building to a point of frustration, until I can't hold it back any longer.

"Ow!" I cry out.

"Are you in pain?" Nicolas asks.

"Not physical pain," I say, "more like a very tender spot and that's just the sound coming out of it," and I keep saying "Ow," half laughing and half crying, through the entire session.

Jeanne comes to me when I ask for her help. I feel her hands resting on the sides of my face, holding me steady, and I hear her voice. "*Go with it, just go with it,*" she says, "*let it out, let it go.*"

Nicolas leaves me for a few minutes when we're done, and I lie on my side underneath a blanket and cry. I have the strongest desire to just be held, but I don't know how to ask him to do that. It feels like too much to ask. I'm afraid that deep emotions will spill out, this first real release just the precursor to a flood of pent-up emotion, and deep sadness beneath it all.

Nicolas gives me a mantra: "Shivoham," meaning "I am Shiva, I am spirit," good to use as one awakens to one's own spirituality, he says.

"Say it slow, say it fast, say it all the time," he says. "In the day or in the night, always come back to it."

He also suggests that I do shavasana at night and ujjayi breathing before bed to relax and sleep better. And to do it again if I wake up at night; it will help me get back to sleep.

As I drive away, I begin saying the mantra. It has a nice hum at the end that feels good in my throat.

I get home late, after a meeting at the artists' gallery. I started to laugh at one point during the meeting and I began to fear that I would dissolve into tears, that I wouldn't be able to stop. I'm so stressed, on the breaking point, but I also know that I am no longer as willing to hold it in.

Shivoham!

May 14, 2004

I woke up early, at four, but was able to fall back asleep after doing shavasana and breathing, as instructed by Nicolas. I see Chuck this morning, though I have no idea what I'll talk about. I just feel like crying. I can't keep up the old façade anymore; I can no longer be stoic. There's no reason for it. I discovered that yesterday, during my session with Nicolas. It's time now to just go with the flow.

Chuck hands me the EMDR pods and I focus just on breathing and centering.

"You're going to be fine; you're going to be fine," he says, suggesting that exhaustion can increase the sense of giddiness that attacked me last night during the meeting, and that the work with Nicolas is certainly cracking my old façade, making the giddiness more likely.

"Try not to worry about the sleep issues," he says.

"I won't, I promise," I say.

When I get up to leave, I'm dizzy. I have to sit back down again for a few minutes.

"Get centered," Chuck says. "Breathe."

I realize I hadn't eaten dinner last night, and I didn't eat breakfast today either. I just forgot, didn't even think of it. I don't tell Chuck this, but I get some food before I head out to work.

May 15, 2004

I'm trying to keep the waves of emotion calm. It's as if I have an extra veil of skin floating on top of my real skin, shifting and emulsive, like an oil slick on top of water, all the emotions having risen to the surface. I call it *epidermis emotionalis*, and it vibrates all the time.

Art studio tour day. I'll be spending the day at the studio, but first I have to drive out to my client's house and varnish the floor, plus get the kids set for a day with friends, and then put out signs directing people to my studio in the building. The weather looks good. I feel slightly panicky at the prospect of such a long extraverted day, especially with my emotional skin so raw and tender.

I'm not home again until eleven at night. Things got better as the day got busier, and I was taken out of myself by the amount of people to deal with. After the studio tour ended, I worked at the artists' gallery and then helped with cleanup after the opening. Just starting to unwind now.

I noticed that I was unusually chatty today, but then my throat closed up tonight and felt raw, as if saying, "Enough, enough talking. Stop." Something else crept in then, a feeling of how much memory I have sitting there in my throat, all the oral sexual abuse, all the blocked words, the silence imposed on me, the secrets that wove into the fabric of my life. I don't have to dwell in silence now; I don't have to hold it in. I can release. I can talk. I can say my mantra.

Thank you for helping me through the day.

May 16, 2004

I don't want to think so much today, I just want to breathe and rest, say my mantra, and see where life takes me. I want to stay focused on the good internal voices, and on my spiritual advisors. Contact with them assures that I will get through my life fairly unscathed, firmly upon my path of heart, heading in the right direction. If I lose contact, even briefly, the other voices speak louder to fill the gap. Immediately sensing an opening, they sneak in and begin their battery of taunts.

I head out to see Nicolas in the early afternoon, feeling slightly stressed, aware that my mind is revving, churning out old scenarios again. I turn it off by reciting my mantra. Shivoham! Shivoham! Shivoham!

I lie down on the thick matting Nicolas prepares, my legs resting comfortably over a low pile of folded blankets. As soon as we begin, I go where I don't want to go, though I know I must. I don't fight. I just go with the flow, aware of how necessary it is, almost immediately hitting the lonely empty place where I was always left after my abuser was done with me. I'm surprised it wasn't all that difficult to get there. I sense myself pulling sideways, as if to get away from something. I know I have to just go with it, encounter it, and relive whatever the feeling is. I experience a pulsing, releasing sensation in my lower spine. And then I feel my spine widening and becoming loose and open, after a half century of closure. I remain alert to what's happening with my shoulders too, automatically loosening them when they start to hunch.

My forehead chakra, my third eye, constantly releases during the session too. At one point, I say, "Ow," when Nicolas is working on my spine at the level of my heart. He asks me to describe what it feels like.

"Like a bruise," I say, "like you're touching a bruise."

"Well," he says, "that may well be what it is; your heart is bruised."

For the rest of the day, I feel pulses in my sacral area; grief releasing. Pulses in my heart; pain and sadness releasing. And pulses in my forehead; my third eye constantly sparking.

"Thank you, everyone, for being with me again," I say, at the end of the day. I'm sitting on my bed in my room, but as soon as I say this, I'm back in my childhood bedroom, a young girl again, sitting in my childhood bed, gazing out my window, talking to the moon, as I once did.

"Thank you, moon, for keeping me alive another day."

May 17, 2004

I dream that I'm sitting at a table and money is being handed to me. A transaction is being made; I am the recipient of a large amount of cash.

Indeed, in spite of everything, I do feel rich. I see every day how well I'm doing. When I walk into other people's homes and see the messes they live with, encountering all kinds of domestic chaos, I take note that, comparatively speaking, I'm doing remarkably well.

Stuff came up yesterday during the Embodiment session, rapes that occurred when I was twelve, thirteen, and fourteen years old. I'm inundated with the emotions that arose with them and I feel myself beginning to withdraw, dissociating, just like I did when I was a teenager. An old sense of increasing distance between myself and reality creeps up on me too. I can still hear, see, and act, but I'm hidden inside myself, empty and lost. I can't let the dissociation take over now, though I know I must go through these experiences as they arise. I must feel again what the rapes felt like, experience every nuance of them so I know exactly what happened, so I'm clear on the truth of them, but still not get swallowed up by them.

There's a fine line between re-experiencing trauma and being overcome by it, because being overcome was truthfully part of the experience, but I must not allow my dissociated self to take over. I must stay in my body this time and find out what happened while I was out of it back then. The dissociated state is so well known to me, a normal state; since childhood I have lived in that dissociated place. To return to my body fully would have meant encountering the annihilating qualities of the trauma, and that was not an option. As a child, I had to find a means of survival within the context of my life, a life that did not adequately provide an outlet for expression of the trauma. In a sense, I had to find a way to block the experience not just once, but twice. The first time was to protect myself, and I did this by leaving my body during the rapes—my consciousness sent outward—and the second time was to ensure that I stayed dissociated, disconnected from my body once I returned to my body and my normal life, so that I didn't go insane, for there was no person and no place to go for support.

I do the sweeping breath to alleviate some of the feelings and tensions around the memories that came through yesterday, but breathing is hard today. I feel more like curling up and crying. I feel anger too, pulsing, ready to unleash, and I know I'll have to find a way to release it, but for now I must comfort my teenage self.

In the afternoon, anxiety does a steady climb and I sense another memory coming. My body clenches, reacting, but to what I'm not sure. Do I feel threatened? After a half hour, with no further recapitulation coming through, I push the feelings away and head out to work on setting up the garage as a studio. I'll be doing my furniture painting there now, at least until the weather turns cold.

As I move around and make space in the garage, I simultaneously seem to move something around inside myself. Suddenly, a recapitulation floods through me, and those teenage rapes that came up yesterday during the Embodyment session reveal themselves in greater detail. When they're over, I'm left lying in the barn where my abuser often took me, and where other men often came. I am fully enclosed in devastating feelings, a shattered young girl picking up the pieces of herself, stunned by the total silence of the darkness within. I wanted desperately to get away from that dark loneliness and emptiness inside myself, where there was nothing and no one, to something and someone. I both hated and craved that loneliness and emptiness though, craved it because it meant I was safe and hated it for the obvious reasons; it was too much of a reminder of all that I had experienced.

I am much more relaxed afterwards, the anxiety and heavy depression of the recapitulation lifted, so that by evening I'm in a fairly good mood. It definitely makes a difference to feel better inside!

May 18, 2004

I dream that I'm traveling to some destination, crossing over dangerous railroad tracks. Trains are whizzing by. I'm with an old college friend and a few others. All of us are trying to figure out how to get somewhere.

Where am I going, and why? What for? It all seems so meaningless. Why am I doing this recapitulation? What's the purpose? I seem to be on an endless pursuit of nothing, following endless train tracks that don't go anywhere, and my train never arrives! Am I just going and going because there doesn't seem to be anything else to do? It seems so hopeless. All this searching, constantly seeking, waiting. And why? Just to keep doing it some more? What's the point?

I seek little rewards as I take my journey, signs telling me I'm on the right track. Little things offer a boost; they carry me to the next day and to the next hope and desire, but I wake up in such frustration, spiritually and physically. Right now, I feel like a hamster on a wheel, endlessly running, numbingly going in the only direction the wheel spins.

I felt pretty good last night. Now I believe I'm suffering the fall from the heights of the contentment that set in, what Carl Jung termed *enantiodromia*; a sudden shift caused by the unconscious reacting to something that challenges the status quo, making an extreme turn toward its opposite. What goes up must come down! At least until I've completely changed my inner makeup that is, until I've gotten to the point where there's no longer anything to challenge, when things have evolved, when greater inner equilibrium is established and status quo is nothing more than my own calm heart. Someday, true equanimity will be my natural state.

In spite of all that, my energy is good. I work in the garage using my electric sander to sand old paint off twenty doors, a dirty and noisy task. I'm covered in sawdust and exhausted when I'm done, but contented with my new work space. After a satisfying day of work, I am made more fully aware of just how true Jeanne's persistent message is; everything *is* going to be just fine!

May 19, 2004

What's going to happen today? This is the first question I ask myself every morning. My life is uncertain, my direction unclear, the past recovered and left behind, at least for the most part, and the future is an open road. I've learned to just go with the flow, focusing on my path of heart, taking one step and one day at a time.

I made the tremendous decision to begin this journey of self-discovery, to become an explorer, throwing myself out into the universe, allowing myself to be transported to other times and events. I made the decision to discover who I truly am in order to become a better person, in order to be better for myself, my children, and my world. By doing this recapitulation, I do believe I will make a big difference in all of our lives.

I notice that my jaws are cracking constantly. A lot of releases have been taking place, my body seeking to be rid of the past. It doesn't want to wear the old armor, and neither do I.

May 20, 2004

A transformation truly has been taking place over the past three years, ever since I first stepped into Chuck's office and began to see and understand myself, and the world, differently. I never would have gotten this far in such a short period of time without his guidance and knowledge, but I also had to be ready for the journey and all that it entails.

I'm learning about myself from scratch as I undergo this recapitulation, rediscovering, and discovering for the first time in some instances, my greater potential. As I relive many episodes from my childhood, I gain a new perspective on my life, but I also gain a new attitude about who I might become in the future. I recall that I made many promises to myself as a child, intentions that actually did manifest, that successfully fueled a future me. I became a fierce warrior of my own destiny. Now I'm changing and I have new intentions based on what I've learned about myself over the past three years. I opened myself to the magic of recapitulation, and during my journey I've let myself be open to new worlds of possibility. And that's what I'm looking forward to in my future too. But first, I head off to see Nicolas.

The session gets off to a rocky start, with painful releases and a lot of discomfort. Nicolas notices.

"It's okay," I say. "I'll just go with it."

"You always do," he says.

I go into some deeply stored emotions and feelings. I don't know what they are, but they make me cry. I feel lonely, alone and sad. I feel brutalized, traumatized, and empty all at once. I sense that something very important has been taken from me and I don't know if I'll ever get it back. It's my deepest inner self that has been so brutalized, my innocence. I curl up in a fetal position at the end of the session.

"It's hard to come back," I say, "and I can't talk."

"You don't have to," he says. "Keep coming back to the body throughout the day. Ground yourself in your body. Do some breathing and yoga. It will help."

I go home, and even though I feel like curling up I decide it's better to eat something and get to work. I have to paint all those doors in my garage. It's the most important thing now, to stay in this body and this world, to both keep moving and get grounded.

As I work, I also work through feelings in both my body and psyche that emerged during the Embodyment session. The need to curl up is strong, but I fight it. There's something I haven't gotten to yet. I'm not sure what it is. Some truth? Emotion? Feeling? I must get to them all, and fully express them, or I won't be able to fully access my total self. I must accept this process and how it unfolds too, facing whatever comes up, showing me where to go next. I must return to that place of sadness and loneliness and look for what it is that I didn't access in the session with Nicolas. But, as soon as I even think about going there, fear comes. It staunchly guards those deeply buried emotions, still seeks to keep me from them. Buried a long time ago, they were meant to be kept hidden, supposedly forever, though now they require release. I won't survive if they aren't released. That I am sure of.

As I work, my back keeps opening and releasing. By the end of the day, I am just a tired and cranky mess.

May 21, 2004

I find the article in the *New York Times* that the reporter wrote after his day in the area, a tiny, 2-inch article about real estate in the region. What a bummer! We, the artists that make the region so interesting are not even mentioned! The guy was such a fraud! What was he trying to prove? BOO to him!

I'm depressed, with little energy during my session with Chuck, barely dragging through it.

"I think I need to just open up more," I say, "to just take the leap and let things happen, as they will, but I'm afraid. I'm afraid of what my unconscious will show me."

"Don't question it in the old ways," Chuck suggests, "but do allow yourself to make the leap to confidence and success."

"But I'm afraid," I whine. "If I could wish for anything it would be to not be so afraid all the time."

It's an old sentiment, and not very helpful.

It's really humid and the paint dries slowly on the doors. I set up some fans around the garage to get the air circulating. As I paint, I realize I'm trying not to cry. Why do I hold it in? Chuck said I looked angry today, and I said, "yeah, I'm angry, and I'm frustrated." But really, I was trying not to cry, though I didn't tell him that. And why didn't I tell him? He always encourages me to tell him everything, to not hold back, but he would want to know why and I don't really know why. I guess I still think I'm not allowed to cry, that it's not permissible. He wondered if the work with Nicolas was going too deeply, too quickly, but I totally disagreed with him. I have to continue it.

When I take a walk in the evening, I realize that I must push myself even further if I am to break this impasse, that I must somehow force a breakthrough. It becomes exceedingly clear to me that it's vitally important that I do just that. I've been preparing myself for this moment and this work forever, and I'm ready to deal with everything that comes. This I know. I also know that the most important part of this process seems to be openness, that it's not just about releasing things, but it's also about being open. I must remain physically open, to allow for things to leave my body, whatever those things may be. I must allow old energy to leave and new energy to come in. I must become more receptive.

I watch a movie and have a glass of wine, trying to stay mindful and aware, telling myself that I'm relaxing now and also intentionally keeping things away, that I need a break. I notice my sacrum opening more and more as I sit on the couch. As I relax into the releases, I know I need to allow for even more, that it's important. It means that my body wants to do this, that my body needs this release as much as my psyche does, that it too has been holding onto this stuff for way too long. I need Chuck to understand this, that my body itself is pushing for this release, independent of what I or he might think needs to happen. I know I need to go where it takes me. It's the magic I crave.

In spite of my efforts to stay mindfully present in the moment, I am assaulted by a sudden recapitulation. I turn off the movie and let the memory come, unwinding like a film inside me. I stay physically and mentally, mindfully present as the memory sweeps through me.

I am a child again, and grown men are kissing me. I feel the disgust I felt then, and the fear. Penises force their way into my mouth, gagging me. I think I'm going to die, not able to breathe. The nauseating smell of men, of sweat, alcohol, and tobacco fills the room. I feel the stubble of beards scraping against me. Okay, I'm not questioning it, I'm going with it—there must be a reason. I feel spreading heat in my lower back and the memories coinciding with it, crashing into it, melting like cold butter in a hot frying pan. They are undeniably linked to me; they are *my memories*.

"This is what you've been holding inside you," my body tells me. I accept these truths, and I acknowledge how strong I am, and how strong I've always been.

May 22, 2004

I dream throughout the night of deep self-hatred and dark anger, but then I find the means to change those feeling. I find that if I shift my body, I also shift away from the incessant negative feelings. I become aware that I must constantly keep moving, keep actively working on myself. If I don't, I'll stagnate and things will get increasingly worse. Taking action on my own behalf, including staying active in dreaming, as well as in waking life, is my salvation.

Last evening, as I walked, I saw once again the shape of a cadaverous figure in a hollowed-out tree alongside the edge of a field where I often walk. I'd seen it before and was struck by its dark shape, a head with a gaping mouth, turned just so, gazing in the direction I was walking. Who were you? I wondered. And how did you end up here, seemingly caught in some spell? I found myself thinking, again, about suicide, the two voices, the old and the new, inside me, arguing in their usual way. Why am I thinking still about killing myself when I know I never will? Why the arguing still? As I asked myself those questions, I heard Chuck's voice interjecting: "It's the old stuff; it's only the old stuff making its last efforts to get you."

I have to keep going, not pause long enough for the old stuff to catch up with me, because it's running behind me at a rapid pace, seeking my energy, as always. It showed up in my dreams last night too. It came and tried to take me back with feelings of self-hatred and anger. I knew yesterday that I had to remain open, to continue to allow for the flow of energy, now and forever. If I don't, I'll end up stuck in my own tortured pose, the one I lived in for most of my life, similar to the one I see in that old tree. When the old stuff comes back in search of me, I must physically shift, get ahead of it. I must stay focused on the good work I'm doing to free myself.

I also realized, while walking last evening, that it's essential that I continue the work with Nicolas, at the pace we're going, that I need to do it. I'm strong enough and determined enough to handle it; I'm ready. It's important that I honor the pace and the intent of this process, that I don't ever shut down again. I must continue the work, so I can become free. It's an opportunity I can't deny myself.

I write every day, effortlessly filling a new journal every week. A lot of pain flows out of me onto these pages. I am lost but also not lost, because the ground beneath my feet is familiar. I walk the same paths, but each time the air around me swirls differently. I am presented with the same views, but they are always different, always changing. And each day that I walk those same paths, I see new things that I never saw before, because I too am different. I too am changing.

Yesterday, the fields smelled summer sweet, the bright green grasses pungent with wildflowers, the scent of honey and strawberries on the breeze. As I walked over the rolling fingers of farmland reaching out toward the river, I thought: "Oh, look at me in this beautiful spot, come all the way to this beautiful place where I feel like I own the whole world." The pure happiness of having gotten to this place ran through me, and I felt the joy at being able to walk these trails beside the river every day, if I so choose. My life is rich in this beautiful river valley. I feel like a queen as I look out over the river, queen of all I see. My life is rich indeed.

I must stay calm, grounded in this new body where I'm making room for my new self, a body that walks and talks differently, that stands differently, that even thinks and breathes differently. I still deal every day with the depression though, still must find ways to get myself to a place of functioning, push myself to be an active life participant, a member of the world, and not stay behind the closed doors of my room where I know I'm not safe either anymore, but where I feel comfortable and connected, even if it's only to old habits. Still, it's something familiar. But instead of staying there I have to drag myself out the door, and continue my journey into the unknown. This part of my journey through life, this recapitulation, has been to reexamine the past in order to discover myself, to thoroughly understand all that I am, all that has held me back, and all that still awaits me.

In a happier mood, feeling grateful for all I have, I get out of bed, put a coat of paint on the doors in the garage workshop, and then go to the studio, hoping to sell a few more items from my collection of painted furniture before I close my gallery. Fingers crossed!

In spite of my earlier happier mood, I've been fighting depression all day, trying to stay focused. I can't seem to decide what I need to do with my life, the morning's resolve drifting away like a puff of smoke. I begin to perseverate again about how to make a living, how to survive this world and support my family. This kind of thought pattern always sends me into a place of fear, and panic easily sets in too. At four, I close the studio for the day and head home, depressed once again.

I lie down for a few hours, in a near catatonic state. What is wrong with me? Why must I sabotage every attempt to get myself together? I feel myself beginning to disintegrate again.

"I'm falling apart," I say. "I'm just a house of cards and I'm falling into a heap. There isn't anything inside to keep me up. I'm merely air, empty except for the Invisibles, with their pain and anguish, and their sadness. The Invisibles are getting me. The demons are coming, the invisible demons."

I jolt myself out of it, grab a glass of wine, and head out to the garage and paint the doors again, giving them another coat as the sun goes down. It's seven thirty by the time I'm done and I'm at a loss for how to handle the Invisibles. Maybe I'll get drunk. I'll just have a horrible weekend and then it will be over, because right now I can find absolutely nothing to look forward to; nothing makes me happy. I feel like running away. Or I could cry. I didn't buy food for the weekend, but I could make some eggs; that will give me something to do.

Instead, I am swept into a tornado of self-destructive thoughts. I acknowledge my lack of self-confidence and that, with no faith in my abilities and no motivation, I am nothing more than a dismal wreck of a failure. I declare myself a fake, a charlatan. I turn out the garage lights, close the door and, once back in the house, fall into a heap on my bed where I continue calling myself names, riding the tornado until it loses its power, until I am back in reality.

The self-destructive storm has passed. It seemed to help, as I finally truly let myself be the failure that I feel I am. Now I'm calmer, ready for sleep. Tomorrow morning, I must step out of bed and find the path again, and find my spiritual helpers again too. They do seem to leave me alone to work through these bad stretches on my own.

May 23, 2004

I dream that I'm waiting for my brother to help me fix up a house that has no bathroom, and no running water. I have all the supplies ready. When my brother finally arrives, he decides he won't do the work. I'm disappointed but decide it's time for me to take over, that I'll hook up something on my own, so at least I'll have water.

War

I woke up at every tiny sound throughout the night, the first drops of rain, the sigh of a cat, every sound hugely magnified and intrusive. I feel like I'm in a holding pattern, waiting for takeoff, but not knowing where I'm going, or when, or why. I've already determined that I'm going to see this process through to the end, that I'm not a quitter, that no matter how difficult it gets I'll allow it to take me where I need to go. I'll follow the clues and signs along the path and just continue to tough it out. I'm afraid of the feelings and emotions that I'm confronting daily, but even so, I'm not going to slow down or stop the process; it's absolutely necessary for my growth and sanity. I must stay focused and grounded as I reclaim my energy, my body, and my calm mind. I think that's what my dream is trying to tell me; that I'm in charge of my own destiny. Only I can provide what I need.

Yesterday, I went to some really bad places, and it ended up being a very unpleasant day. Today, I resolve to keep moving, to put another coat of paint on the doors, and continue tackling the enormous project of dismantling and transporting my studio equipment and supplies to the garage, one carload at a time.

I hear the neighbor's peacocks screaming in the woods, their sound unpleasant to me. What are they crying about? Being in captivity? Well, I feel the same way. A bird sings when it opens its mouth, and its voice pours easily out. I want to cry, but when I open my mouth nothing comes out. It's like being in a nightmare, mouth wide open and not a sound escaping, though inside I'm screaming my head off. I've been stuck in this nightmare on and off for weeks now, losing touch with the magic in my life, seeing only the veils created by the invisible demons. The Invisibles are trying to sabotage my journey. This is real, this is not some imaginative science fiction story or crazy diatribe; this is my real world at this moment, a constant battle against the Invisibles.

I force myself out of bed and go for walk, a fast one, running from the Invisibles, looking for the magic instead. Where is it? I've lost the magic.

I drive to the studio, pack up a load and bring it home. My body resists, weighed down by depression. I have absolutely no energy, but I don't let that stop me. I keep going. I unload the car and vacuum the garage, hoping the noise will scare the Invisibles away. I can't see well; I'm under the veils again. I hate it here. I call Chuck and tell him that I'm going crazy. My demons are after me again, and I'm too tired to do anything about them.

"I'm ready for a new world and it's just not happening."

"Don't worry, it will, in an instant; things can change in an instant," he says.

"Shouldn't I be through this by now?" I say. "I want it to be over."

"Create a new world for yourself," he says. "Somewhere, somehow, get beyond it; push through to the other side."

He's right. I need to shake things up, make a new world for myself, just as my dream was indicating; I have to take over. I do Shavasana and Ujjayi breathing, the only yoga I'm able to muster, in spite of Nicolas's suggestion that I do lots of it this weekend. I go out food shopping, cook some fish, and finally eat.

I'm hunching my shoulders. Does my body pose attract the Invisibles? Have I drawn them to me because of my haggard, sad and lonely energy? If I stand up straighter instead, shoulders and body relaxed, with my heart's intent strong, will that produce a different outcome?

The veils lift right about the same time a heavy rainstorm comes through in the evening, shaking and rattling things. It's just as if I've woken up from a nightmare! Suddenly, I clearly see that I have enough work for the next three weeks to earn enough money to get through the next few months. This alone is cause for celebration, though I couldn't see it clearly while under the veils. I've gone from a terribly down mood to a very good one, with new energy. Chuck was right, things certainly can change in an instant!

I look over my horoscope and see that Mars and Saturn have been directly opposed to each other in my sign, and that tomorrow they will come together. These two energies represent the old versus the new, the same battle I've been engaged in for months! Perhaps it represents the last tangle with my old friends, fear and depression, my lifelong invisible partners. Tomorrow is going to be a day of big thunderstorms, so it'll be interesting to see what transpires.

I sense Jeanne's presence in my darkened bedroom. I see the soft white flutter of her energy, letting me know she's with me in energetic form. She assures me that magic is on its way, that it's already in the works. I ask for help as I face what comes next, as I sense things changing more rapidly now. She responds, showing me something I haven't clearly grasped, that all of this drama is about *change, and that change is good.*

May 24, 2004

I get up early and go out to the kitchen to put the coffee on, walking off the cramps in my hips, wondering what triggered them, knowing that I'm earning a new life as I go through this recapitulation process. Haven't I earned it by now? Haven't I reached a point now where I can receive some good? In spite of the pain, I notice that a new kind of calmness pervades me today. Perhaps the final battle is almost over.

My father calls. He doesn't call to talk, to offer advice, comfort, or understanding. He doesn't say a thing, really. He can't seem to perceive of me as a thinking, feeling adult. He sees only something he's imagined, something on the surface of his mind, his own fears projected. He treats me as if I were nothing more than a mirror, only a reflected human shape, not real. I tell him I'm fine, since that's all he wants to hear. I put some energy into my voice, and he's happy. I can't confide in him and I have no desire to be truthful. I see no point.

My parents, foreign beings that they have always been to me, exist only on the periphery of my life now, devoid of need or attachment. I'm going through too much now to even think about them, though I know it seems cruel, especially when my father is so sick. At the same time, that's his journey to take, as he will. I admit to a feeling of sadness for them as I watch them face old age, and yet I stay detached, going my own way, as I encourage my own children to do. We all have our own journeys to take. I'm preparing my children as much as possible before sending them out into the world. I wonder, every day, if I've done enough for them. Keep talking, I remind myself, just keep talking; stay connected to them, to who they are. I also understand that my parents did all they were capable of, and so I hold no resentment toward them, and I send them off with love to take their final journeys, as they choose.

Some more doors arrive today and I get paid for the work I've done so far. Now I can pay some bills and start to relax about things. It's time to face the fact that I'm making a living, that I've been doing so for far longer than I give myself credit. I must stay mindful to not get caught in old places of fear, worry, and stress. I remember what Chuck said, how things can change in an instant. A realization takes only an instant too.

A big thunderstorm rolls in with a loud boom. Jumping up, I run outside through loud claps of thunder and flashes of lightning to close the garage door. The fresh scent of rain fills the air. Let the battle begin.

Late at night, another heavy storm, with violent winds, lightning and thunder comes barreling through. The lights flicker off and on a few times. After much searching, I find a flashlight and keep it handy. The night feels volatile, ferocious energy whipping through, clearing the air, a purging and shaking-up kind of energy; the kind of energy that can change things in an instant.

May 25, 2004

While it storms outside, I dream all night of the battle going on inside myself, my body aching. I'm aware of the crashing of thunder and the flashing of lightning in the background of my dreams, even as I know that I am the storm itself, that I have become it. And I'm fully aware that it's the final battle of the old versus the new.

My body crackled and sizzled throughout the night, as the energy of the thunderstorms enveloped me, as I became the thunder and the lightning, engaging it physically, riding with it and also letting it ride through me, crackling and alive with electrical tension too. Then, as the storms passed and the energy got calmer, something inside me got calmer as well. Something has shifted. The coming together of the two warring energies of Mars and Saturn produced, as predicted, a clash and then a release, my own body following suit.

Today, I'll be working at a jobsite on the other side of the river, but first I have an appointment with Nicolas.

In the session with Nicolas the releases come quickly and are pretty uncomfortable, with sharp pains across my hips, just like during last night's storms. It's as if I'm being struck by lightning. It's hard to breathe too. My diaphragm and throat clench repeatedly, until I begin to relax, and then the breathing is easier and the releases are easier too. Soon the pain is gone. I realize that the constant holding and clenching are more painful than the discomfort of the releases. Once released, the pain goes and it doesn't return.

I tell Nicolas that I often wake up at night very angry, that anger is one of the emotions I've been accessing and working with lately, and that under the anger are tears, tears that I try to keep in, fearful of the deep well of sadness at the bottom of it all.

"Why don't you want the emotions? Why don't you want the sadness and tears to come out?" he asks, gently, rhetorically, as he works.

Why indeed? What am I so afraid of? Do I think they're signs of weakness? The tears are somehow equated with intense shame, since tears and crying produce sound, which produces fear that someone will hear me and know that I'm filled with pain. My body is steeped in shame, for what it did and is capable of doing. I fear I'll be found out, my shame exposed, my disgusting past revealed to the world. If people find out what happened to me, what my body did, the heavy shame will cover me, slowly suffocating me. A quick death would be preferable.

After the session, Nicolas tells me that he'll be away for ten days. He shows me some simple yoga poses that I can do to support the releases, effortless poses that I can even do in bed. I thank him for all he does for me. He tells me it's an honor to be working with me.

"It's an honor on my part," I say; "it's lifesaving work."

"Are you eating?" he asks.

"I'm trying," I say.

"Nourish yourself," he says, "and drink plenty of water."

I try to notice what's happening in my body when things shift, such as when the tension broke the other night after the thunderstorms and I began to feel better. I want to figure out what's happening so I can use it later when things get tough again. At the very moment the tension breaks it feels as if my brain switches to a different channel, gets rid of the static, and I slide into a different, clearer wavelength.

I paint ceilings for six hours and come home exhausted. The kids have dinner with their dad tonight, so I don't have to worry about them. I'm very sleepy, which is a good sign. I need sleep more than anything.

Thank you for everything. I know the magic is working all around me. I know I'm being taken care of like never before.

May 26, 2004

I dreamed that I was traveling on a bus with children. I sat next to a little girl of about five years old. She scolded herself for singing and talking to herself. She kept scolding herself for things I didn't think she needed to scold or apologize for, normal things that a child would be expected to do. I noticed that for such a young child she had set some pretty strict rules of conduct to live by, and that she was way too hard on herself.

This is exactly what I do to myself, as I constantly scold myself for the old postures, day and night. Last night I was aware of how I was sleeping and kept trying to relax the tension in my body, to keep from ending up in the old positions, but I ended up curled in the old fetal position anyway. In the end, I slept better and didn't wake up as often, but even after the releases of tension gained during the thunderstorms the cramping goes on.

Home at seven, after painting all day. I have a glass of wine with my meal, which relaxes me, and then take a bath. The kids are having dinner with their dad again and when they get home, I plan on heading right to bed. I painted walls and trim for eight hours today and my arms and shoulders aren't even feeling it, but the bath feels good.

I have another eight hours of painting to do tomorrow. When I'm there, it doesn't seem like real life to me. It's like traveling to another country, and discovering that the place you are in is the only thing that feels real. You know another life exists far away but your sense of it fades in this new environment. Real is only relative to place. When you travel, where you are is the only thing that's truly real, everything else is like a dream, distant, less important. So, each day, I get in my time capsule SAAB and drive to the job, and at the end of the day I get back in my time capsule and return to my real life. The dream feeling is okay, because it keeps things away, though I know the night will bring them all back again.

I wake in the night with excruciating pain shooting through my legs as another violent thunderstorm rages outside. I feel the heavy pounding of rain on the roof and in my body. The flashes of lightning followed by the crashing and crackling of thunder ride through me like electrical currents, as if I'm being struck by lightning. So, what else is new? Will I feel better after this storm has passed too?

The storm rages for an hour, and then gradually calms down. The cramping in my legs calms down too!

May 27, 2004

I wake at four thirty with residual cramping, and do some yoga poses that Nicolas taught me the other day. It helps. I hold myself together very tightly all day and when I finally get into bed and begin to relax, my muscles react. The pain seems to be directly related to the intense amount of holding I've been doing each day. This is psychosomatic pain, but it's more real than other types of physical pain, if you ask me; ancient pain come to greet me after all these years. I've been so like that five-year-old girl in my dream, scolding myself for having feelings and reactions, for being natural, but I refuse to hold back any longer. I give the pain permission to release, and not just during thunderstorms.

This is the week when everything finally comes together. This weekend, I'll be doing the final move of the studio. I'll have help one day with some of the bigger items, but otherwise I'll be doing most of it alone, though I'll have the kids help out a little too. I'll be moving upstairs to the new shared studio, as well as bringing the bulk of my stuff home to my garage workshop. I'm also working fulltime, earning a living, and for the first time in a long time I'm allowing myself to accept that I really am going to be okay, just fine, as Jeanne always told me I'd be.

I drive to the jobsite, saying my mantra aloud all the way, and work another long day. By the end of the day, I can't see the difference between the peach color on the walls and the white on the trim. I go home, grab a bite to eat and rush out to my daughter's honor's night. She rakes in six awards and I'm happy for her. She's a great kid and has handled the divorce and the changes over the past few years marvelously.

It's raining again as we head home, my daughter bubbly and happy, me tired and empty. I take a bath, have a glass of wine, and say my mantra before bed.

The pain stays away during the day, I realize, because I'm focused, quietly painting, staying in the moment, intently aware of what I'm doing, present in the surroundings I find myself in. But being in the moment is a kind of Limbo, a holding place, an unreal world. The real world is being in the turmoil of my inner work, confronting the issues I have to deal with, being innerly attuned and aligned with my inner journey. The real world is my recapitulation, and my search for wholeness. Everything else pales in comparison.

May 28, 2004

I meet with Chuck and immediately sense that he's upset or annoyed with me. Indeed, he confronts me, expressing again his concern about the Embodyment Therapy.

"I've noticed a regression over the past few weeks," he says, wondering if I'm pushing too much, trying to force a change and thus creating the current situation. He suggests I throw the *I Ching* and ask for guidance.

"Should I continue with Embodyment Therapy?" I ask.

Repeatedly returning is good for renewal, the *I Ching* advises, but the "tail biting obstinacy" is not good. So, yes, the Embodyment itself is good for me, but the approach I personally am taking is not. The *I Ching* warns that more stormy weather is in store for me if I continue in the manner I'm going, bringing to mind the synchronicities of the recent thunderstorms and my simultaneous pain. Without care and nurturing, I will only bring disaster upon myself, it advises.

"I get it," I say. "I *have* been forcing things. It's time now for renewal and rest. It's exactly what you've been suggesting and everything that Nicolas has been stressing, that I must be gentler with myself. I've rejected this advice for the more well-worn path of the tough and stoical self. Nicolas had already suggested that I withdraw from the intensity, but I've insisted on pushing it."

Chuck's intuition regarding the position I've landed in is correct in one sense, it *is* related to the Embodyment Therapy but more directly to my own intent to finish this recapitulation, and my determination that I can handle anything. I've imposed a strict agenda on myself, and without mercy I've been pushing through to resolution. It's the exact approach that little girl in my dream was using, and which my dreaming self found so absurd.

"I've been so intent on toughing it out and pushing forward that I forgot about everything else," I say, "but Nicolas is constantly pushing a softer agenda, asking me to do yoga and breathing, to nurture and give myself the care I need, the kind of self-care that's so hard for me to enact. I always think I have to tough it out, to forge ahead at all costs, but I see now that such an approach will only be costly to my health."

It's an old approach. I must reconcile with my tough self and find a way to take care of myself in a new, softer way; to soften without giving up, to nurture and nourish while still forging ahead with my recapitulation, to rest and allow a new side of myself to emerge, because that is what my main agenda is, to emerge from the depths of my recapitulation a new person. I must find a way to do the things that Chuck and Nicolas suggest. Ironically, I, a mother, must listen to these two men giving me advice on how to mother.

"I must stop the intensity of the pushing, and ask the warrior self, so used to constantly being on the frontline, to pull back, to retreat from the battlefront because she's wearing down," I say. "She must rest. It's time to take care of myself, or I'll just end up destroying myself."

I acknowledge that I've actually been going against the flow of my life lately, fighting it rather than going with it. The truth is that everything *is* going my way; I don't have to do anything to make something happen. I just have to let go, and go *with* the flow. It would be so much easier than all this resistance.

As I drive to the jobsite, I acknowledge that the tail-biting obstinacy makes me feel powerful, but this is a false sense of empowerment. It has been my source of strength for so long, but I don't need or want that kind of strength any more. I have a new source waiting to be accessed; love and gentleness.

I get home at six, have something to eat, and then sit in front of the television, exhausted, watching a movie, with no energy to do anything else. Afterwards I take a bath. Sitting in the hot water I contemplate where I am. I'm doing the best I can, trying to find ways to get better, to find things that work for me. I know that I'm not good at taking care of myself, in fact I am so bad at it that for years I refused to admit there was anything wrong with me. I was fine, everything else in my life was wrong. It was always much easier to make myself stronger, to go to battle than to pamper and nurture. I know that even though that tactic has worked in the past for the old me, the new me can't function under those old guidelines. The new me is not going to be so hard on herself, or angry with herself. She will no longer just tough it out.

I can take some simple steps to begin a shift, though sometimes, when I'm in a bad place, I can't even feed myself, as if I don't deserve to eat, as if I'm not important enough. But I also know that these acts of self-denial are part of the recapitulation process. They are the issues to confront, all the garbage I must sift through and find out why I carry around with me, all the old thoughts that constantly pop up telling me that I'm this or that, totally inadequate for the most part; that incessant internal dialogue. Oh, how I know it so well!

I can be such a great mother to my kids, but I don't really like being good to myself. I don't think I'm worth it, so why bother. I can manage the way I am, I say, but that's the same attitude as "toughing it out." I can push myself to exhaustion because it makes me feel strong and accomplished, and then I feel somewhat good about myself, but I can't seem to go in the other direction, to really soften and feel equally good about myself. Being hard has an immediate affect; I end up feeling strong, like a warrior. And that's okay, even though it also may feel like punishment.

So, why do I punish myself? I don't have to feel any emotions then; I don't have to have feelings. And I can bypass all the other stuff I've been refusing to acknowledge.

I don't really know how to like myself.

May 29, 2004

The *I Ching* warned me that if something doesn't change in the obstinacy department then disaster and devastation would ensue. So, I return to the path of heart, the path of healing, by focusing on one step at a time. It's okay to go back if it propels me two steps forward, but not if I get stuck back there.

"I've noticed a regression over the past few weeks." It struck me when Chuck actually said that yesterday. I now know that I must deal with this current regression differently, not returning to the old way of handling my feelings, but by doing more caring things. In the old way, I'd push myself until I'd achieve numbness. That's what was happening again. I don't want to do things that way anymore. I don't want to be mean to myself anymore.

Lara has been repeatedly telling me: "Don't go back, it's not good for you." My process has been to be dismissive of such cautionary concerns, electing always to toughen up, stiff upper lip and all that because I can handle it; I can handle anything. But I know it's not just about being strong and handling things now, it's about changing. I did not heed Lara's advice either, and now I must deal with the consequences.

I have to learn how to take care of myself, to quell the old voices within me who still want control. They're threatened by my impending independence because it means the end of them.

On the drive to the jobsite, I think about the old self-hatred and how that has been the thing to sabotage everything I've ever attempted to do for myself. Even when I write the word "self-hatred" I see my mother's face, scrunched up with a look of disgust, and I wonder if I got this self-hatred from studying how she treated herself. Or did I inherit it from her, embedded in our DNA? This attitude of self-hatred kicked in again recently, full force, and it continues to do so to some degree.

I keep busy, painting till midafternoon, anchored in the Limbo of another world, then go to the studio to pack some more things. I move two carloads of stuff to the garage. I stay busy all day and by midnight I curl up under the covers, exhausted.

The need to be comforted is intense, for the kind of comfort I never got or only got very briefly, very early in life. By the time I was a year old there was a new brother to take the lap of my mother and from then on, I took care of myself, as best I could. The child's needs that were never fulfilled by responsible adults are still present, hitting me full force at this point in my recapitulation. All at once, I am overcome with stuff I've been so successful at ignoring. Now I find that the old way isn't good enough anymore, nor is the impact of carrying around this amount of need good either. I remind myself that I must stay the course and tackle one thing at a time.

As Chuck often says: You wouldn't be dealing with this particular thing if you weren't ready for it. The unconscious knows and presents exactly what we need, when we need it.

May 30, 2001

I moved six more carloads of stuff home from the studio, did the grocery shopping, and got the kids to take turns mowing the lawn. And I even went to the laundromat and got the laundry done too!

I woke up several times last night, feeling the fullness of the needy and abandoned child. It put me into a lonely mood. Thinking about it now reminds me of the numbness I felt today as I went about moving the stuff from the studio. I went solidly numb so I could do it. Every time I got back into the car to go get another load I wanted to cry; just the act of getting into the car brought on feelings of aloneness. I would push them away and go pack another carload, bring it to the garage, unload it, and then get back into the car and drive back to the studio for another. I did as much as I could. There are still things to move, but I left it for another day.

I do know, however, that my old tendency, learned in early childhood, to hide my feelings and needs, or to ignore them in some other way, or to find some comfort by curling up and hiding under the covers, are no longer acceptable means of dealing with them, ingrained though they are. I must re-ground; find new stability within myself by meeting my feelings head on, no longer refusing to face them. They're coming to the fore for a reason, for me to finally accept them. None of this is being forced out of me or upon me. My unconscious has been preparing me for this moment for a long time. I really am ready.

On the other hand, I felt really good about all the hours I worked this past week. I came away from the job with a new sense of myself as very steady and capable, and entirely worthy of the nice paycheck I received.

May 31, 2004

I dream that I'm walking around a construction site. There's a lot of work still to do, but I see that I'll be able to get it all done by being patient, tackling one thing at a time. I also know that it doesn't matter how long it takes. I tell myself that I am just one small person; I can only do what I can do. "I'm doing the best I can," I say, somewhat comforted.

I turn over in my sleep and the movement wakes me up. I sit up and can't help but admit that I'm really sad about leaving the studio. It's been a depressing process. I feel as if I'm grieving, suffering through a great loss.

When I walked around the construction site in the dream, I felt overwhelmed at first by the amount of work still to be done. Eventually, I realized that it's the process of *doing* that matters, in paying attention to and attending to my true feelings, as well as attending to moving what must physically be moved. I must not stagnate again and pretend that this doesn't matter; it does matter, and the more effort I put into being honest with myself the better outcome I'll have. It doesn't matter how long it takes. It's the incremental push forward, one small step at a time, that really matters, tackling not only the moving of matter but incrementally attending to my spirit as well, in a positive and self-caring manner. Even if I feel alone and exhausted, it's not overwhelming when seen in this light. Taken in increments, it's totally doable. With this in mind I lie back down and visualize the color green, then blue, then green, then blue, going back and forth between these two calming colors until I fall back to sleep. Then I dream another dream.

I'm standing in a green field, looking up at a deep blue sky. The huge wheels and underbelly of a giant plane come soaring low overhead. As I watch, the plane lands awkwardly, skidding and bumping along the green field and down a steep hillside. The wings of the plane retract, and it turns into a bus. I watch anxiously as this bus careens out of control down the steep hill toward the crowded streets of a small town, filled with people and traffic. The driver hits the brakes in the nick of time and the bus comes to a screeching halt. All is well.

Switching back and forth in my mind, visualizing green and blue, seems to have invited the second dream. The plane, big and cumbersome, flew out of the clear blue sky and skipped across the green fields. I was both the plane and an observer of it, in two places as once. One part of me was soaring forward at great speed, almost out of control, as if the plane were too much to handle, while the other part of me watched in horror, suffering the anxiety of impending disaster. My unconscious seems to be reining in an old cumbersome tendency, essentially putting the brakes on self-destructive behaviors, letting me know that I have to shift away from the negative mindset, the numbness, and the old internal dialogue before it takes over. In so doing I will effectively put a stop to the war with my old self.

This dream portends a good ending, and new life to come, if I can remain spiritually and physically alert and aware, with all parts of myself in balance. And indeed, I wake up feeling quite exhilarated, back in the magic again!

Chapter 6

Redeployment of Energy

June 1, 2004

Frantic energy courses through me in sharp, hot pains like electrical shocks. I toss and turn trying to get comfortable, wanting a little more sleep, but it's impossible. I have to get the kids up and off to school anyway. Then I see Chuck. I wonder if he's still angry with me about my recent regressive behavior.

"I would never judge you, Jan," Chuck says, kindly. "Did you think I was being critical?" He tells me he was only concerned, that he needed to find a reason for why I was stuck.

"I made the decision to be hard on myself, to just get through this time," I say. "It's an old model, I know."

"I know how hard the struggle is, and how desperate you are to get someplace new," he says. "Start by being gentle with yourself, not harder in the old way. Feed yourself, nurture yourself, be kind to yourself," he says, mimicking Nicolas exactly. "You're half in another dimension, in another reality. It's a tentative time, but it won't last forever. You will get through this time and go on into new life."

"Yeah, and that's another problem, I'm so afraid of life!"

"You have to allow for life," he says. "Somehow, you have to learn how to open up to it."

"Well, I still keep myself pretty isolated, hidden behind the wall I constructed so long ago. I admit that it's probably time to knock it down."

"Probably by exhaustion," he says, "exhaustion will be the reason the wall comes down."

Oh, he knows me so well!

"Give yourself kindness," he says, as I depart.

Dreaming All The Time

I work another long day at the jobsite, in a melancholy mood. Work keeps me tough and hard, physically and mentally, when I actually need softening. I need to listen to what's going on inside if I'm to find an opening for a shift. Intense inner pressure has been building for weeks, and some release has happened, but there's been a stoppage. Something's holding back. And I don't think it's just me being hard.

June 2, 2004

At least I now know what's wrong with me, what has always been wrong with me. I know that I was raped, tortured, and neglected for most of my early life. And how did I manage to survive, to grow up into a fairly well-functioning adult? The same energy that kept me going then still keeps me going: the hard, tail-biting numbness, and a thick wall of obstinacy.

It's clear to me that I must allow the wall to crumble completely, and even though it will leave me exposed and vulnerable I must allow for it. Nothing will change if I can't allow myself to be vulnerable, to be open to new life.

"*Everything will be okay,*" Jeanne says. "*Just take one breath at a time, one day at a time. Okay?*"

I get the kids off to school and then spend some time meditating myself into a calmer state and a better frame of mind. I don't have to fight anymore; the threat is no longer there. It's just the remnants of the Invisibles trying to keep me attached. Time to let go of the old, inside and out, and allow for entry into new life. I've been stalking a new self for a long time now, and I've had glimpses of who she is. Time to let her come forth. And there's no need to hold that old wall up anymore either. It isn't protecting me from anything anymore. It's just keeping me away from what's on the other side, from the new, good, free and unburdened life I've been working so hard for. Why is it so difficult for me to let go?

Lara works over me for a long time. My stress level is extreme, electric, she says, exactly how I've been feeling lately.

Redeployment of Energy

"No sugar whatsoever," she says, and I feel immediately guilty for the few chocolate chip cookies I usually eat with my lunch. "And drink lots of water."

"Paint," she says. "Why aren't you painting? Don't nod; just do! You have to have that outlet. It allows you to forget about everything for a little while."

By nighttime I am so stressed out that I call a client and cancel our meeting for tomorrow. I don't have to be back at the jobsite until next week, so instead I can have tomorrow totally for myself. I can finally straighten out my piles of paperwork, and my house is a mess. I haven't vacuumed in two weeks, and with three cats it's really beginning to show.

I'm so cold! I'm actually shivering! Not sure why, but for a few minutes it seems to be a memory. If I let myself go there, to the sensations I'm feeling, all I intuit is that I'm inside a closet, or someplace small and dark, and I'm picking at the doorframe to get out. I noticed something strange as I painted the trim around a door today—I got a flashback—but not when I painted window trim, only the door trim. While I was painting, I thought I was re-experiencing a dream I'd had but couldn't remember, because it was so dreamlike, but there was fear associated with it, and then I knew it wasn't a dream. I haven't had flashbacks in such a long time, but that's exactly what this feels like, and there's incredible stress and tension around it too. I know the exhaustion is playing a part, and possibly the session with Lara too. Some channel that was previously blocked has opened up, I'm sure of it.

"Take care of yourself first, then everyone else," Lara said today, and my first reaction to that statement was that it's almost impossible for me to take care of myself first. I don't really care as much about myself as I do about others, especially my kids, and I'm not sure what to do to take care of myself either. All three of them, Chuck, Nicolas, and Lara, are all saying the same thing: *Be kind to yourself.*

I'm feeling vulnerable. I wonder if that's why the anxiety and memory are coming through. Or am I feeling vulnerable because of the memory? I do know that the memories never came through unless I was ready to handle them. And so, I also know that I must let this memory come on its own, without resisting or blocking it.

I've forgotten about the high anxiety that accompanies a memory, and the intense feeling that I'm actually going crazy, as I get drawn back in time, down the rabbit hole, pulled by something invisible. My entire body hurts as I go tumbling down. I catch myself from disappearing by doing the sweeping breath. I look around in the memory and see that I'm trapped in an unfinished closet, which is inside a room, inside a house under construction. It smells of wet plaster and dust. My stomach hurts, my back hurts, my neck and shoulders hurt. My stomach cramps and I roll into a ball of pain.

"Jeanne, are you there? Are you with me? I need you."

June 3, 2004

I dream that I'm standing on a mountain road with a little girl. The road is familiar. It looks like the old neighborhood where I grew up. The girl points out that a devastating fire has ravaged the area, destroying everything. Houses are burned to cinders, cars are melted, trees are blackened skeletons. I cannot see clearly at first. It's only after the girl points it out to me that I see the utter devastation.

I'm exhausted, my energy utterly depleted; my legs and arms are so heavy I can barely lift them. The dream accurately points out my own total devastation as I've gone through this recapitulation, as I've recalled the past, reclaimed the memories, and systematically dismantled the belief systems I once relied upon. The innocent little girl has been my traveling companion throughout this entire journey, pointing the way, and pointing out the truth as well. The dream indicates that change is no longer a thing of the future; it has already come to pass.

I meet with Nicolas. We don't do Embodyment therapy, but instead go directly to my memory, the energy of it sitting in my body, waiting for release.

"Breathe in through the tip of your nose. Right here," he says, as he very gently and lightly touches the tip of my nose.

"I feel like I'm vibrating."

"You are vibrating," he says.

"I don't know what the memory is specifically about," I say, "except that I'm locked in a small space, left alone."

Intense fear floods my body as I talk.

"What is it associated with?" Nicolas asks.

"Childhood," I say, "childhood, and what was happening to my body, something was happening."

Working from the tip of my nose down to my knees, I breathe into and release different areas of tension, gradually working back up to my neck again. There are short pauses after each release, which come like ocean waves crashing on a shore. As soon as one wave recedes, there's a slight pause before the next begins, coming up out of nowhere, from somewhere deep within my body, pulled out by the movement of Nicolas's hands over a sensitive area and my own acquiescence to the process, the two of us working in synch. We work each separate section at a time, opening the energetic passageways, until my energy is flowing, until finally I can breathe so far down into my body that I can actually feel my sitz bones receiving breath. A full hour passes before we stop.

"I feel a huge amount of release," I say.

"You can do that on your own; your body can do it, you have that in you," he says. "There's a tremendous amount of heat in your body wanting release; a lot is coming out. I can feel it."

"Walk with your whole foot, flex it and lengthen your leg so you feel your sitz bones," he says, as we finish up. "Ground yourself and you will begin to feel like you are in your body."

"Sometimes I think I am," I say. "But it doesn't last that long."

"Not yet, but it will," he says.

"Take good care of yourself. Breathe, eat, walk, and do some yoga, if you can," he suggests.

Exhausted, feeling almost ill after the session, I head over to the new studio to pick up a key that's been left there for me. I don't want to see or talk to anyone.

I picked up the key, came home, and got right into bed. I'm trying to focus on the present, trying to get my equilibrium back, but wouldn't you know, my car's acting up again! The radiator's doing something weird, trying to explode again. I have to call the repair shop.

I am out-of-body, looking down at a little girl. That girl down there is me. I have to go back to her, to save her after he's done, after he leaves. She needs me or she'll die. She needs me to make her strong, so she can get up and get away. I have to go back and get her up and dressed and away from there. I have to make her run as fast as she can and forget, forget, forget. Be strong! Be in control! Don't let anything show! Don't let pain or hurt or sadness or fear show. Pretend nothing happened. And forget. I have to keep her in control, and I have to keep her quiet.

For the rest of the day, I'm tired, a little strung out and edgy, like a rubber band that's been stretched out and then let go, snapping back. This feeling of stretching and snapping goes on all day.

I think I'm finally knocking through that imaginary wall. I'm getting greater clarity about how the memories are strongly embedded in my physical body, as well as fixed in memory. My body has been that strong wall, supporting me, but also blocking me from more fully experiencing life. It's crumbling a little bit more every day.

Today I was able to release more of what I have stored in my body. As we worked, Nicolas would wait for me to tell him where I was feeling the release and how my body was reacting. I noticed that energy was stuck in my upper chest, my shoulders and neck, with a tight blockage in the throat. There's definitely a bottleneck at the throat chakra. He felt it too, because at the end of the session he demonstrated what I'm to look for as I continue the releasing on my own. He held his hand above my chest, my heart chakra, and the other under my neck, the throat chakra, telling me that these two areas needed attention. Nothing could be truer.

June 4, 2004

I dream that I am a young woman, perhaps sixteen. I'm wearing a flowing white dress. I walk through the large double doors of an ancient building of higher learning and along a winding road, happy and contented. I'm moving on, having graduated, having passed all the tests and gotten awards for my good work. I know that I'm changing rapidly now, moving on into new life, that there's no stopping me. I walk through a tunnel of trees, ready to embrace my new life. Woods surround me, but soon I'll be out of them. I know this for certain, because I see light at the end of the tunnel of trees, not that far ahead. Suddenly, I stop walking. I turn around on the path. I have to go back for something; there's something I forgot, something important. But I feel sure that I know how to find this path again, that I will be back. My intent is strong and I am more self-assured than ever.

My dream shows me that I will get through this, but I can't move on into new life if I leave unrecapitulated memories behind. I must finish this process of recapitulation. I must allow the memories to flow out of me, without holding anything back, no matter how difficult or painful. But it's also certain that I won't lose my way. The path is so clear, my true path of heart.

I meet with Chuck. We go through the memory I worked on in my session with Nicolas.

"Your release got cut off at the neck," he says, "because you haven't fully remembered. You have to recapitulate the full memory in order to release it fully."

He hands me the EMDR pods and I close my eyes and go back into the memory. It's so physically painful, more painful than any memory I've yet recalled, centered in my lower abdomen, second chakra area. I've been feeling the pain there for the past three days. The deeper I go into the memory, the more intense the pain becomes. Chuck calls me back to the present, keeping me grounded, while simultaneously leaving me alone to discover the fullness of the memory.

"Can you tell me what's happening?"

"Yes, I'm locked in some kind of closet," I say, "but it seems that it's after he's done with me. I'm in great pain, and I'm also afraid he won't come back and let me out. The space is small, like under a shelf or under a staircase. I can hear his angry voice, yelling at someone, and that increases my fear. I know I must do exactly as he says. He said to shut up, so I know that I must shut up. Did he put me in here as punishment? I don't know. Who is he yelling at, me?"

It's all I can recall.

I go home and crawl into bed with my clothes on. I lie there for an hour, dealing with the pain. The warmth of my hand over my abdomen seems to help. My energy is depleted. I don't know if I can get up. I want to stay under the covers all day, but that probably isn't a good idea.

I think I understand the dream from the other night, where everything on the mountaintop had been devastated by fire, a little better now. The little girl was showing me not only that it had already happened, but that it had happened a very long time ago. It had a look of ancient history about it. Even as the girl was pointing everything out to me, I was blinking and trying to clear my eyes. I was waking up in my dream, dreaming as a shaman dreams, lucidly, and aware of it, but try as I might I just could not clear up my eyesight. But I did see that the entire area was blackened, devastated, and that it had been that way for a long time. I just couldn't achieve the clarity in the dream to acknowledge that this was so, as vivid and real as the experience was, but now I see it all very clearly. The girl was trying to get me to understand that only the ancient ruins are left. It's like Chuck saying: "It's not now, it happened a long time ago."

I do the recapitulation breath, intentionally clearing the memory away for now, removing it from processing. I'll go back to it later. I have work to do. I get something to eat and head out to take photos for an illustration I'm doing.

I stay fully focused on the road while driving, careful to not let anything from my inner world interfere. If I keep busy, I can get through the day, but I've forgotten how debilitating the whole reliving of an experience can be, how exhausting, and how it takes over, disrupting this reality.

I go to the artists' gallery to sit my four-hour timeslot in the afternoon and stay for the evening's opening too. I'm able to be the new and different person I've been stalking for so long, a totally different personality, someone I've only imagined. I'm totally at ease, funny, fully enjoying myself until the exhaustion sets in again. When that happens, I immediately know that I'm just like Cinderella, and I'm forced to leave before anything devastating happens. And wouldn't you know, as soon as I get home the intensity of the memory revs right up again, and Cinderella is back in her rags.

June 5, 2004

I do the recapitulation breath, sweeping my head slowly from side to side. I hear Chuck saying, "you can do it," and I see him holding a door open just as he holds the door to his office open every time I visit. I just have to step in and begin the journey. It's my job to accept each and every challenge, to step right in and find out what there is to discover about myself.

A memory comes easily. I'm running down the hallway to my abuser's daughter's room, in terror, but he gets me before I get there. He catches me around the waist, pinning my arm, and it's hard to breathe, my diaphragm squeezed too tight.

"Keep the panic and terror down. It's not now," I say to myself, "breathe; keep breathing."

Where is my abuser's daughter? I don't think she's in the house. Later, when she asks where I am, he tells her I went home. I hear him say this when I'm locked in the closet. It's *after*, because my body hurts so much when I'm in the closet. I think he's forgotten about me.

I stop the memory. I don't want to go through any more of it. I need help. I put in a call to Chuck and tell him that I feel like I want to run away from it, to harden up, push it away, and ignore it. The terror of running down the hallway, with my abuser chasing after me, keeps rewinding and replaying. I can't stop it. If I think about something else for a while, maybe I can stop it. I must stay grounded and take care of that terror-stricken little girl, but I also notice that something is different now: I'm feeling the emotions, they're finally breaking through.

"You just have to go through it," Chuck says, when he calls back. "You're in two places at once now, but as intense as it is, you know how to do it. Don't push it, but when it comes, just let it happen."

"I can't really stop it anyway," I say.

"It's like being in labor," Chuck says. "You just have to go through it. You can't control or stop it. It's happening, and no matter how much it hurts, you know you are going to go through it, so let it happen."

We hang up and the memory replays: He grabs me in the hallway and takes me downstairs to the basement, squeezing me around my waist, holding me like a football, a tiny three-year-old girl, his hand over my mouth. I can't breathe. I can't breathe. The breath is squeezed out of me. Then my mouth clamps shut and my teeth clench tightly.

This memory is very early, before I learned how to deal with him. Before I learned how to escape by going numb, and before I knew of his true evil. I was still in the process of learning that quiet was essential, that not fighting back was essential, that playing his game was essential, that if I did as he required, without resistance, it would soon be over. If I resisted it took longer; it just dragged out the agony. But in this memory, I haven't figured all that out yet. By the age of four, I already understood him and how I had to behave. By four I was already totally groomed as his slave girl.

Okay, that's all for now. I will get out of bed now. I will put my feet solidly on the floor and go, just go, *with intent*. No running, just firmly planted on this earth. It's not a great place, but I live here, so I have to figure out ways to deal with it. I may always have the memories and the pain. I may have to live with them forever, but I'm a survivor, and I'm strong.

I get out of bed, eat, wash the dishes and get ready to go to the studio. I still have some more things to move.

Seven thirty at night. I'm happy to report that I made it through the day, though at times it felt impossible. Many times, I just wanted to lie down and cry, but I kept going. I concentrated mostly on getting the studio packed up and I did an illustration that was pending. It didn't take too long and came out all right. Now I just have to write a press release for a local art exhibit. I took home four more carloads of stuff; the house and garage now packed to the gills.

I'm totally exhausted, but I cooked myself some salmon, rice, and vegetables for dinner, and ate it all.

The memory has stagnated for now. I have the beginning in the hallway and I have some of the end, in the basement, but I don't have the memory of what happened to bring on the pain. I still have the intense lower abdominal pain though, reminding me that there's more to remember.

I prepare to sleep, knowing that I may have to deal with the memory, but knowing I can handle it too. I'm an adult, a grown woman, and I *can* mother that child self.

The following has thus far emerged: he takes me to the basement and into the bomb shelter. It's the 1950s and the Cold War is in full swing and many homes are being built with bomb shelters. It contains an inner door that leads into a closet like crawl space, possibly an alternate exit too. This seems to be where he locks me up. This is where I experience the lower abdominal pain, and where the terror surrounds me in the pitch-blackness of that silent space. I pick and claw at the door frame with my small fingers. I just want to get out. I think he's forgotten about me. I'm more afraid of being in here and of being forgotten than anything else. But what did he do to me that made my abdomen and vagina hurt so much? What did he do that pushed my insides up into painful bruised awareness?

I must try to sleep now; it will all come when it's ready. Jeanne, I know you're with me, even though I've been lost in that in-between world. Please stay with me. I need you. I need your help. Thank you for Chuck.

June 6, 2004

I dream that I'm walking through old warehouses of sad stories, my own sad stories. Suddenly, the dream shifts and I'm with my daughter, a tiny three-year-old girl again. We're holding hands, slipping and sliding down a steep and muddy mountain road. I'm wearing socks with no shoes. I tell my daughter that we just have to go with it; that there's no stopping what's happening. We quickly and easily slide down the mountain, almost flying.

There's no stopping the unfolding of this process, or the momentum of the recapitulation of memories. Once they start, it's just like my dream, a slip-sliding adventure.

Something terrible happened.

How did my mother react when I returned home from playing with my abuser's daughter, all traumatized? What did my abuser tell her, that we played "operation," that he found us doing that? He could have said anything. I doubt she even looked at me properly. She was a hands-off mother and already had three kids, with a fourth on the way by the time I was three. By then I was already putting myself to bed at night. Already I didn't need anyone.

This memory may be the actual first rape, the first penis-in-vagina rape. Before that it was fingers and objects inside me, probing and poking, but this one is different, so full of terror. I don't understand what he's doing or why, only that he's hurting me most painfully and I'm terrified, and then he locks me up!

I call Chuck. I'm uncertain about whether or not I should go to Nicolas this afternoon.

"It's important for Nicolas to know where you are, and you feel so safe there," says Chuck. "That container he offers you will be good for you. As far as the memory is concerned, this is very early and you have gone very, very deep already. All the other memories have been leading up and preparing you for this one. You are ready for it," he says.

I hear the compassion in his voice as he says this and I know I must be ready for it, because I don't fight him, nor any of this process.

"I'll go see Nicolas," I say. "Thank you."

I'm careful to act as normal as possible so as not to disturb the kids. I have to be able to get them focused on homework and the things they need for the day. They came home early this morning from their dad's. There's not a lot of food in the house, so I'll have to do some food shopping later too.

My mother calls, as if she knows she's being thought about, talked about, studied. She seems rattled, angry about something. Even now she implies, as she always did, by the accusatory tone of her voice, that everything is my fault. The fact that my car is not fixed properly yet is my fault. I must have done something, she says. What have you done?

I don't want to deal with her, nor do I need that kind of guilt heaped on me. I hang up as soon as possible. I have more important things to attend to.

I go to my session with Nicolas. I tell him where I am, in the midst of remembering, that I think the memory is about the first time my abuser raped me, that it's full of terror and physical pain, and that it's coming in bits and pieces.

"You can't remember while your body holds it in," he says, in contrast to what Chuck said the other day, which was that I have to recapitulate the full memory in order to fully release it. I know they are both right, that I must both recall and release, and that each process happens when I'm ready.

"I'm ready now," I say, and we start.

Nicolas begins working on the left side. The releases come immediately. Before long I'm releasing a lot of wild animal sounds. Eventually, the groans, moans, and howls turn to sobs, dry sobs without tears, as my body cries out its pain. By the time he begins working on the right side I'm releasing wave upon wave of body wracking sobs, but still there are no tears. My body is crying. Starting in my pelvis and working its way up, coming from deep within my body, each sob makes its way along a musty, cobwebby tunnel. I am dredging up old pains, moldy and ancient, and the sounds coming out of me are terrible to hear.

I am tight in my body and throat, as I sob. Each release difficult but necessary. I'm not an openly flowing channel but a tightly clamped tunnel, almost hardened against the sobs, but they want out so badly that there's no stopping them. It's utterly painful and wrenchingly satisfying at the same time.

"My whole body was crying," I say, when we're done.

Nicolas suggests that I lie on my side for a little while.

"Can you do that?" he asks.

"Yes," I say, as I turn onto my right side, my back to him.

"Do you want me to stay?"

"Yes. Don't leave me. Please stay with me," I say, finally able to say the very thing I have longed to say. "Please don't leave me alone."

"Close your eyes," he says. "I'm here. Close your eyes."

"How does your body feel now?" he asks, after a while.

"Tired, exhausted," I say, and tears begin to flow. "I don't know where I am."

"It's okay, you're in your body, and it's a new place for you. That's why it feels unfamiliar," he says, and it's true, I do feel different, totally unfamiliar to myself.

Now come the difficult hours of darkness, the middle of the night and the early morning hours. I feel the rest of the memory is not far away. If I let it come, it will come.

June 7, 2004

In a dream, I am back in my old neighborhood, standing in the road outside my abuser's property. An evil man yells at me that he wants my money. He spits on me, attempting to grab my wallet, but I will not allow him to take it from me. I run from him. Other people stand around watching, as if it's perfectly normal to see two people fighting over money.

I wake up in the night and walk around, anxious. I want the fullness of this memory to emerge so I can function. I want my own energy back, as my dream suggests. I will not let anyone take it from me ever again.

I still feel a little lost after that deep physical release during the Embodyment session, my body aching with residual tightness in my chest, throat, and abdomen. The anxiety of remembering is fully upon me now too, but I noticed that real emotions were somehow absent from the release of the physical memory; they seem to be stored in a totally separate place. A solid wall separates them from my body. They've been apart for so long that I can't cry when I hurt; I can't even seem to connect the two, pain with crying. I head back to bed, hopeful for sleep.

The memory starts up again during the day, uncalled; it simply begins playing. I hear frantic crying and him yelling, "Shut up! Shut up!" I'm with him in the bomb shelter underneath the concrete front porch. Someone is crying. As I listen to the crying in the memory, it becomes clear that it's me, I'm crying. The crying is coming out of me.

Remembering comes in waves now. I tighten physically as the anxiety and terror pass through me, and as the waves of memory pass through me too. My emotions are beginning to thaw. I'm not sure where I am. I'm lost. I call Chuck.

"Mother yourself," he says. "Watch your energy."

"I don't have any," I say.

"That's what I mean, don't overexert yourself," he says, "be careful."

"I don't want to do this alone, it's too hard," I say.

"You don't have to; save it until tomorrow when we meet. Did you see Nicolas?"

"Yes, it was excruciating."

"The experience of your emotions being totally separate from your body is a symptom of the experience. That's what we're trying to bring back together. The disembodied frantic crying you hear *was* you. It was you hearing yourself, but from a dissociated, out-of-body state," he explains, and with this clarity I attempt to put the memory to rest, but the nightmare scenes keep intruding.

June 8, 2004

I woke up hourly throughout the night. Once I got up and went to the bathroom, but every other time I just told myself to go back to sleep, that everything will be fine, that I'll be with Chuck tomorrow, and all will be okay, that after this is over, things will get better. It does feel that way, that this is the last memory.

I'm finally beginning to feel hopeful that there truly is life after recapitulation, but I must not let the outside world in yet. I must not think of wants and desires, nor jump too soon; it's still too early. I must stay focused on my inner work, and not get distracted in any way, even with thoughts of goodness to come.

This memory that sits here now, on the rim of my soul, had shown itself before, long before my recapitulation began, coming in bits and pieces of flashbacks, in jabs at my heart, in fear and trembling, as I wondered what it could possibly mean. I remember the bomb shelter and the closet like crawl space. I remember something terrifying about them, their darkness, their earthy, musty smell, the cobwebs. I was aware that something mysterious, old and frightening lived there. Words are not adequate for the terror I feel in this memory, but adequate enough to help me understand how devastating it was for me, how it ended my life before it even began, how evil came and got me, left me ravaged, damaged, traumatized. But strength always returned, energy always replenished, and it will again. I will be strong again. I will survive, but I will do even better than that; this time I will *live*.

I meet with Chuck and as soon as I look at his face, I think to myself: Oh God, you look really tired. When I say this to myself,

Redeployment of Energy

I notice his features soften, as if he heard me, and then I hear his thought: Yeah, but what about you?

"How are *you*?" he then says, out loud, and I see that he did read my thoughts, and that he knows I read his. We let it pass, again.

In a fairly calm and pretty detached tone of voice, rather stiffly, I go back into the memory and report to him all that I can remember. In the telling I am confronted with the difficulty of putting words to all that I experienced. As always, this telling seems like such an anticlimax, compared to the reliving I've already gone through. But it's a most necessary step, for he is my witness and this is a crucial point, to actually speak aloud, to another human being, words that describe what happened to me. So, as best I can, I explain what went on, the feeling that my abuser is stabbing me and then the screaming starting, and then the yelling, and then the locking up and the pain in my abdomen.

"I don't want to go back there," I say, at one point.

"Who said that?" Chuck asks. "The little girl or the adult?"

"Both of us, I think, both."

He nods.

"I feel like I've already been through most of it," I say, but really this statement is false, because I know I don't have a full memory yet, but I can't explain why I say this; it just comes out of me.

"Yes, it seems so," he says, not sounding too convinced.

"I find it so difficult to be fully functional with the past bearing down on me like a speeding train!" I say, abruptly switching away from the memory. "But I feel better after this telling, mentally at least, and probably emotionally, although I don't feel stable yet, still tentative."

"And you survived the abuse and remained sane! Well, pretty sane!" he says, jokingly, as we finish the session.

He gives me a hug, which I barely perceive, as I am still "back there."

"You'll be all right," he says, "everything will be all right."

I leave Chuck's office and drive across the river to drop my car off at the repair shop. I only have to wait a few seconds before my Benefactor shows up.

"I miss you," he says, as I get into his car. "I told myself I have to figure out a way to have a relationship with Jan without frightening her. So, I thought, can I be her brother? But I'm too old to be her brother. How about father? So that is what I've decided to be to you. So, anything you need, you call and treat me as if I were your father, and I'll help you," he says, quite seriously.

I note how weird this admission is, how uncomfortable it makes me feel, not sure his proposal is a good idea.

"I did call you, didn't I?" I say, letting it pass.

"Yes, you did, and I'm glad you did."

When he drops me off at home, I notice how shaky I am when I get out of the car. I realize I haven't eaten, and I'm physically exhausted too, but my head feels better, lighter. I'm sure it's the result of having spoken to Chuck this morning. The heaviness has definitely lifted. It's almost as if I'm floating, not quite in my body, not quite touching the ground either. I'm almost weightless, as if in a dream.

So, is this healing? Is this what healing feels like? This sense of having unburdened myself? The hopelessness is lifting too, at least for today, and that is certainly a gift. A day without hopelessness is indeed a good day! In spite of the exhaustion, I feel more energetic today as well, whereas yesterday I could barely lift my feet. I'm physically tired yet feeling more whole today, for the depression is leaving with the memories, making room for me. But I know that even with this new feeling of lightness I have to take things slowly, pace myself, conserve my energy.

For more than a week now I've been stuck in the past, gathering the bits and pieces of this memory, but I'm seeing glimpses of possibility again today, feeling like I'm getting back on a positive track. Those glimpses, however, are overshadowed by my old pal fear, sticking close, pointing out that I still have things to face, and that depression lingers still. I can't find inner stillness or balance when fear is present. However, I have to be grateful for fear, for it points out to me what troubles me still, showing me that I won't achieve real balance and true peace until I face *everything*.

I'm so close and yet still so far. I see where I'll land in the future, though I'm still a distance away. How do I get from here to there?

I must stay focused on possibility, on the certainty that everything is possible. I've seen my own bright energy, felt my own strong vibration, and I know what my true state is; I've experienced energetic wholeness. I must remain focused upon total healing, going with the flow of what life offers, for I trust it now, that I will be guided properly, and that I will know now what is right choice and what is wrong choice as I make my way forward in life.

In one sense, I'm choosing instability as a way of life, electing to follow where my spirit takes me, choosing a path of heart over a known path of conventional stability. I've chosen the work path of a freelance artist because it's the only job that feeds my spirit. My spirit's path and my work path are one and the same intertwined path. This is how I envision my wholeness, a true path of heart. And I'm ready and willing to face all the fears that block that path.

I finally write the press release I've been procrastinating about, feeling pretty good by the time it's done, but when the SAAB dealer calls and tells me that the repair on the car is another five hundred dollars, I cry, feeling sorry for myself. My Benefactor gives me a ride to pick it up at the end of the day and I put the charge on my credit card. At least it's fixed and I can get to and from work safely now.

June 9, 2004

While sleeping on my left side, I dream that I'm in an old house with wild animals running through it. I'm waiting for something to be delivered, as well as waiting for someone to help with repairs.

My dream seems to indicate that I have yet to access my emotions, those wild animals running through the house, or perhaps it's the energy I've been dealing with inside me. By the end of the day yesterday I felt scattered and unsure of everything, in spite of my earlier intent. I suffered through a lot of back-and-forth energy, and a sense of too much new stuff inside me needing to be calmed down. Perhaps I was feeling residual energy from talking about the memory with Chuck, but at the same time I felt I must not go back there, so I let it be.

I paint all day at the jobsite, feeling detached from life and the past, feeling like I'm not really here. My body is here but I'm someplace else. When I get home, I mow the lawn. It's very hot and I'm tired, but the grass is almost up to my knees, though luckily not too thick. Afterwards I go into the bathroom to take a bath and find the tub crawling with small red ants and some larger ones with wings, which freaks me out. By the time I'm done cleaning them all out, I opt for a shower rather than risk sharing the tub with any stray ants. It's hard to relax and I keep my shower brief.

I'm being tested. I refused yet another offer of a fulltime job today, one I easily would have gotten, the second one this week, but I would have been miserable. I know that now. It's not where my path of heart is leading me. I am a solitary being.

June 10, 2004

In the morning I'm exhausted, having slept little; the heat of the night making it especially difficult. I did my usual tossing and turning, attempting to find a comfortable position but to no avail. As I tossed and turned, I really dumped on myself, with lots of self-deprecating accusations.

"Look what you've done! You've wrecked everyone's lives, and for what? For this really bad place? Is it worth it? Are you happier? At least you were more secure before; at least you had something!"

But I know none of that is true, that I was dying before and by now might well be dead, or totally numb and dead inside, if not truly dead. No, this is better! This is what I need.

As soon as I start to feel good something always tries to pull me back into negativity. I've proven that so many times. I just have to step back and look at the pattern. All the challenges really teach me that everything works out, that everything is right in my life, that I haven't in fact crumbled and lost my sense of balance. In fact, the next day always does come along, and whatever it was that loomed so huge and frightening has gone. The lesson is about finding the means to detach from the past and what I was controlled by in the past by being open to what is new, thus achieving a sense of safety in the world by being open to life. When I allow myself to be open, I teach myself to trust the unfolding of my own life.

During my Embodyment session, I discover that the little three-year-old girl in this unfolding memory is energetically trapped in my lower pelvis, in the first and second chakra regions. It makes sense, the area of the womb, and like any real human she wants to get out, her birth long overdue. She wants to go where all children go when they grow up, to join me in adulthood. Getting her out proves difficult. When I begin to feel a release, like a labor pain creeping up on me, it causes me to clamp down. Even though I clamp, the release happens anyway. There's no stopping this process. I'm not in control anymore, no matter what I think. So, I try not to clamp down, but I don't really know how not to; it's so a part of my makeup. In the end, I do achieve some good physical releases and after the session, as I head off to work, I realize I feel pretty good, that something definitely moved out of me.

June 11, 2004

I meet with Chuck. I'm stuck, I tell him. I'm afraid to let my inner child out of the dungeon where she's been locked up for nigh on half a century. The truth is, I have no recollection of getting out of the crawl space and the bomb shelter; I'm still there, at least that frightened little three-year-old self is. At the same time that I know I must go to her and recapitulate her entire experience, extricating her from her dungeon, I worry about letting her out, that it won't be safe for her in the real world.

"Yes," Chuck says, "you're afraid something will happen and you'll get hurt again."

"Exactly!"

I realize that the little girl herself is desperate to get out of the dungeon though. Who wouldn't be? But I'm frightened for her because from my current vantage point, I see him, my abuser, standing outside the door, waiting for her, and she's still tender, so young and unaware. It's as if I know something she doesn't know, but at the same time I don't, at least not yet, since I don't have a complete memory. But I couldn't bear it if something else happened to her.

I stay detached from the little girl while working, so I don't have to deal with her, but she's persistent. She won't go away. She's pushing me to finish the memory and rescue her.

I realize that my recapitulation has been a series of lessons, coming in a myriad of ways, from flashbacks and memories, to bodily pain and mental anguish. Even Jeanne has presented me with lessons in her own unique way, sometimes with symbols or riddles, things to figure out as I go along. Sometimes I wonder why I don't just get things handed to me straight, but I guess the real lesson is in what I learn as I take this journey. If things were just handed to me, I'd never have the amazing experiences I've had over the past few years, as I've worked through the mysteries of my own past and my own psyche. The only way I believe that any of these things happened to me is because I have relived every bit of every single memory. But I'm different, in a stronger and wiser place and I'm ready for a new approach now. And so, on the drive home, I shout my intent for this to happen.

"PLEASE! NO MORE LESSONS! I DON'T WANT ANY MORE LESSONS! I GET IT, OKAY? YOU DON'T HAVE TO TEACH ME ANYMORE. JUST GIVE IT TO ME STRAIGHT!"

"No more lessons please; just the magic."

June 12, 2004

I have to unite my body with the past, confront the screams of that child as my own, the pain as mine, the fear as mine, the anxiety and panic as mine. I have to face that at the age of three

I was raped, for the first of many times. It's in my body, all of it. I feel it. I've always felt it.

Here's the truth as I now know it: my abuser raped me inside a bomb shelter in the basement of his house and then he locked me in the dark of a crawl space adjacent to it, punishing me for screaming. I don't remember being let out. I only remember hearing a child screaming. They were however my own screams, but I have yet to claim them as my own. I must have been dissociated, out-of-body, and that's where the disconnect lies, as Chuck mentioned. I heard things I could not relate to myself, for the out-of-body state provided protection from what was happening in-body. But I do truly understand that they were my own screams and that the little girl locked in that space was me.

I finally got everything moved out of the studio. The garage is now full. Organizing it is my next task.

It hits me suddenly that I have actually moved on. It's as if I'm finally taking it in and understanding the surprising truth that I enacted another big change. Something that was so important to me is gone, along with old ideas of myself. New realizations of who I really am take their place. A part of myself is left behind as I begin a new phase, in a new configuration. I'm saddened and amazed at the same time.

An old desperate need to run and to keep running stirs in me, but a secondary need emerges, to just curl up and hide; two very old standard reactions to disturbances within my psyche. But I will do neither now. Instead, I accept where I am now and I look to the future. I must also continue my recapitulation. I must face the locked door of that crawl space and be the safe and trustworthy adult who greets the child this time, when she is finally freed from the darkness by my own hand.

If I continue refusing to connect with the little girl, I'll never resolve any of this. I reach a certain point where I'm able to admit that, okay, that's me and yes, that did happen to me, and I know it for certain by the pain, because the pain is real. But I can't get to the emotions; I'm still emotionally dead. Even though I'm aware of what happened, awareness alone does nothing to further the journey. The only thing that counts is the act of recapitulation, the act of re-experiencing the trauma and reclaiming what has been lost. I've done it enough times to know that it's the only way to fully integrate all parts of the self.

I acknowledge that there was a secret world that never merged with my everyday reality. I realize how much fabrication it took in order for me to cover up the bitter abusive reality. Eventually, the fabrication became my reality, protectively composed, artfully realized so I could at least survive. The past has been murky for so long, but now it has turned clear, concise; a life explained, a life revealed for the utter raw truth of it.

I spend a few hours arranging the garage, stacking things neatly on shelves that line the back wall, trying to make it more spacious and workable. By five in the afternoon, I'm totally out of energy, but I have just enough left to make a trip to the grocery and video stores.

"Go slowly," I tell myself, "take it slow. You are driving. Focus," I say, noticing that I'm not in my body, for the truth is that I'm far away, and I stay that way until I'm safely back home.

Later, I watch a movie called *Leo*, about a man who, while in prison, begins writing letters to himself as a young boy. As he recapitulates, he returns to his home in Oxford, Mississippi where they meet, the boy and the grown man, each having been searching for the other, each with a message for the other. It's where I am now, trying to meet up with the child self, that abused and sad little girl. I must not be so afraid of her.

June 13, 2004

3:15 am. I am awakened by intense vaginal pain. Why? I breathe, trying to refocus it in words, in breath, in getting it out of me. Is this the pain I felt at the age of three? First, it's cold and shivering pain. DAMN! Then I'm hot, so hot! So much heat; the pain burns inside me, the pain of rape, the pain of the memory of rape. I breathe, trying to release with each breath, trying to release both the pain and the heat.

I get out of bed to walk it off, going from room to room, the three cats following me, as restless as I am. They must think it's time to eat, but no food bowls are appearing. They rub against my legs as I stand at the back door, looking out at the dark night sky. As the last of the pain finally eases out of me, I realize the only way to deal with it is to accept it, to relax into it, and let it go. It's always the same answer, to *acquiesce*.

The cats follow me back into my bedroom and we all jump back into bed, hoping there's nothing more. I sense their continued restlessness, their watchfulness. They're alert to my every move, aware of my painful nights. I drift off to sleep at around five.

I dream that I'm at a large resort. The season is over and the resort is closing. I have to find a way to get home. I don't have a car. I watch as everyone else drives away, leaving me standing alone in the empty parking lot. A kind man comes along and guides me through a tunnel. At the end of the tunnel, he points out that I have two clear choices. I can either take the wide, open yellow brick road that's right in front of me, or I can take the steep mountainous path that he points out to the left. It's totally up to me. I choose the mountain path, because I think I have to. Frankly, I don't see that there is a clear choice. I think I have to go the hard way because it's what I'm used to; in fact, it looks very familiar.

As I begin to climb the mountain path, I teeter, each step more precarious and dangerous than the last. I fear falling down the mountainside as I take one shaky step after another, going higher and higher. As I work my way up the steep mountainside, I'm aware that I must still cleanse my body of the pain, that I still have a lot to release. I feel better by the time I arrive at the top. From there, I can see the wide yellow brick road that the man had first pointed out to me. It's still right in front of me, crossing my path.

As soon as I wake up, I feel like such an idiot! Of course, I could have taken the yellow brick road to begin with; a much easier route! It's where I end up anyway, right where it intersects the steep mountain trail. It makes me laugh; how blind I can be! But the truth is that when I first saw the yellow brick road, I couldn't at all take in that it was easier. I just automatically took the more difficult route, out of sheer habit, because I still feel that everything has to be a challenge or I'm not doing it right. Life is supposed to be hard!

Breaking old habits is hard after having lived a life where habits kept me safe. I did whatever my abuser told me to do, for sixteen years having it drilled into me that this is how you survive—do what he wants and you'll survive! So, for the rest of my life that became my *modus operandi*. It was safer than fighting, safer than certain death, but I've remained captive to its power, unable to accept that I do in fact have other choices, that other roads might yield better outcomes. Life doesn't have to be as hard as I make it out to be.

It's time to challenge the status quo, my own inner habits that have guided and dictated the choices of a lifetime. My dream was pointing this out to me, how I habitually choose a difficult path because it's what I've come to expect of life. But I'm changing; I have new expectations of myself now. I'm learning to take back my power, learning that I have the power within myself to choose a different life.

The pain signals that it's still with me. I don't care! GO AWAY! I have to accept that it's where I got hurt. My abuser didn't hurt my heart. No, he hurt me down there, and from there it spread throughout my body. Does the pain come back because I refuse to own it? But I recognize it; I know that pain intimately. That's where it all started. From there all those other pains, phobias, and fears grew. My innocence was replaced with pain.

I can't do anything when the pain comes except be with it, become it. The only thing to do is let it take over, like the labor pains of childbirth, like the releases in my Embodyment sessions, because there's no other way to deal with it. It's going to happen anyway. But it's the worst pain imaginable, and when I'm in the midst of it, I can't think or gain control of it. I can only whimper and gag and drool like a baby, because that's just what I did when he raped me. I couldn't stop it then and I can't stop it now. I can't ease it or erase it; I can't do anything except let it happen. Until I have experienced it, relived it all, it will remain in my body.

It's only eight thirty in the morning and I'm already worn out. I must shift out of this recapitulation in order to remain sane, present and grounded in this world, but I must also go back into the memory and relive it fully. Sometimes the shift out of that old world isn't total and I have to be careful when I'm out in the world, especially when driving, like yesterday, when I felt so distant from reality. It can be frightening when that happens. The world remains out of focus and I feel the distance, but I'm also aware that I just can't bridge it at the moment.

I go for a quiet, solitary walk, needing to be in nature. I walk for a mile or so and sit in the grass, feeling so exhausted that I fear I won't make it back, but I do, walking numbly, just putting one foot in front of the other. I think about the dream I had last night, about how I keep choosing the familiar, but also about how I can't yet seem to fully make the other choice, the one right before my eyes. Maybe I'm just not ready for it yet; I may have another mountain or two to climb.

After my walk I drive over to the new studio space. I sit there quietly absorbing its light and energy. I'm full of hope at the prospect of having this new place in my life, needing and wanting desperately to have something that will keep me sane and balanced, a sacred space in which to be creative, where I can safely, within the cloak of my artwork, express my pain and hopefully, eventually, my joy.

I'm not being dragged through this recapitulation, I'm going willingly, following the signs that guide me. Some deeper part of me is leading the way, cheering me along, so grateful that I'm taking this journey. However, there's another part of me that still feels that I must be punished for the sins of my past, guilty or not. I participated in every act that my abuser perpetrated upon me, and that complicit part of me needs the excruciatingly torturous path. She still chooses punishment over the ease of no blame.

I'm fully aware that I'm the only one who can release my child self from her dungeon. I must do that before I can embrace any new life. I must take back all parts of myself, restoring all of my energy. I believe this is the last mountain.

"*Trust,*" Jeanne says. "*Cleanse yourself first of all the old stuff and then you will be free to take the new road. With the burden of the past and those steep mountains still there, you will never be able to choose the easy road. Find a way to unleash the past from your body and soul, and then you will truly be free."*

Nothing will change if I don't deal with the past, that much I already know. The yellow brick road is in plain sight but still unreachable at this point. The solution, however, lies within my grasp. It's time to fully confront the physical and emotional pain that little girl was left with, and the fact that after all these years she's still, symbolically, locked away in that crawl space, for I have no recollection of ever getting out. I surmise that my abuser would have let me out, and by then it probably felt more like a rescue. He was a child rapist, yet he did not kill me. And in this instance, how ironical that he would appear as my rescuer!

I wander through the day, doing one thing and another, unfocused for the most part. The kids come home from their weekend with their dad at eight in the evening and by ten I'm in bed, trying to sleep, but thoughts keep coming. I wonder how someone ever overcomes lifelong phobias and fears, how you cure someone of sadness and distrust, of fear and pain, and how you get all the hidden things, the invisible, untouchable things out of a body? It seems impossible.

I finally fall asleep and wake up a few minutes later with a strong soapy taste and smell in my mouth. What is that from?

June 14, 2004

I dream that my right side and left side are arguing over my lack of energy. I'm so exhausted that I just can't go another step, but at the same time I know I must keep going. One part of me is sure that I'll be forced to quit out of sheer exhaustion, while the other part refuses to give in or give up.

"Just keep going. Tap into the reservoir," I hear, just as I wake up.

This is exactly what goes on every day. The intensity of my recapitulation encourages forging ahead at all costs, while at the same time I am becoming increasingly exhausted. I know if I keep going in this manner that I'll either break down or become sick in some way. This is exactly what the *I Ching* warned me about, to suspend the tail biting obstinacy or face breakdown. The recapitulation is getting harder, not easier, but even so, I must keep going. And what is the reservoir? The reservoir of strength? The reservoir of energy?

The kids leave to catch the bus and I go back to bed for a while, feeling negative, the Invisibles back again. I know that as long as I stay stuck in the old way of thinking—that I can't do something—then I won't do *anything*. If I don't get out of bed and do something for myself, nothing will happen. I'll just stay stuck. Nothing new will happen if I don't make it happen, if I don't actively invite it into my life. I know this.

Yesterday, I finally felt an inkling of hope as I sat in my new painting studio, felt lucky to have it, felt assured that in the end, everything will work out just fine. I have to remember that good and positive feeling.

My lower back releases in spasms of burning pain throughout the day. What am I still holding onto? And I have the taste of soap in my mouth again. Another memory?

June 15, 2004

I wake up with the taste of soap strong on my lips and in my mouth. This is accompanied by a sensation of choking. I have to get the complete memory. It's really the only way to process it, by getting the entire story. I'm aware that this recapitulation process has a life of its own, that I don't control it, but that it presents me with what I need and what I can handle, when I'm ready for it. As much as I want to jump ahead into new life, I realize that's impossible until I'm totally freed of the past. It's the past, after all, that won't allow me to move on. It catches me up whenever I think I may be ready to move on, presenting me with another facet, showing me what I've missed, another feeling, taste, or smell to process.

I realize I have to allow myself to get angry and upset as each memory emerges. It's part of getting in touch with my feelings, even if they're bad feelings about myself. Even those kinds of feelings are related to the memories.

Lately, I've been experiencing the collapse of all that once upheld me, but I think it's good. It feels like acquiescence and acceptance of the truth, but it also feels like I'm finally letting go of the ingrained need to constantly be in a heightened state of alertness to potential danger in my environment. It's such an old and exhausting stance, and no longer necessary. I'm not being threatened as I once was. It's really the clash of the old and the new that I'm experiencing as I go through this collapse, the loss of the old me and the challenge of the new me, as I figure out each day who needs the attention and where to place my energy. Is that the reservoir my dream suggested, my own pool of retrieved energy, as I learn how to redeploy it?

I meet with Chuck. I piece together as much of the new layer of memory as I can. It starts with soap in my mouth and ends with the rape, but in actuality, the soap came after the rape. The memory of the soap in my mouth led the way down the rabbit hole of the memory, back to the most painful aspects of it.

"It's okay," Chuck says. "You're safe, you're safe, you're safe," as I rock and writhe in pain. I am like a little baby and his gentle words allow me to accept my child self in pain, and I go even deeper into her experience as a result.

"Ask for help," Chuck says. "Ask for help."

I tell him that my abuser washed my mouth out with soap for screaming and crying. *No screaming allowed! No crying allowed!* He washed the crying out of me.

"He was grooming you, teaching you the rules," Chuck says, "his rules, the only rules he played by."

"But why, why me? Why did I have to have these things happen to me?"

He tells me that Jeanne struggled for a long time with that same question, wondering why she had to get cancer, but eventually got to: Why not me? Why not? I'm not special.

"Don't look too far ahead, just deal with what's right in front of you," Chuck says. "Just continue taking one step at a time, and when you're in the throes of a memory, when you can't seem to relate to reality, call for help. Just say, *please help me*."

    I go home afterwards, eat breakfast, put gas in the car and drive to a new job. I work until late in the afternoon, painting a decorative motif on a built-in china cabinet. My client is thrilled with the work I'm doing for her, an old customer who's been collecting my work for years. She's bustling and cheerful, neighbors stopping in to say hello. I sense life returning to me too, my own bustling energy not far off.

    By the time I arrive home at the end of the day, I'm still feeling the after-effects of the morning's recapitulation, which hung over me all day like a veil, although I was able to push it to the side while working, knowing that later I could pull it back over me and revisit the memory if I wanted to. While I painted and chatted with my client, I wondered why, indeed, I had the early life experiences that I'd had. Why was I confronted with such horrific stuff at such a young age? I know there must be a reason that I've taken just this life's journey and not some other. There's a reason for everything that happens. I may not yet know why I've lived just this life, but I trust that eventually the reason will reveal itself. And it will be meaningful. In the meantime, I will plod along dealing with what comes, taking life one day at a time, moving one more step forward.

    As I lie in bed, quite tired and hopeful for sleep, I feel detached from my body. In spite of having relived the memory, I remain numb. My body may have recapitulated the experience, but I did not wholly participate. Part of me was absent, perhaps the same part of me that was absent when the rape actually happened, my detached, dissociated, out-of-body self.

    I'm so grateful for where I am in my life now, how Jeanne is guiding me, and the wonder of it all.

June 16, 2004

I wake in the night, coming out of a deep dream, my body leaden, heavy. I'm hot, but a cool breeze comes through the open window, soothing me.

"Help, please, I need help!" I call out, as I struggle to fall back to sleep. "I need help inside my body!"

Eventually, I drift off into restless dreamless sleep for the rest of the night. I get up at five, make coffee, and shake off my tiredness. The day has begun.

I go back to bed and lie there for an hour after the kids go to school, trying to get balanced, talking to the child inside myself, still dissociated, still untrusting.

"It's okay, baby, you're safe now. It's okay, baby, you're safe now. I'm safe now. We're safe now. You're safe now."

It seems to help, addressing her in this way, for I sense her growing calmer. I feel her nestling in, beginning to trust that I can do this for her, that I am her salvation, the rescuer she has been waiting for all these years. It feels similar to the work I did with my sixteen-year-old self, as I reunited with her in the same patient and loving manner.

By nine o'clock I'm ready for the day. I head out to the garage to get some work done, intending to stay focused on today, and today only, nothing else. I have my to-do list and I have my work for the day lined up, so it's just a matter of staying on task, focused and functional, grounded in reality. The soapy taste is still in my mouth. I'm getting used to it, though soapy tasting foam constantly forms in my mouth. I keep stepping out of the garage to go spit it into the grass.

I've been having mild hot flashes and no period since early May. Maybe that phase of life is over. Time to shift into a new phase of life, with new parameters and new awarenesses.

"Awareness is what allows for life," Chuck said yesterday, when I told him I sometimes lose all confidence that my life will ever change.

"It will change," he said, "it will get better, it's all part of your journey; the tough stuff, the old stuff, and the shock of reality is all part of your journey to awareness."

June 17, 2004

In a dream, I'm out driving around, supposedly to pick up children, though I can't remember who, where, or when I'm supposed to get them, so I turn around and head back home. I stop my car on a steep hill, and get out for no apparent reason. As I do, the car starts to roll. I stand there, with a sense of helplessness, watching the car roll down the hill, unable to do a thing about it. This is what it feels like in reality now too; I am not in control.

I try to decipher if I'm experiencing hot flashes—typical menopausal hot flashes—or a memory triggered by the soapy taste in my mouth. The flashes come all day. While I quietly work, they come like clockwork, every thirty or forty minutes. In the beginning they last five minutes, but by the end of the day they last less than a minute. I time them, and I also take my temperature to see how hot I get, but all thermometer readings are normal.

There seems to be a connection between the hot feeling and crying. I used to experience a very similar feeling when I cried as a child, a desperate panicky feeling that I must not cry. This was accompanied by a hot red heat creeping into my body, rising into my face as I attempted to hold the tears back. Intense anger rushed over me when I could no longer hold them back. A hot river of shame, embarrassment, and guilt swept through me along with the tears.

I believe now, after dealing with this all day, that the hot flashes may be memories of just those crying episodes. I noticed that when I thought about some aspect of the past, such as the recent memory with a lot of anxiety attached to it, a hot flash arrived simultaneously. The hot flash didn't produce the anxiety, but rather the anxiety produced the hot flash. The heat came up from the middle of my back like a winged V, spreading to my shoulders and head. I did not turn red but simply felt very hot.

Nicolas mentioned that I have a lot of heat in my body around this stuff, as did Lara. Is that what I'm releasing now? I have no other menopausal symptoms, no palpitations, dizziness, nausea, just sensations of heat and feeling sweaty, just like I did as a child. Today, I got control of the heat by calming myself down and breathing into it, by getting centered, focusing my attention on breathing into my belly, exhaling long breaths. It's been a very bizarre day.

June 18, 2004

Once again, I dream that I'm driving. Things keep falling out of the car. I stop and pick them up. I arrive at a house where I find a little girl of three, sitting on a toilet. She stays on the toilet through the whole dream, wanting me to stay with her. I go back and forth between her in the bathroom and going outside to find the things I had lost along the way. I tell the little girl not to worry, that the rest of our belongings will be arriving soon.

I wake with a start when Cosi, the little cat, jumps off the windowsill onto the bed, landing with a thud an inch from my face, her sharp claws digging into my pillow, her fluffy tail swiping my face. It was not a good night. I slept restlessly, though I was able to control the hot flashes by relaxing and breathing into them, slowing everything down by first emptying my mind and then by slowly and calmly breathing.

My dream seems to be letting me know that my three-year-old self and I still have some things to work on. Perhaps what I'm actually retrieving in my dream are the memories specifically associated with that three-year-old self. While she waits patiently for me, I bring back to her memories of rape and pain. At the end of the dream, I'm certain that we'll soon have gathered everything we need.

Pain across my ribs startles me more fully awake. It's as if I'm being grabbed and held. Is this the memory of being grabbed in the hallway, as I tried to outrun my abuser? It's as if something is calling me, enticing me to go back in time, to let the anxiety take me. Am I being set up for another memory? Panic sets in. Oh shit! I feel sick. There's soap in my mouth, my throat is closing tightly, and I feel helpless. I can't stop it. I calm myself down. I'll go through it with Chuck. Another hot flash builds. I calm it down too. It comes to a stop at the back of my neck. I breathe it out. Relief.

When I meet with Chuck, I try to release, try to cry, but I can't emit much more than a few strangled cries, and no tears come. Chuck reassures me.

"Don't hold it in," he says, "let it go, let it out."

"There's pain and danger associated with crying," I say.

"Crying is very healing," he says. "It's good for you."

"The hot flashes are probably related to holding it in," I say. "I'm holding in so much fear; it's created heat in my body. The holding in and the heat are one and the same. I've built up a tremendous fire."

"There's a synchronicity around all of this," I say, as it suddenly dawns on me. "The water pump on my car is leaking now. It isn't holding liquid, which is pouring out of a worn ball bearing. The whole cooling system has been affected by pressure failure."

"The car is reacting in direct correlation to what's happening within you!" he says, making me laugh.

"I get it," I say, "but unfortunately, the car is a lot more expensive to fix than I am!"

I get the car problem fixed, another charge on the credit card, but at least it seems fine now and it should be okay, as long as I work on my own internal pressure problems.

In another synchronicity, I get home to discover that my daughter has a fever of a 102. She alternates between hot and then chilly, showing me the proper, natural means by which to address a feverish system, how a proper cooling system works. I tend to her, telling her that everything will be okay, to just sleep, that her body knows how to heal itself, and that I'll check on her in a little while. Then I head out to paint in the garage, and I keep telling the little girl inside me that everything will be okay too.

"Crying is very healing," Chuck said. I have to remember that, and that this journey is a journey of healing.

When feelings come and the heat begins to rise, I say a new mantra—*I am safe*—remembering that indeed I am safe now, and that it's okay to cry because it's healing. I say the mantra and breathe through the hurt, through the pain across my ribs, and through the pain in my throat. I breathe, gently at first, and then deeper and deeper, as I release the heat, naturally, without holding.

With time and patience, I will find a way to allow the child inside me, and the adult self, to cry. We both need to, but mostly it's the child who has suffered, having held back for so long, resulting in this burning up. Just thinking about it sparks fire within me. It's going to be a hot night tonight!

When I said, "thank you, for everything," to Chuck today, he said, "you don't have to thank me."

"But I want to," I said.

"Well then, you're welcome!"

Someday I will have to grow up and leave him, but for now I will take it one moment at a time, accepting and working with what he teaches me. So, indeed, thank you for him.

Jeanne comes into my room at night. I felt all day that she wanted to tell me something, that she had a message. I finally listen to her, but I don't really want to hear what she has to say. She says that Chuck loves me.

"I know he does," I say.

"*He is discovering deeper connections to you.*"

"Well, we knew that too," I say.

"*No, he is going to discover that his desire to be there for you and to be a part of your growth and transformation are going to increase.*"

"Well," I say, "I can't go there. I can't think about that. I just have to think about now, that he's my anchor, my teacher."

She says I will maintain a long-lasting connection with him, that I don't have to fear losing touch with him, that we need each other, that he listens to me and hears my need now, but, as I continue to grow and transform, he and I will understand what I can offer him in return.

I can't accept what she's saying. I tell her that I can only take it one day at a time. I love him today for what he offers me, as I journey through this recapitulation process, and for the guidance he gives me. He is on a journey that has intersected with mine and so we journey together for a while. For how long, we don't know, but for now we are here. It's all I can accept right now. I'm not ready for anything else. I still have work to do.

June 19, 2004

I dream of a small girl standing all alone in a huge empty room, like a vast gym or exhibition hall. I feel her starting to cry and sense the hot heat of emotional repression rising inside her, as if it were happening to me. There is no comfort anywhere in sight, and no one comes to her rescue. She's totally alone.

In the dream, the floor of the vast room stretched into infinity; there were no walls and no ceiling. There was darkness all around, as if a spotlight were shining on a scene in the center of a vast stage. I was in three places at once in this dream, experiencing three different perspectives. First, I was the child, standing all alone. Second, I was my adult self, standing in the shadows, watching the child. Third, I was myself as the dreamer, dreaming the dream and watching these two other figures, the child and the adult. The adult self was on the left in the scene, and the child on the right. I knew what each of them was thinking and feeling, but they couldn't communicate with each other and I could not communicate with them. I could not, as the dreamer, assist them, nor could I tell them what I now know. Even though they were all me, we were detached from each other, in our separate dreamscapes.

The adult self, the character on the left in the dream, knew the child needed help and wanted to go to her, swoop her up, hug her, and tell her she was safe, like I've been yearning to do during this recapitulation. In the dream I was unable to do so. Invisible barriers kept each dreamscape separate and apart. They could not be penetrated by any of us.

My dreamscape perspective, as the third character, the dreamer, was outside looking in at the entire scene. I was just an observer, even my adult self, the second dream character was not aware that I was present. The truth is that the different parts of myself have each remained in their own dreamscapes all these years, though now, through my recapitulation work, they are being brought into consciousness. In the dream, the child is totally alone in that vast expanse of space, transfixed by fear, the same space she has occupied in my psyche, just as my adult self has lived in her own dissociated dreamscape in my psyche.

My dream shows me the truth of what happened as a result of the trauma of childhood, but also that I'm in a different place now, able to observe and understand what the child needs, indeed, what she always needed. My dream also points out the growing awareness of my adult self and her desire to finally unite with her lost child self. The dream shows me that though we have evolved, we are still in fragments, and that somehow, I have to find a way to penetrate the invisible barriers that prevent us from more fully communicating and integrating. That is the challenge we now face, getting beyond the barriers that separate us, to final reconciliation.

As the adult self in the dream, I was aware of still being detached from the child, and frustrated that I was prevented from getting to her, but I also knew that she, the child, could not help herself. I could not blame her for anything; she was just too young at the time of the rape. She didn't have the necessary developmental skills to protect herself or get herself safely away. She was innocent, barely out of infancy, and although she very cleverly survived, that's all she could do. She has remained all this time in the vast limbo of survivorhood. In the dream I see her pain, feel her fears, and know she needs rescue, but I can't figure out how to get to her.

As the dreamer, the third character in this dream, I see how each of these two parts, the child and the adult, are stuck in their own separate worlds, where they have been for so long, compartmentalized, unable to truly connect or acknowledge the existence of the other. They've been separated by the painful memories of the past, which sent each of them scrambling for safety and oblivion.

This is an important moment in my recapitulation. The adult has learned new skills that will be able to take her beyond oblivion now, beyond the limbo of just surviving. She knows what needs to be done now, as she learns compassion for herself and for her child self, whom she has kept at a distance, locked away in that vast empty arena. The child self doesn't let anyone get too close. That has been her means of survival; by keeping others away she remains safe. In the dream, the child clearly exhibits that she still believes this is the solution. Now I've come to finally rescue my child self, after all these years, to get her out of there and bring her safely home, to the home within. I'm learning what that really means.

I must maintain a calm and healthy maturity while remaining fully aware and connected to the needs of the child self. I can't let the old hard personality take over again, though she hovers nearby, ready to swoop in at a moment's notice. I must keep both the child and the adult in happy, healthy balance.

I stress to them that we are safe now, that nothing bad will happen to us, that it's over, that the old way isn't necessary anymore. I tell them that we can handle this, get through this, that in the end we will be together as never before, in our own wholeness, more safe and solid than ever. I repeatedly say the mantra: *we are safe now; nothing bad is going to happen*, continually calming myself, my whole self, with those reassuring words. At the same time, I keep track of where each personality is and why. I watch for the signs of where to go next to facilitate my recapitulation process, to bring us into unified wholeness. And I remain alert to the guidance from the universe, providing a link beyond the known human self, to the divine self.

My recapitulation journey has been much like waking up from a terrible nightmare, "the shock of reality," as Chuck called it the other day, all part of my journey to awareness. When I look into the mirror now, I see a grown woman, not a frightened child but a woman who has had a life, birthed children, published books, had relationships, and been married twice. In fact, I see a woman who had a pretty full life, but it all feels like a dream because I wasn't really present. I was numb and detached from what that woman was experiencing. It was impossible for me to fully be part of her life because the other parts of myself where far away in their distance dreamscapes, doing what they needed to do in their own way. It was all a matter of how best to survive. It was as if we were all on the same train, going in the same direction, but all riding in our separate compartments, meeting only occasionally, as we passed each other in the aisles. Then, one day, I stopped the train.

"I can't take this trip anymore," I said. "I just can't do life this way anymore. Something is missing."

And thus began this journey of transformation.

I notice the inner rise of heat comes when something causes anxiety, be it a thought, something I'm reading, anything that triggers a situation where I'm confronted with having to feel intense emotion. This is followed by the need to hold it in, to not release. My body is burning up with this heat, but whenever I check my temperature, it's always exactly 98.6 degrees.

After a trip to the laundromat and the grocery store, I spend the rest of the day sorting through and straightening up all the stuff I brought home from the studio. Little by little I am turning chaos into order.

I found some books on psychoanalytical subjects at the free book exchange at the recycling center. At first, I wondered if it was a good idea for me to be reading them, fearing I might be influenced or confused, better to just let my process unfold, but instead I'm finding them very helpful. In fact, I'm hungry for more knowledge about this process I'm going through and what it all means, about how memory works, how we store stuff in our bodies, and how it interferes later when we least expect it. I've been reading about the psychological aspects of this inner work, but also the spiritual. They're really in alignment, just different parts that come together as we learn more about who we really are, not who we *think* we are.

What I've experienced as I've taken this recapitulation journey goes far beyond what the human mind is capable of understanding. I can't believe something simply based on hearsay, nor do I expect anyone to believe me or my experiences, but what

I've experienced shows me just how incredible the human mind and body are, what they can do and perceive, what the human spirit can withstand and what it is really capable of. Through my own experiences—which have proven to be more mysterious than anything I could have ever imagined—I discover that I must abandon science and religion both and shift to a new perception of the world. I have complete trust in my own experiences to continue to guide and inform me. I could only get to this perspective because I dared to break away from old ideas of a limited self.

"Please, I need some magic," I begged the other day, and then I looked up to see a deer standing right in front of me. We stood and stared at each other, straight into the eyes, only a few feet apart, head-to-head for several minutes. As I stood there, looking into those dark pools of nature and instinct, I thought, "you are the magic, this is my magic," and suddenly I thought of Jeanne.

"It's Jeanne," I thought, "I see her now in those big brown eyes."

And I whispered her name under my breath. It seemed impossible that the deer could hear me, but it immediately kicked up its heels, as if delighted. And then it ran off, as if to say, "that's enough for now, enough magic for today!"

Last night, Jeanne was in my room again, fluttering about, keeping me company. I felt she wanted to communicate something, but I didn't understand what it was.

The night is cool and I'm hoping to sleep better tonight. I hope the cats remain calm. Some nights they run around all night, racing over my bed like a herd of miniature buffaloes. Now I just want sleep. Thank you for today, thank you for coolness, inside and out.

June 20, 2004

I wake at six to the sound of cats fighting outside my window. It's so cold that I lie under the covers shivering. A cold front must have come through in the night. The wind kicks up and my three cats, spurred by the sound, race around the house, running in and out of my bedroom, trying to squeeze onto the windowsill over my head, attracted by the catfight and the blowing and scratching of branches outside. I didn't have any hot flashes in the night, in fact, it was so cold I had to pull my quilt over me to get warm!

The child in me is making a big plea for affection. She's never asked for it before, but she feels safe asking now. I must pay attention to her and help her through this final phase. I must allow her to cry, which both she and I need to do, but we also both need to feel safe in order to do that. This damaged adult self must feel safe too.

Over time, I hope I'll get to a point of being able to trust others as much as I trust Chuck and Nicolas. The inner me feels safe enough to open up, talk about, and explore my experiences, past and present, with Chuck, the man who knows. That's how I always think of him, as *the man who knows*. I have never trusted anyone like this and I've never allowed anyone into my inner world the way I've let him in. My body feels safe in Embodyment Therapy with Nicolas too, after years of studying yoga with him. I feel safe enough not only to be touched but also to talk with him about what I've been going through.

It's taken a long time to get to this point, and I want to keep going, keep changing, but I still feel pretty emotionally detached, uncaring and unfeeling as I plod along. I just point myself in the direction I must go and push myself to keep moving, but I go through each day with no joy and no anticipation. I expect I'll stay like this until I connect with the child self, until I rescue her. I tried to dream my way back to her last night, but couldn't. I must keep trying. The only way I can figure out how to reach her is by first feeling safe enough myself, because we've both had the same experiences and we both need the same cures.

I've supplemented my work with Chuck and Nicolas by making sure I have as much time as possible to recapitulate. I am driven by an urgency that is much more than just the need to recapitulate; my spirit is equally driven. But I must also temper that urgency a bit so that I'm in a good stable place to handle what comes. I know this.

I feel like I'm almost done, almost finished with this recapitulation. I see the child self clearly now. I see what she's had to deal with and how she's done it. I'm learning compassion in this slow agonizing process, and it's leading to self-acceptance and loving kindness for myself. I also understand why the child won't let anyone near her, because I'm the only one who can approach her and truly help her.

I go out for a walk and then return to bed, the only place I want to be, curled up and safe. I lie quietly and tend to the child, listening and feeling all the old pain and confusion. I'm stranded on the vast open space, that empty floor of my dream, deciding that since there's no one to help me, I'll withdraw and take care of myself by staying separate. But I know I don't want to stay here, even though the urge to stay is pressing, if only because it's familiar and safe, in its own strange way. The reality is that it's a completely dissociative state and the security lies in avoidance, because when I'm here, I totally avoid life. Part of me desperately wants to stay here, the child part, the extremely damaged child, who is still so afraid of everything. The adult me, however, desires new life.

There's not much heat inside me today, but that could be because I'm actually dealing with the child, finally listening to and feeling what she's all about, trying to figure out how I'm going to get her and bring her with me into new life.

I'm beginning to understand that I must go back to all her feelings. I've been covering them up, running from them, not wanting to face them because they're so painful, but I know now that they must be confronted, that the adult self must confront them too. And if crying is the way to retrieve those feelings, then I will find a way to cry, to take back the ability from those who denied me access to it, including myself. It's a natural ability all humans possess. My eyes actually have tear ducts so I can cry.

But it's Father's Day, so there will be no crying today. I have to get up, get the kids up, and go be the daughter my father wants. I can still act, play the part, but that isn't who I am anymore. It's not at all who I am.

When I'm with my family, I become someone else. I notice that I become someone who is up in my mouth, talking and being entertaining, funny, and louder than I'm used to being, the daughter they want, the entertainer. But inside is that child looking out and wondering how all that still goes on, not being truthful, not being real. It's like stepping back into an old movie, the reruns of old lives where nothing has changed, though my siblings and I have moved on. We are no longer interested in being the main characters. We've all gone, but the old scenes my parents once fabricated, and demand replays of, are still in place, and my parents are still in place in their same costumes too, sitting in their same chairs, doing and saying exactly the same things, just a little older and a little more worn each time the movie gets replayed, each time we visit. It's an alien, lifeless environment now, a boring story. I don't enjoy going back into it, but I acquiesce, don my costume and makeup, and become the character they expect to see, acting my part in the family drama.

I'm happy to shed the actor's clothing and persona and return home, to get back into my own quiet skin, even though that's no longer that comfortable either, but at least it's honest.

June 21, 2004

It was slow and painful going, all night long, as I drove around in dreams looking for parking spaces. Sometimes I found one, sometimes I didn't. In the last dream, I was driving a car on a very busy street in bumper-to-bumper traffic with my son in the passenger seat. We had to pick up my daughter, but first I had to deal with the traffic and the slow-moving line of cars. Then I saw a parking space and maneuvered into it, quickly and precisely. My plan was to wait in the car and have my son go look for my daughter.

Normally, my daughter appearing in dreams represents my inner child. It looks like I was trying to avoid having to confront her directly, the work that I must now do, consciously and without fear reliving the pain of that very young self.

It's a beautiful day today, the first of summer. I feel lazy. All I want to do is stay in bed, even though it's the most beautiful day in the world. I'm just so physically exhausted after the deep inner work I've done over the past three years. The journey has been both enlightening and exhausting, and I grant myself the rest

Redeployment of Energy

that is a necessary part of this healing. The issue now is to rescue the child, but first I need to conserve my energy so I can handle the emotional onslaught that is sure to come as I face the truth of that three-year-old child self. But first I face that I'm exhausted. Some days the only thing I can do is center myself. Some days all I can do is breathe and find a modicum of calmness inside myself. Today I will rest.

Short bursts of heat come every now and then during the day, reminding me of the work I still have to do with the child. No one else can rescue her. I'm the only one who knows how alone and abandoned she is, how frightened. I too have been caught in that place of abandonment and fright with her. I've found ways to become an adult, while at the same time I've kept myself as protected as possible, kept the child safely at a distance. But keeping her cut off doesn't help. It just keeps her in a fragmented, lonely and abandoned state, unable to interact.

I know that exposure to that which is frightening will, over time, reduce the fear. It's the same experience I've had with the memories of my childhood. Repeated exposure to them has reduced their hold on me, lessened the fear attached to them, as well as reduced the amount of personal energy attached to them. I know that exposure to life will eventually reduce my fear of being in the world too, that someday it just won't be so frightening out there.

I feel, inside my body, a memory of pain, nudging me into recapitulation. The other day with Chuck it was nudging at me too, anal/vaginal pain pushing at me, perhaps to remind me that I hurt all the time, in some fashion, or perhaps to get me to cry, to release. I admit that I'm in pain all the time. I forget about it for short periods, mostly when I'm really busy and focus is off my body, but it's always there when my attention returns, when I come home and crawl exhausted into bed. The old pains show up to keep me company through the night, begging me not to forget about them, pleading with me to let them stay, old friends that they are, lifelong friends. When I go to that child standing alone on that vast arena floor, the pain is unbearable. It's only through facing the memories and releasing the pain attached to them that the pain will leave my body; this too I already know. As soon as I confront a memory, the pain leaves, as if it never existed, its job done.

By the age of two, when the abuse began, my developing personality and emotional health were squelched by the violent behaviors inflicted. This sent me on a particularly dissociated journey. When the abuse started, I turned inward for strength, soothing, and protection. Life as a healthy human being, with the capacity to learn about the world in a safe and nurturing manner, suddenly halted and the world took on a frightening pallor.

Do I view myself as a victim? I never have before; but yes, I was definitely the victim of someone else's evil intent. I find it difficult to do the "poor me" thing, but I think I do need to apply it to that child still back there in that nowhere land. If I picture her as a victim it allows for compassion to emerge, which is so difficult for me to feel for myself. However, I'll never be a complete, feeling human being if I don't tap into my emotions, if I can't allow for good and positive feelings about myself, if I can't love myself. If I can fix myself, I know I will be a better person in the world.

I'm learning what love means as I take this journey of recapitulation, what it means in a bigger, broader sense, but also on a personal level. I admit that I need it and want it, deeply and intimately, even though I may tell myself that I'm done with love in this life, saying that I'll just be happy living alone. That's just the child inside me talking. To her, being alone is safe. Nothing has worked for her except her solitariness. And I agree with her that the idea of intimacy is frightening, though I'm beginning to understand that I won't have lived to the fullest if I don't allow love back into my life. Even the fear of rejection, of being hurt must be confronted or I won't evolve. I understand my own situation now more clearly, the realization that I too have needs. They are valid needs, and until they are addressed, I won't live wholly in the real world but only continue to hide in my old world, dissociated, incomplete as a human being.

I get out of bed at noon and make something to eat then go back to bed. I work a little on some writing assignments but mostly I read and doze. My daughter calls at two-thirty for a ride home from a friend's house, so I drive over to get her. Upon return, I make a cup of coffee and get back into bed. I submit to exhaustion, stating to myself, one final time, that this is where I want to be, where I need to be.

At six o'clock in the evening I get out of bed to feed the kids and the cats, then retire to my room again. Maybe after this long and contemplative day in bed, of reading and writing, of consolidating energy, I'll be okay for the rest of the week.

June 22, 2004

I feel sad and wonder where that sadness is coming from. Is the adult beginning to allow for feelings? Is the child? I haven't gone back to her in my dreams yet. I haven't been able to, though I've tried. Is she so far away that I can't access her, the distance so vast I won't be able to find her again? I hope not. Our union is crucial to the completion of this journey.

My body has been like a car lately that I get into when I need to do something but then get right back out of again when I'm done. It looks terrible, skinny and neglected, my boobs all droopy and flat, my face sad and long. My shoulders slump, and I have no energy. There's no gas in this car.

I meet with Nicolas. During the session I concentrate on being in my body and staying in it, just going with what comes, surrendering to the process. I can't control it anyway. There are some mild releases in the beginning, in which I focus on allowing myself to feel safe, both with Nicolas and with being in my body.

"The heat you feel is karma burning off," he says.

I notice that this is similar to what Chuck has said, that the heat is tension, long stored in the body, old holdings needing release. I let myself go with the flow and before long I feel some very deep burn offs in my pelvic area, huge flare ups, like flames shooting out of an industrial smokestack. It feels as if something immense has left my body. By session's end I am empty and yet also full, back in my body, at least for the moment.

"Do yoga, say your mantra—Shivoham—and continue to allow for release until I see you on Thursday," Nicolas prescribes. I promise I'll try.

In contrast to my quiet day in bed yesterday, I don't slow down until almost eleven at night. I work all day on writing jobs and preparing my artwork for an upcoming show. In the late afternoon I take a long pleasant walk with my daughter. When we get back home, I cook dinner, take care of the cats and do the dishes.

My horoscope suggests that I take advantage of this time to get my personal and professional life in order. Apparently, it's a very creative time for my sign. I should use this time wisely, not let it slip by without doing something to enhance my life. There's a suggestion that I should give myself what I want, and also that I should ask for things. Beyond that, I am advised to tell people the truth, to trust my instincts, and to acknowledge that I do have needs, and to not be afraid to make them known. That's a high order! And right in alignment with this transformative time in my life.

In keeping with all that, I've been concentrating on turning off the incessant chatter in my head before it really starts up, all those negative voices of the Invisibles that pull me back into old places. I've been shutting the door on them, though they keep banging to be let in. For the most part I can ignore them. For most of the day they've only been faint murmurings in the background.

I feel that, indeed, I'm getting somewhere, not wasting this good time in my life but staying aligned with the intent of the cosmos. Even so, I've remained detached from the child self. I see her out there in that vast arena, no one in sight to help her. In a way, even at her young age, she made the decision to surrender to her circumstance. Very quickly she ascertained that there was no one to rescue her. So, in a most devastatingly lonely way she took care of herself as best she could. She knew there was no hope, and yet she found a way to cope, by closing down.

"Don't have needs because nothing you ask for will ever be answered," she told herself. "You will not be provided with what you need. So isolate, become independent so you don't need anyone or anything. Shut down."

And that's what I very cleverly did. My horoscope is telling me that now is the time to challenge all that, to creatively confront the old guard, to let it go and instead ask for help, be open to receive help, and finally make the real changes that are so apparent and so necessary. Today's Embodiment session was a good start, because something really did shift.

June 23, 2004

I don't hear the alarm for a long time. It seeps into my dreams, a distant annoyance. When I finally pull myself out of a deep sleep, I see that I've let the alarm ring for five solid minutes. I get out of bed, wake my daughter, and get her ready to go off to take her final exam of the school year. By nine I'm back in bed, exhausted, falling right into a dream.

I'm staying at a retreat center. I'm teaching a yoga class, but crazy circumstances keep interfering. First, I have to take my daughter to school to take her test, which I do, but she comes right back, saying it's too early; the test is not until later in the day. She'll need a ride later. I go back to teaching my class but am continually interrupted by people needing one thing or another. There are locked doors that I must open, things get lost that I must find. I get lost and can't find the room where I was teaching. People talk to me through windows, asking me for things, and for help. I am completely inundated with requests, running around taking care of everyone else, unable to focus on my own needs and my own class.

I wake up a second time, groggy and frustrated by the tensions in the dream, steeped in old feelings. I roll onto my good, right side to make some sense of it. The dream leaves me feeling that life is too hard to handle. With constant blocks thrown at me, with so many problems to solve, and everyone needing me, how will I ever evolve? Just before I woke up, I asked this question in the dream: "Why me?"

I drag myself out of bed for a second time and plan my day. I have to keep going. In spite of the depressing and scattered quality of the dream it leaves me with renewed interest for this challenge before me: how to not be overwhelmed by life but only intrigued by it.

I've been walking in my sleep lately. I wake up at night to find myself in the hallway or living room, my body absolutely leaden. It takes great effort to lift my legs and get back to my room and into bed. My son says I stumble into his room at night and mumble stuff at him. Yikes!

While working in the garage, I notice that I no longer automatically block the heat as it builds up in my body. I'm not forcing it back down but easily letting it go, naturally. This proves the point of how when consciousness is applied to effect a change, change does happen. This is certainly progress.

I'm aware that I've been on the path to this place, where I find myself today, for a very long time. I've finally arrived at this very day and this very moment in time, where I am fully able to accept what happened to me as a child. I've stayed detached from feeling both compassion and horror for myself as I've recapitulated, but I'm now able to accept them both as equal parts of this healing journey, the two sides of life, the dark and the light, the good and the bad. I'm at a new level of acceptance now, clear on the issue of abuse and finally beginning to feel depths of compassion and sadness for my child self, while coming one step closer to my long-buried emotions.

I finally accept that I was deeply wounded as a child. How can I heal if I can't accept that there was a wounding to begin with? I don't *see* a wound, but the memories stored in my body show just how much pain I actually experienced as a child. If I won't let myself *feel* the wounding, I will never achieve the fullness of healing that I seek.

I must continue going back into the past, while at the same time I must plod along on the path before me, as it unfolds each day. Lara instructs me not to look back, as she whisks away my frantic energy, worried that I'll be overwhelmed, too depleted by what I encounter there, but I know I won't totally heal if I don't go back and finish what I've started. I must go back in order to move forward. I must fully know what it is that I'm healing.

I feel more confident today that I'll be okay. I sense things changing more rapidly as I get further along the path and farther from the resolved memories, which no longer haunt me or hold me captive. I still have the feelings and the emotions to deal with. I must find a way to tap into them, to allow them to become part of this person that I am becoming. Without them I will remain incomplete and unknown to even myself.

June 24, 2004

School is over for the year. The kids are sleeping in. I'm granting my son two weeks of freedom to stay up as late as he wants and to sleep in as late as he wants, and then he'll begin working a summer job as an usher at a local concert venue. He's enjoying the freedom. My daughter has been a little harder to please. I've already heard her say that she's bored. While she waits for her summer camps to start, I've given her jobs around the house that I'll pay her a weekly allowance for. Trying to keep a good balance all around!

I have a good session with Nicolas. The child is present, telling me where the pain lies. In the hips and around the waist, on the right side, she indicates, where my abuser's hand has left a burning imprint.

When I mention to Nicolas that I've lately been able to read other people's energy, he says it's my sensitivity to other people's pain, a psychic sensitivity, related to all the second chakra work we've been doing. I notice it's the same thing with my own inner child, I'm reading her pain. As the session continues, I hear her speaking clearly, as if she's lying right next to me, speaking directly into my ear. She's so full of pain, she tells me. I try to release from the hips and the place where my abuser's hand has left its mark. My middle back is so sensitive. At one point, I cry out. My spine feels totally bruised; my whole body feels bruised.

"I'm not even touching you and you cry out as if in pain," says Nicolas.

I know I'm still dealing with the last memory, which is just a mess of feelings. Caught in the confusion of it, I experience only pain and fear. When I turn to the child, she knows I'm here to rescue her, finally. She sports a "what took you so long" expression. She's been waiting so patiently, knowing that eventually I'd show up. But I can't quite get to her yet. In order to do that I have to go back to a very painful place, to that rape and the brutal swirl of pain and confusion of it. I must experience my feelings. I must tell myself, and believe, that my abuser really hurt me in a most devastating way. I must convince myself that the rapes and molestations were indeed horrific, that he hurt me in my body and in my soul, that no one should have to suffer that, but I've pushed the truth away. It doesn't matter, I always say, I don't matter. But that's not true. It does matter, and I matter too.

As the memories returned over these past three years, the tendency was to not acknowledge that I was in the picture at all but to completely obliterate myself from the equation, because it was too painful to bear. I'm at the place now where I can acknowledge the depth of pain and fear I suffered. I understand how it affected every aspect of who I am and how I chose to live. It was horrific. Instead of pushing the pain away, as I've always done, I must go through it now, though the old pushing away tendency jumps right in to protect me, as it always has. Feeling my abuser's hand on me again, knowing who it is, and realizing that he did indeed do great damage, is where I arrive during the session with Nicolas, out of the mess of chaos and confusion into clarity.

After the session, I go home and dress for a memorial gathering of a friend's husband, who recently died.

"You know I won't be around for a while," she says to me afterwards, and as soon as she says it, I sense that I'm losing another important anchor in my life.

"I love you," I say to her, knowing that she needs time for herself, time to grieve and feel, just as I do.

I cook dinner and then go out and mow the lawn until I'm too tired to keep pushing. Afterward, I lie on my bed unable to move, depressed and empty, exhausted from all the activity of being out among people, meeting and consoling. I have nothing left except tears. Is that all that's left?

I feel like I worked very hard on myself this week, on a track of discovery, the child setting the course. I've been reading voraciously all the books I can find on personal and spiritual growth, on the psyche and the unconscious. I understand more fully what I'm up against, what I experienced, hopeful that someday soon I'll figure out why. I'm desperately trying to *feel*, still pretty detached though probably closer than I think.

I'm discovering what feels right and what doesn't, how best to use my energy and where to go next in this journey to wholeness. The one thing I am certain of is that I have to keep allowing myself to be open and sensitive, and to be vulnerable.

June 25, 2004

I woke in the night, hearing a voice speaking to me, and wrote the following: "*The sky is not enough.*"

What does that mean? That I have to wish for more? Must I not settle for anything, but just keep going? Is the idea of reaching for the sky limiting? Must I go beyond even that?

I see Chuck at our usual early morning time. I talk about all the stuff I've worked on during the week, but in the end feeling that I let the child down, for I couldn't quite complete the rescue.

"She's pretty smart, figuring out ways to deal with things," I say.

As we sit and talk quietly, I notice that my body is all scrunched up, my legs and arms crossed. I'm sitting on one side of the chair, tilted, not uncomfortably, that's just the state I'm in, out of whack. At one point in our conversation, I clearly know what he's thinking, what he doesn't say, but I brush past it as usual, because it makes me uncomfortable to read his thoughts. I know it doesn't matter, what matters is how I feel. And then I begin talking about how I'm trying to feel enough so I can get to the child, so I can reach her. She distinctly stood up in my dream of the vast arena and told me to come and get her, that she's been waiting, but I still have some invisible barrier to work through.

"Perhaps you could paint that barrier, paint what it feels like," Chuck suggests. "If you can paint or draw it, perhaps you can find a way through it."

"Well, at this point I'm just looking for some kind of equilibrium in where I am at this moment in time," I say. "I've been doing a lot of reading and it helps me step out of the nightmarish aspect of the whole thing, taking the experiences out of the horrible context of sexual abuse and rape and putting them into a different place, into other perspectives that offer a kind of distance. I've always envisioned this recapitulation as a shamanic journey, a spiritual journey where everything is meaningful, and I easily see the unfolding of that journey, but it helps to have other perspectives too. It helps make the whole process feel less selfish and more meaningful. And I actually feel that I'm not so weird, that I have lots of company out there, that many have gone before me, taking the journey into the darkness of their own souls. And knowing that the crazy mind I sometimes feel I'm burdened with has been studied so intently, in different fields, is comforting. I don't feel so alone."

I work at the gallery in the evening. Since it's a quiet night and not many visitors, I sit and write in my journal. There's an open bottle of wine left over from the last opening and I sip a cup as I write. I feel relaxed and mellow.

I envision what that invisible barrier between myself and my three-year-old child self might look like. It suddenly looms up in front of me, an impenetrable thick glass wall, soundproof, bullet proof, as thick as it gets. I can see through it, see the inner child, but I can't get to her or speak to her. It's as if my dream recreates itself, right before my eyes. I know that I must somehow break this glass wall, shatter it or explode it.

An elderly man comes into the gallery. We chat easily and comfortably. We discover that we share the same birthday and that neither of us like surprises, especially surprise parties. He fears that his wife has one planned for him in a week and he's not happy about it. I know how he feels. A few more people come in. I notice that I easily read their energy, each of them, as soon as they step through the door. Should I be doing this? Invading their personal space? I can't help it. It just happens; I know things about them.

Finally, the time comes to lock up. Back at home, I just want to sleep, too tired even to watch the movie I'd gotten earlier. The kids are staying up late so I ask them to keep it quiet, to clean up after themselves and that we'll see each other in the morning. They're enjoying their autonomy, actually seem to be basking in it, especially my son. He's even doing the chores I ask of him. For my part, I've learned not to jump up and do their every bidding, letting them get their own glasses of water, and fix their own food to eat. I'm pulling in my energy to take care of me.

Thank you, Chuck and Jeanne, and the rest of you too!

June 26, 2004

I wake at 6 a.m. in the midst of a burn-off, just letting it happen. It's a rainy morning and the cats are meowing for food. Cosi, the little one, is running around like crazy, freaking out about something. I know how she feels. Perhaps the sound of the rain is causing her anxiety.

The child still needs me to get her, and the adult is still struggling. But I do feel that in small ways I'm beginning to change the old habits of self-denial and self-hatred, trying to be nicer to myself, not so hard and demanding. My stomach begins cramping as I write. I don't feel good. I'm fully aware now that physical pain is usually a sign of some emerging mental anguish. The fact that I'm changing perhaps? Challenging the status quo, the reliable habits and patterns of life? The body does not lie. I already know that it's a sure indicator of something in my psyche wanting me to notice and attend to it. Not ready to go into it yet, whatever it might be, I get out of bed. I'll go there later.

I go out and buy wood to make picture frames. When I return, I eat a bowl of cereal and climb back into bed for a little while; the need to just sit and be silent is strong. I feel slightly lonely, longing for something. I long for intimacy but that just isn't in the cards right now. I still have too much to do, like learning to love myself first.

I spend the day working in the garage. I keep busy, finishing up painting those twenty doors and then building frames for my paintings. I'm pretty depressed, but also slightly anxious. The Invisibles are loud. Surely something is brewing.

Late in the afternoon, my daughter and I go see a *Harry Potter* movie. I'm struck by his encounters with evil and magic, though it's nothing compared to the stuff I deal with on a daily basis, in outer reality and inner reality alike.

June 27, 2004

In a dream I want to go back to an old world. I'm with some new friends, and they don't think it's a good idea for me to go back. I insist that I must revisit old places one last time, to make sure I haven't forgotten anything. After much discussion, they assign a blind and deaf man to accompany me back to these old places. They encourage me to hurry, to not waste too much time, as there's a plane to catch that will take me to the new world, faraway in a foreign country.

The blind man leads me through dark and dreary ancient buildings, wobbly structures crammed full of old antiques, rooms cluttered with junk. Everywhere I go, things block my path. I question whether I really still need any of the things from my past, even old memories. Even so, I feel that I just can't leave and move on without some of my personal stuff. I also need to find my passport. Back in the old buildings I meet a lot of people I once knew. They're sad to see me go. They surround me, begging me to stay. Overriding every aspect of the dream is a great urgency, an awareness that I could miss the plane that will take me away. At one point, a group of children gathers around me. I tell them to go eat some food, because it will be a long journey. By the end of the dream there's one final thing I must do, but I can't quite figure out what it is.

I have clearly moved on in this dream, out of an old life and into a new one. The new place was described as a foreign country, a place that was far away, and indeed that's what this new world feels like. I've landed in a place where I don't know my way around yet, where I don't speak the language, still learning how to be at home here. In the dream, I go back to the old world for a final check, to see if I left anything behind that might be useful or necessary in this new life. This is where I am now, making sure I've completed my recapitulation, that I've retrieved all of my energy that was once bound up in old traumatic memories.

A blind and deaf man leads me, allowing me to make up my own mind, like blind justice, not judging me, just being present as I make the last journey back. Others in the dream clearly express their opinions. In the new world I'm surrounded by goodness, by loving, caring people who only want the best for me. They show me the richness of my new life and encourage me to stay. In the old world, people want me to stay for selfish reasons, for them. The children, whom I encourage to eat before the long journey, are clearly my sixteen child selves, one for each year of the abuse. Now fully integrated, they are moving on with me. As the dream suggests, I'm putting the final touches on this magical journey.

Last night as I was preparing for sleep and this morning as I woke up, I realized that I've been allowing the negative voices, the Invisibles, to speak again, and way too loudly. They've begun insinuating themselves into my life again, interfering in my progress. Even now, they ask me not to get rid of them, to not leave them behind. After all, they say, what if I need them?

I take a walk, intent upon throwing off the negative energy and the old voices of the past. I walk through the woods and across the meadow to an overlook by the river, focusing on walking slowly and deliberately, feeling the ground beneath my feet, the way my legs feel as they walk, the swing of my arms, the steadiness of my breathing. I think about my friend's husband who just died, his large, generous nature, his expertise with financial matters. He offered to help me many times, but I always said I was fine.

"I'm struggling now, but I'll be fine in the end," I would tell him.

He was a very big man, in every way, especially his heart. I look out over the expanse of water, mountains, and sky, the same river, mountains, and sky that he looked at from his house on the river every day.

"Can you help me now?" I ask, calling his name out loud. "Can you help me from where you are now?"

Within seconds a small swallow begins flying in circles around me, circling around and around, and I know he has come.

"So," I say, "what do I do? I don't know what to do. I feel lost again."

"*Use your talents for yourself,*" I hear. "*Stop giving them to other people. They are your biggest assets; use them for yourself.*"

"I need a strategy," I say.

"*Just go with where you are now. Put one foot in front of the other. Stay on the path.*"

"I know that," I say. "You're right. I already know that."

"*Sometimes you may lose the path and you have to backtrack,*" he says, "*not to go back to anything, but simply to find the place where you lost the path. And often, if you just look ahead, you can make out the path, even though it isn't clear-cut. You can see it if you look closely.*"

As he says this, my dream becomes suddenly clearer. I was not going back in an old way but merely making sure I was on the right path.

"What else can you tell me?"

"*It's okay for you not to involve your parents in your life. They take too much, expect too much. You can let them go.*"

This is the same thing that Jeanne recently told me, that it's time to detach my energy from them, that it's okay to move on without regret. I notice that the bird continues circling around while I receive these messages. It fights off another bird then flies back over me again, carving circles around me. I am surrounded by magic.

"Don't run away," I hear my friend's husband say. "*Don't force change, just keep going. Change will find you.*"

Redeployment of Energy

At this, the bird flies closer, right down around my head. I feel puffs of air coming off its wings as it peers right into my face and then scoots off to join its companions in the sky. I stand there for a few moments looking out over the river, grateful for the magic in my life, and especially for these words of wisdom.

Feeling more grounded than ever, I turn to walk back across the meadow. I look for the bird one last time. The sky is empty, but then, out of the trees on the right, one lone bird flies toward me, high overhead now. I know it's my birdman. Then the rest of the flock follows. As I watch them disappear, I carry with me the clear message that my needs must be self-oriented now, that I must pull in my energy and release myself more fully from the negative voices of the past. I fully accept the guidance I received from the swallow, the energy of my friend's husband, finally freed from large, lumbering human energy, transformed into the lightness of that bird. It was how I always perceived him, a beautiful being in a massive body, with a truly light and generous heart.

All my experiences anchor me deeper in my new reality. When I return to groundedness and get heart centered, the guidance is always the same: stay on the path, take one step at a time, proceed without ego strategy but with an open and trusting heart. Always trust the journey, but always remain intent upon personal growth and evolution of spirit as well. All of this is leading me toward a higher purpose. Perhaps one day soon I'll discover what that is.

I must allow myself to go forward with eyes and heart open, and without fear. Something powerful is in the works; I'm certain of it. I sense a big jolt approaching. It could be anything. I'm ready.

I meet with Nicolas. The spirit of my friend's husband comes to me again, my birdman. He instructs me to "ride the bird." It's easy to imagine as I'm already in a dreamy state, lying on the floor, waves of release going through me. We go for a ride, my birdman and I, me holding onto his wings, my energy soaring around the room as if in a flying dream. I feel Jeanne's presence too and then see a small ladybug circling above my head.

"It's your body's time now," she says. *"You are here for your body; just go with it. Just let go."*

Encouraged by her words, I ride the bird effortlessly, the releases flowing easily out of me. Great peacefulness spreads through me. My spirit and my body float suspended on a pillow of peaceful calm on the bird's back. I am at one with the bird, totally safe, soaring, gently flipping, tilting, and whipping around the room.

Suddenly, everything is incredibly quiet, inside and outside of me. There's a feeling of nothingness, and there's a feeling of fullness too. I am empty and I am full. I am tiny and I am large. I am small enough to lie on the back of a tiny five-inch bird and large enough to be on the floor in Nicolas's office, myself and not myself at the same time. I am the light, and the light is crystal clear.

"You are here for your body; let your body receive what it needs," I hear Jeanne say again. *"Let it all go, just let it go."*

I'm *flying*. And in this moment, I know that all the magic I've experienced is true, that without a doubt I am surrounded by magic. I understand now, with perfect clarity, that it's only real because I can accept it, that in daring to ask for it and then allowing for it, it does manifest. Ask and you shall receive.

"A shift happened, a very noticeable shift," Nicolas says. "I noticed it beginning during our last session, but definitely today, suddenly, and full force."

"Yes," I say, "something shifted in me and something happened to me simultaneously."

I am totally accepting and aware of vast amounts of resources to be accessed if we dare to ask, if we trust that they do exist and if we're open to them. If we dare to receive, we will receive. It's that simple. The world is full of magic. We don't need spells, incantations, rituals and rites; we just need to be open.

"Magic exists," I say. "It's really true that magic exists."

"Yes, it is true," Nicolas replies. "Very true."

June 28, 2004

I don't have any jobs lined up for this week, though many pending. I'll have to see what transpires, try not to get stressed out, and trust that I'll be okay, that the universe will provide. My own inner spirit says: "You'll be fine, just hang in there. You'll be fine."

I've been creating a world for myself, both consciously and unconsciously finding my way, one day and one step at a time. I am certain that the work aspect will evolve as I do, that I just need to hang in there, be patient, and stay the course. In the meantime, I'm not totally without work; I have numerous small jobs to fill the interim.

The message from the bird spirit guide, to use my talents for myself now, to stop wasting them on others, leads me to remain steadfastly open to what transpires as I continue my journey of self-discovery. To just *"go with the flow"* may sound unreasonable, irresponsible, and even frightening, but you know what? It works! Today, however, I admit that having more financial security would be nice. I hate worrying about money! The messages coming to me today, however, are all the same:

"Go with the flow, stop wanting what you can't have and be open to what comes. Stop trying to figure everything out and just allow for life to flow. Go with the flow. There is really no plan. Just follow the path, one step at a time."

"Just give it some time! It's only Monday! Relax; forget about all the worries. You know they always work out!"

June 29, 2004

In a dream, I am in the desert sitting on the rim of an abyss, a large hole in the ground, perhaps ten feet across, looking down into endless infinity. The flat empty desert stretches all around me, dry and uninviting. I sit with my legs dangling over the edge of the rim, waiting, knowing that I need patience, the great patience of sitting in stillness, no matter what's present in my environment. *I must sit and wait. The time is not yet.* My legs ache from sitting still for so long. I hear the voices of everything and everyone coming from the great cosmos, telling me to hang in there, to just wait, that it will get better.

As soon as I wake up, I notice that I'm still in a dream state, suspended, my body still, my mind blank. In a quiet trance, I pick up my pen and notebook and write.

Don't depart. Stay a little longer. It will get better. See, the birds are singing. The sun is dancing upon the leaves. The morning is barely begun. Stay a while and see what comes, because it will come. It will come. Before night falls you will have received a gift and you will hear a different message.

Uncork the sadness. Let it flow out of your head and down your shoulders and limbs and into the great abyss before you. Let it flow down your dangling legs and into the great open pit upon whose rim you sit. Let it drip, drip, drip until it fills it full, a pond of tears and sadness, where all thoughts will sink to the bottom, the heavy barrenness dragging old tendencies down to lie buried on the bottom, while you, free, can float on the surface, breathing with each brief ripple. More than still—alive! More than just existing—newly formed from your own ancient wisdom and persistence.

Eventually you will bump against the edge of the rim. And after brief struggle (for there is always struggle) you will climb out and find that, indeed, you are whole, a body that stands and walks, and, if you dare, speaks. Why not? For the past lies down there, unseen now. You have shed it and left it there like old farm machinery rusting at the bottom of a pond, and your first new step plows new fields, and new paths present themselves at each forward movement.

Just go, just go away from this place where you no longer need anything. And, as you gain distance, the pond will disappear in the distant landscape blending in with flat planes of earth, and you will have a deep memory of pain and suffering but it will no longer hurt you. Go, look for life and love and stability and safety, but:

Choose instability.

Choose the unknown.

Choose journeying.

Choose the path that is endless, for although it is seemingly endless, it traverses the most fertile ground, the most

Redeployment of Energy

lush, rich forests and gardens. Take that challenge and your life will indeed be full!

I emerge from my trance and realize that I chose that path already when I began this recapitulation journey. I chose the path of knowledge, the path of change, the path of challenge that would constantly force me to shift. I feel that this choice was made long before I ever entered this life; that my life was set up for all of this to unravel so I could one day find myself on this path of rich, fertile ground. I am here now. In fact, I've always been here, but now I'm waking up to that truth, journeying with awareness, breaking all the old rules so I can travel more freely, open to what comes, rather than held back by old perceptions and ideas of how things are *supposed* to be. In freeing my mind, my spirit will lead the way.

My dream stresses how I must continue this journey with renewed intent. When I find myself in uncertainty, having lost track of where I am, I must intentionally pull myself back to the path and to my heart center. I may have to return to the rim of infinity on occasion and sit patiently in stillness, bearing the pain of whatever comes to disrupt my quiet solitude. The waiting may be excruciating, but I must have patience. In the end my time of recapitulation will be finished and I will no longer be drawn back to old experiences. I will leave the past behind.

I also now know that I must remain an open channel, open to tap into the wisdom offered by the voices of my guides, my spiritual partners in this life. They know.

I meet with Nicolas. It's a very difference experience this time. I am immediately less resistant than normal, having had such good releases last time, but I don't have my bird guide or Jeanne with me this time. And although I open fully to the releases, they don't flow smoothly out of me but rip painfully out of my chest and torso. It's as if I have a huge zipper going straight up the front of my body that is being unzipped in tiny incremental jerks. My flesh and muscles are caught in the tracks of the zipper, tearing painfully. And I can barely breathe, stifled by a pressure that is intensely familiar.

No matter how I try to control my breathing, I cannot draw a deep breath. I relate it to my most recent memory where my abuser is holding me so tightly that I keep dissociating, going out of body. I pull myself back, trying to stay in the moment, to just be with what is presented here and now, even if it's painful. I know I must remain here on the edge of *this* abyss of feeling and release. I must let the full memory come, let it fully go through me, and finally release it.

I remind myself to relax, that I'm here for my body, though more than anything I want to jump up and run! It's just old fear. I must stay with the tension and the pain. I must stay put and allow the pain to flow out of me naturally, in whatever way it happens. I am being asked to *surrender*.

The pain is twofold. It's the pain of a grown man raping me, a three-year-old child, destroying me. I can't breathe and I can't move. I feel his arm holding me so tightly that I'm suffocating. It's also the pain of labor, of birth-giving labor that starts in the lower back and creeps around to the front of the body, gradually gaining in intensity until it's tearing me open. The pain is the same, first experienced during rape at age three and then, many years later, experienced as the pain of giving birth. It's the same kind of pain. In both cases I'm being destroyed, split open, the first time against my will and the second time, although by choice, also against my will, for I cannot control what is happening to my body.

Action takes action; to allow for something to shift you must take action. If you do nothing, nothing will change, but if you take action, as I've done in embarking on this recapitulation journey, there is no guarantee that what arrives will be to your liking. But if you stay with the tension and keep making choices that lead to full recapitulation, no matter how painful, the landscape will eventually change. Gradually the bottomless abyss and the dry dessert around you will all change. I know I must stay where I am now, that I must keep seeking the magic, even while I must also sit on the edge of the abyss and wait patiently.

The air smells so sweet today, like strawberries, roses, and honey. After my session with Nicolas, I deliver my paintings to the artists' gallery for inclusion in a show of abstract art. I then drive to a historic home overlooking the river and sit in stillness on a bench for a while, just taking in the view, the calm beauty of the day, and the wide river flowing slowly by. I am calm and content. I can breathe again, freed of something I didn't even know I carried.

When I get home, I bring in two bouquets of flowers from the garden. They look and smell so beautiful. They're so still and at peace. Like trees, flowers too are rooted and must stay in one place, and that is enough for them. And even in not moving they change, they grow, they evolve; they live and they die. They are beautiful and they are complete. I know that this is my own challenge, to just stay where I am and let everything around me change, without giving into the urge to run away or jump into the abyss. I must sit calmly in stillness, doing nothing, but doing everything at the same time, evolving and changing in quiet equilibrium, seeking mastery of self.

I meet with Chuck in the afternoon. I tell him about the magic I've been experiencing lately, how I've discovered that it's there for the asking, about my dream of the abyss and learning how to really be patient, not doing but just staying put; intentionally dealing with life as it is. I also tell him about the most recent revelations of the earliest rape, and how it's been going through me, slowly but surely.

"I'm nearing the end of this recapitulation; I feel it," I say. "But at the same time, it's slow going."

"Things will change," Chuck says, "everything changes."

"Yes, I know that because every day I'm different. I have new challenges every day, and new insights come every day too. I receive the guidance I need and I dare myself to take advantage of it. And if it isn't to my liking, I can change it, but there will be no more running away."

He yells at me when I tell him that I've agreed to curate another gallery show in two months' time.

"You have to learn to save your energy for yourself. No more commitments!"

"I'm going to tell you something, Jan," he goes on, "when you are in yourself, you are a totally different person. You look different, your face, your eyes, you come alive, your body is different, you transform."

"Yes, I know, I see it too," and I thank him for acknowledging that he has seen who I am; it's important for me to hear this. I am real. I do exist.

"Why is it so hard to stay there?" he asks. "To be her?"

"I have to fight to stay there," I say. "I have to fight to stay in my body. I'm only just discovering it, doing things to make it a good place to be. I really want to be alive like that, to be present here in this world, but it's still an unfamiliar place, and it's still sometimes frightening."

"I know that when you tell me to get back to the work that is most important, you mean the work on myself, the recapitulation," I say. "And so, I promise no more commitments. I promise! And I also know that to use my talents for myself means the same thing, to finish my recapitulation so that my energy can be fully redeployed for use for myself."

Now is the time. The kids will be away for the next two weeks and I must not waste the time. I must do something great for myself; walk, write, and paint. In spite of needing to make a living, I must also intentionally do things for myself.

This morning I felt so hopeless, but then I got a call for more work at the same jobsite I had worked at earlier in the month. They are ready for me again! I also got invited to be interviewed by the local paper for the abstract painting show. Things have changed, just as my morning channeling suggested: *before night falls you will have received a gift and you will hear a different message.*

June 30, 2004

I wake up in pain, clenched and hurting, wondering how I'm ever going to break this bad habit, because I do feel it as a habit, my body automatically setting itself into position, like a cogwheel locking into place. Even though there are other cogs to engage, I am stuck in the groove of this one. But it doesn't have to be this way forever, I know that now. Things *will* change.

Redeployment of Energy

One of my brothers called last night and I told him I was not going to our parent's house for the Fourth of July this weekend. I can't let myself feel bad about that. Chuck said he notices how depressed I get every time I go there, and it's true. I feel the darkness of that place creeping over me the closer I get to it, like a heavy damp fog, smothering and weighing me down.

"You don't owe your parents anything," Chuck said. "In truth, you don't owe them a thing."

I take my car to get inspected and while waiting I wonder about what Chuck said yesterday, about how I look when I'm in my body. Do I even know when I am? Right then, when we were talking, I knew I was fully there. I was aware that I was relaxed, fully present in the moment, not clenched or shaky, not nervous or feeling threatened. It's something to continue striving for, to be conscious of my body and of being in it. It's a good body, a nice body, and I should enjoy being in it.

The mechanic comes out to tell me that the car needs some lightbulbs replaced. They will order them and I can pick it up later. I walk over to my new painting studio to wait.

I cover an entire wall with a large sheet of white paper, scrolling it out from a large roll someone had once given me. I get out a box of oil pastels and begin drawing. The phrase, "*pockets of silence*" comes to me as I draw. I'm innerly quiet, my mind still, and I feel as if I'm drawing that inner quietude and stillness, but then I realize I'm drawing safety, "*pockets of safety*," how it feels to be enclosed and calm inside a tiny warm cell, protected, silent, and safe. I draw small pockets of safety, colorful and delicate, but secure and protected at the same time. They come rolling out of me, through my arm and hand and right through the oil pastels onto the paper. My drawing is freeform, full of life, a tangled braid with small jewels trapped in it. After a while I walk the few blocks back to pick up my car, hoping it isn't going to cost too much. I have so little money to spare. I guess I really am crazy, no money, and I'm just sailing along, open to magic and goodness, trusting that everything will be fine!

I pick up the car and drive over to the park, to walk out to the river. As usual I find myself talking to dead people; like people talking to God, I guess. I have no one else to talk to on a daily basis and they're always willing to listen. As I walk, I try to stay present in my body, in the moment, aware to not panic or allow the Invisibles to intrude.

"Am I going crazy?"

I ask myself that a lot, but I don't think so. I just have a vivid inner process going on, as I attempt to figure things out. I seem to be able to tap into other energy, and I get what I need. I've learned to trust it, so I accept it. My bird guide speaks to me.

"*Just hang in there,*" he says. "*Don't lose hope about anything. Do your work.*"

That is exactly what I did do today. I used my inner resources, my creativity for myself alone. I worked without preconceived ideas. It was quiet and peaceful at the studio, private, no phone, no interruptions; the perfect place for getting away; just where I needed to be.

Chapter 7

Completion

July 1, 2004

The only dream I remember was one in which I was talking to Chuck. He told me to just keep talking, to never stop talking. I read my horoscope for the month ahead and it's totally in alignment with my dream, all about communicating, keeping the lines open.

I turn to Jeanne for guidance. She refers to the fact that everything is in a holding pattern now, that this is a time of waiting. She tells me to hang in there, be patient and wait, that something good will happen eventually. Well, tomorrow is my birthday, and a full moon. Naturally, I wish for something good!

When I get out of bed and go into the bathroom, I find a picture of a high-flow toilet taped onto the top of the closed toilet seat. "It eliminates all clogging," the ad says. When I lift the lid, I see that the toilet is totally clogged. My son has a sense of humor! Very funny. But truthfully, it mirrors my present state, the clogging up of feelings, emotions and memories, all that shit I live with daily.

I meet with Nicolas. As soon as I lie down on the pile of blankets on the floor, I am faced with the fact that it's time to deal with the pain of my three-year-old self. It's time to surrender completely to the truth of the abuse, and to the details of what happened to me when I was three. As the session begins, I find it hard to breathe, as if my diaphragm is frozen in place.

"The pain isn't allowing you to breathe," Nicolas says, "it doesn't allow the diaphragm to move naturally."

"Yes, that's true. I was held there, across the diaphragm, very tightly," I say.

Even now the weight on my diaphragm is too much and I instinctively curl into a fetal position. I do this repeatedly and involuntarily while Nicolas works on me, a reflex response to the pain. It's time to acknowledge it, to accept the pain that I once pretended I didn't have, that I pushed away so deeply that it has taken this long for it to resurface. The refusal to admit to pain was once my salvation, but as the memories have broken through, I've been in near constant pain, as that which I once could not handle alerts me that I can handle it now.

My birdman and Jeanne are with me during the entire session. Jeanne lies beside me and comforts me, encouraging me through the releases. My birdman stays at my head, whispering in my ear, stroking my face, saying: *It's okay baby, you're doing great, just let it go*, as if I were a three-year-old child.

"Oh God, more pain!" I say. "Remind me why I'm doing this?" But I know why. My guides, and Nicolas, all give me the same answer. "*It's good for you, you need to get it out, your body wants it out.*" The child is in there too, pushing out the pain, urging me to release today, fully ready to get rid of it and move on.

When we finish and I finally stand up, I'm shaking, a bit wobbly on my feet but I feel lighter, and freer too. I've expelled a lot of stuff.

I wake up my son, who has volunteered to spend a few hours helping me move some artwork and furniture to a gallery that sells my work. Afterwards, we stop at a friend's house to see his latest work, and so I can take some publicity photos of his artwork for him. Another one of those little jobs I seem to always be doing, but the small jobs keep me going just as much as the larger ones.

My daughter and I walk in the late afternoon walk. The same deer that I've been seeing every time I walk the same path appears. She stares at us for a long time, even going around a tree to continue watching us as we walk past her. We wave at her. She just stands and stares, checking us out, not afraid in the least. I tune into my birdman guide as we walk. He says that I'm doing okay, finding my balance.

"*Keep doing it,*" he says, "*don't worry, your talent is your resource, your living; it will all work out.*"

In the evening, a violent thunderstorm rages for about an hour, bringing torrents of cooling rain, flooding the street in front of our house. A bolt of lightning lights the night, followed immediately by a loud clap of thunder, too close for comfort.

"Fire!" yells my son, and when I run into his room flames and sparks are shooting out of the computer modem, sending white smoke into the room.

We quickly unplug it and discover that it's totally fried. Luckily nothing else is damaged.

July 2, 2004

I wake to a foggy morning and find that my daughter has left me a birthday gift by the coffeemaker, including coupons for chores she'll do, lots of free vacuuming, and even for 30 minutes of silence. Very cute!

I meet with Chuck and then work at the jobsite for six hours. I stay very present. I like it. I like the way my body looks and feels, strong now, definitely centered, with good feelings about myself. All the releases seem to be having a positive effect. Chuck warned me about the negatives, that they will come back. I know they will, but I also think I'll handle them better now.

I come home to find that my son is treating us to pizza for dinner and that my daughter has baked a chocolate cake. I spend a lovely evening enjoying these gifts with my sweet and thoughtful children.

Thank you for today, for my children and all my spirit friends and guides, and for Chuck and Nicolas who give so selflessly. I am full of gratitude.

THE PAIN IS BACK! Chuck was right! It can come out of nowhere! I am fully awake as it hits full force, yanking me out of sleep and into its truth, but I know what it is now and why it comes back—to remind me to fully release and fully heal. I can't control it. The only option is to surrender to it. Once I do that, it fades away.

"I'm okay," I tell myself, when the onslaught is over. "I'm okay." And I tell my three-year-old self the same thing.

"We're okay, we're working through this. We're okay."

July 3, 2004

I wake to a beautiful sunny morning. My legs are achy, as usual, but I'm in a good mood. I've learned how to surrender to the pain, to relax into it. I don't force it away, as I once did, but willingly allow it to incrementally go through me, staying focused on release as the ultimate goal. Now that I've learned how to do it, it feels like such a logical thing to do! But it has taken a long time to get to this point. Normally, my body did what it was used to doing, but the change has come about because I've become aware that I can do something different, and the more I practice, the easier it gets.

When I'm present and feeling good I have no pain, but when I'm asleep, in the vulnerability of unconsciousness, the pain slips easily back in. But I've set a different intention now. Rather than actively resisting, as in the past, I'm actively participating in releasing now. This time of patient waiting is paying off.

I get my son up and we drive to the nearest internet cable company offices to pick up a new modem. They don't want to believe us when we tell them that it got struck by lightning, but as soon as they see the modem there is no more discussion. They hand us a new one and off we go!

I get ready to go to the opening of the abstract painting show. I'm excited because I'm showing a new kind of work that I feel good about. I prepare myself differently. I dress differently too, and when I arrive, I feel like a different person. I talk, for the first time really, about my art, and many lively conversations ensue. It isn't just me, because the whole show begs to be spoken about, and for the first time in a long time the conversations are about the art, not about the appetizers and wine, or who's there, but about abstract art specifically: how we do it, how we define it, the meaning behind it, where it comes from. I have a fabulous time. It's also interesting to hear the reactions people have to my own work, as many people come up to me with their comments. One man says he picked out one of my pieces as possibly his favorite in the entire show. It's good for me to hear this, as my ego could still use a little bolstering, especially since I paint directly from my unconscious and always wonder if it's too personal, but something seems to be landing on the canvas that others find relatable.

Back home around eleven, I'm tired but still wound up. The intensity of the experience tonight was exhilarating in a lot of ways, for it proves to me that indeed, art still feeds my soul like nothing else. I'm excited but a little scared at my daring self, as I dare to stay with the instability of the artist's life, even with all my commitments and duties as a mother and provider to my children. It feels like such a momentous decision, as I reinstate my intention to go it on my own, as an artist and a mother. I know it's the right inner decision, and so it's also the right outer decision too. I will no longer be a divided individual but at one with myself, and besides, I've come to really understand and trust my journey through life in a new and surprising way. And I do have a lot of support!

I dealt with a lot of anxiety today, examining it as it came up, wondering where it was coming from. I knew, as I released the pain last night, that there was something else behind it that I wasn't able to grasp at one o'clock in the morning. I felt angry and hostile on and off today, as well as anxious. Not sure why, but I was aware that something deep inside, having to do with the pain that emerged in the night, stayed with me to some degree, lying in wait under my skin. I guess I'll find out what it is soon enough.

July 4, 2004

I've been questioning my stubbornness, my ability to say no to jobs that will allow me security and a nine-to-five schedule, in order to pursue my art and writing instead. My strong spirit self wants me to continue with my creative life, although I have no plans per se, except to go with the flow and follow my muse, so to speak. However, my muse doesn't appear to have much money either, or else I'm just not finding where she hides it.

I'm wondering if it's the scared child who wants to be the artist and writer because it feels safer than going into the world. Perhaps she's keeping the adult captive, not allowing for growth outwardly; i.e., the introvert keeping the extrovert from engaging the world? But, on the practical side, how do I intend to pay my bills? Right now, I have no plan. I do have some money coming next week that will pay some of them, but as I look over my checking account, I see that this is worse than I thought. I feel like I need some advice. I decide to go for a walk.

I meet the deer almost immediately, as I round a turn in the path. She crosses in front of me and then stands alongside the path, looking at me. I ask her what I should do and she turns her head towards the woods, nodding, which I interpret as *"keep going, just keep going."* Lara said to me the other day: "Jan you will destroy yourself if you stop now, don't stop. Stay on your path." She's exactly right.

I feel that once again a question is answered, and the answer remains the same, to stick to the path that my heart points out. I realize that yes, the wounded child in me has certain needs, but I'm not catering to her anymore. Instead, I'm allowing the adult in me to set the standards for the future. My intent is that it will be a future based in spirit, in what feels right, not decisions based on old parameters but decisions based on what my heart knows. The adult knows how important it is to bear the tension of sitting through this time of waiting. Eventually, the new creative will come to fruition, that I am certain of.

I have another conversation with my birdman guide. He comes swooping in close, a tiny swallow, to assure me that if I just pay my bills as they come in, I'll manage better. Pay one bill at a time, rather than waiting until the end of the month when everything comes due at once, he advises. In this manner I'll whittle down the large monthly bill total to smaller more manageable payments. What a brilliant idea, and so simple! My normal routine has been to let the monthly bills pile up and then pay them all at once, but this idea actually makes a lot of sense.

"Hang in there," he says, *"good things will come."*

I'm sure I'm in denial about some things, but I am dead certain about others, especially that now is the time for me to stay focused on myself. That's what this entire recapitulation has been about, remaining on the true path and being focused on my own deepest needs, for once in my life. In spite of everything, I've created a good home environment for myself and the kids. The financial aspect is the hardest to contend with at this point, but maybe in a day or two it will be better. I seem to have a terrible relationship with money, feeling that I don't deserve it, ashamed to accept it, even for the hard work I do. In the back of my mind I always think I don't deserve it, that I haven't earned it; humiliation and shame keep me from accepting it as my due. I don't like to say I *need* it. It's almost as if I send a signal that I don't care about it or want it. There's such shame in needing, in being in a position of having to ask. Somehow, I have to believe in myself, and that I have a right to the money I work so hard for, that I do deserve it, because I've definitely earned it!

July 5, 2004

I tell myself over and over again: don't panic, don't panic, everything will be fine, everything will be fine, but the stress is almost unbearable. Often when the kids are away, like this weekend, I think of all the things I'll get done but generally end up doing nothing, except getting more depressed. Although, to be fair, I did send off several short stories the other day to various publications, and even though there's probably little chance they'll be considered, I feel really good about taking that daring step.

My dreams last night were depressing, a continuation of how my day was, a rash of problems spiraling through me. However, I got through yesterday and I'll get through today, and each day to come, and I will figure things out. Perhaps I'm too hard on myself, demanding that I do the impossible. After all this time and effort, it's not right to take the tail-biting, obstinate route anymore. Far better to acquiesce to spirit and finally really trust that I'm in good hands. I should only be taking advice from my guides and my own heart center, the soft, feminine self, not the hard, masculine self.

I realize that one main reason I'm in such debt is the underlying need to make everyone else happy, to make my customers happy, and the desire to be seen as a nice, good person. Although these are largely unconscious needs on my part, they have been at the core of my interactions in the world. In giving everyone else great deals, in accommodating everyone else's budget, I have financially ruined myself. My business obviously can't work like that, and I'm left in a bad spot, too generous for my own good.

I work at the jobsite until six-thirty, drive the half hour home, take a bath, eat and flop into bed, my body exhausted. I made enough money today to make a dent in the bills. While I worked, I thought about working in an office, driving to work an hour or so every day, and I just don't find anything appealing about it. Sure, I'd make a living, but I'd be bored and unhappy. I'd done that before, worked in publishing in New York City, and every day for three years I made plans to quit and go back to freelancing, until I finally did. The reality is that I keep choosing the unstable creative life, over and over again, and I'm being very stubborn about it, so it must be right.

"Follow your bliss," Joseph Campbell says. Well, how long does it take to finally get there?

July 6, 2004

I dream that I'm sitting and talking with Chuck. Hunks of stained glass surround my chair, as if a large stained-glass window has shattered and is lying in pieces all around me. I try explaining to Chuck that I'm giving up now, finally acquiescing, pointing out the broken stained-glass window.

"Here are all the pieces," I say, "pieces of my dream." He refuses to believe me or allow me to accept that the window can't be fixed. I try to justify why I'm giving up, pointing to the chunks of glass to prove that everything is over.

"I can't do anything with them anymore," I say. "I can't keep it together."

"It's only a temporary setback," he says, refusing to look at the evidence, as if it doesn't even exist.

Completion

I slept well, until almost eight. I feel a little stiff after nine hours of painting yesterday, but I had no night clenching for the first time in a long time. In fact, I was pretty limp all night. Exhaustion has its benefits.

My dream seems to suggest that perhaps fear is in the way of fulfilling my dreams, that fear is at the root of everything. I'm afraid perhaps of actually achieving my dreams, as that beautiful stained-glass window may imply. Maybe it isn't broken. Maybe it just hasn't been assembled yet. Maybe I'm not at the end stage but the beginning stage.

I meet with Chuck. We talk about my ability to shift, to do what the shamans call *stalking*, being able to step into who I need to be. I *stalked* when I stepped seamlessly into being an abstract painter the other night at the opening. Stalking means being right *in the moment*, when nothing else exists, except that moment, and who you are, in that moment. On Sunday I shifted into being the writer, stalked being a short story writer. Yesterday, I shifted into being a housepainter, stalking that life on the jobsite, the lone female among the workmen, and I had that really good strong feeling about myself as I played that role.

"Who are you today?" Chuck asks.

"I'm the woman who feels unworthy, with an inability to understand that I should get paid for the work I do, that I've earned it."

"You don't owe anyone anything; it's simply okay and right to be paid for the work you do," Chuck says.

"Yes, I deserve to be paid because I work, and I work really hard," I say. "I have to learn to say, 'yes, write me a check' when someone offers to pay me, rather than act like I don't need it. Sometimes I actually say, 'oh, you can pay me next time,' when I actually desperately need the money right away. I sometimes act as if I don't care if I get paid, as if I don't want the money. Wanting exposes a need, a vulnerability, but I must appear totally unneedy to stay safe. I already did the work, so why can't I just accept what's owed me?"

"You work, you get paid," says Chuck, "you work, you get paid; you work, you get paid."

He's right. I'm in a different world now and it works in a different way. It's a world where I get paid for the work I do, and it stops there. I work and I get paid.

I tell Chuck about the encounters with the deer. He seems intrigued by these episodes, listening intently, which helps me to accept the validity of them as meaningful events in my life—the deer on my path, appearing over and over again, offering insight, guidance and advice. There's no expectation of payback, just simple giving, and it's so simple to accept.

"You're all right," Chuck says. "You're all right."

In the afternoon I have a session with Nicolas. None of my guides accompany me, but it's painful. At one point I spontaneously yell "OUCH" really loudly. After that, Nicolas gently encourages me to focus on breathing and relaxing my body on the exhale, to incrementally let go. "Breathe," he says, "breathe... relax... breathe... relax." I am lulled by the sound of his voice and before long a lot of burning releases issue forth. My throat keeps closing up, as usual, and I feel like I can't breathe. It's almost as if I'm choking, or on the periphery of a memory that might sweep me away. Instead, I breathe, relaxing into it, whatever it is, letting it go without a hitch.

While I walked this evening, I felt like I was on top of the world, alone in it as the sun set over the river. I saw a few deer, but not mine; she didn't appear tonight. One crossed the path far ahead of me and kept walking. I took it as a sign that we're all on our own paths; you on yours, me on mine. Sometimes paths cross, sometimes they join up for a while, but the main thing is to just keep going on your own path of heart, following your bliss.

I walked into the woods tonight for the first time in a long time. Mostly I've been staying in the open fields, but tonight I conquered my fear and entered the shadows. Squirrels in the trees kept dropping things on me, leaves and hickory nut casings. Birds chirped loudly, and I wondered if they were warning me or if they were just happy to see me, urging me on, telling me I'm safe, that it's a different world now and I'm safe in it. It was very quiet the deeper into the woods I walked, the last of the sunlight flickering among the dark shadows. Only the animals moved. I was fine, I was okay. I made it through without fear; I heard only distant rumblings within myself that I was able to let pass without attachment. Instead, I stayed in the sensations of the moment.

I am full of gratitude and love for all who assist, nurture, guide, and love me. I'm working hard to get to a new place. The going has been tough, but I'm getting to a better place. I now know that it truly *is* possible to change, and to heal too.

July 7, 2004

I had nightmares all night long about being locked away in darkness. I suffered deep loneliness and fear, and lost all trust in humanity, men especially. I lost all trust that they would ever be kind to me. Men represent only pain and fear, I thought. I was certain that I would never trust or believe that help would come, because help never came.

In my dream last night, an adult, a man I was supposed to trust, came back to me in my dungeon over and over again, and each time he returned another flame of hope that he had come to save me was extinguished. Finally, by dream's end, there was not even a flicker of hope, not a hint, just dead certainty that I was totally on my own and the only escape was shutting down completely, going as dead as possible. I feel, very intensely, that my body did exactly that to protect me; it went dead. My own body, the one thing that suffered so immensely, found a way to protect the little three-year-old girl that I was, allowing me, my conscious self, to escape by going out of body.

I feel the old deadness as I write this, how it felt, how my body shut down all feelings, went numb, and in so doing pushed me up and out, so that I could escape the brutality and the knowledge of it, so I didn't have to be there. My own body took the pain and let me go, finding the solution to the dilemma of choosing life over death. There was no other means of salvation; there was no other person to turn to for help; I had to find a way to help myself. However, as a result, I never quite got back in all the way; I remained always split. There was me and there was my body, two separate entities that stayed fragmented, separated from each other in order to survive. The effects of what happened were so long-lasting and painful that to reenter my body would have shattered and crippled not only my body, but my sanity as well.

"Why does he hate me so much?" I often wondered about the man who abused me. "Why does he hate me?"

I never expected kindness or goodness from people. I remained cut off from feelings and expectations, safe in my split. I'm in the process of merging those two halves of myself now, and finding that they do belong together. I now know that rediscovering the pain, and reliving and releasing it are all parts of a successful merger. For most of my life, however, I found only deadness in my body, fear in my mind, and a desperate need to find a quiet place in which to hide. I was always seeking safety, a place where the two parts of my broken self could reside in peace. It was like putting a broken toy away in a box, not playing with it ever again, not even looking at it. There was just an instinctual need to store it away. But now I have a great need to fix it, to take it out of the musty box and repair it, to put the head back on the body, reconnect the veins and arteries, try to get it to work and feel, the way it's supposed to work and feel, like a real human being. I'm a broken doll that I'm trying to fix. That's who I am today.

I drop my car off yet again at the mechanics for another repair, hoping it's just a fuse that needs replacing, as is suspected. I walk over to the new studio to wait until it's done, feeling a strong need to be there. The nightmares hang heavily, and I take it as yet another validation of my condition, and the deep split I suffer as a result. I still need to find safety more than anything, to feel secure in my life in order to continue growing. It's what I've always been searching for and what I know I'm searching for now, because I cannot continue to grow and change if I don't feel safe in myself and in this world.

Though remnants of dreams from last night stay with me, adding a tinge of depression to the day, I also feel how urgently necessary it is that I get my story written down, that I continue my personal healing work, that I learn to trust the people who have come into my life, who travel this segment of the journey with me. But I also know that I must find the safety and security I seek within myself, for that is where I must ultimately find the healing I seek too, within myself.

I draw with my left hand, letting the three-year-old child speak through me, for that was her nightmare I dreamed last night. I watch as she puts her feelings down onto the large sheet of paper that I'd fastened to the wall the last time I was here.

"It hurts," little Jan says, "it hurts."

"What hurts?" I ask.

"My body, my vagina, my heart, my head, down there, down there really hurts, down there where no one is supposed to look or touch, not even me; down there hurts the most of all."

She draws the hurt, a small round circle a few inches wide, coloring it red and pink, placing it inside a slightly larger angry black circle.

"I only made a little drawing of hurt," little Jan says, "because it isn't that bad," but I know she's only saying that because she thinks that's what I want to hear. But it's time now for both of us to admit that the pain was devastating.

With the red oil pastel in my left hand, I redraw her drawing, making the red area as big as it needs to be, because the real truth is that the pain is HUGE!

Chuck told me that I should keep shifting now, as often as I need to, that I've learned how to stalk like a pro. So today I am stalking my three-year-old child self. The goal is to really connect with her, let her speak, and finally release the pain.

As I shift from drawing with my left hand (the child) to my right hand (the adult) I notice that the adult self just wants to create a calm center of blue-green and stay there in its utter calmness, but the child can't even go near it. She's only interested in dealing with the dark devastating colors of pain. As I/we draw, the red hurt abuts right up to the pool of blue-green calmness; only a thin line separates them, as fragile and thin as a membrane, not very strong. If I go deep into the blue-green pool of calmness, I can pretend it's safe there, but it's only an illusion because as soon as I do, the red hurt pushes up against it, and I feel the pain pressing in on me. I can't really get away from it. For most of my life it has been the most important thing to keep them apart, to keep them from spilling into each other, to keep my safe place safe, as best I could, and my sanity intact.

When I put my right hand on top of my left at one point, in order to guide it, it feels like a strange adult hand, separate and foreign, not my own hand at all. I tell it to go away; this is not your day for drawing.

"She needs to do this on her own," I say, "let her deal with it. It's important and she has to do it alone."

Is my left side dominated by the child? When I sleep on my left, am I allowing the child to dream and express her emotions? My nightmare last night came directly from my experiences as a child, and I was sleeping on my left side.

"It's okay, it's over, he's gone," she said in the dream, "it will stop hurting now, the hurt will go away. He's gone, he's gone now, it's okay."

My spine cracks and snaps with tiny hot pockets of release as I work, as I speak soothing words, as I describe the pain in color and line and form. There seems no end to it. I realize that all aspects of the protective endeavors my child self was able to establish were temporary, but effective nonetheless. But the truth was there wasn't safety to be found anywhere, and the pain wasn't really out of the picture. But it became a matter of dealing with it as best I could. There was nowhere to take it except more deeply inside myself. What a brilliant tactic for such a young child to take! As I accept this, anger explodes onto the paper, and the whole red and pink drawing becomes encased in darkness, surrounded by fury, just as the sadness inside myself still is, for I already know that the anger is just a cover for what really lies in the depths of the self: sadness, utter sadness.

I walk back to the garage to pick up my car. As I walk, I realize that I'm not in my body, not fully anyway. I have difficulty putting one foot in front of the other and getting centered. I can't catch my breath, can't walk and breathe at the same time. By the time I've walked the few blocks I'm better, having pretty much talked myself back into my body, slowing down to a pace that fits my mood, not pushing myself to be the way I used to be. I'm accepting that I'm different now, that my body is different and I am different in it. I have to respect that.

I realize how important it is for the child to be able to speak now. By listening to her, I'm reopening to my lifelong desire to live the creative life; there is no other me. Now I just have to expand on it. I've been an illustrator. I've been a children's book illustrator and author. I've been a furniture painter. I've been a graphic artist & designer. I've been a teacher. I've worked in publishing and advertising. I've been an editor. I've been a house painter, decorative painter and muralist. I'm a writer and an abstract artist. What will I be next?

The whole day wove together creatively. The three-year-old child was given voice. I gave her the opportunity to express herself in drawing during the day, and, in the evening, I wrote a short story about her. I feel good about it. And for the first time in a long time, she feels calm.

Thank you to all who guide and encourage me, to all the animals and ethereal spirits, and to my earthly healers too. I am full of gratitude and love for all of you.

July 8, 2004

It was hard to fall asleep last night, I tossed and turned until one o'clock and then finally slept. I woke at seven and have been snatching half hour snoozes since. The three kitties meow loudly every now and then, asking for one thing and another, waking me out of fitful naps.

I dreamed the same dream I dreamed the night before. I was locked away in a dungeon and a man came visiting whenever he pleased. The atmosphere was dank, dark, cold, and sad. He was an ugly, mean man. The abuser came back.

In a session with Nicolas, I go to a very dark place, much like my dungeon dream. I'm surrounded by badness, alone with it and I can't keep it away from me. The badness gets into me and I have no power or control over it. I become immediately lost in what it does to me, leaving me an empty and sad shell of a being. I can't find my way back into my body. Nicolas tells me to keep breathing until I feel that I've returned.

"Come back," he encourages. "Come back to your body, it's your garden."

Somewhere between getting the laundry done at the laundromat and making some phone calls I have returned; I am back in my body, energized! Whatever it was that came in my dreams stayed with me until just a little while ago. It revved up during the session with Nicolas and when I felt it surrounding me and seeping into me, I knew there was fear along with it, my own fear. It felt as if the badness was not mine but that it was negative energy left inside me by the abuser. The abuser made me feel bad about myself, telling me I was a bad girl, a dirty girl. I've carried those ideas around with me since I was two and three years old. It was what came through when I was working yesterday as well; both in the drawing I did at the studio and the story I wrote last night, and it was what permeated those two dark nightmares.

During my session with Nicolas, I went back into the empty place inside myself where I had to find a way to deal with the confusion of feelings and words that my abuser spoke to me. It's impossible for a young child to make sense of such confusion. An adult is torturing you and you don't understand, first of all, what exactly he's doing, but then on top of that he makes you feel ashamed of yourself, that you should know better. He also tells you that you have chosen to be there with him because only a bad girl would do such a thing. His evil gets hammered into you and you become what he grooms you to be, his slave girl, and you know he's right when he tells you that you like it; you prove it by being there! His body touching your body makes his words true. You are so full of shame it's impossible to imagine being anything but bad. You try to figure things out, to make sense of it, soothing yourself by looking for ways to alleviate the constant mental and physical pain.

Every evening I write, working on short stories, and every week I send one off to a publisher. This is my intention now, to stay focused on perfecting my writing skills, to keep telling my story in some fashion, whether cloaked in fiction or not. I must release it into the world, even in small drips and drabs, until I get to the place where I can tell it in its entirety, without fear. That day will come, though I'm not there yet.

Today was such a mix of void and reality. For part of the day, I wasn't totally present, I was out of my body, but then I'd notice I was partially back. I functioned better then. I even set up a few appointments today for new work, lining up some faux finish painting jobs. I made the decision to charge by the hour now too, no more flat rates for a job but time and materials only. It works better for me. I'll give guesstimates based on time expected, but charge an hourly rate. *I work and I get paid. I work and I get paid.* I must stay strong and remind myself often that things do have a way of working out.

July 9, 2004

I dream of being a child. I have to figure everything out without any guidance. I know *nothing* and yet I have to try and make sense of *everything*. I'm in a state of confusion and yet I'm determined to not let the confusion overpower me. I have no understanding of how anything works and yet I create out of what is presented to me. I have nothing but myself and my own intuition and creativity to rely on.

My dream is right on target. That's what my life was like as a child and it's what I seem to be recapitulating now. I had only my own wits to rely on. I acknowledge this truth, and yet I still cannot acknowledge the bigger truth; I won't let myself accept the fullness of the truth of my past. Instead, I push it away. Far easier to accept the straightforwardness of my usual anxiety, so known and doable. But the truth is, I feel deep, intense sadness whenever I contemplate the real truth. It's like a dark lake inside me that I have yet to explore. I try to make it not be important, but it keeps reappearing. It's been forming all week, getting into bed with me, arising with me in the mornings, seeping into my days and into my nights. It's something I haven't wanted to go to, that I haven't been ready to dive into. I pretend I'm okay, but that dark lake of sadness is rising higher inside me.

I meet with Chuck. As soon as I sit down, I am a three-year-old child locked away in a dungeon. I hear sounds outside. I want it to be someone else at the door, someone coming to rescue me, but in the end, it's always him, the abuser. But I, the adult, want that child to learn that it isn't him anymore, that *I'm* at the door now, that *I'm* her rescuer. She has to find a way to release herself from her incessant expectation of disappointment, to expect kindness, and to once and for all accept that things have changed.

"I think I'm still looking for ways to avoid being present now, in this life," I say, "still looking for reasons to remain in the dungeon instead. The biggest problem may be that I actually like it there!"

"Do you *really* want to stay there?" Chuck asks. "In spite of everything you know, do you *really* want to stay buried alive in there?"

"Right at this moment, in all honesty, I spend more time trying to figure out how I can *stay* there. Not how to get out, but how to stay there, protected; how to keep the dungeon intact so I can at least go back when I need it, because it feels safe there. Even though I know that fear is bedded down with me when I'm there, at least it's familiar. It's a known fear that I've dealt with all my life. At this point I'm quite comfortable with it. When I'm there, I almost don't want it to be taken away from me!"

"I feel like someone just getting out of years of solitary confinement and finding the world totally unfamiliar, preferring to replicate that solitary existence, to the sparsest degree, outside the walls of the prison. So why not just stay there? What is there that will really be different?"

"Help the little girl by drawing a hole in the wall of the dungeon. Break through it; go in and lead her out," says Chuck.

"I sometimes feel that she made the decision to stay locked up in that dungeon because everything she encountered in the real world was painful and scary," I say. "She chose to deal with it by hiding from the real world, remaining institutionalized, in a sense, but it kept her sane. I, the part of me who went ahead into real life, chose a different path; I chose to find a way to stay sane while remaining in the real world."

I've been dreaming the little girl's dreams and drawing her reality, letting her speak and writing her story, and as much as I know that she hopes for a different life, I also know that she just doesn't see the possibility of it. She doesn't recognize that we're living it already, that I'm already breaking down the walls that surround her. I offer fresh new life, the opportunity to *stalk* with me, to live and feel life in a totally new way. If she won't come out, then, as Chuck suggests, I'll have to go in and get her, so we can begin this new life together at last, as one.

"I guess I'll have to stalk a new integrated me," I say, finally, "try to become the person who can save both of us, the reluctant three-year-old child and the equally reluctant adult."

We had spoken about *stalking* before, but Chuck corrects my interpretation of it. He says that it needs to be natural, not a conscious decision but something that happens without consciousness, that I suddenly find myself there, in the moment, being who I am not normally.

Normally I'm not stalking, because normally I have to tell myself, right up to the last second, that I can do something, that I can lead the artists' gallery meeting, that I can meet this client or that one, that I can make that phone call. Normally, I prep and pep myself up for what I must encounter, telling myself to push through my fears and just do it. True *stalking,* on the other hand, is a natural, seamless occurrence.

"You don't even know you're doing it," Chuck says, "until all of a sudden you find that you are someone else."

"For the most part, when I go out into the world, I push myself out of the way so I can play the chosen roles," I say. "But it's another thing, and very surprising, to all of a sudden find myself in a situation, totally flowing and not even realizing how I got there, like at the opening last weekend. I *felt* different as I was getting ready, but I didn't have my usual awareness of having to get into costume and perform; I just had a sense of *feeling* different."

"That's the difference," Chuck points out, "and that's what you must prepare yourself to be available for, without fear or self-dismissal, but wholly and energetically become someone else entirely, as naturally as being yourself."

Chuck also reminds me that the other things that happen to me, when I'm walking and encountering the deer, for instance, or when I'm engaging in the magic, communicating with nature and my guides, that those experiences are as real as the things that keep that child locked up, that they are all occurrences happening in another world, as real as this world, what the shamans call the *second attention*.

"Yes, I understand," I say. "The child, however, doesn't know that. I've experienced so much of the magic that surrounds us, the magic that we have access to, but she hasn't. Her experiences have only been on the dark side. She hasn't yet experienced the light."

I have a creative spirit and I believe that is what has kept me with one foot in reality, anchoring me throughout my whole life, offering me sanity in this world, what the shamans call the *first attention*, even while the pull to go over to the other side, to the second attention, has at times been tremendously persuasive, cunning, and inviting. To go completely over to the second attention, never returning to the first attention, would have meant giving up my sanity. Instead, I was offered an identity, one that I didn't have to work too hard at. It's who I am in the real world, an artist, a creative person. It came most naturally, but at the same time I knew I was only playing a part, unable as I was to believe that I truly fit into the artist's world. As capable as I was of playing the role, I always knew that a part of me was missing, the part that was left behind in the second attention. I see that now. It now also makes sense that the thing that has kept me most sane, my creative artist self, is also the catalyst for breaking through the walls of that dungeon and to saving the three-year-old child self.

Again, I ask myself: do I really want to stay in there? Does she, the child, want to stay there? The answer is: yes, right now I see no reason to come out. I see no good reason to give it up. I would be at a total loss without it. I would become that prisoner who needs his prison in order to survive. The fact is, I like solitary confinement because I'm safe there; nothing can get in, but obviously I can't get out either. I think that's partly what I'm up against; the child doesn't dare have hope, because it means leaving the safety of the dungeon. As bad as it is, it's comfortingly familiar. Although I know she's been calling to me for years, I also know that she won't come out on her own because there has never been a reason that is more powerful than safety. Something else, something more powerful and enticing than feeling safe has to draw her out. Love has to draw her out; it has to be love.

I try to relieve her of some of the torment she holds by painting, drawing, and writing. Even the nods of acceptance I get for my work are important; people reacting and feeling things when they view my work validates the process. I have something to offer, something that affects people, but in the process, I am also pulling up the debris that has blocked me from the child inside. I am energetically transforming it, giving it new form, and forging a new kind of connection to her in the process. She, in turn, is being offered glimpses of me in action in the real world, learning the art of stalking, of flowing naturally in the world, proving to her that I am as comfortable to be with, as trustworthy, as powerful as the safety of her dungeon, offering her something new to believe in. I also hope that she sees that I am a loving being who wants only the best for her. It's a slow but necessary process.

Some aspect of my personality allows me to be daring, and I've always relied on and cultivated that part of myself to a certain extent, kept it alive and viable. And so, I am able to offer the girl inside the dungeon a representative in the real world, the part of myself that knows her way around, a creative spirit that is willing to take chances on her behalf. What it all comes down to is that I am all things for myself. I am the little girl; I am the walls of the dungeon; I am the jailer; I am the creator of the dungeon itself, but I am also life, and love, and freedom. In the end it's this place, this awareness that matters, the *third attention*, where the first and second attentions are seamlessly experienced and lived, the place of dreaming all the time.

I take a walk. Something gets in my eye and bothers me for the first half of the walk. I can't see, can't focus, can't calm down or enjoy the walk at all. I attempt over and over again to remove whatever it is from my eye, wiping at it, folding my lid over, but nothing helps. Everything is out of focus. Eventually I shake it off by drawing attention away from my eye, focusing on being in the moment instead, enjoying the beauty of the day, but I am unable to find balance.

"Come on!" I say, finally, commanding myself to be more present, "at least enjoy this place that's so special. At least enjoy the walk." I know the magic is here, somewhere behind the haze before my eyes, but unavailable today, the girl in the dungeon pulling me back to stay with her in the gloom. Perhaps it's the little girl expressing her fear of the world, afraid to look at it, to face it.

"It's okay, baby," I say, "everything will be okay."

For the remainder of the day, I feel scattered and vague. I have energy, but I also have a heavy desire to stay in the dungeon. But I think the universe is clearly trying to tell me it's time to get out of there. Why do I still want to stay in a place where I feel suffocated and hurt, where I can't breathe or see, where I feel like crying all the time? What is so comforting in all that? Just because it's familiar?! Chuck is right, I do need to make a hole in the dungeon, even just a small one.

I go to the studio and paint over an old painting. Retaining a hot pink edge from the previous work, I paint a dark blue background with a small white hole smack in the middle of it, no bigger than a Quarter. I may want to stay locked in, but I've punctured a hole and there is light seeping in now, if even just a little. My dungeon has been invaded.

I also work on the big ball of orange pain that I painted a couple of months ago. I'm not sure where it's going. It doesn't feel finished; something else needs to happen with it now. It feels like it needs containment of some sort. It's so painful to look at, almost shocking in its intensity; its color and vibrancy dizzying. I can't stand it. I paint small dark rings over it, over the whole painting, so that it dulls the intensity, hides the pain a little, so that when I step back, I can actually look at it without feeling pain in return, for that is what it did to me every time I looked at it. As beautiful as it was it pained me.

Completion

As I walked today, I thought about *stalking*, how Chuck explained that it must become a natural act. To me, right now, it's as if I have a bunch of suits hanging in the closet, made out of different types of energy and personas, and depending on what I have to do I reach for the most appropriate attire, like a costume to put on so I can act a part. A mask makes a person become that mask. If I put a mask on, I become the expression on the mask even though I'm behind it, and even if I've never seen what the expression is; once I put it over my face I change. I act differently with a mask over my face and people react to me differently when I'm wearing one. This is what happens when I take the persona out of the closet and clothe myself with it, when I step into the skin of the person I need to be at the moment. I become that person, but as soon as I am able, I run back to the closet and hang it up again. I get some satisfaction out of the adventure, but I'm still more comfortable once I'm done, when I take the costume off and crawl back into the dungeon. One day, I expect I will seamlessly and naturally stalk again, but even as I write this I think: "No! I don't want to! I don't want to come out of the dungeon!"

"Why not?" I ask.

"Because, it's my home," says little Jan, "it's my home and I feel safe here."

"Even though you constantly hear *him* at the door?"

"Yes, even though I know what he'll do and even though I live with fear surrounding me," says little Jan. "I'm very comfortable here. I know what to expect and how to deal with it. And I'm finding ways to at least express myself now, different ways, and I do leave the dungeon for things that are nurturing. I do go out into the world every now and then, and I'm working very hard at finding ways to heal. I just don't want to leave the dungeon forever."

Chuck will tell me that if I refuse to leave the dungeon that I am essentially putting the brakes on the process, that I'm quitting. The adult me doesn't want to stay there all the time, I just want to stay there for the good parts; for the comfort, for the solitude, and the safety I find there. But I realize that means continued isolation from interacting with people, keeping me from the possibility of having relationships, of experiencing everything the world offers. Maybe this is enough exposure for me though, maybe this place I've gotten to now is enough. Maybe I won't require more freedom and interaction than this.

Why do I say such things when I know I will never stop the search for my total freedom? Because I'm afraid? Yes, I'm afraid.

I'm tired, feeling lonely and frustrated by the end of the day, which as usual turns into anger at myself, and my energy level drops precipitously. I did spend three hours at the studio though, essentially working on myself, which is the only way I'm going to get anywhere. Of course, I need to let this negativity blow over, not let it attach or sabotage my process, or steal my focus from my real work of completing this journey of healing. However, at the moment, I feel myself getting drawn back with such intensity that the dungeon is looking mighty homey and inviting right now. It calls to me, saying: "I told you it wasn't safe out there! I told you this is where you belong. Why don't you listen to me?"

I told Chuck that I'm not regressing but confronting the dungeon, that I need to find out why it draws me so strongly still. It's pretty clear that I'm in this world to engage in something creative, to engage my solitary nature in a healthy way that will eventually benefit not only myself but others as well. I just haven't found out how that's going to come to fruition yet, but part of that entails leaving the dungeon behind.

It's noisy in the neighborhood tonight. I hear voices outside my dungeon, but I'm tired. I shut them out and go to bed.

July 10, 2004

I slept well, as it was a cool night, good for sleeping. I intend that today will be a better day, and that it will be more productive. Maybe I can get beyond this void, this suffocating feeling of being under a spell.

I take a walk. I ask my birdman for guidance.

"I can't seem to do it right now," I say, and I actually cry as I reveal this weakness. "I just don't feel capable."

I ask that I continue to have enough work.

Completion

"Just enough is good," I say. "I don't need more than that, but enough so I don't have to go into more debt, because I can't handle that right now."

"*Don't worry,*" he says, and I know he's already taking care of it.

"*Just stick to the path,*" says Jeanne, when I also ask her for guidance. "*Just stick to the path.*"

So, I hear sound advice from both my financial advisor and my spiritual advisor: *don't worry, and stay on the path.*

Goldfinches, bluebirds, red cardinals, shimmer-backed swallows with scissortails cut the air around me creating a buzz of energy. I feel it, like a cape draped lightly over my shoulders. Green bottle flies come buzzing like bad memories, but I shoo them away. I want to keep this moment pure and magical. Magic is all around me; it surrounds me.

My child self is entombed in darkness, thinking she's safe, but she's in a mental hospital of her own making. I need a better world than that; I have to make mine better than this fragile attempt at living. I may have to sacrifice the child self in order to advance, if she refuses to journey onward...

I work at the artists' gallery in the afternoon. It's very quiet, just me and a few flies. A few people wander in, though for the most part it's quiet.

Today feels like a day of culmination, as if all my potential is finally coming together. I feel good. I guess my walk today really was magical, because I feel present, in the moment.

An artist friend comes in and tells me I look gorgeous. I say thanks, but she keeps repeating it, insisting that I accept her observation. I can't quite take the compliment in. Then I let it in, a little. Maybe I believe her and maybe I do look "gorgeous." The more persistent she is in her declaration, the more I begin to accept that what she's saying is possibly true. I'm changing in spite of myself.

In the evening, I feel good, in balance. I reach the realization that all this work I'm doing on myself is really what life is all about; doing inner work, learning to embrace constant change, and becoming a better, more spiritually evolved person. The only way I can do that is to continue the journey out of the dungeon, away from the old comforts, no matter how strong they are and how intensely they attempt to drag me back. I have to get myself away from them. The challenge is to not do it by avoiding them as in the past, but to initiate change by confronting them.

As I get ready for bed, noises outside rev up. Someone in a house behind mine is having a party. Kids are up late; the energy is rambunctious and intrusive. A car roars loudly through the neighborhood. I could get attached, fearful, but I know I must focus only on what's important at the moment, on what's necessary for now, and only that. Otherwise, I'm just wasting my energy.

Thank you, all of my spiritual guides. I know you are all working on my behalf as intensely as I am. Thank you.

I wake up at two, startled out of a swirl of frustrating dreams where nothing is resolved. Clearly, that's just where I am at the moment, where nothing big is happening and so much remains to do. However, my dreams point out, there are lots of tiny increments of change taking place, things I might not notice until much later. When things shift so subtly it's often not clear that anything has happened at all. I understand this now, how things work in the slow incremental process of everyday reality, magical or not. I do see changes every day, and that is some of the magic I experienced today.

I understand also that Jeanne has been not only guiding me but protecting me as well. The energy that I perceive in my room, that I *see,* as the shamans say, is *mine.* I've perceived it as Jeanne's energy, which it is as well, but now I understand that it's also my energy, that she has been watching over it, protecting and guarding it for me, bringing it to me as I've grown ready for it. She shows me every day what I'm really capable of, that the magic is real and that it's available. It comes in small increments because that's the only way it's acceptable to me, otherwise I won't trust it.

Completion

So, little by little, I receive what I need. Thank you, Jeanne. She knows me so well.

July 11, 2004

In a dream, I'm walking along a road with another person when a big Cadillac comes along, packed full of happy women coming from a feast. They're all dressed up and heading to church. They seem to be relatives of the person I'm walking with. It's decided that they'll come to my house later to continue the feast. In the meantime, this person I'm walking with, and whom I can't clearly detect as either male or female but merely as an illusory energetic presence, walks me back to my house, a house I don't recognize, and shows me around. We wait around for the women to return from church. Then, suddenly, the illusory being gets up and leaves. I continue to wait alone. I wait for a very long time and eventually fall asleep.

I sleep and sleep, eventually waking up to discover that no one has come. I also discover that the house is much bigger than it previously seemed. There are several large rooms I hadn't noticed before. The more I look around the house, the more I see that it's quite derelict, was left unfinished and uncared for a long time ago. I'm fully aware that the place needs work and I grow more determined that I'll do the work myself; I'll fix it up and use it in the future, I decide. As I imagine renovating the house, I am also aware that first I need sleep and food, that I must take care of my own needs first.

I look out a large picture window and see, outside in the yard, a row of banquet tables piled high with food, ready for the feast that the women in the Cadillac promised to attend. I'm really hungry and I think about going out to get some food, which looks really fresh, steaming hot, and delicious. I also imagine that the carload of women might come and see me eating.

"What's wrong with that?" I ask. "Someone has to eat it. Why not me?" I look around for a sweater to put on so I can go outside to the banquet tables. I find one and put it on, even as I imagine the carload of women coming back any minute, catching me in the act, eating the food that I believe is not meant for me. I imagine getting scolded for not only eating the food but for not covering it or taking it inside because it looks like it might rain. Other thoughts enter my mind too, that those women don't care, that they aren't coming back anyway, and that I should just go ahead and eat. They were just showing me that it's possible to be relaxed and happy. What the heck! Why can't I just go out and enjoy the food? But I remain inside, afraid to move, certain the food isn't meant for me. As the dream ends, I am still there, gazing hungrily at the food, unable to take the next step.

In this dream, I find myself suspended in time, in an old rundown house, and yet there's a bountiful feast right within reach that I don't dare touch. What am I waiting for? Do I think I don't deserve it? Yes, I think I don't deserve any of it. I feel threatened by anyone who might catch me enjoying it, fearing I'll be scolded for taking what's not mine. All those happy women in the Cadillac, enjoying life simply because it's available to them, can have it, but not me. It's so beaten into me that I'm not allowed to enjoy anything, even to fulfill a basic human need, such as hunger, or enjoy the sheer pleasure involved in satiation.

I've had dreams like this before where I've been confronted with the bounty that life offers and I've been afraid to partake, but this time is different because I *want* some food. I'm hungry, and the voices keeping me from it don't belong to the new me; they're coming from the old me. I try to reason with them, but I still can't take the next step to fulfillment. I'm still stuck in the dungeon, unable to fully enter into life. This dream points out the dire necessity of finishing my recapitulation, freeing myself from the dark, dank, lifeless dungeon, and finally embracing life. If I don't, I will never be a partaker of the bounty of life, but only an observer.

Interesting that I have this dream right now when the kids are away and I'm denying myself food. When they're away, I usually don't cook for myself. I don't even bother buying groceries. I eat whatever I have in the house, buying only a few necessities, but not spending much because I think I'm not worth it, that it will just go to waste, that I won't eat anyway, and most of the time I don't. So, yes, I don't buy food for myself because I feel that I don't, in fact, deserve it or need it. I deny myself things because I feel that I shouldn't have needs at all, in fact.

Completion

Can't I accept that hunger is normal? Why so ashamed of a basic human need? I have to figure out a way to understand that I deserve to eat, and that everything out there in the world has been waiting for me to partake of it. It's life out there. And yet, it's enjoyment of life that I keep denying myself.

I've been working very hard to get out of the dungeon, that place of comfort that's really just a hiding place. All I do inside that dingy tomb is sleep. I'm not alive in there; I am dead tired asleep, my energy zapped.

This dream points out the dire necessity of completing this journey. I have to, once and for all, reclaim all my energy, and fully take on this new life I've been fashioning for myself during the last three years. The end is in sight. It's as close as that banquet table was from where I was standing in the dream, mere yards away. I have to stop denying myself what I really want and need, what really sustains me, and proceed as if I belong here in this world. It's about time.

What I also confront in the dream, is my lack of self-esteem, a sense of unworthiness, feeling that I don't deserve anything. Even with no one else around, and with only a windowpane separating me from the feast in the yard, I still hesitate because the old voices are still strong, the negative voices that hold me back. I am still obedient to them; I still listen to them.

The illusory being who brought me to the house and showed me around, told me to eat, and then went away and left me to deal with it alone. This is exactly what recapitulation has been about, discovering what needs to be done and finding the means to do it. It's a very solitary journey, facing not only what lies deeply inside the self but also what's holding one back from greater experiences of life, and finding the means to reconcile with it. In the end, I do know that I must do this on my own. Only I can renovate those old rooms of that rundown house of my dreams; my inner process can only be done within my own psyche.

I meet with Nicolas for an Embodyment session. As soon as we begin, I visualize a calm place. I am alone in a cabin in the New England woods on a still lake. In my imagination I go to the lake and float in the calm water. Allowing incremental openings to happen in my body, I float and float, getting more relaxed and comfortable until I get to a good quiet place within myself. From this place, I am aware that it's my choice where I decide to go next. I can choose to go to a calm place like this instead of back into the old dungeon. There are better, safer places that are calm and non-threatening. I don't have to retreat back into that dark place that feels like comfort simply because it has always existed. The fact that it's a habit doesn't make it a good place.

I accept that I have hidden from much of life by partially keeping one foot inside that dungeon. I could always run back inside when I got triggered and needed to find a familiar place to retreat to. Even though it was so debilitating a place, it did its job of protecting me from the onslaughts of pain that sought to remind me of my childhood. When I go to this new place of peacefulness, lying on this calm lake of my imagination, I find that I enjoy life, that life is easy and beautiful, the way I want it to be. I must accept that it's normal to enjoy life, that it's perfectly normal to eat too. I deserve to partake in all that life offers as much as the next person.

"Go back to that place now when you need it, not to the old dungeon," says Nicolas. "You do have choices."

"Yes, I do," I say, "and they can be as simple and effective as visualizing an enjoyable and calming place."

As I leave Nicolas and head out to meet a new client, I realize I must still confront my thoughts, that they are old dungeons too, old ideas that lead me only down old paths. Even as I allow my body to show me that I can let go of old habits and achieve calmness within myself, I must also direct my thoughts to change as well. I must face what remains in all the old places in body and mind. One day soon, I will wake up and go eat from the banquet table without a thought or a care in the world!

I'm in a happy mood when I meet with my client. She wants her bathroom painted with a faux finish that looks like the walls of a Tuscan villa. We agree that I'll drop some samples off for her later in the week since I'll be in her area working on another job. As I drive away, I notice that I'm excited about the prospect of this new work. I'm glad I was able to get to such a calm, happy place during the session with Nicolas. I feel the beginnings of a new shift, subtle but present nonetheless.

My dream keeps me company. My inability to step up to the table and partake still puzzles me. Why do I continue to deny my needs rather than face them? In the dream, I am caught right smack between an old way of acting and the new choice I so clearly see and so clearly understand as the right one. But the choice to take action, as always, is mine. I do have choices, as Nicolas pointed out. I haven't always been in a position to take action on my own behalf, but things are changing now. It's time to do things differently. And with that thought, I decide it's time to get some food, cook it, and eat it. It's time to get over my guilt and my fear! It's time to live more fully, to make healthy choices that are totally different from the old behaviors. That's how I'll break the old cycle of depression and stagnation, how I'll find my way to the banquet table of life. When I feel drawn back to the old comforts, I must seek and do something totally different.

When I left Chuck's the other day, I felt very strongly that I really wanted and preferred the old comforts, that if I had a choice I would still choose the old dungeon, thinking that I needed something from it, that I would lose a big part of myself if I left it, a part I was fearful of losing. Today I know that it's only fear I will lose, and of course fear would prefer I stay. It's like a vampire. In order to survive, the fear needs a body and it has been attached to mine for so long. It has totally relied on my staying available.

I also know that I need time to work on all of this, that this recapitulation must remain a major part of my life for yet a while. I elect to be poor by choice in order to spend time on this process, confronting my fears. I can't stop now and I can't give up, it would be the end of me. I have to keep going, and allow my helpers to continue helping me while I work on myself. The truth is, I *am* doing new things, different things, heading right straight towards that banquet table.

I feel as if I'm on a rollercoaster all day. I dip down into depressive states, but quickly snap out of them, rising high above the shadowy underworld. One moment I am lost, and in the next I am found. One moment I am inundated with a swirl of old thoughts, ideas and bad feelings about myself, coming at me fast, but today, rather than getting caught by them, I've been saying no to them and pushing them away, for they do not belong to the new me.

I need sleep tonight. Last night each time I woke up I panicked for a minute or two, thinking I was going to get back into that awful pattern of sleeplessness again, but I calmed myself down, pushed the intrusions away, and fell back asleep fairly quickly. I realize that I'm being challenged to accept this slow recapitulation process, to accept that it will take the time it takes. I must hang in there and continue to trust that all is working in my favor.

July 12, 2004

I dream that I'm being taught how to properly sell my artwork. I'm trying to sell a long, vertical canvas. It's a red painting of pain, my own pain, but I know others will recognize it too, for I know there are others out there who have the same pain within themselves, and if they could paint their pain, it would look as red as mine.

I wake up in total body pain, sad and depressed before I even get out of bed, writhing in the red pain of my dream. I set my intention for making good choices today, to shift away from pain and sadness like I did yesterday, focusing instead on moving forward. I'm frustrated by the pain though, and the slowness of this change, but I know I'm still in the time of patient waiting, and that progress is destined to be slow and steady during this phase. It does no good to rush ahead; it's not the time for it.

Sometimes, I wonder if I'll ever be fully functional and live more in the world, though I also realize that I must not dwell in negativity but look to a stronger place of power. I have the sense that lots of things are happening behind the scenes and that sooner or later the pieces will fall into place, and the old stuff will be replaced by something new and better.

    I get an email from a publisher who offers me a job. I'm interested, I like the people in the office. I'd feel okay working with them, safe. Is that what I want, safety?

    I meet with Chuck and talk about all the feelings I've been juggling lately, wanting at all costs to stay back in that old protective dungeon, afraid that I'll lose an important aspect of myself if I don't, but also aware that it isn't a good place to be, but the draw to go back there is magnetic, getting me when I'm vulnerable or tired. I have to shift away from it quickly or I'll get caught.

    Chuck suggests that I go back to my dream of the other night, when I was so afraid to take something from the banquet table, so that I can begin to explore outside of the dungeon, have a taste of what real life in the world might be like.

    In my imagination, I creep up to the table quietly and covertly, like a little mouse. I take only a tiny mouse nibble. I'm afraid that someone will see me, but when I look around there's no one there. I go back again and again, gaining in boldness each time, until the mousy attitude disappears completely. Finally, I walk boldly up to the table laden with food and dig in. Suddenly, it dawns on me that *life and all that it offers is here for me too!*

    "Keep painting," Chuck says, as the session ends. "Paint everything you're feeling and experiencing."

    "Yes, I will," I say. "And I do need to go and get some real food now too. I'm hungry!"

    I've been denying myself for too long and it isn't good. And so, I head off to the grocery store and buy some food. Back home, I eat lunch and spend most of the day writing. It's quiet without the kids around. In the evening I don't have much of an appetite but my stomach is growling, telling me I should eat again. I pay attention.

July 13, 2004

"Why is it so necessary for me to eat and to heal?" I write in my journal while I sleep. "Do I really matter?" I dream of escape, but I can't move. I am nothing but pain, tight heavy cinderblocks of pain. Just leave me alone so I can disappear. Chuck appears in my dream and tells me to keep doing my paintings. "You need to keep painting," he says in the dream, just as he did yesterday in real life.

I lounge around in bed, and finally get up at nine. I have to meet some people to go over the publicity for the upcoming show I'll be curating at the gallery, but the depressive energy of my dream hangs heavy over me.

I send out my intentions to the universe, asking for help in noticing the signs that come to guide me. I ask to be reminded that I'm safe in this world. When I'm back in the dungeon that's the most important thing to me, feeling safe. When I'm in my new world, I want to be open to adventure, to new experiences and excitement, but I also want to feel equally safe. However, I still expect the darkness to come back, the feelings of loneliness, desolation and fear, and the pain too. I expect the psychological stresses to come back, to overwhelm me so that I'll once again be incapable of functioning in the real world, incapable of almost everything, of eating and earning a living, of going out in public, of talking, of even saying hello or greeting someone I know, afraid I'll have to say something back, to lie and say, I'm fine, and it will be too hard to keep it up, to stay calm and act like I really am fine. Some days it's just too hard to imagine that life could be anything but hard, for the old world still lies so close.

I go to the meeting as planned and then return home, not feeling too spiffy. The depression weighs heavy on my heart, but I won't let it take over. I did pick up a movie and a bottle of wine to have this evening with dinner. I won't let myself feel guilty about splurging on myself. I won't be the mouse at the banquet table but a full-fledged adult. What the heck, I am an adult! I ought to be able to give myself some small pleasures once in a while. The hell with the depressing dream!

Completion

I make sure to eat some lunch and later in the day, toward evening, I take a long walk. I see the deer. She sees me coming along and walks down the path directly toward me, getting closer and closer. I see a couple walking towards us.

"Someone's coming," I say softly.

She walks off the path and into the grass and stands there waiting. The couple sits down on a bench. They seem to be reading something. It gives us the extra time we need. The deer comes right up to me again, standing her ground, her eyes scanning up and down my body, as if sizing me up or memorizing me. She seems to want to know something from me.

"Do *you* want a message from *me* this time?" I ask. She comes closer and closer as I speak and I hear her asking if *they* are okay.

"They're okay, everyone is okay, everyone's fine," I say, and I notice a dark storm brewing in the mountains behind her, on the other side of the river.

"I have to go," I say, "a storm is coming and I don't want to get caught out here in a lightning storm."

"Do you have something to tell me?" I ask her, since she is still staring fixedly at me.

She says that everything is going well for me too, that I'm almost there, at the end of my journey, but overall, I feel that the message I gave her was the most important one. She tells me that the waiting is almost over. I'm pleased by what she says.

"Someone is coming," I say, hearing voices again.

Her energy feels sad, as if she's not happy to hear this. She goes back into the woods at the same time that I turn and walk away. I glance back where she stands quietly in the shadows of the trees, keeping me in sight too, but soon I round a bend in the path and lose sight of her. Suddenly, I hear loud snorting. Turning back, I see her standing on the top of a rise in the field, calling after me. Her forceful snorting sends chills up my spine.

"Oh my, this *is* real!"

I take it that she's encouraging me to believe and trust that good things will happen, that this magic is real, and that I will always have magic in my life, if I continue opening myself to it, *innocently*. I thank her for her communication, noting that this is exactly what I intended this morning, to be made aware of the signs and help coming my way. Well, here I am, totally immersed in it.

Tomorrow, I see the lecherous doctor, the dermatologist. Usually, he looks at my entire body, and I let him. I let him lift my clothing, peek around my waistband, between my toes, let him touch my face and neck. He does it so crudely. I'm afraid of him. Why do I even go to him? Why do I think I have to? I'll just go and get it over with. Everyone in the office is so friendly and happy, maybe I'm just imagining what I feel when I go there, maybe it's just me.

July 14, 2004

I'm still struck by the deer incident from last night. What did she really want? There was something very sad about her; that much I understood. It was as if she missed someone terribly, and she looked so intently at me, as if searching for something recognizable, as if we shared something. She didn't want me to leave; I knew that. I'll have to go back and find her again.

Is she the embodiment of Jeanne's spirit, as I've often perceived? Or is she something else; the essence of hope, wisdom, knowledge, awareness? Is she a symbol of patient waiting, how to go about it? She was also telling me that the waiting time is almost over, that the coming together of everything is very near now. She came and stood so close to me; it was uncanny!

"Wait, wait don't go yet," she said. "*I want to take a good look at you before you go,*" and then the couple walking towards us sat down, giving us time to communicate.

I felt that she either wanted to memorize me, or that she was making some decision about me. I do feel that my time of recapitulation is nearly finished, as she said, that I'm in the home stretch. It was the same deer that I've seen so many times. I felt such a longing in her.

I don't want to go to the dermatologist today, but I will. I'll go and get it over with. It won't take long. I no longer fear skin cancer returning, as I once did, now I fear him. He doesn't actually do anything to me, it's just the feeling I get that he'd like to, that he takes pleasure in looking and touching. Maybe if my attitude is different, he'll be different.

I found out something about myself today: *I've changed since last year.* I didn't have the same experience with the dreaded dermatologist because I'm different. It was as if I had a shield around me. Rather than poking at me without my permission, he asked me what he should look at, and we went over the same old suspicious moles, suspected problem areas, which are not really problems at all. I felt that he was trying to implant some new fear in me, telling me that I'll have problems because he's the expert, he knows. Well, I don't buy it. He treated me differently today because I appeared differently, my energy was stronger, changed, no longer fragmented, no longer servile to masculine energy.

Why do I even go to him? Because I don't want to have skin cancer again? But that isn't how I won't have skin cancer. Going to the doctor won't have any effect on that! It's me, I'm the only one who can change that, by my intent to change and to heal. And I did, I've changed.

I couldn't go to the deer today, too many thunderstorms.

July 15, 2004

I have another rough night, waking up at 2 a.m. in a panic over my financial situation, the Invisibles taking over. I don't really know how I'll survive; the only plan is to get work. Of course, now that the sun is up and it's a new day, I feel a spark of hope that I'll be okay, as usual, but then I wonder if I'm just being naïve. I long for an answer, a plan, but there seems to be no answer. I will hold out and stave off panic as best I can.

"I'm in a void," I say to Nicolas, when I arrive for our appointment.

"Is it inside you or outside of you?" he asks.

"It's definitely outside of me," I say. "When the void is inside, I know the feeling. This is different."

"Well," he says, "when you find yourself in the void, stop and look around; see what's there."

As the session begins, I experience confusion and hear the loud racket of it. It feels like I'm about to go shooting off, a rocket out of control. I let it take me, go with the flow of it, while at the same time I remain intent upon achieving equilibrium. I have to get back to where I can feel alive, on a good playing field. By the end of the session my energy has spiraled back down to a hum, less confusing, though everything is still unclear.

"The whole world is inside you," Nicolas says, as I leave.

All this week I've been verging on panic. Is it the three-year-old child, waiting for what's going to happen? Knowing that she'll be leaving the dungeon? I've tried to reassure her that all will be well, just as Jeanne and the deer have told me. I've tried to be calm for her. I've let her innocence guide me to speak to the deer, to communicate, showing her that the world is indeed a safe and magical place. I've spent time writing about her too, trying to stay focused by being creative, the only thing I seem to be able to concentrate on that's stabilizing. Maybe this void is a productive one!

I have such a need to move, to walk, to shift that I get into the car and start driving. As I round a curve and glance up through the rain splattered windshield into the negative space between two pointy pine trees, I experience an intense moment of total paranoia. I am sucked into the "V" of sky between the trees, into a dark room where a vivid scenario plays out in the blink of an eye. It's as if I'm inside an old black and white movie set, the room sinister, creepy. I understand that I'm being offered a choice. In this moment the magic and the good in my life are depicted as evil; Chuck, Nicolas, and Lara become evil entities, partners in a plot created and manipulated by the deer, or whoever is controlling the magic, all part of a plot to keep me from "true" sanity, from "true"

Completion

reality, the old world I've worked so hard to escape. I hear my father's voice speaking, as the voice-over in a silent film.

"It's all a conspiracy," he says, repeatedly, his words echoing inside the dark chamber. "It's all a conspiracy! It's all a conspiracy!"

In that split second of time, I am fully aware that I have entered a crack in the universe. It drew me right in, offering me its negative version of reality, while indicating that my whole recapitulation journey and everything I've learned is all a conspiracy. In that moment, as I experience that dark reality between the two trees, I feel truly insane, crazy, paranoid! I could so easily tip into it and be lost. In the next second, a voice pipes up, loudly directing me.

"Look away! Look away!" the voice commands.

I turn my eyes back to the road and see that I'm still in the exact same spot, driving past the pointy pine trees. I don't glance back at them a second time but instead keep my eyes focused on the road. I notice that I'm shaking violently.

"What just happened?!"

In that instant, I clearly understood that I was being offered a choice, that it was time to make a final decision. I can either go into that crack in the universe and the paranoia that it offers, back to the old-world reality where everything was dark and depressing, back to the oblivion of sleepwalking through life, or I can keep going on the path I'm on, my path of heart, more committed to this healing journey, more committed to waking up each day in the magic that's offered, and to all that may be offered to me in the future.

This moment is crucial. I must face the truth of this journey of recapitulation. I must accept everything I've learned about myself and experienced over the past three years. I must choose my path of heart once and for all. It's time to totally trust the journey, to face it without fear or compromise, to leave the old world behind once and for all. Time to fully trust my heart.

I drive to the park where I normally walk and get out of the car. Still shaking with fear and amazement I begin to walk. The rain has stopped and although there are still dark clouds overhead,

I don't care. I must walk and figure this out. As I walk, I get calmer because I know, in my heart, that I am indeed on the right path. I walk quickly to shake off the negative energy I still feel trying to entice me back into that crack in the universe, to the old world of fear and paranoia.

By the time I've walked for about twenty minutes I feel much calmer, more like my normal self. Then I see my deer. She stands in the field, looking at me. Other deer in her company nibble calmly at the grass, unthreatened by my presence. I want her to confirm that the magic is indeed real, that I'm not going crazy, even though I had that momentary glitch. She doesn't move but just stands still, watching me walk past.

I see rain falling in the distance, over the mountains on the other side of the river, moving north up the river, away from where I'm walking. At the same time, I notice a dark and ominous cloud moving rapidly toward me from the south, barreling over the bridge that spans the river, sailing right toward me like a great gray whale.

I notice there's no rain falling from this huge cloud, which comes in low and fast, rumbling soundlessly toward me. I wonder if I should start walking back to my car, but I hesitate, for I am struck by how massive and silent this cloud is. I watch as it soars quietly over me. Instantly, I am nothing but a tiny creature standing on the bottom of the ocean looking up at the wide expanse of a giant beast. As it floats over me, I swear I can almost hear the beating of its heart reverberating on the hills around me. Raw nature, ferocious, filled with unbending intent, heading where it will—nothing can stop it. There's no rain, lightning or thunder coming from this cloud, just its enormous silent gray bulk floating right over my head. If only I were a little taller, I could touch it. Then I notice that it's dragging wind, rain, thunder and lightning behind it. I see sheets of rain and gray swirling mist like a long tail trailing behind it, jagged lightning shooting out from it, and suddenly I am in the middle of it. I am standing in the center of a massive storm, in the undertow of the great silent beast, drenched in an instant.

It's both thrilling and frightening. I wonder if it's safe to stay here, at the center of this great gray void, in the middle of utter chaos, annihilation so close I can smell it. I stand my ground, because more than anything I want to be inside the belly of this massive beast of nature. Then fear kicks in. I fear the lightning most of all, the smell of it in my nostrils. I turn and run as fast as I can. Trying to outrace the storm, I head back up the trail. There's a gazebo at the top where I can take shelter.

I run as fast as I can, but I can't win, the rain comes down in torrents, spitting in my face; lightning flashes, loud thunder crashes, the wind whips my hair and clothing. I tell myself to relax, to not attract the lightning with fear. But I also instruct myself to stay connected to the truth that my time on this earth is not up yet, that I have many years left, that indeed I have just begun to live. I will not die tonight.

I'm in good shape and barely winded from the run but I'm soaked to the skin by the time I reach the shelter of the gazebo. I stand under it looking back toward the river and see the massive dark cloud as it drifts slowly and sedately northward, an enormous harbinger of something to come, sheets of rain and jagged streaks of lightning still shooting out of it. As I stand and watch it leave, I almost hear it grumbling, protesting that it can't stick around any longer, for it was so close to the ground that it could have sat down and stayed for a while. Without a doubt I know this experience is personally meaningful, though it's too early to decipher its meaning.

It's then that I see my deer again. She stands in the field exactly where I had left her, not having budged an inch. Through the grey sheets of rain, I see her watching me still. As the rain begins to let up, I see her more clearly and I wonder what she thinks of me. Was she guarding me, or just observing? All the other deer had gone into the woods to escape the rain and they begin to come out again now, as the rain lightens, but she stays solidly in her place. And I get it, the message from her, once again, is that yes, the magic is real. She doesn't come any closer because I know she's showing me that I need a good dose of this new reality to keep me awake, to alert me to its power, to shake me up as loudly as the storm, the rain, and the lightning did, more potently than the crack in the universe between those two trees did. Indeed, which reality will I choose?

Then I see that I'm not alone. Off to the right I see a man running out of the woods, a jogger in shorts and a tee-shirt.

Obviously, he too has gotten caught in the storm. He takes off running back toward the parking area like a scared rabbit. For a moment I feel an old panic that he might come to the gazebo where I stand, that I will have to speak, to interact, to fend him off, that perhaps he's a rapist! But then the new voice pipes up and tells me to calm down.

"Don't use your energy that way!"

With the rain coming down only lightly now, I start walking back to my car. I must question my own sanity. It's only appropriate. I am living in a fantasy world, talking to deer and believing in magic, and at the same time pretending to be normal, to be sane. However, I know the real evil is the old negative stuff trying to entice me back. The further away I get, the harder it tries.

"Let's make her think she's crazy, then she'll come back to us!"

The world I've inhabited as I've taken this recapitulation journey has many times offered me the option of sanity over insanity. Sometimes I've wandered around wondering what's real and what's not, constantly forced to face the truth and meaning of what I'm being confronted with. At the same time, there's a part of me that's still fragile and sits around in a daze, like an institutionalized patient in a mental hospital, because she's afraid it's not safe in the world. That part of me fears that it will never be safe in the world. That part would like to depart from reality, but I won't let it. So, we have this constant battle to stay present, but it's really only the fragile part that's so afraid, the three-year-old girl, who still doesn't trust. The rest of me is quite strong, sane, and adventuresome. That part of me knows that Chuck, Nicolas, and Lara are the good guys in my life, that the magic is definitely real, and that the only thing that really matters is that I stay on this healing journey.

I must be patient and stay grounded rather than let the old negative energy get to me. That's what showed up tonight. I got drawn into an alternate reality, sucked into that crack in the universe, another dimension. In the space between those two trees, a curtain ripped open and I entered a room where I was presented with a choice between one reality and another. I had to decide what to do. Which world would I accept? I only spent an instant in that space between the trees, but I knew instantly I could not stay there.

In the blink of an eye, I pulled out of it and, looking straight ahead, drove onward, away from it, knowing I had to get out of there and save my ass. Funny, that right after that I had to run from that storm and save my ass a second time!

It's pretty clear that something is playing with me, that something doesn't want to let me go, that something is being fought over—my energy, no doubt. There's an entity out there that still wants me. I was beginning to think it no longer cared!

July 16, 2004

QUESTION REALITY! This statement on a bumper sticker on a car directly in front of me while on my way to meet with Chuck blows me away. By the time I get to Chuck's I'm shaking uncontrollably.

"What's going on?" he asks.

"I don't know," I say, "but I'm scared."

I tell him about my experiences of the previous evening, about the crack in the universe, the paranoia outright offered to me as an alternative to the magic, and then how the deer stood her ground while I experienced the fury of the storm, and then that bumper sticker!

"I feel like I'm losing my mind!"

"Don't worry, Jan," he says, very calmly, "the shamans have explanations for everything you've experienced."

"Okay, so tell me."

"You *are* losing your mind!" he says, chuckling loudly. "The world as you know it is shattering, and you automatically try to hold onto it, but when that happens the shamans say don't try to fix it, just stay with the experience. It's another shift of the assemblage point, which we've talked about before, and which you've experienced before, where your view of the world shifts suddenly and you view it from another perspective. That's all. You got to see into another reality."

"I wish I wasn't so afraid."

"It's okay to be afraid, just don't stop."

"All of those experiences *were* kind of magical. The crack in the universe did show me another reality, and even though it freaked me out, it was kind of magical, but in a dark way. The storm was frightening but magnificent, and thrilling as well. The deer is magical in her own way, and I realized yesterday that she always seems to communicate that she is both a young deer, a child who is longing for and missing her mother, but that she's also an older deer, the mother who is steadfast and determined."

"That deer is part of you," he says. "I think she may be a manifestation of another part of you."

"I agree, both the child and the adult I see in her *are* me," I say. "So how come I can't seem to help myself. I can do anything, I prove it all the time, but only for others. I can't seem to allow myself that same energy, and that's when I feel most depressed. I feel myself sinking lower and lower. I don't know what I'm going to do."

"You are going to continue your recapitulation journey!"

July 17, 2004

I have, since the divorce, been trying to figure out not only who I am but how to resolve simple living, how to eat, pay the bills, and attend to my kids. So far, my tactics have been to keep my fingers crossed that everything works out, while at the same time I wait for something unknown to occur. I wonder, though: what is it that I'm really waiting for? I don't really know the answer, but today is a new day. I'll have to see what it brings.

I take a walk. I walk fast because I'm being chased by the vicious voices of self-hatred and self-doubt. As I walk, I calm the inner storm down and breathe, let the Invisibles go and relax in my body. I have to admit that I've been looking at myself very closely for years now, with a microscope almost, but it hasn't been until now that I finally understand how all the tiny fragments of me fit together. The truth is, I really have made a tremendous amount of progress, especially lately. I examine everything differently now. I question reality differently. I'm different. I have to accept that progress is being made, all the time. I'm really changing now.

Completion

I work at the gallery in the evening and recount the depressed feelings of the early part of the day, how incredibly self-defeating I can be, how an old tendency to self-negate still has such power. Why do I let myself get like that? All the signs, all the guides tell me to stay the course, that everything will work out. And I know that it usually does, but sometimes I feel like I'm losing more than just my mind, that I'm having a real breakdown. But probably, as Chuck says, it's good. Maybe it's the best thing that can happen to finally break through to fully embracing new life.

I read a book of short stories while I sit in the empty gallery to take my mind off my own troubles. I think my writing is really pretty good in comparison to what I read. I drive home at nine and go right to bed, exhausted.

Please help me. Please help me get some work this week. That's all I ask for. Thank you.

July 18, 2004

I dream that I'm a deer caught in headlights, but I don't flee. I am no longer stunned or triggered by what comes at me. I stand my ground, aware that I have lots of resources to help me handle any situation. I've been to school and learned my lessons, for that's what life is all about—Earth School.

Then I dream that I have to mow an enormous lawn and all I have to work with is an old broken-down lawn mower, but I crank it up and start mowing, simply because I have no other tool and the job must get done. People stand around watching and commenting, saying things like: Are you kidding? You're going to mow that whole thing with that? I just keep at it.

My dreams are telling me to just hang in there, that this is Earth School after all, that I'm here to learn, and sometimes learning means having to plod along one step at a time, with inadequate tools, like the derelict lawn mower in that last dream. With determination it will do the job, but it's woefully inadequate for the huge task. There has to be a better approach.

Dreaming All The Time

On top of everything else, the IRS says I owe $1300 in back taxes! What am I going to do? I guess I'll have to get into further debt and just hope that this dry spell doesn't last forever.

What is the most important thing for me to do now, for myself? Do I allow my old fearful and abused self to destroy all my opportunities again? Do I let the child in the dungeon rule? How do I break this cycle of defeat?

I walk, needing to shed the negative energy trying to engulf me. I've only gone a short distance when something makes me look up, and there's the deer, staring at me.

"Okay, I see you," I say, "but not now, okay? I can't now."

She stands there staring at me, but I just need the walk. She turns and runs into the woods while I continue on, this time at a hard, fast jog. Looking down at the ground, I think that I've come to the end of all I can stand, that I don't want to keep digging, that I don't want to learn anything else about myself. I can't take any more of this recapitulation because it just leaves me feeling helpless and full of self-hatred. I'm going to quit; I quit! No more of this! No more Chuck, no more Nicolas, no more Lara. I can't do it anymore. The whole damn thing is over now. I'm giving up.

I slow to a walk, go past the gazebo and down into the next field. Steeped in a dark inner muddle, I look up and notice two people and a dog standing on the path ahead of me. They stand perfectly still, looking in my direction. Their dog is also perfectly still, looking toward me too, a silent tableau. I wonder what's up with them, why they're standing there like statues. I push away old fears and continue walking towards them. As I near them, I see them more clearly, a man and a woman and a large black poodle still standing perfectly still and quiet. I see that they're staring at me with mouths agape, as if seeing a ghost. What the heck! Perhaps they recognize me?

"Did you see the deer looking at you?" the woman asks, excitedly. "She stood perfectly still watching you."

"We couldn't see you because you were around the bend," says the man, "but we could see the deer and she's been standing there for a really long time watching you come down the path. You walked right past her, close enough to touch her. Didn't you see her? Amazing!"

"No, I missed that," I say, and then I know it was her, my deer, and that the magic is real. They had seen her too! I speak to the couple for a minute, then say goodbye as they walk on, shaking their heads in disbelief.

I start to cry because I know I can't give up. I'm almost at the end of this long journey. I can't stop now! Somehow, I'll have to figure out a way to keep going. I know that even though I feel totally lost, my deer is still here, steadfast and strong, letting me know that it'll be okay, that I'll be okay, reminding me of my strengths and all the things I've been learning about trust, about allowing for things to unfold, about letting things happen. I'm more certain than ever that I'm being guided and protected. I have to accept the innocent child in me that allows for these moments of magic to happen as well, for she is not just living in the old dungeon anymore but actively partaking in this new and changing life, just as I've hoped she would.

I breathe a sigh of relief, because I've been given the message I've been seeking: *"Don't give up on everything you've worked so hard for, not this time! The depression will come and go but always remain steady, sure, and focused on the journey and everything will be okay."*

I truly live in a magical world. I have to remember that.

I cry a lot the rest of the day, surrendering a little bit more, letting something unleash. It feels also as if the child is stepping out of the dungeon more and more, meeting me and guiding me, just as I have guided her. I truly am the one she's been waiting for all this time, and just as she needed to be ready to meet me, I had to be ready to meet her too. We both had to get to this place of innocent trust. We seem to be a good team.

I don't know exactly what it is, perhaps the tension of everything I've been through from the time I was a three-year-old child, but I let the tears come. I don't stop them or think negative thoughts about myself. I just cry real tears. Later I eat, do some yoga, and get a call that the faux finish samples I'd dropped off for review the other day have been accepted. I have a new job now. It was exactly what I'd asked for last night, that I get new work this week. Ask and you shall receive!

I've also been offered another writing assignment, to do a three-part article on the local art scene. I also have the show to prepare for at the gallery and I also need time to figure out how I'll handle this new reality I've landed in. *Question Reality*, said the bumper sticker, and ever since I saw it, reality has certainly been questionable! Thank you, Earth School!

In the evening, something shifts again, this time within my physical body. I experience an effervescent fizzing in my brain, and the depression lifts up and out of me, right through the top of my head. After going through hell for days, the fog and fear are suddenly gone! The void is gone! In a matter of seconds, I go from heavy darkness, where I can't get clarity on anything, into a lighter, more even and balanced tone. It's like magic! I'm not sure what just happened, but suddenly I feel alive again. After a weekend of hopelessness and apathy I am suddenly flooded with optimism. I want to live, really live! Has the child exited the dungeon? For good? Are we done with that? Ever since I painted that white circle of light in the middle of that dark painting, the hole in the wall of the dungeon, she really has been stepping out into life a lot more. Time will tell.

My dream last night was pointing out that everything is about learning, that what occurs in everyday life is a lesson, hard and tedious though some of them may be. I am a deer caught in the headlights, but the headlights are me too, turned inward as I shine a light and experience my whole life playing out in intimate detail, everything illuminated for my benefit.

I take another look at the tax letter I've received from the IRS. I can't make heads or tails of it. It looks like they recalculated my income downward, and yet they want more money from me? It doesn't make any sense. I'll call and get it straightened out in the morning.

July 19, 2004

I dream that I am a child being held down and something is being forced into my mouth. I don't want it. A voice shouts: "Change! Change! You don't have to do it anymore! You can change!" It's my own adult voice; me telling my child self to change position, and I do, rolling over so fast that I wake up!

This dream is telling me what I already instinctively know, that physical shift, as well as mental shift, is necessary to get away from situations that previously had power, situations in which I went numb and could not move. But in this dream, I was teaching my child self what I've learned, continuing our progress in Earth School. Similar to the dream of the other night, of being the deer in the headlights, it shows me that I already know how to take back my power. I have the tools and the personal power to shift, whether awake or asleep, and now the child is learning the same. She actually rolled over so fast I woke up! Good girl!

"The shamans say that the mind is nothing more than messages planted there by outside forces looking for control. Combat it with awe. Remain in awe," Chuck says. "The fact that the old stuff is so strong is because it's battling for control. It goes to your most vulnerable places, but it doesn't have staying power. Release the mind, change, shift, and then try to find the awe again. As your dream insists, stay with the awe."

He describes the energy of the body as being circular, open and flowing, as opposed to the sharp back and forth energy of the thinking mind. I know what he's talking about. My mental energy is indeed back and forth energy, caught somewhere up in the frontal lobe of my brain; I can actually feel it when it revs up.

"Look for the awe. Track it, watch for it," Chuck says. "That's why the movie, *The Matrix*, is so interesting to me. It deals with letting go of the mind, the matrix. What you are going through now is the scene where Neo is being unplugged. It's frightening, and there's a constant battle going on because the matrix wants you back, and yes, it does go to where you are most vulnerable."

Dreaming All The Time

Jeanne is part of the awe. The deer is part of it. I need to remind myself that they are both as real as the horrors that visit me daily, trying to lure me back.

I work at the new job all day, painting the bathroom with its Tuscan faux finish. I try to stay attached to the awe, as Chuck instructed, looking for it, recalling it, realizing its potential. I breathe it in and try to remain as calm as possible. The house is empty and calm and I have the place to myself. No uninvited guests appear. All is well.

The kids are back after being away for two weeks. So nice to have them home. My daughter and I take a walk together in the evening. There's no sign of the deer until we're heading back. Suddenly, I see her, standing in the middle of the path, waiting for us. My daughter remarks on this, and I tell her that she looks for me, that she communicates with me. The deer perks up. We greet her. She stamps her feet, bobs her head in an up and down motion four or five times, as if saying "yes, yes, I see you, yes, yes."

"Hello," I say, "everything is okay."

"*Yes, I see that you are back*," she says. "*Yes, everything is as it should be. Yes, it will be okay. The waiting is almost over. Yes, you will be happy someday soon.*"

She hops happily about in front of us for a few seconds before running off into the woods.

"She acknowledged us," my daughter says.

"Yes, she did," I say, "most definitely."

"That was awesome," she says.

The old stuff has receded over the past few hours, since the kids came home. Now, alone again in my room, I feel its presence. I turn away from it, refusing it. I remember the instructions in my dreams and I remind my inner child that we are safe. I remember how the deer makes me feel happy, how she makes me feel safe too. I know now that the experiences of her are real; I have witnesses. Those two strangers were in awe of what they experienced, as was my daughter. I'm not simply imagining it; the communications are real.

July 20, 2004

I dream of two options, to either: "*face it now*" or "*don't face it now.*" These are buttons to select on a computer, the only choices I have.

I had a tough night, waking up a lot with pain in my legs, anus and vagina, the old pains of rape and torture. My dream presents the truth, that there really are only those two options, to face it now or face it later, because if I don't face it now, I'll only have to do it later. So, excruciating though it was, I faced the pain that came in the night. I let it go through me without letting it get to me. I didn't want it to attach someplace else, to move to some other part of my body, so I just let it go. I didn't *tell* it to go, nor did I allow it to take over; I simply released it. It doesn't belong here anymore.

"It's over now," I told myself, "the whole thing is over."

I confess that I harbor anger at the world for letting such things happen to children, but I also know that if I can get out of my head, out of the vicious cycle of anger and terrible thoughts, and remain in awe, away from the back-and-forth energy of the head, as Chuck says, I know I'll eventually release the anger too. The truth is, I'm tired of always waking up feeling like I'm still in the same place, with the same pains and the same anger too. It's getting pretty boring!

I turn my thoughts to the deer instead, see her nodding and looking directly at me. I see my daughter's bright little face shining with awe. "Remain in awe!" I hear Chuck saying.

Relief does come from getting out of the head; I see that now. It seems to be the only relief I have access to most days, the ability to stop thinking about the old stuff, to stop trying to figure out how to deal with it, to stop wondering why I'm still so afraid. Far better to turn off the mind and instead turn toward the letting-go and releasing process in the body itself. At the same time, I practice letting go of the old mind and the old self too. I've worked hard to achieve a new place of utter calmness, a new emptiness of mind and body that is peaceful and fresh, totally within myself, created by myself, for myself. This place of utter emptiness is what I want more of! The surety of this new self as a viable being is my new anchor, connected to a new and different world, unfamiliar to the old world but as beautiful as it gets.

Communicating with Jeanne, with my birdman, and the deer are all part of this new world of healing and awe. As I leave the old world and enter this new realm more fully, I find nothing to be quite what it seems but everything is full of awe indeed!

I suddenly remember a dream I had last night. I was on my way to meet with Chuck. I had something wrong with the sole of my foot. When I got to his office, I sat down in the waiting room and picked at the skin on the sole of my foot until it began to fall off in huge chunks, until there was a big hole in my foot. The hole was full of a black beadlike fungus or mold, or some type of parasitic invasion eating away at my body, deeply embedded in my foot. I was horrified and disgusted. I tried to hide it because I didn't want Chuck to see it, but as soon as I entered his office, he knew immediately that something was up.

"What's going on?" he asked. "What's wrong?" He finally convinced me to show him my foot, which I reluctantly did. I was so ashamed of it. "No problem, we can fix that," he said, not even flinching when I showed him the disgusting black hole. "Trust me," he said, taking my foot between his hands and telling me not to worry, "we can fix this!"

I guess this is how I actually feel about myself, that I'm rotten and disgusting, full of shame and ashamed of needing help. I prefer to cover the truth of what's eating away at me. Why am I still so ashamed? Why do I still have a hard time telling things to Chuck? In spite of all I do tell him, I am still so private, keeping back things I haven't dared to go near yet, though they have a way of appearing and making me face them. I haven't even written down some of the memories because they're too frightening and horrific. I just don't want a record of them.

In the dream, I didn't want to admit that I had let myself get that bad, that I still had things to face, that I'm not in fact done with this recapitulation yet. There are still some deep issues to face, like that black anger I just wrote about, festering inside me. But Chuck was so calm and matter of fact about it in the dream, just as he is in real life; nothing seems to faze him, nothing is too difficult. There's always a solution.

I go to an Embodyment session with Nicolas. Just as my dream revealed, it becomes almost immediately clear that there really is something inside me that I'm reluctant to deal with; perhaps it's anger but it feels more like sadness. And indeed, I feel one slow tear fall out of my left eye as Nicolas begins working on my left side. I'm so uncomfortable that I try to separate my head from my body, so I don't have to think about it or wonder what's up. Suddenly, I remember something that happened last week at the dreaded dermatologist's office.

"You have lots of hair, lots of long thick hair," he said, as he stood behind my back. It felt as if he were smelling it or caressing it, and it made me not want to take care of it anymore. In fact, I have not washed my hair for a whole week now, as if making my hair attractive would make me attractive. The thought of him touching me was subconsciously disgusting to me and my dirty hair is protection!

Oh shit! This is kind of pathetic on the one hand, but it shows me also how my subconscious works or has worked in the past to both protect me and confound me! It kept the painful truth from me that the doctor was actually lecherously drooling over me at the same time that I thought I was acing my protective shield. In fact, as I go back into the experience, I can feel the doctor touching and smelling my hair, but I blocked this from myself in order to get through the ordeal.

I haven't thought at all about his remark about my hair. I barely took it in. I was so intent on not breaking my protective shield, and it really did work, because I came away feeling so strong and capable. Meanwhile my subconscious was plotting away, having latched onto his remark. It kept it inside, working it, creating a real mind/body conundrum. For some reason, I just couldn't wash my hair this week, nor could I figure out why I didn't want to, when usually I love to have clean and beautiful hair. My subconscious gave me the subtle suggestion that if I make myself unattractive, I'll be safe. Now I understand that this is what has been going on all week!

I'm able to finally get to this during the session with Nicolas. I notice that there's a dual process going on here, for while he works on my body, not only the known issues release from my physical body but what's in my subconscious as well.

I do mindless tasks; cleaning closets, doing laundry. I try to suppress the depression I feel creeping in, but it overpowers me. At first, it's just a trickle, like a small stream, but soon it's a lake that I'm drowning in. I realize I'm still dealing with mental and somatic repercussions of sexual abuse, that not everything has been released yet. The Embodiment Therapy stirs what's still in the body, as does just about every aspect of life. I'm so open to this process that it's hard to turn it off. I still can't work full time yet; I need days off in between jobs to rest and rejuvenate. Nicolas suggested that I nap during the day, which I will try to do. I have to stop worrying, have to shut my mind off.

I'm not even aware of triggers sometimes, as in the case with the dermatologist. There's some shame around this thing with him. Perhaps I still go to him because he's an older man who's attracted to me? I sense the tension of his desire to touch me in a lascivious way, but he pulls back at the last minute. I get the feeling that he enjoys the titillation, and I allow him to have that moment by being there. Am I ashamed about that; that I have knowingly continued to go see him for the past five or six years with this titillation in mind? And I get to have his full attention on me for a few minutes. Am I as titillated and lascivious as he is? Is this what it means to face the shadow; the part of the self that is as devious as we accuse others of being?

Chuck did point out that I have to admit that I knowingly went to see him, in spite of how uncomfortable it makes me feel, because it's the way I do things; I follow orders. I admit that I've been taking the conventional, well-charted route, never even questioning why I do it. I muster up and force myself to get it over with, but I could actually do it differently if I chose to. Chuck is right to confront me about this aspect of myself that tends to follow the rules, even rules that leave me feeling depressed and inadequate, or that put me in compromising positions. A part of me has continued to be a rule-follower even though I know better. Far better to take a new approach. I have the power to choose a new doctor, or none at all. I have to start thinking for and acting on behalf of myself, doing things that are empowering in a healthy way.

The rule-follower, that dutiful automaton, makes me feel bad about myself. She's a depressive bore who just muddles through life, doing what she's told, without thinking. The truth is that's an old part, not the new evolving me, but I have to face her too. She's part of my inner makeup that needs to be put to rest along with all the other stuff that I no longer want ruling my personality.

I sense a fight going on inside, the three-year-old child arguing with the Invisibles, those voices that insist things stay the same. It's as if she's been listening to my thoughts around the dermatologist and is having to face her own desire for change and new life, simultaneous with mine. That's a good sign; we're on the same page. The Invisibles offer terrible advice and make terrible decisions, and I don't have to listen to them anymore or do things their way. I can live life in my own way now.

When I called the IRS today, I found out that I do owe $1,135 in self-employment taxes, by August 2nd. Yikes!

I finally break the stalemate with the dermatologist and wash my hair—after seven days! Bad memories can really wreck a life!

July 21, 2004

I deal with the everyday struggles to meet my financial commitments and raise my two children, but what I really feel is an urgent need to just take care of myself. Fewer responsibilities would make the whole process easier, but I do know that my responsibilities keep me present and grounded, constantly pull me back to cold reality, though I feel tortured by guilt about not working enough and not earning a better living, that I'm not being a good enough mother, that I personally am so needy at a time when my children still need me so much. However, I do understand that I'm as important as the process, and that I won't get anywhere good if I don't take care of myself too.

I must be patient as I maneuver through this time of patient waiting; it's a crucial time in this recapitulation. It's not time to jump ahead but time to go slowly and methodically, waiting and listening, pursuing only that which has heart. Even though I often can't see the path before me, I know it's the right one, and that I must focus on following it, one day and one step at a time.

The depression lifts slightly as I write; getting my thoughts down renews my commitment to myself and to this journey. If I stay focused on the path and remain connected to Jeanne, my birdman, and the deer, I know I'll be okay in the end. They urge me forward, telling me to go bravely, to trust. Even though there's no plan, it's still the right path.

"*If you look around you,*" I hear, "*you will see signs proving this. See the deer, and Chuck and Nicolas, and all the caring people around you; see the new life that is developing. See how, when you ask, you receive. It does work; it's right.*"

"Okay," I say, "but I still have to pay my bills. How do I do that? How do I get enough work to do that?"

"*Try not to let everything overwhelm you. Everything works out. It will all work out in the end. Stay focused. Believe in yourself. Trust yourself, trust your gifts, all the gifts you are given!!!*"

I look forward to the gifts that today will bring. Maybe that's exactly what I need to do, begin to expect gifts every day.

I got through the morning okay but I'm back inside my head now, in the back-and-forth racket of the mind, with the terrible voices of the Invisibles badgering me. In order to not drive myself even more crazy I turn my thoughts to the creativity that sustains and nurtures me. I must keep to the path of healing and the path of the creative. I must not be so afraid. I must turn my creative energy inward toward myself now.

These are the things I decide I can do for myself immediately: I must cease the inner badgering, stop the negative racket in my head, the voices of the Invisibles. Breathe. Continue the integration of my three-year-old child self. Continue walking. Continue healing practices. Make time and space for writing and painting. Keep my workspaces at home and at the studio in good shape so they're ready for me when I need them.

The kids go out to dinner and a movie with their dad. They'll be home late, which gives me a quiet evening. I take a walk and see lots of deer. They're all over the fields, crossing the trails. I even see my deer. She nods her head at me a few times, as has been her habit, and then goes back to eating. The others all look at me, staring at me, as if she's told them who I am. After taking a good long look they too go back to eating. The deer never run from me, unless it's to communicate something. Tonight's message is clear.

"*Yes, we're all still here and we all just need to keep going, to take care of what's most important and necessary; eat and take care of yourself too*," they say. It's the message I most need: take care of myself.

I leave the deer and cut across a field. Suddenly, I hear every single sound in the evening air, every buzz and every chirp, loudly and clearly. It's as if I've walked inside a concert hall during the middle of a performance, where the sounds of every instrument reverberate off the walls. It's as if every single cricket and bug in the field is singing in my ears, all with something to tell me. The sound is deafening.

"*Keep going,*" I hear, "*do it the way you need to do it; do it your way. You don't have to listen to the voices that shriek at you, to those negative voices. If you listen only to what's happening deep down inside you, you will always know what to do and you will always find the right path.*"

"Yes, I know that," I acknowledge, but at the same time I can't help wondering about the boldness of some of my decisions, at how blindly and willingly I stick to my path. I've decided to shirk certain conventions, to break away from them and do what I've always been warned against, to trust fate, the universe, God, whatever you want to call it; to let life unfold before me and show me what to do, staying in the moment rather than having a previously laid out plan in place. I'm letting go of the rule-follower;

she's no longer in charge. It's both a frightening and a fascinating place to be, proceeding without a map, and without a compass too.

I have, to some extent, always operated on this free-flowing principle, but now I'm doing it consciously while also letting go of the old fears that have kept me so attached to the conventions of life. I now *trust* that I will be taken care of. This is the trust that Jeanne has taught me about, and my experiences lately have supported this letting go and trusting. I now trust that the only way I'll achieve the peace, security, and fulfillment I desire is by continuing to push forward until I've gotten rid of the old self, all of her old attachments too, and fully achieved the new self. So that's where I am now, pushing onward, despite all odds.

July 22, 2004

In a dream, I'm taking a walk. I see a black and white police car come racing out of the woods. I know it has something to do with me. I lurch awake as it speeds toward me. Fear and anxiety invade as I attempt to fall back to sleep. They sneak into my bed, and when I feel their cold fingers embracing me, I jerk awake again.

I was finally able to get rid of the fear and anxiety by relaxing body and mind, breathing and letting everything go, resorting to the new me, the one who knows how to handle things, the one who has so many new tools by which to achieve a calm inner state. The dream points out that there's obviously a part of me that feels like a criminal for breaking the rules, for daring to be different, to be so unconventional as to go with the flow rather than following a well laid out plan or adhering to the status quo. I'm breaking the rules and that might get me into trouble, but I must continue my journey, even though I'm pursuing something I can't see or validate, something that's just a feeling. Where am I going? The truth is that I don't know. I just know that if I don't fully surrender to this healing process, and if I don't pursue a creative life, I will be destroyed, either pulled back into living a numb life or actually die, for I am sure that something inside me will kill me.

Lara, the energy healer, had a brain tumor as a young woman that almost killed her. She interpreted it as blocked energy and cured herself. I view all sickness as blocked energy. I know I must release all this depression from my body, which shuts down access to my creative energy. I must find a way to allow my own creative energy to blossom inside me and keep me healthy and alive. I can't let it be blocked by depression, old fears, or anything else that doesn't belong to me. I must continue this recapitulation to the end, and find the means by which to live a vital and fulfilling creative life.

      I meet with Nicolas. Feelings of great terror and sadness poor out of me as soon as we begin. I realize how terrified I am of throwing myself out into the unknown, and how sad I am too, because I'm leaving all the old stuff behind (even the terror), and leaving the old comforting ways of dealing with life behind too. But I have to accept that I've already moved on, that I'm just not living in the same world anymore. I have to face all the changes I've already gone through and accept that I don't have to live in the old darkness anymore. I don't have to desire death over everything else. I don't have to hide under the covers, or keep my shoulders hunched and my legs pressed tightly together anymore. But I do have to allow myself to experience this new life and allow it to bring me to new levels of consciousness. Every day I progress a little bit more. Even if it's slow and incremental progress, it's change nonetheless.

      I assure myself that I'm safe, that there's nothing to fear. I'm safe in Nicolas's hands, I tell myself. I feel such love for him and understand that he loves me too, but then conflict arises. The old voices come, telling me that no one will ever love me, that I'm just delusional if I think he means it when he says it. I push the old voices away. I'm not delusional, I tell myself, he's the most sincere, honest and safe person I could possibly work with. His energy is pure and without conflict during our sessions; his energy is beautiful.

      I reassure the three-year-old child inside me that we won't go to that creepy doctor anymore, that I won't put us into awkward situations like that again; I won't place us in danger. I promise that I'll cease listening to the voices of the Invisibles. They create fear where there is none, insisting that I'm doing everything wrong, that I'm incapable and stupid, but I'm not. I'm daring and brave.

I'm fine. I don't have to listen to them anymore. I'm leaving them behind too.

As the session continues, I begin to more fully understand the deer as manifestations of myself. They used to flee from me, unable to sustain being near for very long, frightened by every small intrusion into their safe world, but now the deer hold their ground; they are less afraid, even as I am. They go about their own important business even in my presence, even when I stand fairly close to them. They've even reached out to me, as I have to them, not wanting me to leave, following me. They observe and assess, decide how close is comfortable, and how much to trust, the same process that I've been undergoing over the past few years. The way they react and interact mirrors me in my own life. They send me clear messages that I should go carefully, with caution, "*as we do,*" they say, "*but by all means continue the process.*"

"And by the way," they say, "*don't forget to stop and nurture yourself along the way. Continue the healing; it's essential. You'll get what you need, like the animals in nature, enough to sustain you.*"

Perhaps that's all I'll ever need, just enough to sustain me, but I also have a rich creative life to compensate for the meagerness of other aspects that may not be so rich. I get the message that my creative life is also my spiritual life. I also get the message that it's time to stop giving my energy away to others; there's no reward in that. I'm merely wasting the energy I so desperately need for healing, and for the pursuit of my own wholeness; it slips from my grasp when I spend it on others. This is my time for myself now; I understand that. After the next show at the gallery I'll stop, I promise myself that. I'll announce that I'm retiring. There are plenty of others who can take over; the place ran fine before I came along and it will run fine after I'm gone.

When the session is over, I feel very relaxed but also very tired, as if my body is signaling me to pay attention to the exhaustion I feel, signaling that I'm exhausted for good reason. After fifty years of being on heightened alert, my body constantly poised and ready for attack, constantly in fight or flight mode, it's finally time to let down my guard.

"Remember, you do have a support system," Nicolas says, as I prepare to leave. "Say the mantra all the time, not just when you feel the tension, but say it all the time, and do yoga. It will help with releasing tension and unblocking energy."

I take the kids to the eye doctor. They have their eyes dilated and both of them are cranky afterward, even ice cream doesn't help.

I get a call from an artist friend who invites me to be in a group show in the fall.

"You are very good artist," he says, in his thick Polish accent, "just very unconventional and hard to place, but I'll do good job."

It would be an opportunity to be in a big regional show and not have to be involved in any way, except to get my work in on time. I accept the invitation.

"Thank you, I love you," he says. "I'll be in touch."

As the day wears on, I feel the terror caving in on me again, but I remind myself to stay focused on remaining calm and not letting it get to me. Old feelings that I'm crazy, that everything's falling apart and I'm going down, hover above me like dark clouds, ready at any moment to pour down torrents of cold insults, accompanied by the flash and clash of negativity.

I shift my focus to what's positive in my life now. As I give up my old controls and let go of the old anchors, I see new people in my life surrounding me, helping me, wishing me luck on my journey, even as I feel exhausted and fragile, even as the old darkness waits for me to totally collapse so it can rush back in and whisk me away to its old dank tomb. I hang in the tension between worlds, sometimes dipping within hearing distance of the Invisibles, but as soon as I do, I kick them away, turning more fully toward the present.

I take a walk at the end of the day. My intention is to move on more fully now, to find a way to break the cycle I feel trapped in, on the edge between worlds. I know I'll still have triggers to contend with a while longer, and that I'll also get through them. I also accept that my life may be pretty rough and uncertain for a while longer, and that I'll get through that too. I just know I have to keep going, one step at a time. I also think about the writing I'm doing. Whether anything comes of it or not, it's important to give voice to those who can't speak for themselves, especially to those many abused children who didn't make it. That may be the ultimate reason I eventually tell my own story, as a tribute to all who didn't make it.

When I return home there's a message on the answering machine from Chuck; he has to cancel tomorrow's meeting. It's funny because as I was walking, I thought he would do that, and here's the message.

"Don't worry," I say, when I return his call, immediately putting my new decisiveness to the test. "I'll be fine. I'll see you on Tuesday instead." But the truth is that the three-year-old child inside me feels abandoned when he cancels. Feelings of sadness and terror that I've been dealing with all day swirl up again. I had been looking forward to talking with him tomorrow and now I can't. Well, that's not really true, because he said I could call and we could talk on the phone if I needed to.

I didn't see any deer while I walked tonight, until the very end. Maybe they were signaling that I just have to be patient and work through this time on my own. Then I saw a mother and her fawn and I knew I had to take care of myself, take care of my inner child, that it's my job now as an evolving being to be there for her, to understand her and support her, but also to help her resolve her deepest issues. The mother stared at me for a long time, as usual, even when her fawn leaped at her, urging her to move along. Finally, she turned and gave me one long last stare before running off after her baby.

I have that child inside me right now, feeling hurt and abandoned, sad, and terrified at being alone. I know that the depression is keeping me from getting out into the world, keeping me isolated, perhaps perpetuating the fears and terrors that I have yet to conquer. I'm in free fall now, I know that, but I'd really like to land soon. I've been in this stage for a long time, and I find it extremely uncomfortable, terrifying, in fact. I'm just trying to survive each day without some disaster happening.

I have to be careful. I've been so distracted lately that I've been doing things haphazardly, which is not like me. I'm usually so detail-oriented and attentive, but lately I've had to keep pulling myself back into reality so I don't screw things up.

July 23, 2004

It's raining lightly but I decide to walk anyway. It gets me out of myself, shifts my perspective away from my inner world and my depressed feelings and stirs up positive energy too. As I walk, I acknowledge that I'm alive and healthy and that my problems can be handled; they are no longer life-threatening issues. The rain picks up, so I turn back. By the time I get home it's darker, pouring steadily.

I sense this is going to be a strange day. I feel something phenomenal happening, something entering me and going through me, and it reminds me of the buzzing energy I felt the other day as I walked across the fields, through the bugs and crickets. It feels good and energizing; perhaps it's the final push through to the other side of this time of patient waiting. I understand just how receptive I am now, and that the more work I do on myself, the more open and receptive I become.

I get a vision of two clotheslines, running parallel to each other. On the first line, photos are clipped with clothespins, hanging outside in the sunshine. Behind them, on the second line, are large white bed sheets. The wind starts to blow and the photos blow off the line, along with the clothespins that were holding them in place. Everything scatters, blowing into the sheets hanging on the second line, where they all swirl together. The wind picks up again, blowing stronger and stronger until the sheets blow off the line too. I watch as they scatter into the blue sky, mingling and merging with the clouds, carrying the photos with them. When the wind dies down there's nothing left, just empty clotheslines.

This vision is about all of us, about life and death. For me it's about the past swirling off, leaving me free. The pictures are all the little girls, who are part of me, finally free too. I've studied them enough and can finally let them go.

My personal journey is certainly progressing. My known world has disappeared and I find myself in the unknown, the yet to be known. I am no longer sitting, pensively waiting, no longer hesitant. At some point along the way I took a leap of faith, probably that night of the storm, when I stood my ground beneath the great belly of that giant whale of a cloud and rode the fury that dragged in on its tail. From that moment on, I have been in free fall, wondering when and where, if ever, I will land. I am with Mother Nature now, a student of her universe, flowing with her, learning how she works, how to listen to her, how to act on her principles, and how to understand her magic. I am open and ready to receive, but also ready to act.

In order to anchor myself in this new world, I decided I needed to adopt a new attitude about my past and confront the fears of my present situation in a different way. I decided that I'll accept the triggers as they come, working through them with all I've been taught. But I decided that I'll also accept the magic into my life too, that I'll surrender to it, be open to it, as much as I've surrendered to this recapitulation. It's the only way to be now, in full surrender mode.

I accept also that although I may be terrified of becoming a channel, I'll surrender to that as well, because as each day unfolds, I am offered the most wonderful and amazing insights. And finally, I surrender to the fact that I'm in free fall and that yes, I'm afraid, but I will learn to embrace this stage in my recapitulation as I have every other, for this is my life. I surrender to it all.

July 24, 2004

I floated all night on a choppy ocean of sleep, never quite dipping deeper into it. It's the way I feel about my life at the moment, that I'm floating along, searching for the right moment to land, seeking not only the right time, but also the right place.

As I ponder the depths of the magic that I encounter and the ability of insight and vision I've been granted, I find myself in awe. I have to trust it, not push it away. I have confirmation of its trustworthiness almost daily, and I need to start listening more closely. I notice it, but I haven't fully embraced it yet. If it truly is a gift for me to use, then I must find a way to use it.

I was falling in my dreams last night and there was no end in sight; no bottom, no tethers, nothing to grab onto, and the speed of plummeting was picking up and I was falling faster and faster, totally out of control. It's as if my thoughts of surrender sped into action in my dream, showing me what it really means to surrender, to give up all control and be swept away. In fact, things *are* totally out of my control. However, the one thing that remains constant is a certain clarity, which arrives in clearly heard statements, words whispered in my ear. I'm learning to not just acknowledge that I hear them, but to really pay attention to them, to take them seriously, and to act on their advice; in the end, to trust them.

In the past, before I began this recapitulation, when I heard such words being whispered in my ear, I knew they were absolutely true, but I couldn't act on them, for I was too numb, too embarrassed, too afraid of what I would unleash if I did. I also knew the day would come when I would finally surrender, finally pay attention, and that was the day that my recapitulation really began, long before I ever met Chuck or heard of Jeanne, long before I even knew what recapitulation was, but at a time when I knew I had to change or I would surely die. Now, however, I understand the journey I've taken as a well-planned journey, the events of my life stringing together like a long, beaded necklace, each bead an event in my life, each bead snuggling next to the one that came before it and the one that came after it, each one necessary for there to be a necklace, for there to be a life, for there to be continuity and growth, for there to be this journey.

"Remain in awe," Chuck said, "it's how the shamans embrace the world."

I meet with Chuck. I tell him that I've been feeling lost and untethered lately, uncertain of what to do, and then I go to look for the awe and I find it, right there, waiting for me. I ask and I receive; I ask for messages of guidance and I get them. I tell him that I still bottle things up, that it's still hard to talk sometimes, even though I wait all week for our meetings.

"Why not talk?" he asks. "Talking can't hurt you."

"I know," I say. "A few years ago, I decided that the truth was the most important thing and I've been working on it ever since, but this sensation of free fall, which seems to be taking all the time in the world to end, is difficult. I remain terrified."

"Of what? What are you so terrified of? The unknown?"

"Yes, and not finding anything familiar to grab onto and no sign of anything either, just plain emptiness all around."

I tell him that I'm too depressed to work full time, but I feel so guilty about it too. I'm spending more time on healing, which feels important, but it's difficult to justify sometimes.

"You're just not used to the new position you're in, that the old is gone and you can't quite find a new place yet. Shifting, you're shifting," he says. "It's just the old stuff, the Invisibles, the old patterns trying to reestablish their positions of power, fighting like heck to stay in charge."

"I desire the old," I say.

"Why? Why do women go back to abusive situations?"

"There's still a degree of comfort there and at least it's better than the loneliness. The loneliness and suffering alone are very difficult, so when you go back at least you aren't alone."

"Well put," he says.

I talk then about the guilt and shame and the stuff that lies very deeply embedded around the yearly approach to the dermatologist. I tell him about my experiences this time, how I felt so good on the one hand, but then for some reason unknown to me I could not wash my hair. Every time I got into the shower, I ignored it, letting it get dirtier and dirtier until I finally figured it out. It took me seven days and some very deep probing to release the fallacy, the belief that if my hair was unattractive, I would be safe.

"I'm trying to find a better place to view all of this from, even the awe," I say. "Right now, all of it terrifies me and I can't even seem to be in awe of the awe for very long."

It's a beautiful, cool day and my energy is unusually good. I get the kids up and we do some outdoor work. My son mows the grass while my daughter and I work on the flower beds. Afterwards, I vacuum and wash the big picture window in the living room. In the evening I drive out to a winery where a couple of artist friends are having a showing of their work. I say the mantra, Shivoham, as I drive. It calms and centers me.

  The reception is sparsely attended but the show is nicely hung, the work good. I feel uncomfortable in my body, as if not quite in it, with low energy, much depleted from my early morning high. In fact, I feel so totally burnt out that I don't stay very long. I do talk to some old friends, a woman and her husband whom I haven't seen in a long time. I'm surprised by how delighted they are to see me, wanting to know how I'm doing, thrilled to hear that I'm writing more. They had read some of my published work and really enjoyed it.

  I talk to a few more people, congratulate the artists on their show, and make the long drive back home, trying to figure out how I can stay in awe. Can I wake up every day and decide that I'll be different today, do everything differently, and just see what happens? Tomorrow, I decide, I'll give it a try. I'll have a new attitude from the start and see what develops.

  "You send your energy out into the world and you get something back, you attract something to you," Lara said to me the other day, "little bits and pieces are enough."

  I have a lot of myself out there now, in press releases, writings, artwork, intentions; bits and pieces of myself floating in the universe, all my positive intentions to change.

July 25, 2004

  I dream of being with some women friends, sitting on a blanket underneath some trees on a muddy driveway. I get up to get something. It's raining hard and my feet sink into mud up to my ankles. My feet are so muddy, I can't imagine I'll ever get them clean. I go inside a building, which appears to be a motel with bland, unappealing commercial décor. I see an open doorway leading into a long corridor. I decide not to go through that doorway because one look at the long, ugly corridor and I realize it won't be worth it; it's too impersonal and I know that what I want is not there. I go back outside. Cars are coming down the road, cars full of people; there's life out here.

Then I dream that I'm staying in a hotel in New York City with my son and daughter when my daughter just walks out of our hotel room and is gone. I wake my son so we can go look for her. I try to figure out where she might have gone, to something cultural I surmise, and the idea of a film festival at the library pops into my mind. I am full of anxiety since she's only a young girl who doesn't know her way around the city.

I wake out of the latter dream with a start, leaving it unresolved. I lie stiff and paralyzed, unable to move; the pain intense. Drowsy, still half asleep, I withdraw from my frozen body. I look down at my sleeping face on the pillow, studying it, looking for a way in. Slowly and carefully, I move, incrementally, back into my body until I am fully back and fully awake. Still in bed, I do some simple yoga poses, breathing and releasing slowly. Finally, the pain and stiffness release.

The dream of my daughter, alone in the city, leaves me full of worry, feeling a little sad, but at the same time I know it's not really about my daughter but about the little girl inside myself. She's letting me know that this journey of recapitulation is nearing its end. The picnic dream is about making different choices now; it's time to embrace a more gregarious lifestyle. And the child, in the second dream, has made a choice as well; she has left the dungeon. It's not about selecting old doors or walking down old corridors anymore, searching among the ruins of the past, rather it's about consciously taking completely new and different, unknown routes.

I really am throwing myself out into the universe now, heading in new directions, trusting life itself, and the child self is doing the same. I don't have to fear for the child alone in the city, for I already surmise that she's choosing her own path of learning, going to the library, a wise choice. These dreams indicate that life itself really is showing me the way now, as I dare to enter more fully into this new life that I've been fashioning for myself. All parts of myself, the three-year-old child included, are fully ready and on board now for new kinds of exploration.

Completion

I go for a walk in the cool and fragrant early morning air, hoping to see my deer; I miss her. As soon as I see someone else on the path, I immediately tighten up and hold my breath. Unable to bear my personal space being brushed up against, I draw inward, guarding myself protectively. After the intruders pass by, I can barely get air back into my lungs, barely return to my body. I understand how what happened to me in the past totally controls how I react to the world in general; I am guarded all the time. I study the physical effects of this process as I walk, noticing and analyzing what happens in my body every time I see another person. I want to stay aware so I can change my reaction in the future, react differently. I know it's the reaction of a victim and I'm trying to change that. What was once normal must now be questioned. My dream last night points out the need to make new choices, and for the most part I am doing so, even unconsciously, and I think the more I do so consciously the more natural it will become. And then I realize that I'm a better person for having contact with others, that they are my mirrors. How else do I understand things about myself if not by constantly seeing my reflection in others?

I see my deer, out in the field, flicking her tail at flies.

"I see you," I say to her, "I see you."

The morning is beautiful, the air tranquil. I sit on a bench and try to get into the Tao of it, to sink into the utter calmness of this beautiful spot in nature, where butterflies greet me, and a sparkling jewel of a bluebird whistles me a tune. A groundhog comes out of the weeds and sits near me for a while, until it becomes aware of my presence. Then it shoots off back into the weeds; more like me than I like to admit!

I get the kids up and take them to the river for a picnic lunch. My son complains at first, not wanting to get up, but we have a very pleasant time, hiking along a trail, skipping rocks out over the water, collecting driftwood, and inspecting the garbage that has washed up on shore. I have a sense of contentment, a feeling I haven't felt in years; I'm happy. The tide is out and a bit of sandy beach is revealed. We stand barefoot in the shallow cove, letting the gentle waves lap over our bare feet. Sinking into the sand, I am reminded of my muddy dream. I let the energy of the old self wash away in the water, in this river that leads to the ocean, letting it take from me all the energy that does not belong to me, sending it downstream to mix with the unwanted energies of others doing the same thing, also standing at river's edge, releasing and letting go of what no longer works.

In the evening, I take another walk along the trails where the deer live. They stand in the fields and watch as I walk out to the place that I call the "magic spot." My deer is waiting for me there. I walk up to her, as close as I feel is acceptable. I sense she's been expecting me, that she wants to show me something. She comes closer, peering into my eyes. Trust—she wants to show me what trust looks like. It's time to allow myself to experience safety, she says, to let myself be safe in the world. She is showing me how to do that, showing me that she feels safe, reflecting back to me that this is how you do it, a little at a time until you are comfortably safe. I understand the message. There's utter trust with certain people that develops slowly over time, a kind of bonding having taken place, and which automatically invites in feelings of safety.

The deer wanders slowly away after we communicate, calmly eating as she goes. I stand and watch her, and then I begin to cry, like I did when those people told me the deer was watching me so intently. I realize I'm working out a lot as I take these daily walks, as I confront the final issues of this recapitulation, within myself, where the finishing touches are being made. Darkness begins to descend as I start back to the car. I have no fear. I know I am safe.

I get a call from the woman whose bathroom I had recently painted with the Tuscan faux finish. She gives me rave reviews, absolutely loves everything. She's perfectly satisfied. Her call lifts my spirits immeasurably. I feel really good.

"People love your work," says my sweet little daughter.

"Yes, they do," I admit.

This makes me realize that if only I had more painting work, which I love doing and am really good at, I would probably have less overall anxiety. This is a dumb "AHA" moment, but it's important. I have never before put money in its proper place, solely as income. My feelings about money have always been directly related to my feelings about myself. Money has always carried so many other connotations, supreme among them being that it was a measure of my worthiness and value, or lack thereof. But I'm struck now by the clear implication that with a better income, the amount of anxiety surrounding *all* the changes I'm going through would decrease drastically, making this time of transition flow more smoothly. Yes, money is key to life running smoothly, at least in the real world; you can't do without it. Also, I would be released from a lot of my personal problems if I experienced a better sense of self-esteem and self-worth, like I did just now after receiving that positive feedback. Maybe I've gone through this process around money before, but for some reason it feels enlightening at this moment.

I resolve to not give up, for I sense that I'm on the verge of getting very busy, with lots of work. And with that new perspective on just what it means to have an income, I suddenly feel a lot more positive. A friend at the opening last night told me not to worry about money, that it will come.

"Everything will work out. You'll see," she said.

I prepare for bed, hoping for dreams, aware that my entire waking life is also a dream, that I'm dreaming all the time. I struggle still with my evolving self, struggle to fully embrace the magic, to take on the weight of it and the seriousness of being Jeanne's channel, for I know that's what she's been training me for, to become her connection to this world. Without even fully understanding what it might mean, I face the grave responsibility of it. I must make sure that I'm doing it for the right reasons, that it's truly the right thing for me to do, and I must figure out how to best apply it.

July 26, 2004

I dream that I'm in a large house with older children, teenagers, boys and girls. People are coming to see me, asking me for advice. Meanwhile, I'm packing up; the time has come to move on. I watch as the children leave the house, carrying suitcases and travel bags. I give them each something to take with them, mementos of our life together, as well as food for nourishment, and monetary gifts as well.

I've sent them all off. What began the night before, my young daughter heading off into the great unknown city alone, continued in last night's dream. This time I was fully present as the children left, and I didn't let them go without them knowing how much I love and care about them. I'm clearing my inner house, preparing for what comes next. Even my three-year-old self is calm and contented now, for she has learned to feel safe with me and safe in the world. I have taught her well, just as she has taught me.

I notice myself clenching and tightening for no apparent reason and I remind myself that it's an old habit from a time that no longer exists. I tell my inner child that none of the past exists now, that I've fully recapitulated it and released it from my body, that we are safe now. I must begin to use my awareness of this fact to relax and remain fluid all the time. I must flow through life without attachment to the past and all that it entailed. I intend to remain open now, optimistic and trusting, as trusting as the deer. And I intend to remain fluid, in body and spirit, as if I really am dreaming all the time, because it's the right thing to do—all the time.

I noticed yesterday that as long as I stayed energetically fluid, in mind and body, everything was not as depressing as it once was or could become. My need to run away was reduced, my need to clench disappeared, and I looked around and saw very clearly that everything was perfectly fine. Without the anxiety, fear, and sadness, I realized that I was living in a totally new and different world.

A yellow butterfly comes to me while I'm walking. It's so in my face I can't ignore it. It flutters around me, staying with me while I walk. Suddenly, something clicks, and I realize that it's showing me all the intricate beauty of my life, and I have this epiphany: *I already have the life I've been waiting for. I already have everything I want.* I have time to care for myself, to work at healing, to paint and to write. I have it all, *right now*. It's all inside me and always has been. It's not what I *don't* have that counts; it's

Completion

what I *do* have, and there is plenty! I'd been concentrating on what I didn't have, my feelings like a tight glass bottle, ready to shatter, but meanwhile I'd failed to notice that inside that glass bottle was a beautiful golden pear, and it's been there all along.

I sit down on a bench overlooking the river and realize that I've had this epiphany before, but not with such clarity. It's as if I'm wearing magnifying glasses. Suddenly everything is brilliantly clear, and just as suddenly I break out of the tight glass bottle of the old fearful self and transform into a small, contented golden pear, sitting in my golden self.

"I am a small golden pear sitting on a bench in the sun," I say to myself, feeling calm and contented, and then I realize that the yellow butterfly is still near me, on a small clover flower, and beyond that butterfly lies immeasurable beauty, all around me. I realize that it's always been there but I had to be able to *see* it. I realize that I *am* where I want to be. This thing that I'm constantly waiting for I already have in my life, in fact, *I've always had it inside me!*

The process of having lived as the torturous glass bottle self and the long and arduous journey out of its constricting container—the recapitulation journey—has finally reached its point of transformation. In the blink of an eye, I am transformed into this contented, shiny, golden pear self. With a profoundly tiny shift of the assemblage point, I experience how my own energy feels as it flows in the universe. I'm in another world. Only this time the crack in the universe doesn't pull me into darkness, but quite the opposite, for I am almost blinded by the light, by the utter clarity of what I see and feel, the utterly beautiful oneness of everything.

When the mind stops agonizing, when the thoughts stop dictating, the body can relax and the energy flows. That is what happened as I walked and watched the butterfly today, and as I surrendered to the energy of nature and let it flow into and through me. It's what makes the difference from one day to the next, how my energy flows in my body, how relaxed I can be so that it flows most freely and naturally. This is what I intended this morning. This is what healing feels like, being able to drop the constrictions of an old way of life and open up to a totally new concept of life as beautiful energy flowing through us all. In contrast, when my body reacts negatively, largely because of habit, my own bounty of energy is blocked. Every time I fall into an old familiar depression, the vital energy inside me stops flowing; it gets dammed up. As a result, everything inside is trapped and my creativity and my vital energy are stuck; it's a vicious circle.

I'm finally figuring out what Nicolas meant when he told me I had the whole world inside me. Now I understand not only that it's inside me, waiting for me to discover it, but that I create my own world simply by my choice to be aware or not, to go with the flow of my life or to block the flow of energy inside my body. In freeing my mind from the old ways, I free my body, and when I free my body, my life energy is fluid, and from that fluidity comes *knowing*, that which I receive, that which I channel.

Last night the deer was telling me to trust, but she was also stamping her feet, telling me that right here is everything I need. I don't have to go looking, or keep waiting; it's all right here and now. The message is to just stop and look around; trust, feel, and know.

I must remain alert to triggers and address them as quickly as they arise. This is my challenge, because even as aware as I am today, I have the same clenched reaction to people I pass along the trail, even though I'm in the midst of revelation and clarity. My body reactions are so ingrained and immediate that I don't even notice them, but I do know I can consciously change them. I must learn the simplest relaxation techniques of all and just drop my shoulders, unclench my jaw, relax my throat, and loosen my hips. In release upon release, this is how I'm changing myself and my world.

I watch for triggers throughout the day. I change my physical stance and shift my mental state whenever I notice an old pattern emerging. I notice that in so doing an emotional shift automatically follows. Everything inside of me is interconnected. I remind myself to stay true to *knowing*, to stay connected with the magic. I remember the deer telling me to trust and to look around me, *here, now*. I stay present. I am here, now.

July 27, 2004

    I looked for Jeanne last night and saw her very distinctly, a flutter of iridescent wings, like the butterfly I saw on my walk. I asked her to come closer and she did. I got the feeling that she cares deeply about me and that she won't give up on me, in spite of how long it has taken me to really embrace her presence in my life, beyond the help she's offered during my recapitulation, for I am still reluctant to be her channel. When I'm feeling whole and centered, like that golden pear self, I'm certain of being on the right path and I have no reluctance whatsoever to being her channel. When I have such clarity, everything flows, including me and my energy.

    With such clarity I also understand how I tend to panic and what happens as a result. For instance, in reality, my continual dilemma about whether or not to find a full-time job, although obviously a real issue, is also due to financial stresses. I go around and around about this issue, driving myself crazy, even though I've already decided that I won't get a full-time job, that my freelance work is sufficient. But when I panic, I forget my decision. Now when I feel strong, even though I still have no idea how I'm going to survive financially, I know I'll do it without stepping outside of the world I've worked so hard to create. And I know that I will more than survive; I'll thrive, because that's my real intent.

    Everything looks different when the dark blanket of depression lifts. There's really no way I can fully function when I'm that depressed. It's like being stolen away to another world, in a different body, trapped and lost. And when in that state, I look for something to hold onto, something to give me a sense of security, and often I have nothing more than the act of getting out into nature and taking a walk to see me through it, to help me find answers. I ask the deer to advise me, and I discover that what they show me or communicate to me is as good as anything else I can find at the moment. They offer me very sound advice, the simplest being to just stop and look around at what I have.

    "Look how much I trust you," my deer says, *"me, a wild animal known for being skittish and nervous. Even I have learned that your world is pretty darned safe right now."*

And if those deer are manifestations of a part of myself, as Chuck suggests, then I'd say I'm offering myself some pretty darned good advice.

I spend the rest of the day at the gallery hanging the paintings for the upcoming exhibit. At one point, I feel a slight hint of old negative energy, as if a door has opened and one of the Invisibles is peeking through, assessing whether or not it's a good time to attack. I feel a cold chill and instantly know I'm being watched. I go over and literally slam shut the open door of the gallery. No uninvited guests allowed!

I feel stronger, clearer now. Maybe my time is finally here, though I know I must take more control of my destiny without jeopardizing all I've gained. I'll figure it out. I'm not going to give up what's so important to me, the reason for my survival—my connection to spirit. I'm not totally clear on what that means yet, but I'm certain it will be revealed as time goes on, especially as I venture more and more out into the world. I have many talents and many things to offer, but I need to stay focused almost entirely on myself for a while longer, preserving what I've gained as I take this final leap into the unknown. Everything will work out. I know I've been saying that for a long time, but I'm still here and still okay, just to prove the point!

I know that my next challenge is to JUST DARE! I must dare to accept my role as Jeanne's channel. I must dare to put the trust I've worked so hard to build to the test. I must dare in every aspect of life in order to move things along. The deer stamping her foot means that too.

"*Damn it, Jan, just do it,*" she taps with her hooves. "*You have all you need! What are you waiting for? We are ignoring you now, turning away, because we need you to take over. Go for it. Do something! Get going. Now is the time. Don't waste it; make it happen! Dare to do it, dare to do it, dare to do it!*"

July 28, 2004

I dream of being in an apartment building that's being evacuated, section by section, and sprayed for roaches and bugs.

People and things are being moved out. It all looks very much like a deserted concentration camp. I watch from my windows. A child comes wandering through my door looking for someone or something. I leave and go to see my kids, who are staying with their dad, and then I go to a large bazaar. There are tables laden with clothes and household items; you can buy whatever you need for very little. I don't need anything. I had seen people walking around with art supplies earlier, but then decide to look for clothes for my kids. In the end, I ask someone where to find the art supplies. I give a woman three coins, even though I don't buy anything from her. I go off to look for canvas and paints, needing that more than clothing, more than food, which can also be bought at the bazaar. I know what I need in order to sustain myself and that is to be a creative person, in whatever form that may take. I know that now's the time to fully pursue it.

In another dream I meet with Chuck. We sit with our foreheads touching, engaged in quiet spiritual talk.

Today is my day to be daring, to begin the next phase in my healing process. As the first dream points out, the old days are over, everything has changed; it's time to look in the spiritual creative direction now, to that which is most important.

I have learned, and am still learning, that I can trust all that I have, that my life is full of people and magic, and that the entire universe is supporting me. My dreams, day and night, fully support me in everything I endeavor to do. Now I have to take that understanding and use it by daring to be bold, by following my dreams, pursuing them unafraid. I must force fear into retreat and refuse to open the door to it again. If I see the door opening, even a little, I must go over to it and slam it shut, telling the Invisibles to go away, just as I did yesterday while hanging the show at the gallery, saying, "Things are different now, and I'm in charge. I live in the present now, and the present doesn't include you. You can't touch me anymore. I'm free of you."

Jeanne was in my room again last night. I asked her to come closer and she came so close that I realized she was inside me too. Everything, the whole world is inside me, and it's up to me to utilize it now. I must be bold, be daring, and do this new work. It's not about me; it's about something bigger.

I am no longer in free fall. I have solidly landed in the present. I am alert, unharmed, and definitely *here*. It's time to use my energy for myself and those closest to me; for my kids and those who need me. I must continue seeking the means to sustain this life I have created. I will find a way. It's time now; it's definitely time.

"Your energy is unblocked. You are open now. You are here and very grounded," Lara says, corroborating my feelings of change. "Your stress and anxiety, the brittleness, all are gone."

"Yes," I say. "Yes, yes, yes!"

All the things I feel, she feels energetically. While in free fall I wasn't just falling, I was shedding as well, letting go of a lot of stuff. I was aware of it all around me, floating past me in the air as I fell.

"Now is your time," Lara says, reiterating my own words.

"You need to eat," she says, "lots of protein, and also drink lots of water," and indeed, I feel the need; my body is asking for such nurturance.

"Your energy is flowing in and out now; before it was blocked. Make sure you paint," she says at the end of the session. "Just go and do it!"

As great as I feel, a door to the past suddenly opens and pure darkness stares out at me, looking for my weaknesses. I slam it shut, for I intend to keep my body in a fluid state so the energy can keep flowing. I won't go back.

I drop my son off at an evening music rehearsal and then stop at my usual place to go for a short run, my energy so alive, bubbling over. Running feels like a happy thing to do. The sky suddenly turns dark and threatening, and I see lightning and hear thunder in the distance. I see my deer on the hill, at the magic spot, the dark broody sky behind her. She's standing in the field where I usually see her, staring right at me. We gaze at each other for a few

Completion

minutes, no need to communicate, we're saying goodbye. I wave. She too knows I'm going to be okay now.

On the walk back I step on a snake slithering across the meadow, half buried in the grass, a long black one. Its head flares up at me, as surprised as I am. I feel its body beneath my sandal and jump quickly aside as soon as I detect it. It freaks me out! I wonder what it means. Perhaps it symbolizes my conquering the evil that took my innocence when I was a child. As it slithers away, I see the other deer, the younger one, standing nearby, quietly observing.

"It's okay," I say. "I'm fine." In fact, I feel extremely present, grounded, and alive, as if the snake's energy enhanced my own. The energy inside me is much more even, as Lara mentioned today, flowing in and out without obstruction, all previous blockages gone. Everything that I was feeling today, she described, even how I'd been so tight, like glass, so brittle and ready to break, but that now I'm flowing and balanced. I am healed; I have healed myself as much as anyone else has.

"You are much more grounded now," she said. "You are right here, right now, in the present. You shed the past. You were in that swirl of all that bad stuff and now you are here."

This free flowing of my own energy is not only invigorating but I feel safe within myself for the first time. I feel strong and capable. It's such a foreign idea, but I do believe that I have achieved a state of no fear. For the first time in my life, I am unafraid.

The old stuff, the Invisibles have made brief appearances today, but I've banished them and they have since only dared peak out through a crack in the door. I'm tired of them now. I've sent them away, bored with them. I want something else now. I need something else now.

It's time to use the channeling ability I've been honing, that Jeanne has been training me in. I must find ways to make it useful and helpful, to myself and to those close to me. First, I must listen for and follow that clear, heart-centered voice that tells me what's true, and then I must dare to heed it, unafraid.

Dreaming All The Time

The days have been better and better. During the daylight hours I'm doing marvelously well, but at night the old stuff clamps down on me with a vengeance, the pain returns and everything with it, but I quickly work through it now, telling it to go away, that it doesn't really exist, that it's only an old mindset. It moves along pretty fast when I say that. I'm taking my energy back now, and I won't allow it to be taken from me again.

Something has happened; something has really shifted inside me and in my perceptions of the outside world as well. In spite of all the problems I still have, real life problems, I feel incredibly energized, contented, satisfied with the deep work I've done on myself. The little child is calm inside me, nestled in, asleep beside that sixteen-year-old self, everyone home at last, safe at last, in the best place of all, inside of me!

I've had a major breakthrough. Somewhere, over the past few days, I landed, and I landed right on my own two feet, solidly, and in one piece. I left all that old stuff swirling behind me, sucked into the vortex of that old world.

Gravity is certainly wonderful! I *feel* it. I've discovered what it means to someone like me, who has barely set foot in the present, having spent most of my life caught in the past. Look how long it has taken for me to arrive! The key, I now know, is to not exhaust my supply of energy because if I do then I won't have the strength to save myself again. So, it's important for me to still maintain a high level of attention to healing.

Healing should be a lifelong project anyway, and part of that is remaining creatively active, to keep painting and writing, to always be the artist. Healing means also doing the physical work that's so important, the yoga, meditation, and breathing that have saved me and kept me alive through all of this. And finally, healing means continuing to remain open to new ideas and new experiences, to keep talking to Chuck about the shaman's world, and to maintain the spiritual connection with Jeanne, to never close that door.

I understand more fully what Nicolas said about everything being inside me, that I have the whole world inside me; it's such an abstract concept, but you do know it when you experience it. I know that even Jeanne and the deer are inside me, all the channeled words and visions are inside me, the past and all the horrors of the past are inside me. Everything is inside me, including the free fall, the vortex, the void, the darkness, the Invisibles; all of it is inside me. And I hold the key to accessing it all, and to locking it up again too, transformed and redeployed as my own energy. What I sought to heal from wasn't outside of me, it was inside of me, though I projected that it was still something outside of me. Now I carry it all inside of me with full awareness, recapitulated and laid to rest, no longer a burden but a means of evolution, for in its full revelation that which once darkened my spirit has been my means of transformation.

    Now that I've worked through my darkness, I have access to whole worlds of light inside me, through my openness, trust, innocence, and daring to venture beyond what once held me spellbound in fear. What lay inside me led me to not only go deeper into myself but beyond myself as well, for I have gone beyond anything I could have ever imagined. I have been to the light and back. No one can see any of it, though, for it's my private spiritual journey, but it's real. If it were outside of me you would see it surrounding me like an aura. I would see it every time I looked into the mirror. I would be able to touch it. But it only exists through my openness to fully knowing what lay inside myself. The inner self, once opened is infinity itself. And in that infinity lies as much potential for good as for bad, for that is where everything exists. It's a matter of choice which way to go, but somehow, I feel there has to be a balance if one is to maintain a healthy equanimity.

    Now, however, the good stuff is having its turn to be in the forefront of my life. I no longer have a need for the old stuff in my life. There's been a changing of the guard. The good guys have finally captured the castle of so many of my dreams, and *I have been set free.*

    The next few days will be interesting. I have enough money now to pay a bunch of bills. I have work lining up, both writing and painting work. I may even be able to buy some new canvases and start some new paintings without having to paint over the old ones again for the fourth or fifth time!

I'm tired now. It's been an amazing day. I can't wait to see what happens tonight when I sleep. My legs hurt already, anticipating the usual night fight. But maybe not this time!

July 29, 2004

I dream that I'm with Chuck, on a ship on the ocean in the middle of a hurricane. I hold onto Chuck, steadying him so he doesn't get swept overboard as he struggles to steer the ship and keep it afloat. I have a firm, strong grip, and am not intimidated by the situation, though water is leaking into the ship. We scramble to find the problem and fix it before it gets worse, or before the ship sinks. A man comes along and says: "I can fix anything." He then proceeds to pour truckloads of cement all around the ship, filling up the ocean and covering the ship too. When he's done, we all stand on top of a huge mound of concrete, like the back of a great gray whale. I wonder if it's okay to be on top of it, worried that it might sink, or that it isn't solid enough.

"It isn't going anywhere; it's not going to budge," the guy who poured the cement assures me. "It needs water to solidify and become as hard as rock. It's going to be okay."

Even though I stand on this very solid surface, I still feel the rocking and the tossing of the ship in the ocean waves, but I also see how rock solid everything is now. I feel the firm surface beneath my feet. Buried in the cement all around us are still visible some of the things that have caused me such pain, my past lies buried but not totally forgotten; some things still stick out, bits and pieces of memories and things from the past. We stand there elated, excited, happy, but I'm also still worried that the cement won't hold and the ship will shift, but Chuck reminds me of what the guy told us; that it will not budge now. In spite of the fact that I see a tiny hole in the cement, I believe him.

I wake up after sleeping a solid seven hours with my body clenched and in pain, as always, but I now know why I clench; the old habit is so ingrained and I haven't yet found a way to shut it down at night. I shake off the pain; it doesn't belong here anymore. I return to fluidity and to the beginnings of a brand-new day.

Completion

In the dream, I was so grateful that we weathered the storm okay. There was such a finality to it. My recapitulation is coming to a close. It ends on water, the deep unconscious that I have delved into so deeply over the past three years, bringing what once was hidden to the surface, to consciousness. It ends on the healing waters of the great wide ocean, the ultimate feminine expression of lifegiving birth, yet I stand on the solidity of the work I have done. It is an expression of the Tao, fluidity and solidity in equal measure, the balance of nature that I have so sought to achieve. I have indeed weathered through the storm of my recapitulation, and indeed Chuck was crucial to that journey, helping me steer through some of the densest and most unsettling aspects of the journey, teaching me how to view the world in a new and different way, showing me the shaman's way, the warrior's way of approaching and interpreting life. I've passed the tests, gone through the turmoil of the storm, and now stand on solid new ground.

I feel strong. I've landed in a totally different place from where I started. I've gone from living in total darkness to incredible light. I have survived the vortex; I've been inside the most vicious tornado imaginable, and I have survived. My heart has achieved equilibrium, my spirit the alignment it so wished for, and although I still have further healing to do, I know I'm well on my way to getting wherever it is that I'm going.

I've learned to trust the gifts I've been granted, and I will continue to study and nurture that side of myself, the open and innocent part that is connected to all that is and the channel that Jeanne has taught me to be. This is part of my healing process too, and the next step, as I see it, is to do something with those beautiful gifts from the infinite realm.

In the dream, even though Chuck indicated that the poured concrete was rock solid and would not shift, I saw at the bow of the ship that there was a small opening, big enough to look inside, a crack in the solidity. I wondered why it was there, and I still do. Is it a reminder of where I've been? Is the past something you can never completely close off; does it need access to the present? The concrete did indeed feel very solid, but even mountains can move; nothing is permanent. And that's one of the lessons I've learned during my recapitulation, that everything is in constant flux, that permanency doesn't really exist, that change is endless, that we are beings of endless energy ourselves.

I have no fear of death anymore, for I have experienced the lightness and abundant energy of my own spirit outside of my body. Obviously, having a sense of permanency makes it easier for us humans to go on living our lives without questioning or confronting the truth of our existence. It allows us to live in ignorance, but I'm not interested in that anymore. I'm only interested in knowing the truth, and so, I'm sure the crack will reveal its secret before too long.

I go for a walk. The deer notice me, but mostly I notice the world around me, my focus shifted from looking inward now to looking outward. I have my quiet alone time on the "magic spot" and take in the busyness of the natural world. Two yellow butterflies flit about in front of me. They chase each other, playing before me, as if saying: "*Look at us! This is life! Look how happy and carefree we are! You too will be happy like this!*"

On the return walk, my usual desire to not meet anyone kicks in. This is immediately challenged, for as soon as I think it, people suddenly emerge from every pathway and I am caught in the middle with no way to avoid any of them. I have to laugh at the tricky way the universe teaches!

People are what life is about. Life is all about interacting. Being in the world means being around other people. So, I accept the challenge and barge ahead, greeting everyone I meet with a smile and a happy greeting. I know that people are not all that frightening, it's just that I've lived at such a removal from them for so long, dissociated and fearful as I was. I've been looking inward for such a long time, but that's changing now.

I have a pain attack as soon as I get home, reminding me that something still needs recapitulating, showing me the reason for the hole in the concrete in my dream: that I am not totally done yet. The hole offers an opening to all the stuff that's still to be accessed and released; it's a two-way opening. Things can go in and things can go out, like the blowhole on a great gray whale, the exact image that came to me in the dream. I will not shrink from encounters with pain; I intend to welcome them, acknowledge them for what they come to teach me, as I have learned to do.

I tell today's pain that I'm grounded now, that I'm not interested in getting overwhelmed by it, that I'm strong, ready to finish up what needs finishing. As I let the pain go through me, I remind myself to not get too inflated but to remain humble, for this is a powerful process.

"I'm no longer numb," I say to the pain. "You won't ever find me in that state again. You can still bug me, remind me of what I must still recapitulate, but you will never again hold me captive. I've come too far now."

As I speak to it and breathe it out, the pain lessens and finally goes away, leaving me slightly energetically depleted, but I'm okay. I'm strong now and getting stronger every day. I'm more grounded now than I've ever been and I've gained a certain amount of knowledge and awareness about myself. I've learned to listen to and trust my body and my spirit, to take seriously what comes to guide me—all the gifts I am given.

I head out to scout out some places I might sell my painted furniture and talk to a few business owners. I stay grounded, in the moment, noticing that my spirit, my mood, stays up without my even doing a thing. I do have to fight off the Invisibles, as they pop up every now and then with their tired old negativity, as expected, but it's nothing compared to what I've been through, and I have no problem refusing them.

In the evening I take another walk. I see my deer. We stand and stare at each other, a strong current of connection palpable between us. Suddenly, I feel my legs and feet get very heavy, as if someone or some energy were pulling me into the ground. I look down, wondering what's going on, expecting to see my feet sinking into the earth, wondering what energy this is, for it feels as if I am actually being sucked into the ground. When I look up again, I see the deer still staring at me. She nods, as if letting me know that it's true, *the earth will protect me now, nature is where I will find my grounding now*. Then she runs off crashing into the woods, loudly and clumsily, as if to alert me to the fact that she is not a figment of my imagination, but a real live animal.

July 30, 2004

  I meet with Chuck. I feel grounded, very still and in my body as we talk. I mention stepping on the snake a few evenings ago and how I interpreted it as a sign of conquering my abuser and his negative energy, but Chuck reminds me of the healing aspects of the snake too, that it's a symbol of consciousness and knowledge entering into the Garden of Eden, and that perhaps it symbolizes my own healing, everything I've overcome as I've journeyed on, and how grounded in a new world I am now.

  "That makes a lot of sense," I say, "because it was after that that I realized just how grounded I did feel, how much more aware I had become of trusting myself, and how strong I felt I had become as I took this journey. I felt so alive after I stepped on that snake! I felt how present I really am, grounded here in this world. I've never really felt like that in quite this way."

  "I'm glad you're feeling grounded and safe, you deserve it, after all the work you've done," says Chuck. "You're doing very well, Jan."

  "Yes, I am," I say.

  I realize just how much my work with Chuck has helped me, how it's brought me to this place of grounding, clarity, and awe. He's shown me the way back to my true self, to my soul. He's helped me to understand and see the magic and awe in the world. He's shown me what true compassion is, taught me how to be nonjudgmental, taught me what it means to trust, what it means to be a thinking, feeling human being. He's taught me how to overcome pain, fear, anger, and sadness. And he did it all so selflessly, in the most humble, gentle, supportive, and nonthreatening way. I love him for that!

  "I'm so grateful to you," I say. "Thank you for taking this journey with me."

  "My pleasure," he says, "but you did all the work!"

I pay all the bills. There is no lack of money this month, for things are indeed looking more fruitful in the work and income-generating department, for suddenly I have plenty of work lined up for the foreseeable future. It's almost as if getting to this point in the recapitulation has released me from more than just my own past but also everything that was attached to that past as well, including my own feelings of unworthiness. I am suddenly open to abundance because I have freed myself of all the old ideas of myself that blocked the universe from getting through to me.

I change daily now, rapidly, in unexpected ways; my body, my thinking, but also my feeling ability has kicked in and my emotions are finally coming on line like never before. And right now, my stress level is zero, at an all-time low. I feel absolutely none. Amazing! I continue to trust this journey, as I focus now on my work and achieving still greater stability. I'm calm in a totally new way, and yet I'm also ablaze with wonder and awe.

Midnight. I'm still up, my energy buzzing, the excitement of the evening running through me, for it was the opening of the last show I am curating at the gallery. The show is off with a bang, with work selling like hot cakes, and this is only the first night. I feel so good about this. I'll be going out in style.

July 31, 2004

It's gray and cloudy today, and will probably rain, but I decide to take an early walk. I want to see if anything happens. It's quiet as I walk. I see the usual early morning runners, some with their dogs, but it's fairly quiet and peaceful. The old internal dialogue revs up as I walk, but I halt it immediately.

"I don't want you here, get out of my head!"

I flick my arms outward and away from my body, whisking away the old energy on the wings of my intent. As I do, a red-tailed hawk squawks loudly and flies out of a tree and right down the path in front of me, an awe-inspiring synchronicity. As the large bird leads the way, I am reminded of what the deer inferred the other night, that *nature is my teacher now*. In awe, I follow the hawk, asking it to show me where to go next. What new path, what new journey lies ahead? Whatever it may be, I intend to remain open and in awe. Remain in awe! It's my new motto, not only reminding me to remain open to the magic in this world, but also to remain open to the magic of the shaman's world, where, in the blink of an eye, one can be transported and dropped into experiencing the world as a truly magical place.

I do errands after my walk and spend the afternoon at the gallery. By the time I get home at six, I'm hot and sweaty from sitting in the stuffy, unairconditioned gallery all afternoon, but I have so much energy! I'm fully HERE, and it feels really good! I got such good feedback on the show, which was very gratifying, and a lot of work got sold. The show is definitely a success!

I'm somewhat surprised, as the day goes on, that I don't have one of those old veils falling in front of my eyes. I notice how stable I've been for the past few days and how I don't feel any of the old stuff. It's such a new experience, something to get used to, but I'm happy to remain present and grounded, in this new state of awareness, fully conscious that I am at last in the new world I've worked so hard to create. It suddenly dawns on me that I really have been on quite a courageous and tremendous inner journey. I haven't wanted to really think about myself in any of this, kind of leaving myself out of it, considering it a journey of the spirit, separate from me. But now I'm ready to accept that it was me who took the journey, the human me, right from the start. And I haven't fully appreciated my child self yet either. I haven't given her credit for being so strong and brave. So, thank you, little girl! Because of your bravery I have survived; we have survived, but more than that, we've gone beyond survivorhood; we have evolved. Certainly, a job well done!

And I also have my spirit guides and my human guides to thank as well. Thank you, all, for taking this journey with me.

Epilogue

Over the next few months, I continued my recapitulation on my own, still meeting occasionally with Chuck. Also, while still deeply committed to working with me on my recapitulation, Jeanne proposed another project as well, that the three of us, Chuck, Jeanne and I, join forces and work together, beyond the constrictions of time and space. In essence, I agreed, though somewhat reluctantly at first, to become her channel, and Chuck and I agreed to see where it would take us. This agreement led us on a totally different journey resulting in a totally different kind of relationship. All of that is another story, but there are still parts of this story to be told.

For me, everything fell into place in 2005. That was the year my mother stated that twins were a common proclivity on her side of the family and that I possessed the family gene, passed down from her own father who had been a twin. It was during a family gathering when there was speculation about a newly pregnant relative and whether or not she could possibly be carrying twins. My mother mentioned the possibility and, looking directly at me, said, in her usual dry manner, "even you, Jan, can have twins." My immediate reaction was that, of course she knew this about me. And if I had any vestige of doubt, this cemented the facts of my pregnancy with twins and the subsequent abortion at the age of twelve.

My father died in the fall of 2005, and soon after his death I told my mother that I was channeling Chuck's deceased wife, for by that time we had greatly explored the possibilities that such a connection might offer and had published several channeled messages from Jeanne. When I told her of my channeling ability and gave her some of the channelings we had published, she told me she'd always seen me as an "Indigo Child", a spiritually connected child, saying that it was hard to know what to do with such children.

In addition, in that same year, I bumped into the man who had abused me. It was only in unexpectedly meeting this man again that I fully grasped what Chuck and Jeanne had been teaching me about the shaman's world. As with all ventures into that world, nothing is fully realized until experienced, and even then, the full impact may not be understood until recapitulated. As I returned to my old neighborhood to attend a relative's funeral in the spring of that year, I had no thoughts but to pay my respects and leave, as quickly as respectfully possible.

I was in the viewing room of the funeral home, talking to an acquaintance, when all of a sudden, a man materialized next to me. I turned to my left and recognized him instantly.

"Oh," I said to myself, "it's him."

We looked at each other and nodded, though no words were spoken between us. Instead, he greeted the other person I had been conversing with, for they knew each other. I noticed that I felt nothing, neither fear nor hate. No memories flashed; no desire to demand an apology and no need to blame arose; nothing jolted me. In a completely detached manner, I simply took in the fact that he was a shriveled old man now, bent, rather hawk-like. There was a dead man lying in a casket behind him and other people milling about in the subdued atmosphere of the funeral home.

Suddenly, something shifted, another position of the assemblage point was achieved, that keen point of perception that Chuck so often spoke about in our meetings together. Suddenly everything dissipated. The room went quiet and it was just the two of us, back in the woods, surrounded by trees.

It was then that the man who had abused me so many years ago transmogrified in front of my eyes. No longer just a wrinkled, bent old man, he took on the guise of an ancient sorcerer wearing a dark, hooded garment glistening with specks of light. The skin on his face and hands turned dark and weathered, blending in perfectly with the rough bark of the trees. Resting one gnarled hand on the trunk of a tree, he peeked at me over his right shoulder and gave me an impish wink. In that second, I exploded into full heightened awareness.

Full knowledge of everything that had happened to me flooded into and through me. And in that instant, I *knew*, without a doubt, that everything I had recapitulated was true, but also that what happened to me as a child was planned, laid out for my training; all I had to do was meet every challenge and pass every test, impeccably. In that split second, I understood that everything I had been through was set up for this man to *teach* me, that he was my personal guide into the world of the dark side of shamanism, the dark sorcerer's world, beginning at the age of innocence. But I also knew that I had signed up to be his pupil, that I chose him to be my teacher, that we had made a pact together a long time ago.

He looked pleased, nodding, as if he were reading my mind. I could hear him saying: "Yes, and yes, that too; yes, that's so." He was always a sorcerer; I saw that very clearly and then, just as clearly, I heard him say, though again no words were spoken aloud: "You've done well. Congratulations!" And then he bowed ever so slightly, the trickster sorcerer releasing his pupil, for I knew we were done—forever—and with a final brief nod he moved away, out of sight, blending into the trees.

A flash of white light blinded me for a brief second as, somewhat stunned, I found myself still standing in the same place in the viewing room, though he was nowhere to be seen. Still stunned, I made my way through the room of mourners and out to my car. It was only as I pulled out of the funeral home parking lot and was waiting to make a left turn onto the busy county highway that I snapped out of it. As I turned my head from left to right and back again, as in the recapitulation breath, looking for an opening in the traffic, I was suddenly shifted back into present reality. As I drove away, the full impact of my early years became clearer and clearer.

I had met the man in the woods once again, but this time nothing could trigger me, nothing could captivate me, nothing could shift me. Indeed, I had passed every test. I felt no fear, no self-pity, no self-importance of any kind, nor any attachment to him whatsoever, to what he had done to me or what he could possibly do. I felt completely whole and stable within myself. There was nothing to get attached to. Indeed, I had taken back my energy; there were no energetic strings binding me to him.

In those few seconds, when the universe cracked open and I faced him in the woods again, under totally different circumstances, I understood that I had been initiated into the ways of the warrior barely out of infancy, that I grew up a warrior child, though I did not know it at the time. I had to recapitulate everything in order to understand that. Now I was ready to fully embrace the warrior woman I truly was. Suddenly, the teachings of the shamans of ancient Mexico were no longer just words and concepts from a strange world. They now fell into place and made perfect sense in my own world. They became a means of perceiving my experiences, offering valid viewpoints from which to understand the past and from which to live the future.

As I drove away, I saw, I understood, and I accepted the bold truth that I had indeed done well. I had learned to not take the predatory nature of the universe personally but to use it to grow and advance, to evolve beyond victimhood. I had learned the art of detachment, I had gained knowledge and awareness and, ultimately, I had *transformed*.

"Yes, finally, it is done," I said. "I have evolved."

I would not have advanced had I not fully recapitulated the part of my life that was spent in the world of a sexual predator. I always knew I was supposed to wake up and remember something, but I would not have taken a recapitulation journey nor gained a unique perspective if I had not dared myself to reenter that dark world of the sexual predator, going back through the filmy, shadowy curtains of the past to take a closer look with new eyes, and with a new set of ideas leading me. If I had not dared to reenter that world, I am not certain that I would be here today, writing about it, still able to go back there at will, returning unscathed to talk about it. The pact of silence that once controlled me has been broken; words to explain my childhood experiences have been found. Words now exist for me to speak about and understand the journey I took.

My recapitulation reintroduced me to my child self, whose life in the world of the predator began with an ostrich bite, but ended when I rediscovered my innocence, having retrieved it from the dark woods of the frightening past. The coyote I came upon one day in my backyard signaled what was to unfold as I began to

Epilogue

investigate who I was, what was to be reawakened as I learned from my past. The runaway horse that bolted down the highway and into my yard another day, showed me the process, the ups and downs of the night sea journey that would lead me back to myself and to my innocence. The fox I met one wintry day while running, signaled that the time had finally come to take the journey that I yearned for and feared yet knew to be so necessary. The deer in the meadows taught me immeasurable lessons about trust and love. These animal guides, whom I have written about in my books, were indeed significant figures during my recapitulation, showing me where I would go, how things would unfold, and what to look for as I traveled.

As I journeyed back and recapitulated my past, I also took back all the lost parts of myself, the sixteen little girl selves who were lost and waiting. I was the only one who could find them and rescue them. And I succeeded in my task, not only finding them but lovingly integrating them into my being, becoming whole in the process, for I am no longer fragmented; I am whole, and my wholeness is complete.

But what was I supposed to learn from knowing that man so intimately?

In my mind's eye, I have killed the man who abused me a thousand times over, payback for all he did to me. I have decapitated him, dismembered him, disemboweled him, impaled him, and imagined his ghastly natural death as well. The release of these smoldering emotions and acts of retribution were critical to my healing, but the real challenge was facing the demons inside myself who continuously tormented and tortured me, bringing me to my knees in pain and despair. I knew it was not the man who abused me that I had to confront but those demons inside myself if I was going to be able to fully recapitulate and move on. And indeed, it was not until I fully faced those inner demons, dismantling them one by one, that I could more fully take on the challenge of embracing a new self. I had to reconcile with my own darkness before I could own the being of light and love that I had worked so hard to become. If we stay attached to victimhood we will never heal, become whole, or advance. That was the lesson I was supposed to learn, and that is the guidance I offer anyone who is intent upon healing.

I have done a tremendous amount of healing work on myself; I have recapitulated my entire life. Every day during my three-year-long journey into the past I asked myself the same questions: Could I take the next step? Could I really go behind the curtains again and see what was hidden there? Could I revisit who I had been and discover what I really went through as a child? Could I face the truths as they were revealed? Could I mentally, physically, and emotionally withstand the torment of breaking apart and rebuilding myself? Could I love and nurture myself through the process? To answer all these questions, the lesson was that if I was to keep advancing on my journey, I had to suspend all the old judgments I'd had about myself and learn how to be open to receive the unconditional love and the many gifts being offered to support me on my journey. I had to learn to trust the process and discover that I too was worthy of a life of goodness and abundance and love.

I found that there were other challenges to face as well, for as I took my journey I was confronted with another world, the world of the paranormal. As I began having experiences that I had no explanations for, often frightening experiences that would have been interpreted quite differently had I been in a different place and working with a different person, I felt so blessed to be working with a person with knowledge of the shaman's world, and of the vast and far-reaching spiritual components of our lives. Under Chuck's tutelage, I allowed myself to explore other worlds, in which I was confronted with a far greater reality. I learned that the world of everyday reality is only a subsection of a far greater reality. I learned that in order to be prepared to enter that far greater reality we must not only move beyond the limitations of victimhood and judgment, we must learn how to maneuver and perceive as energetic, spiritual beings, for that is ultimately our destiny, to become fully aware energetic beings. I learned that that's not only what life after death is, but that is life now, in human form.

As I recapitulated, I began to let in the light a little more each day, slowly removing the energy of the predator that I had carried within me for fifty years. Eventually I basked in the light of transformation, totally healed of the mental, physical, and spiritual pain that had plagued me for decades. I returned from recapitulation not only with my child's innocence intact but also having reawakened in the light of a new and different world. I

Epilogue

emerged fresh, alive, and free, having jolted myself into full consciousness, having reconnected with my spirit in a totally new way, with a whole new perspective on life. I learned that to fully live in this world, we must retrieve all of our vital energy from where it lies entangled in the violations of innocence that everyone experiences, in one form or another, as we live out our human lives. For myself, what was restored to me was a matured innocence, encased by a vital energy that is fully trusting and fully capable of opening to and enjoying life, despite the certainty of woundings still to come.

During my journey of recapitulation, I was able to pull together the fragments of my life, each memory another puzzle piece, until finally the last piece was added on that spring day in 2005 when I met a master sorcerer in a funeral home. Such an appropriate place of ending! In the presence of death, my journey ended. I had come full circle, for as death signifies, when something ends, something new begins.

In the end, I discovered that what mattered were the experiences I'd had, what I took from them, and what I decided to do with them. Now, many years later, as I complete this book and share with you what happened to me during the final months of my recapitulation, as I impart the lessons I learned, the insights I gained, and the meanings I discovered, I also share that the only lesson I look for now is the lesson of today, the only insight the insight that comes today, the only meaning the meaning for today. And yet, I do not attach to any of it, for I know that today will end and something new will come to shed new light, new insight, new meaning. And that is what I look forward to each and every day... to whatever happens.

I wrote *The Recapitulation Diaries* for three specific reasons. First, to educate, to tell the truth about sexual abuse and its repercussions, for how can we rid such behavior from society if we do not acknowledge the utter pervasiveness of it? Secondly, to demonstrate that total healing from traumatic complex PTSD is possible, though it takes a strong commitment. Actually, all one need do is truly embrace the intent to heal and the journey will begin. Thirdly, I wrote my books in an attempt to show the evolution of the human spirit, that not just healing is possible but access to inter-dimensional energy states, that a deeper sense of the self as more than just a physical being may be accessed, that we can experience so much more than this solid world we live in.

After the publication of my first book, *The Man in the Woods*, I contacted a well-known Manhattan District Attorney who personally knew the man who had abused me. I sent him a copy of my book and wrote him a letter regarding this man, what he had done to me, and my process of healing. I asked for nothing from him, only that he investigate the man who had abused me to ensure that he was no longer molesting, raping or causing harm to any children. I never did hear back from him, but then again, I didn't ask him to contact me in return either.

I end this book with the same words that I began it with, words that now make perfect sense to me, words that I hope will inspire you to seek the healing only you can achieve. May you too hear your own spirit say these joyous words to you:

"*I have turned you into this beautiful thing called love.*"

Acknowledgments

I wish to thank several people who were instrumental in my journey to wholeness. Each of them had a special role in my life. I express the deepest love and gratitude to them all.

To my parents for giving me life, for being my vehicle into this world. They did the best they could.

To my children, two of the most beautiful spirits I have had the pleasure to meet, who took this shamanic recapitulation journey with me, though they did not know it at the time.

To my husband, Chuck Ketchel, my radiant companion in love and life, who guided me during my recapitulation journey and taught me about the shaman's world.

To my stepchildren, who didn't know me then but know me now; three of the most nonjudgmental beings I have enjoyed getting to know.

To Nicolas Dalton, my wonderful Embodyment therapist and teacher of Svaroopa yoga, a beautiful person.

To Lara Chekhetiani, gifted energy worker and artist whose innate knowledge of how energy works has assisted many.

To Jeanne, my beautiful spiritual mentor and guide, who still guides me, and whom I still channel to this day.

To the man who abused me, who taught me what it means to be a warrior and without whom I would not be the person I am today.

And last, but not least, I dedicate *The Recapitulation Diaries* to the abused children who didn't make it and to those who did, to those who dare not speak or write, and to those who still live with fear, warriors all.

Books by J. E. Ketchel

The Recapitulation Diaries:
The Man in the Woods: Volume 1
The Edge of the Abyss: Volume 2
Into the Vast Nothingness: Volume 3
Place of No Pity: Volume 4
Dreaming All The Time: Volume 5

The Book of Us with Chuck Ketchel & Jeanne Ketchel

www.ingramcontent.com/pod-product-compliance
Lightning Source LLC
Chambersburg PA
CBHW071232160426
43196CB00009B/1034